聞いて覚える英単語
キクタン
TOEIC® Test
Score 990

一杉武史 編著

英語は聞いて覚える!
アルク・キクタンシリーズ

「読む」だけでは、言葉は決して身につきません。私たちが日本語を習得できたのは、赤ちゃんのころから日本語を繰り返し「聞いて」きたから──『キクタン』シリーズは、この「当たり前のこと」にこだわり抜いた単語集・熟語集です。「読んでは忘れ、忘れては読む」──そんな悪循環とはもうサヨナラです。「聞いて覚える」、そして「読んで理解する」、さらに「使って磨く」──英語習得の「新しい1歩」が、この1冊から必ず始まります!

Preface
TOEIC990点獲得に必要な単語と熟語がこの1冊で完ぺきに身につきます！

TOEIC最高レベルから満点=990点へ！この1冊で英語最上級者に近づけます！

本書は、「Non-Nativeとして十分なコミュニケーションができる」と評価される860点=レベルAに到達し、さらに満点=990点を獲得するための単語・熟語集です。このレベルになれば、日常会話はもちろんのこと、新聞・雑誌・ラジオ・テレビなど、あらゆるメディアが発する情報を理解する力が身についたことになります。それでは、レベルA到達に必要な単語・熟語とはどのようなものでしょうか？

まずは、「十分なコミュニケーション」に必要な5000語レベルの日常表現が挙げられますが、それだけでは不十分です。レベルAに入り、そこから990点に近づいていくためには、expire（期限が切れる）、premium（保険料）など1万語レベルの語彙のほか、reimbursement（払い戻し）、itinerary（旅行計画）など1万語を超えるものまでが必要です。では、こうした表現は何を基準に選ばれるべきなのでしょうか？

話題の「コーパス」を徹底分析！頻出単語・熟語を楽々マスターできます！

まず挙げられるのは、TOEICの公式問題です。また、TOEICに精通したネイティブライターによる模擬試験のデータも参考になりますが、いずれも量的には不十分です。本書では、上記2つに加え、膨大な数の話し言葉・書き言葉を集めたデータベース、「コーパス」をコンピューターで分析して見出し語・熟語を厳選していますので、レベルAを突破し990点に到達するために必要な表現を、「頻度順」に身につけることができます。

「十分なコミュニケーションができる」レベルとは言え、それは「Native Speakerの域には一歩隔たりがある」とのただし書きつきです。990点に近づいていくことは、この「隔たり」を狭めていくことです。990点を獲得しても、Native Speakerと対等に渡り合うにはさらなる学習が必要です。本書で身につけた英語力を基に、皆さんがNative Speakerを相手に世界で活躍することを心から祈っています！

Contents

1日16単語・熟語×10週間で
TOEIC990点攻略の1120単語・熟語をマスター！

Chapter 1
名詞：超必修240
Page 13 ▶ 75

- Day 1 【名詞1】
- Day 2 【名詞2】
- Day 3 【名詞3】
- Day 4 【名詞4】
- Day 5 【名詞5】
- Day 6 【名詞6】
- Day 7 【名詞7】
- Day 8 【名詞8】
- Day 9 【名詞9】
- Day 10 【名詞10】
- Day 11 【名詞11】
- Day 12 【名詞12】
- Day 13 【名詞13】
- Day 14 【名詞14】
- Day 15 【名詞15】

Chapter 2
動詞：超必修112
Page 77 ▶ 107

- Day 16 【動詞1】
- Day 17 【動詞2】
- Day 18 【動詞3】
- Day 19 【動詞4】
- Day 20 【動詞5】
- Day 21 【動詞6】
- Day 22 【動詞7】

Chapter 3
形容詞：超必修112
Page 109 ▶ 139

- Day 23 【形容詞1】
- Day 24 【形容詞2】
- Day 25 【形容詞3】
- Day 26 【形容詞4】
- Day 27 【形容詞5】
- Day 28 【形容詞6】
- Day 29 【形容詞7】

Chapter 4
名詞：必修240
Page 141 ▶ 203

| Day 30 【名詞16】
| Day 31 【名詞17】
| Day 32 【名詞18】
| Day 33 【名詞19】
| Day 34 【名詞20】
| Day 35 【名詞21】
| Day 36 【名詞22】
| Day 37 【名詞23】
| Day 38 【名詞24】
| Day 39 【名詞25】
| Day 40 【名詞26】
| Day 41 【名詞27】
| Day 42 【名詞28】
| Day 43 【名詞29】
| Day 44 【名詞30】

Chapter 5
動詞：必修112
Page 205 ▶ 235

| Day 45 【動詞8】
| Day 46 【動詞9】
| Day 47 【動詞10】
| Day 48 【動詞11】
| Day 49 【動詞12】
| Day 50 【動詞13】
| Day 51 【動詞14】

Chapter 6
形容詞：必修112
Page 237 ▶ 267

| Day 52 【形容詞8】
| Day 53 【形容詞9】
| Day 54 【形容詞10】
| Day 55 【形容詞11】
| Day 56 【形容詞12】
| Day 57 【形容詞13】
| Day 58 【形容詞14】

Contents

Chapter 7
副詞：必修48
Page 269 ▶ 283

- Day 59 【副詞1】
- Day 60 【副詞2】
- Day 61 【副詞3】

Chapter 8
動詞句
Page 285 ▶ 315

- Day 62 【動詞句1】「動詞＋副詞［前置詞］」型1
- Day 63 【動詞句2】「動詞＋副詞［前置詞］」型2
- Day 64 【動詞句3】「動詞＋副詞［前置詞］」型3
- Day 65 【動詞句4】「動詞＋A＋前置詞＋B」型1
- Day 66 【動詞句5】「動詞＋A＋前置詞＋B」型2
- Day 67 【動詞句6】「be動詞＋形容詞＋前置詞」型1
- Day 68 【動詞句7】「be動詞＋形容詞＋前置詞」型2

Chapter 9

形容詞句・副詞句
Page 317 ▶ 327

| Day 69【形容詞句・副詞句1】
| Day 70【形容詞句・副詞句2】

Preface
Page 3

本書の4大特長
Page 8 ▶ 9

本書とCDの利用法
Page 10 ▶ 11

Index
Page 329 ▶ 349

【記号説明】

- CD-A1:「CD-Aのトラック1を呼び出してください」という意味です。
- 名 動 形 副 前 接:順に、名詞、動詞、形容詞、副詞、前置詞、接続詞を表します。
- 見出し中の [ ]:言い換え可能を表します。
- 見出し中の ( ):省略可能を表します。
- 見出し中のA、B:語句(主に名詞・代名詞)が入ることを表します。
- 見出し中のbe:be動詞が入ることを表します。be動詞は主語の人称・時制によって変化します。
- 見出し中のdo:動詞が入ることを表します。
- 見出し中のdoing:動名詞が入ることを表します。
- 見出し中のoneself:再帰代名詞が入ることを表します。主語によって再帰代名詞は異なります。
- 見出し中のone's:名詞・代名詞の所有格が入ることを表します。
- 見出し中の「~」:節(主語+動詞)が入ることを表します。
- 見出し下の「Part ~」「ビジネス問題」:該当するTOEICのPart、ビジネス関連問題で登場する可能性が高い単語・熟語を表します。
- 定義中の ( ):補足説明を表します。
- 定義中の [ ]:言い換えを表します。
- ❶:発音、アクセント、定義に注意すべき単語についています。
- ❹:補足説明を表します。
- ≒:同意・類義語 [熟語] を表します。
- ⇔:反意・反対語 [熟語] を表します。

だから「ゼッタイに覚えられる」!
本書の4大特長

1
公式問題・模擬試験 さらにコーパスデータを 徹底分析!

TOEICに出る! 日常生活で使える!

TOEICのための単語・熟語集である限り、「TOEICに出る」のは当然──。本書の目標は、そこから「実用英語」に対応できる単語・熟語力をいかに身につけてもらうかにあります。見出し語・熟語の選定にあたっては、TOEICの公式問題・模擬試験のデータに加え、最新の語彙研究から生まれたコーパス*のデータを徹底的に分析。目標スコアに到達するだけでなく、将来英語を使って世界で活躍するための土台となる単語・熟語が選ばれています。

＊コーパス:実際に話されたり書かれたりした言葉を大量に収集した「言語テキスト・データベース」のこと。コーパスを分析すると、どんな単語・熟語がどのくらいの頻度で使われるのか、といったことを客観的に調べられるので、辞書の編さんの際などに活用されている。

2
「目」だけでなく 「耳」と「口」までも フル活用して覚える!

「聞く単(キクタン)」! しっかり身につく!

「読む」だけでは、言葉は決して身につきません。私たちが日本語を習得できたのは、小さいころから日本語を繰り返し「聞いて・口に出して」きたから──この「当たり前のこと」を忘れてはいけません。本書では、音楽のリズムに乗りながら単語・熟語の学習ができる「チャンツCD」を2枚用意。「目」と「耳」から同時に単語・熟語をインプットし、さらに「口」に出していきますので、「覚えられない」不安を一発解消。読解・聴解力もダブルアップします。

『聞いて覚える英単語 キクタンTOEIC Test Score 990』では、TOEICの公式問題・模擬試験データと最新の語彙研究の成果であるコーパスを基に収録単語・熟語を厳選していますので、「TOEICに出る」「日常生活で使える」ものばかりです。その上で「いかに効率的に単語・熟語を定着させるか」──このことを本書は最も重視しました。ここでは、なぜ「出る・使える」のか、そしてなぜ「覚えられる」のかに関して、本書の特長をご紹介します。

3
1日16見出し×10週間、9のチャプターの「スケジュール学習」!

ムリなくマスターできる!

「継続は力なり」、とは分かっていても、続けるのは大変なことです。では、なぜ「大変」なのか? それは、覚えきれないほどの量の単語や熟語をムリに詰め込もうとするからです。本書では、「ゼッタイに覚える」ことを前提に、1日の学習量をあえて16見出しに抑えています。さらに、単語は品詞ごとに「頻度順」に、熟語は「表現型別」に、計9のチャプターに分けていますので、効率的・効果的に学習単語・熟語をマスターできます。

4
1日最短2分、最長でも6分の3つの「モード学習」!

挫折することなく最後まで続けられる!

今まで単語集や熟語集を手にしたときに、「1日でどこからどこまでやればいいのだろう?」と思ったことはありませんか? 見出し語・熟語、フレーズ、例文……1度に目を通すのは、忙しいときには難しいものです。本書は、Check 1（単語・熟語＋定義）→ Check 2（フレーズ）→ Check 3（センテンス）と、3つのポイントごとに学習できる「モード学習」を用意。生活スタイルやその日の忙しさに合わせて学習量を調整できます。

生活スタイルに合わせて選べる
Check 1▶2▶3の「モード学習」
本書とCDの利用法

Check 1

該当のCDトラックを呼び出して、「英語→日本語→英語」の順に収録されている「チャンツ音楽」で見出し語・熟語とその意味をチェック。時間に余裕がある人は、太字以外の定義も押さえておきましょう。

Check 2

Check 1で「見出し語・熟語→定義」を押さえたら、その単語・熟語が含まれているフレーズをチェック。フレーズレベルで使用例を確認することで、単語・熟語の定着度が高まります（センテンスが入っているDayもあります）。

Check 3

Check 2のフレーズレベルから、Check 3ではセンテンスレベルへとさらに実践的な例に触れていきます。ここまで学習すると、「音」と「文字」で最低6回は学習単語・熟語に触れるので、定着度は格段にアップします。

見出し語・熟語

1日の学習単語・熟語数は16です。見開きの左側に単語・熟語が掲載されています。チャンツでは上から順に単語・熟語が登場します。最初の8つが流れたら、ページをめくって次の8つに進みましょう。

チェックシート

本書に付属のチェックシートは復習用に活用してください。Check 1では見出し語・熟語の定義が身についているか、Check 2と3では訳を参照しながらチェックシートで隠されている単語・熟語がすぐに浮かんでくるかを確認しましょう。

定義

見出し語・熟語の定義が掲載されています。単語・熟語によっては複数の意味があるので、第1義以外の定義もなるべく覚えるようにしましょう。

Quick Review

前日に学習した単語・熟語のチェックリストです。左ページに日本語、右ページに英語が掲載されています。時間に余裕があるときは、該当のCDトラックでチャンツも聞いておきましょう。

1日の学習量は4ページ、学習単語・熟語数は16となっています。1つの見出し語・熟語につき、定義を学ぶ「Check 1」、フレーズ中で単語・熟語を学ぶ「Check 2」、センテンス中で学ぶ「Check 3」の3つの「モード学習」が用意されています。まずは、該当のCDトラックを呼び出して、「チャンツ音楽」のリズムに乗りながら見出し語・熟語と定義を「耳」と「目」で押さえましょう。時間に余裕がある人は、Check 2とCheck 3にもトライ！

こんなアナタにオススメ！
3つの「学習モード」

仕事にも恋にも、英語学習にも忙しいAさんには！

聞くだけモード
Check 1

学習時間の目安：1日2分

とにかく忙しくて、できれば単語・熟語学習は短時間で済ませたい人にオススメなのが、Check 1だけの「聞くだけモード」。該当のCDトラックで「チャンツ音楽」を聞き流すだけでもOK。でも、時間があるときはCheck 2とCheck 3で復習も忘れずに！

将来は海外勤務を目指すBさんには！

しっかりモード
Check 1 ▶ Check 2

学習時間の目安：1日4分

そこそこ英語はできるけど、さらなる英語力アップが必要だと感じている人にオススメなのが、Check 1とCheck 2を学習する「しっかりモード」。声に出してフレーズを「音読」すれば、定着度もさらにアップするはず。

自他ともに認める完ぺき主義のCさんには！

かんぺきモード
Check 1 ▶ Check 2 ▶ Check 3

学習時間の目安：1日6分

やるからには完ぺきにしなければ気が済まない人には「かんぺきモード」がオススメ。ここまでやっても学習時間の目安はたったの6分。できればみんな「かんぺきモード」でパーフェクトを目指そう！

＊学習時間はあくまでも目安です。時間に余裕があるときは、チャンツ音楽を繰り返し聞いたり、フレーズやセンテンスの音読を重ねたりして、なるべく多く学習単語・熟語に触れるように心がけましょう。
＊CDには見出し語・熟語と定義のみが収録されています。

※CDに収録されていない例文音声は、ダウンロードコンテンツとして購入することができます。
　http://www.alc.co.jp/book/onsei-dl/
※コンテンツには「例文音声」「チャンツ＋例文音声」の2種類があります。

＜CD取り扱いのご注意＞
●弊社制作の音声CDは、CDプレーヤーでの再生を保証する規格品です。
●パソコンでご使用になる場合、CD-ROMドライブとの相性により、ディスクを再生できない場合がございます。ご了承ください。
●パソコンでタイトル・トラック情報を表示させたい場合は、iTunesをご利用ください。iTunesでは、弊社がCDのタイトル・トラック情報を登録しているGracenote社のCDDB（データベース）からインターネットを介してトラック情報を取得することができます。
● CDとして正常に音声が再生できるディスクからパソコンやmp3プレーヤー等への取り込み時にトラブルが生じた際は、まず、そのアプリケーション（ソフト）、プレーヤーの製作元へご相談ください。

CHAPTER 1

名詞：超必修240

Chapter 1のスタートです！
このChapterでは、TOEIC「超必修」の名詞240をマスターしていきます。先はまだまだ長いけれど、焦らず急がず学習を進めていきましょう。

TOEIC的格言

A man becomes learned by asking questions.

聞くは一時の恥、聞かぬは一生の恥。
[直訳] 人は質問することで知識を身につける。

Day 1【名詞1】
▶ 14
Day 2【名詞2】
▶ 18
Day 3【名詞3】
▶ 22
Day 4【名詞4】
▶ 26
Day 5【名詞5】
▶ 30
Day 6【名詞6】
▶ 34
Day 7【名詞7】
▶ 38
Day 8【名詞8】
▶ 42
Day 9【名詞9】
▶ 46
Day 10【名詞10】
▶ 50
Day 11【名詞11】
▶ 54
Day 12【名詞12】
▶ 58
Day 13【名詞13】
▶ 62
Day 14【名詞14】
▶ 66
Day 15【名詞15】
▶ 70
Chapter 1 Review
▶ 74

Day 1　名詞1

Check 1　Listen))) CD-A1

□ 0001
premium
/príːmiəm/
ビジネス問題

名 ❶**保険料**　❷割増金、プレミアム　❸ハイオクガソリン
形 ❶高級な　❷プレミアのついた

□ 0002
beverage
/bévəridʒ/
Part 1

名 (水以外の)**飲み物**、飲料

□ 0003
itinerary
/aitínərèri/
Part 2, 3

名 **旅行計画**、旅程(表)
形 旅行の；旅程の

□ 0004
shipment
/ʃípmənt/
ビジネス問題

名 ❶**積み荷**、発送品　❷出荷、発送
名 shipping：❶発送、出荷　❷(集合的に)船舶　❸海運業
動 ship：(商品)を発送[出荷]する；～を輸送する

□ 0005
brochure
/brouʃúər/
❶発音注意
Part 2, 3

名 **パンフレット**、小冊子 (≒ pamphlet, booklet)

□ 0006
inventory
/ínvəntɔ̀ːri/
ビジネス問題

名 ❶**在庫品**、品ぞろえ；在庫品目　❷在庫調べ、棚卸し

□ 0007
pedestrian
/pədéstriən/
Part 1

名 **歩行者** (≒ walker)
形 (道路などが)歩行用の

□ 0008
invoice
/ínvɔis/
ビジネス問題

名 (明細記入)**請求書**、仕入れ書、インボイス
動 ❶～に請求書を送る　❷～の請求書を作る

continued
▼

いよいよDay 1のスタート！ 今日から15日間は「超必修」の名詞240をチェック。まずは、CDでチャンツを聞いてみよう！

- ☐ 聞くだけモード　Check 1
- ☐ しっかりモード　Check 1 ▶ 2
- ☐ かんぺきモード　Check 1 ▶ 2 ▶ 3

Check 2　　Phrase

☐ **car insurance premiums**(自動車保険の保険料)
☐ **at a premium**(プレミアムつきで、額面以上で；品不足で)

☐ **alcoholic beverages**(アルコール飲料)

☐ **plan an itinerary**(旅行計画を立てる)

☐ **a large shipment of wheat**(大量の小麦の積み荷)
☐ **be ready for shipment**(出荷の準備ができている)

☐ **a travel brochure**(旅行パンフレット)

☐ **the volume of inventories**(在庫量)
☐ **take inventory**(棚卸しをする)

☐ **pedestrians crossing the road**(道路を横断している歩行者たち)

☐ **enclose an invoice**(請求書を同封する)

Check 3　　Sentence

☐ **I paid over $3,000 in annual life insurance premiums.**(私は年間の生命保険の保険料に3000ドル以上を払った)

☐ **The waiter is serving beverages.**(ウエーターは飲み物を出している)

☐ **We had to change the itinerary because of bad weather.**(悪天候のため、私たちは旅行計画を変更しなければならなかった)

☐ **A shipment of urgent water and food supplies is expected to arrive tomorrow.**(水と食糧の緊急供給の積み荷は明日届く予定だ)

☐ **This brochure includes detailed information about the product.**(このパンフレットにはその製品の詳しい情報が含まれている)

☐ **We have a large inventory of quality used automobiles.**(当店では高品質の中古車を大量に取りそろえている)

☐ **There are a lot of pedestrians on the sidewalk.**(歩道には多くの歩行者がいる)

☐ **Invoices must be paid by the last day of each month.**(請求書は各月の最終日までに支払われなければならない)

continued
▼

Day 1

Check 1　Listen 》CD-A1

□ 0009
subsidiary
/səbsídièri/
ビジネス問題

名 **子会社**
形 ❶補助的な　❷(～に)付随[従属]する(to ～)

□ 0010
refund
/ríːfʌnd/
ビジネス問題

名 **払い戻し**(金)(≒reimbursement)
動 (/rifʌ́nd/)(料金など)を払い戻す
形 refundable：払い戻しの利く

□ 0011
dividend
/dívədènd/
ビジネス問題

名 (株の)**配当**(金)(≒capital bonus)

□ 0012
warehouse
/wéərhàus/
Part 1

名 **倉庫**

□ 0013
merchandise
/mə́ːrtʃəndàiz/
ビジネス問題

名 (集合的に)**商品**、製品(≒goods)
動 ～を売買する、商う
名 merchandising：商品化計画
名 merchant：商人、商店主

□ 0014
bid
/bíd/
ビジネス問題

名 ❶(工事などの)**入札**(for ～)　❷(～のための)企て、試み(for ～)
動 ❶(bid forで)～に入札する　❷(bid A for Bで)(競売などで)A(値)をB(物)につける
名 bidder：入札者、競り手

□ 0015
warranty
/wɔ́ːrənti/
ビジネス問題

名 (品質などの／…に対する)**保証**；保証書(on ～/against …)(≒guarantee)

□ 0016
detour
/díːtuər/
❶発音注意
Part 4

名 **迂回路**、回り道(⇔shortcut：近道)
動 迂回する

Check 2 Phrase

- a fully-owned subsidiary（全額出資の子会社）

- ask for [get] a refund（払い戻しを求める[受ける]）

- a stock dividend（株式配当）
- dividend on [off]（配当つき[落ち]）

- a vacant warehouse（空の倉庫）

- defective merchandise（欠陥商品）

- make a bid of $10,000 for ~（~の入札に1万ドルの値をつける）
- in a bid to do ~（~しようとして）

- be still under warranty（保証期間中である）

- make [take] a detour（迂回する）

Check 3 Sentence

- The company is a subsidiary of a London-based oil company.（その会社はロンドンに本社がある石油会社の子会社だ）

- You can return any purchase within 7 days for a full refund or exchange.（7日以内であれば、全額払い戻しか交換のため購入品を返品することができる）

- The dividends will be paid to shareholders on April 1.（配当金は4月1日に株主たちに支払われる予定だ）

- The products are stored in the warehouse.（製品が倉庫に保管されている）

- The US exported $248.9 billion of merchandise to Canada in 2007.（2007年にアメリカは2489億ドルの商品をカナダへ輸出した）

- The builder won the bid for the construction of the new city hall.（その建設会社は新市庁舎の建設を落札した）

- The computer comes with a one-year warranty against defects.（そのコンピューターは欠陥に対する1年の保証がついている）

- He took a detour to avoid the heavy traffic.（彼は交通渋滞を避けるために迂回した）

Day 2　名詞2

Check 1　Listen 》CD-A2

□ 0017
specification
/spèsəfikéiʃən/
Part 7

名(通例~s)**仕様書**、設計明細書(≒spec)
名specific：(~s)詳細
形specific：❶特定の　❷明確な　❸(~に)特有[固有]の(to ~)
動specify：~を明確に述べる、明記する

□ 0018
applicant
/ǽplikənt/
ビジネス問題

名(~への)**志願者**、応募者(for ~)
名application：❶(~への)申し込み(書)、申請(書)(for ~)　❷(~への)利用、適用(to ~)
動apply：❶(apply forで)~を申し込む　❷(apply toで)~に申し込む；~に適用される

□ 0019
subscription
/səbskrípʃən/
Part 7

名(~の)**定期購読**(料)(to ~)
名subscriber：(~の)定期購読者(to ~)；(電話などの)加入者
動subscribe：(subscribe toで)❶~を定期購読する　❷(通例疑問・否定文で)~に同意する

□ 0020
intersection
/íntərsèkʃən/
Part 1

名**交差点**(≒junction, crossing)
動intersect：(路線などが)交差する

□ 0021
merger
/mə́ːrdʒər/
ビジネス問題

名(~との)(企業の)**合併**(with ~)
動merge：❶(merge withで)(会社などが)~と合併する　❷(会社など)を(…に)合併する(into …)

□ 0022
agenda
/ədʒéndə/
ビジネス問題

名**議題**、協議事項

□ 0023
supervisor
/súːpərvàizər/
ビジネス問題

名**監督者**、管理者
名supervision：監督、管理、指揮
動supervise：~を監督[管理]する
形supervisory：監督[管理](上)の

□ 0024
transit
/trǽnzit/
Part 4

名❶**輸送**、運送；輸送機関　❷通過、通行
名transition：(~から/…への)移行、変遷；過渡期(from ~/to …)
形transitional：過渡期の

continued
▼

チャンツを聞く際には、「英語→日本語→英語」の2回目の「英語」の部分で声に出して読んでみよう。定着度が倍増するはず！

☐ 聞くだけモード　Check 1
☐ しっかりモード　Check 1 ▶ 2
☐ かんぺきモード　Check 1 ▶ 2 ▶ 3

Check 2　Phrase

☐ specifications for a new computer(新しいコンピューターの仕様書)

☐ applicants for scholarships(奨学金の志願者)
☐ job applicants(求職者)

☐ take out a subscription to ~(~を定期購読する)

☐ turn left at the next intersection(次の交差点で左折する)
☐ a T-intersection(T字路)

☐ mergers and acquisitions([企業の]合併買収)❶略はM & A

☐ the first item on the agenda(議題の最初の項目)
☐ be high on the agenda(最も重要な議題である)

☐ a production supervisor(製造監督者)

☐ public transit(公共輸送機関)
☐ a transit passenger(乗り継ぎ客)

Check 3　Sentence

☐ Please read the specifications carefully before making a purchase.(購入の前に仕様書を十分にお読みください)

☐ There are more than 100 applicants for the job.(その仕事には100人を超える志願者がいる)

☐ A renewal notification will be sent to you 7-8 weeks before your subscription expires.(定期購読が切れる7、8週間前に更新のお知らせが送られる)

☐ There are no vehicles at the intersection.(交差点には車が1台も止まっていない)

☐ The merger of the two companies has created the world's biggest pharmaceutical company.(両社の合併によって世界最大の製薬会社が誕生した)

☐ Let's move on to the next item on the agenda.(議題の次の項目に進みましょう)

☐ He was promoted to accounting supervisor last year.(彼は昨年、会計監督者に昇進した)

☐ The goods were damaged in transit due to carrier negligence.(商品は運送会社の過失で輸送中に損傷を受けた)

continued
▼

Day 2

Check 1　Listen)) CD-A2

☐ 0025
appliance
/əpláiəns/
Part 2, 3

名 (家庭用の)**器具**、機器

☐ 0026
vendor
/véndər/
Part 1

名 **露天商人**、行商人
動 vend：(通例街頭などで)〜を売る

☐ 0027
inconvenience
/ìnkənvíːnjəns/
Part 7

名 **不便**、不都合、迷惑
動 〜に迷惑[不便]をかける
形 inconvenient：(〜に)不便な、迷惑な(to [for] 〜)

☐ 0028
supplier
/səpláiər/
ビジネス問題

名 **供給[納入]業者**
名 supply：❶(通例〜ies)備品；必需品；在庫　❷供給　❸供給物
動 supply：(supply A with Bで)AにBを供給する

☐ 0029
advocate
/ǽdvəkət/
Part 5, 6

名 (〜の)**支持者**、主張者、提唱者(of [for]〜)
動 (/ǽdvəkèit/)〜を支持[主張、擁護]する
名 advocacy：(〜の)支持、弁護、擁護(of 〜)

☐ 0030
landmark
/lǽndmà:rk/
Part 7

名 ❶(陸上の)**目印**、目標物　❷画期的な出来事；(形容詞的に)画期的な

☐ 0031
audit
/ɔ́:dit/
ビジネス問題

名 **会計検査**、監査
動 (会計・帳簿)を検査[監査]する
名 auditor：会計検査官、監査役

☐ 0032
morale
/mərǽl/
❶発音注意
Part 5, 6

名 (集団などの)**士気**、意気込み　⊕moral(道徳の)と混同しないように注意

Day 1)) CD-A1
Quick Review
答えは右ページ下

☐ 保険料　☐ パンフレット　☐ 子会社　☐ 商品
☐ 飲み物　☐ 在庫品　☐ 払い戻し　☐ 入札
☐ 旅行計画　☐ 歩行者　☐ 配当　☐ 保証
☐ 積み荷　☐ 請求書　☐ 倉庫　☐ 迂回路

Check 2　Phrase

- [ ] electrical appliances（電気器具）

- [ ] a newspaper vendor（[露店の]新聞売り）
- [ ] a street vendor（街頭の物売り）

- [ ] put ~ to inconvenience ＝ cause inconvenience to ~（~に不便[迷惑]をかける）

- [ ] an automotive parts supplier（自動車部品供給業者）

- [ ] an advocate of peace（平和論者）

- [ ] a historical landmark（歴史的建造物）
- [ ] landmark discovery（画期的な発見）

- [ ] an audit report（会計検査報告書）
- [ ] external [internal] audit（外部[内部]監査）

- [ ] boost [improve] the morale of ~（~の士気を高める）

Check 3　Sentence

- [ ] The store carries a wide variety of household appliances.（その店はさまざまな家庭用器具を扱っている）

- [ ] The vendor is selling some vegetables.（露天商人は野菜を売っている）

- [ ] We apologize for any inconvenience caused by the delay.（遅れによりご迷惑をおかけしたことをおわびいたします）

- [ ] The company is a leading supplier of semiconductors.（その会社は大手の半導体供給業者だ）

- [ ] She is an influential advocate of education reform.（彼女は教育改革の影響力のある支持者だ）

- [ ] The Eiffel Tower is the most recognizable landmark in Paris.（エッフェル塔はパリで最も目につきやすい建造物だ）

- [ ] Companies are required to establish an audit committee.（企業は監査委員会を設置する必要がある）

- [ ] The management is concerned about low employee morale.（経営陣は従業員の士気の低さを心配している）

Day 1　))CD-A1
Quick Review
答えは左ページ下

- [ ] premium
- [ ] beverage
- [ ] itinerary
- [ ] shipment
- [ ] brochure
- [ ] inventory
- [ ] pedestrian
- [ ] invoice
- [ ] subsidiary
- [ ] refund
- [ ] dividend
- [ ] warehouse
- [ ] merchandise
- [ ] bid
- [ ] warranty
- [ ] detour

CHAPTER 1
CHAPTER 2
CHAPTER 3
CHAPTER 4
CHAPTER 5
CHAPTER 6
CHAPTER 7
CHAPTER 8
CHAPTER 9

Day 3 名詞3

Check 1 Listen ») CD-A3

□ 0033
stationery
/stéiʃənèri/
Part 5, 6

名❶(集合的に)**文房具**、事務用品 ❷便箋 ❶stationary(静止した)と混同しないように注意

□ 0034
altitude
/ǽltətjùːd/
Part 4

名**高度**、標高、海抜(≒elevation)

□ 0035
chore
/tʃɔːr/
Part 2, 3

名**雑用**、半端仕事

□ 0036
venue
/vénjuː/
Part 4

名(競技会などの)**開催地**、会場

□ 0037
liability
/làiəbíləti/
Part 7

名❶(~に対する)**法的責任**(for ~)(≒responsibility) ❷(~ies)負債、債務(⇔asset)
形liable:❶(be liable to doで)~すべき法的責任がある; ~しがちである ❷(be liable forで)~に対して法的責任がある

□ 0038
predecessor
/prédəsèsər/
ビジネス問題

名**前任者**(⇔successor:後任者);前のもの

□ 0039
affiliate
/əfíliət/
ビジネス問題

名**系列**[関連]**会社**、付属機関
動(/əfílièit/)(be affiliated with [to]で)~の系列下である、~に付属している

□ 0040
malfunction
/mælfʌ́ŋkʃən/
Part 7

名(機械などの)**不調**、故障;(器官などの)機能不全
動(機械などが)うまく機能しない、故障する

continued
▼

「3日坊主」にならないためにも、今日・明日の学習がとっても大切。CDを聞き流すだけでもOKなので、「継続」を心がけよう。

- ☐ 聞くだけモード　Check 1
- ☐ しっかりモード　Check 1 ▶ 2
- ☐ かんぺきモード　Check 1 ▶ 2 ▶ 3

Check 2　Phrase

☐ a stationery store（文房具店）
☐ personalized stationery（名入りの便箋）

☐ mountains with altitudes over 8,000 meters（標高8000メートルを超える山々）

☐ boring chores（退屈な雑用）
☐ household chores（家事）

☐ an ideal venue for international conferences（国際会議の理想的な開催地）

☐ joint liability（共同責任）
☐ have liabilities of $2 million（200万ドルの負債がある）

☐ take over a job from a predecessor（前任者から仕事を引き継ぐ）

☐ a foreign affiliate（海外の関連会社）

☐ an engine malfunction（エンジンの不調）

Check 3　Sentence

☐ She works in the stationery section of a department store.（彼女はデパートの文房具売り場に勤めている）

☐ We are currently cruising at an altitude of 30,000 feet.（当機は現在、高度3万フィートを巡航中です）➕機内アナウンス

☐ Husbands should share household chores with their wives.（夫は妻と家事を分担すべきだ）

☐ London is the venue for the Olympic Games in 2012.（ロンドンは2012年のオリンピックの開催地だ）

☐ The defendant denied any liability for the accident.（被告はその事故に対する法的責任を否定した）

☐ The new iPod is thinner than its predecessors.（新しいiPodは以前のものよりも薄い）

☐ Daihatsu is an affiliate of Toyota.（ダイハツはトヨタの系列会社だ）

☐ The pilot reported a mechanical malfunction soon after takeoff.（パイロットは離陸後すぐに機械の不調を報告した）

CHAPTER 1
CHAPTER 2
CHAPTER 3
CHAPTER 4
CHAPTER 5
CHAPTER 6
CHAPTER 7
CHAPTER 8
CHAPTER 9

continued ▼

Day 3

Check 1　Listen))) CD-A3

0041
workplace
/wə́:rkplèis/
ビジネス問題

名 **職場**、仕事場

0042
bankruptcy
/bǽŋkrʌptsi/
ビジネス問題

名 **倒産**、破産
名 bankrupt：破産者
動 bankrupt：～を破産させる
形 bankrupt：破産した

0043
pharmacy
/fá:rməsi/
Part 2, 3

名 **薬局**（≒drugstore, chemist's）
名 pharmacist：薬剤師
名 pharmaceutical：(～s) ❶(集合的に)医薬　❷製薬会社
形 pharmaceutical：製薬の；薬学の；薬剤の

0044
expenditure
/ikspénditʃər/
ビジネス問題

名 ❶(～への) **支出**(on ～)(≒spending)　❷(～に対する)経費(on ～)(≒cost, expense)
動 expend：(金など)を(…に)費やす、使う(on ...)

0045
renewal
/rinjú:əl/
Part 7

名 ❶ **更新**　❷再生、再建
動 renew：❶～を更新する　❷～を再開する
形 renewable：❶再生[回復、復活]できる　❷更新[継続、延長]できる

0046
incentive
/inséntiv/
Part 7

名 (～する) **動機**(to do)；(～への)刺激(to ～)(≒motive, motivation, inducement)

0047
subordinate
/səbɔ́:rdənət/
ビジネス問題

名 **部下**(⇔boss, superior：上司)
形 (～より)下位の(to ～)

0048
discretion
/diskréʃən/
Part 7

名 ❶ **自由裁量**、判断[行動、選択]の自由　❷思慮深さ、慎重さ、分別
形 discreet：慎重な；(～について)口が堅い(about ～)

Day 2))) CD-A2
Quick Review
答えは右ページ下

☐ 仕様書　　☐ 合併　　　☐ 器具　　　　☐ 支持者
☐ 志願者　　☐ 議題　　　☐ 露天商人　　☐ 目印
☐ 定期購読　☐ 監督者　　☐ 不便　　　　☐ 会計検査
☐ 交差点　　☐ 輸送　　　☐ 供給業者　　☐ 士気

Check 2　Phrase

- ☐ stress in the workplace（職場でのストレス）

- ☐ declare bankruptcy（破産を宣告する）
- ☐ file for bankruptcy（破産を申請する）

- ☐ an owner of a pharmacy（薬局の経営者）

- ☐ annual expenditure（歳出）
- ☐ expenditure on education（教育費）

- ☐ renewal of a contract（契約の更新）
- ☐ an economic renewal（経済の再建）

- ☐ have little incentive to do ~（~する動機がほとんどない）
- ☐ economic incentives（経済的刺激）

- ☐ praise [reprimand] one's subordinate（部下を褒める[しかる]）

- ☐ at the discretion of ~（~の裁量[判断]で）
- ☐ act with discretion（慎重に行動する）

Check 3　Sentence

- ☐ Gender discrimination in the workplace is prohibited.（職場での性差別は禁止されている）

- ☐ The number of bankruptcies in small businesses has been rising.（中小企業の倒産件数が増加している）

- ☐ I went to the pharmacy to have a prescription filled.（私は処方薬を調合してもらうために薬局へ行った）

- ☐ We need to reduce unnecessary expenditure.（私たちは不必要な支出を減らす必要がある）

- ☐ The fee for renewal of a driver's license is $30.（運転免許証の更新料は30ドルだ）

- ☐ Bonuses give employees an incentive to work harder.（ボーナスはより熱心に働く動機を従業員に与える）

- ☐ Subordinates must obey superiors.（部下は上司に従わなければならない）

- ☐ The decision was left to the CEO's discretion.（決断はCEOの裁量に委ねられた）

Day 2　)) CD-A2
Quick Review
答えは左ページ下

- ☐ specification
- ☐ applicant
- ☐ subscription
- ☐ intersection
- ☐ merger
- ☐ agenda
- ☐ supervisor
- ☐ transit
- ☐ appliance
- ☐ vendor
- ☐ inconvenience
- ☐ supplier
- ☐ advocate
- ☐ landmark
- ☐ audit
- ☐ morale

CHAPTER 1
CHAPTER 2
CHAPTER 3
CHAPTER 4
CHAPTER 5
CHAPTER 6
CHAPTER 7
CHAPTER 8
CHAPTER 9

Day 4　名詞4

Check 1　Listen 》CD-A4

☐ 0049
surplus
/sə́ːrplʌs/
ビジネス問題

名 ❶**黒字**(⇔deficit)　❷余り；過剰
形 余分の；余った

☐ 0050
petition
/pətíʃən/
Part 7

名 (〜を求める／…に反対する)**請願**(書)、嘆願(書)(for 〜/against ...)(≒request)
動 (〜を求めて／…するよう)請願する(for 〜/to do)

☐ 0051
renovation
/rènəvéiʃən/
Part 5, 6

名 ❶**改装**；修理　❷刷新、革新
動 renovate：〜を改装する；〜を修理[復元]する

☐ 0052
entrepreneur
/ὰːntrəprənə́ːr/
❶発音注意
ビジネス問題

名 **起業家**、事業家

☐ 0053
tuition
/tjuːíʃən/
Part 5, 6

名 ❶**授業料**(≒tuition fee)　❷授業、指導(≒teaching)

☐ 0054
breakthrough
/bréikθrùː/
Part 7

名 ❶(交渉などの)**進展**、打開(in 〜)　❷(研究などの)大発見、大躍進(in 〜)
動 break through：❶大きく前進する　❷大発見をする

☐ 0055
souvenir
/sùːvəníər/
❶アクセント注意
Part 2, 3

名 (〜の)**記念品**、土産(of 〜)

☐ 0056
questionnaire
/kwèstʃənéər/
❶アクセント注意
Part 7

名 **アンケート**(用紙)

continued
▼

「細切れ時間」を有効活用してる？『キクタン』は2分でも学習可能。いつでもどこでもテキストとCDを持ち歩いて単語・熟語に触れよう！

☐ 聞くだけモード Check 1
☐ しっかりモード Check 1 ▶ 2
☐ かんぺきモード Check 1 ▶ 2 ▶ 3

Check 2　Phrase

☐ a trade surplus（貿易黒字）
☐ in surplus（余分[過剰]に）

☐ a petition for healthcare reform（医療改革を求める請願）
☐ draw up a petition（請願書を作成する）

☐ extensive renovations（大規模な改装[修復]）
☐ technological renovation（技術革新）

☐ a talented entrepreneur（有能な起業家）

☐ tuition increases（授業料の値上げ）
☐ private tuition（個人指導）

☐ a breakthrough in the negotiation（交渉の進展）
☐ make a breakthrough in ~（~において大発見をする）

☐ a souvenir shop（土産物店）

☐ fill out [in] a questionnaire（アンケートに記入する）

Check 3　Sentence

☐ When revenue is higher than spending, the government budget is in surplus.（歳入が歳出よりも多い場合、政府予算は黒字になる）

☐ Over 50 percent of the residents signed a petition against the closure of the local hospital.（50パーセントを超える住民が地元の病院の閉鎖に反対する請願書に署名した）

☐ The department store is temporarily closed for renovation.（そのデパートは改装のため一時休業している）

☐ Bill Gates is one of the most successful entrepreneurs.（ビル・ゲイツは最も成功した起業家の1人だ）

☐ Tuition for the private school is $12,500 per year.（その私立学校の授業料は年間1万2500ドルだ）

☐ The scientist made a major breakthrough in cancer treatment.（その科学者ががん治療を大きく進展させた）

☐ What did you buy as a souvenir of your trip to Australia?（オーストラリア旅行の記念品に何を買いましたか？）

☐ Please fill out the questionnaire and send it to the address below.（アンケートに記入して、下記の住所に送ってください）

continued
▼

Day 4

Check 1　Listen))) CD-A4

☐ 0057
surcharge
/sə́ːrtʃɑ̀ːrdʒ/
Part 7

名 **追加料金**、追徴金
動 ～に追加料金を請求する

☐ 0058
mortgage
/mɔ́ːrgidʒ/
❶発音注意
ビジネス問題

名 **住宅ローン**(≒home loan)
動 ～を抵当に入れる

☐ 0059
lawsuit
/lɔ́ːsùːt/
Part 2, 3

名 **訴訟**(≒suit)

☐ 0060
dedication
/dèdikéiʃən/
Part 4

名 (～への)**献身**(to ～)(≒devotion)
動 dedicate：❶(dedicate A to Bで)AをBにささげる　❷(be dedicated toで)～に専念[熱中]している
形 dedicated：❶熱心な、献身的な、ひたむきな　❷(装置などが)ある特定の目的用の、専用の

☐ 0061
sanction
/sǽŋkʃən/
Part 5, 6

名 ❶(～s)(～に対する)**制裁**(措置)(against [on] ～)　❷認可(≒permission, approval, acceptance)
動 ❶～を認可[公認]する　❷～に対して制裁措置を取る

☐ 0062
bulk
/bʌ́lk/
ビジネス問題

名 ❶(the ～)(～の)**大部分**(of ～)　❷(形容詞的に)大量の、大規模な
形 bulky：大きい、かさばった

☐ 0063
vaccination
/væksənéiʃən/
Part 7

名 (病気に対する)**予防**[ワクチン]**接種**(against [for] ～)
名 vaccine：ワクチン

☐ 0064
hazard
/hǽzərd/
Part 5, 6

名 **危険**(≒danger)；(～への)危険要素(to ～)
動 ～を危険にさらす(≒risk)
形 hazardous：(～にとって)危険な；有害な(to ～)

| Day 3))) CD-A3
Quick Review
答えは右ページ下 | ☐ 文房具
☐ 高度
☐ 雑用
☐ 開催地 | ☐ 法的責任
☐ 前任者
☐ 系列会社
☐ 不調 | ☐ 職場
☐ 倒産
☐ 薬局
☐ 支出 | ☐ 更新
☐ 動機
☐ 部下
☐ 自由裁量 |

Check 2　Phrase

- ☐ impose a surcharge on ~（~に追加料金[追徴金]を課す）

- ☐ take out a mortgage（住宅ローンを組む）
- ☐ mortgage interest rates（住宅ローンの利率）

- ☐ file [bring] a lawsuit against ~（~に対して訴訟を起こす）

- ☐ her dedication to volunteer work（ボランティア活動への彼女の献身）

- ☐ impose [lift] sanctions on ~（~に対して制裁措置を取る[~に対する制裁措置を解除する]）
- ☐ give sanction to ~（~を認可する）

- ☐ the bulk of the cost（経費の大部分）
- ☐ bulk buying [production]（大量購入[生産]）

- ☐ vaccination against measles（はしかの予防接種）

- ☐ pose a hazard to ~（~に対して危険をもたらす）
- ☐ a fire hazard（火事の原因となるもの）

Check 3　Sentence

- ☐ Economy class passengers will pay lower fuel surcharges than those travelling in first class.（エコノミークラスの乗客が払う燃油サーチャージは、ファーストクラスの乗客よりも低い）

- ☐ I paid off my mortgage last year.（私は昨年、住宅ローンを完済した）

- ☐ The residents have filed a lawsuit to stop the construction of the mall.（住民たちはそのショッピングセンターの建設を中止させるため訴訟を起こした）

- ☐ I would like to thank you all for your dedication to the project.（プロジェクトへの皆さんの献身に感謝いたします）

- ☐ Economic sanctions against the country will be lifted as soon as a peace accord is implemented.（和平合意が実施され次第、その国への経済制裁は解除される予定だ）

- ☐ Compact and mid-size cars account for the bulk of car sales.（小型車と中型車は自動車販売の大部分を占めている）

- ☐ Children are recommended to receive vaccinations against flu.（子どもたちはインフルエンザの予防接種を受けることを勧められている）

- ☐ Snow and ice on sidewalks is a hazard to pedestrians.（歩道の雪や氷は歩行者にとって危険だ）

Day 3　))) CD-A3
Quick Review
答えは左ページ下

- ☐ stationery
- ☐ altitude
- ☐ chore
- ☐ venue
- ☐ liability
- ☐ predecessor
- ☐ affiliate
- ☐ malfunction
- ☐ workplace
- ☐ bankruptcy
- ☐ pharmacy
- ☐ expenditure
- ☐ renewal
- ☐ incentive
- ☐ subordinate
- ☐ discretion

CHAPTER 1
CHAPTER 2
CHAPTER 3
CHAPTER 4
CHAPTER 5
CHAPTER 6
CHAPTER 7
CHAPTER 8
CHAPTER 9

Day 5　名詞5

Check 1　Listen 》CD-A5

☐ 0065
recipient
/rɪsípiənt/
Part 7

名 (〜の)**受取人**、受領者(of 〜)

☐ 0066
bulletin
/búlətən/
Part 1

名 **掲示**、公報

☐ 0067
payroll
/péiròul/
ビジネス問題

名 **従業員名簿**[総数]；給料支払名簿

☐ 0068
turbulence
/tə́ːrbjuləns/
Part 4

名 ❶ **乱気流**　❷(社会的)動乱、騒乱
形 turbulent：❶騒然とした、不穏な　❷(天候などが)荒れ狂う

☐ 0069
bias
/báiəs/
Part 5, 6

名 (〜に対する)**偏見**；先入観(against 〜)(≒prejudice)
動 〜に偏見[先入観]を抱かせる
形 biased：(意見などが)(〜に)偏った、偏見を持った(against [toward, in favor of] 〜)

☐ 0070
revision
/rɪvíʒən/
Part 2, 3

名 **修正**、改訂、改定
動 revise：〜を修正[改訂]する

☐ 0071
supplement
/sʌ́pləmənt/
Part 5, 6

名 ❶ **補給剤**、栄養補助食品　❷(〜の)補足；(書物などの)補遺、付録(to 〜)(≒appendix)
動 (/sʌ́pləmènt/) (supplement A with B で)AをBで補う
形 supplementary：(〜の)補足[付録]の(to 〜)

☐ 0072
integrity
/ɪntégrəti/
❶アクセント注意
Part 4

名 ❶ **誠実**、正直(≒honesty)　❷無傷の[完全な]状態

continued
▼

Quick Reviewは使ってる？ 昨日覚えた単語でも、記憶に残っているとは限らない。学習の合間に軽くチェックするだけでも効果は抜群！

- ☐ 聞くだけモード　Check 1
- ☐ しっかりモード　Check 1 ▶ 2
- ☐ かんぺきモード　Check 1 ▶ 2 ▶ 3

Check 2　Phrase

- ☐ pension recipients（年金受給者）
- ☐ the recipient of the Nobel Prize（ノーベル賞の受賞者）

- ☐ a bulletin board（掲示板）
- ☐ an election bulletin（選挙公報）

- ☐ be on the payroll（就業している）

- ☐ encounter turbulence（乱気流に遭遇する）
- ☐ political turbulence（政治的動乱）

- ☐ bias against women（女性に対する偏見）

- ☐ make an upward [a downward] revision to ～（～を上方[下方]修正する）
- ☐ revision of prices（価格の改定）

- ☐ vitamin C supplements（ビタミンC補給剤）
- ☐ a Sunday supplement（[新聞の]日曜版）

- ☐ with integrity（誠実に、正直に）
- ☐ territorial integrity（領土の保全）

Check 3　Sentence

- ☐ The number of welfare recipients is on the rise.（生活保護を受けている人の数は上昇傾向にある）

- ☐ Notices are posted on the bulletin board.（ビラが掲示板に貼られている）

- ☐ The company will add 100 employees to its payroll next year.（その会社は来年、従業員を100人追加する予定だ）

- ☐ Please fasten your seat belts; there is turbulence ahead.（シートベルトを着用してください。進行方向に乱気流があります）➕機内アナウンス

- ☐ Racial bias still exists in our society.（人種的偏見は私たちの社会にいまだに存在している）

- ☐ The budget needs significant revision.（その予算案はかなりの修正が必要だ）

- ☐ The doctor told me to take calcium supplements every day.（医者はカルシウムの補給剤を毎日服用するよう私に言った）

- ☐ He is a man of high integrity.（彼は非常に誠実な人物だ）

continued ▼

Day 5

Check 1　Listen))) CD-A5

0073 wholesale /hóulsèil/ ビジネス問題
- 名 **卸売り**（⇔retail：小売り）
- 形 卸売りの
- 名 wholesaler：卸売業者

0074 directory /diréktəri/ Part 2, 3
- 名 **住所録**、名簿

0075 pharmacist /fá:rməsist/ Part 2, 3
- 名 **薬剤師**
- 名 pharmacy：薬局
- 名 pharmaceutical：(～s) ❶（集合的に）医薬 ❷製薬会社
- 形 pharmaceutical：製薬の；薬学の；薬剤の

0076 condominium /kàndəmíniəm/ Part 5, 6
- 名 **分譲マンション**　⊕短縮形のcondoもよく使われる。mansionは「大邸宅」

0077 indicator /índikèitər/ ビジネス問題
- 名 ❶**指標** ❷（目盛り盤の）指針；表示器
- 名 indication：(～の/…という)兆候、しるし(of ～/that節 ...)
- 動 indicate：～を示す、表す
- 形 indicative：(be indicative of で)～を表している

0078 contingency /kəntíndʒənsi/ Part 7
- 名 **不慮の事故**、偶発事件(≒accident)
- 形 contingent：(be contingent on [upon]で)～次第である、～を条件としている

0079 semester /siméstər/ ❶アクセント注意 Part 7
- 名 (2学期制の)**学期**　⊕3学期制の「学期」はterm, trimester、4学期制の「学期」はquarter

0080 radiation /rèidiéiʃən/ Part 7
- 名 ❶**放射線** ❷放射
- 動 radiate：❶(～から)放射[放出]する(from ～)　❷(喜びなど)を発散させる

Day 4))) CD-A4　**Quick Review**　答えは右ページ下

- □ 黒字
- □ 請願
- □ 改装
- □ 起業家
- □ 授業料
- □ 進展
- □ 記念品
- □ アンケート
- □ 追加料金
- □ 住宅ローン
- □ 訴訟
- □ 献身
- □ 制裁
- □ 大部分
- □ 予防接種
- □ 危険

Check 2　Phrase

- ☐ at [by] wholesale（卸売りで）

- ☐ a hotel directory（ホテルの住所録）
- ☐ a business directory（商工名鑑）

- ☐ a pharmacist's office（薬局）

- ☐ a resort condominium（リゾートマンション）

- ☐ an economic indicator（経済指標）
- ☐ a speed indicator（速度計）

- ☐ prepare for contingencies（不慮の事故に備える）
- ☐ contingency plans（非常事態計画）

- ☐ the first [second] semester（前[後]期）

- ☐ a high level of radiation（高レベルの放射線）
- ☐ ultraviolet radiation（紫外線放射）

Check 3　Sentence

- ☐ Wholesale is much cheaper than retail.（卸売りは小売りよりずっと安い）

- ☐ Can you look up the restaurant's number in the telephone directory?（そのレストランの電話番号を電話帳で調べてくれますか?）

- ☐ My goal is to become a pharmacist.（私の目標は薬剤師になることだ）

- ☐ A 30-story condominium is being built near the station.（30階建てのマンションが駅の近くで建設中だ）

- ☐ Various indicators show that the economy is already on track to recovery.（経済が既に回復段階にあることをさまざまな指標が示している）

- ☐ We have to be prepared to deal with contingencies.（私たちは不慮の事故に対処する用意ができていなければならない）

- ☐ Submit your thesis by the last day of class in the second semester.（論文は後期の講義の最終日までに提出すること）

- ☐ Many workers were exposed to dangerous levels of radiation in the accident.（その事故で多くの作業員が危険レベルの放射線に被曝した）

Day 4))) CD-A4
Quick Review
答えは左ページ下

- ☐ surplus
- ☐ petition
- ☐ renovation
- ☐ entrepreneur
- ☐ tuition
- ☐ breakthrough
- ☐ souvenir
- ☐ questionnaire
- ☐ surcharge
- ☐ mortgage
- ☐ lawsuit
- ☐ dedication
- ☐ sanction
- ☐ bulk
- ☐ vaccination
- ☐ hazard

CHAPTER 1
CHAPTER 2
CHAPTER 3
CHAPTER 4
CHAPTER 5
CHAPTER 6
CHAPTER 7
CHAPTER 8
CHAPTER 9

Day 6　名詞6

Check 1　Listen)) CD-A6

□ 0081
autograph
/ɔ́:təgræf/
Part 2, 3

- 名 (有名人などの)**サイン**　⊕書類などへの「サイン、署名」はsignature
- 動 ～にサインする　⊕「(書類など)にサイン[署名]する」はsign

□ 0082
subsidy
/sʌ́bsədi/
ビジネス問題

- 名 **補助**[助成]**金**
- 動 subsidize：～に補助[助成]金を与える

□ 0083
expertise
/èkspərtí:z/
❶アクセント注意
ビジネス問題

- 名 (～に関する)**専門的知識**[技術] (in ～)
- 名 expert：(～の)専門家、熟達者 (on [in, at] ～)
- 形 expert：❶熟達した　❷専門的な

□ 0084
arbitration
/ɑ̀:rbətréiʃən/
Part 7

- 名 **仲裁**、調停 (≒ mediation)
- 名 arbitrator：仲裁[調停]者
- 動 arbitrate：❶～を仲裁[調停]する　❷(～間の)仲裁[調停]をする (between ～)

□ 0085
outlet
/áutlet/
ビジネス問題

- 名 ❶ **直販店**、アウトレット　❷(電気の)コンセント (≒ socket)　❸(感情などの)はけ口 (for ～)

□ 0086
refill
/rí:fil/
Part 2, 3

- 名 ❶(飲食物の)**お代わり**　❷詰め替え品、補充品
- 動 (/rifíl/)(容器など)を補充する

□ 0087
duplicate
/djú:plikət/
Part 7

- 名 **複製**、複写 (≒ copy)
- 動 (/djú:pləkèit/)～を複製[複写]する

□ 0088
specialty
/spéʃəlti/
Part 4

- 名 ❶(店などの)**得意料理**　❷専門、専攻
- 名 special：❶(レストランなどの)特別料理；特売品　❷特別番組
- 形 special：特別な
- 動 specialize：(specialize inで)～を専門にする

continued
▼

名詞と前置詞の結びつきを確認してる？ expertise in ～(〜に関する専門的知識)のように名詞の後ろにつく前置詞にも注意していこう。

☐ 聞くだけモード　Check 1
☐ しっかりモード　Check 1 ▶ 2
☐ かんぺきモード　Check 1 ▶ 2 ▶ 3

Check 2　Phrase

☐ the autograph of a famous movie star(有名な映画スターのサイン)
☐ sign an autograph(サインする)

☐ education subsidies(教育補助金)

☐ expertise in psychology [sewing](心理学の専門的知識[裁縫の専門的技術])

☐ go to arbitration([争議が]仲裁に付される)
☐ refer a dispute to arbitration (紛争を仲裁に持ち込む)

☐ a retail outlet(小売り販売店)
☐ insert a plug into an outlet (プラグをコンセントに差し込む)

☐ free refill([掲示で]お代わり無料)
☐ fountain pen refills(万年筆のインクのカートリッジ)

☐ a duplicate of the key(合い鍵)
☐ in duplicate([正副]2通に)

☐ chef's specialty([メニューで]料理長のお薦め料理)
☐ make a specialty of ～(〜を専門にする)

Check 3　Sentence

☐ The soccer player was signing autographs for kids.(そのサッカー選手は子どもたちにサインをしていた)

☐ The government is planning to increase solar panel subsidies.(政府は太陽電池パネルの補助金を増やす予定だ)

☐ She has experience and expertise in accounting.(彼女は会計の経験と専門的知識を持っている)

☐ The two companies have agreed to refer the dispute to arbitration.(両社は紛争を仲裁してもらうことに合意した)

☐ The pizza chain has about 500 outlets in the US.(そのピザチェーンはアメリカに約500の販売店を持っている)

☐ Would you like a refill on the coffee?(コーヒーのお代わりはいかがですか?)

☐ Applicants are advised to keep duplicates of their submissions.(応募者は提出物の写しを保管しておくよう求められている)

☐ French provincial cuisine is a specialty of the house.(フランスの田舎料理がその店の得意料理だ)

continued
▼

Day 6

Check 1　Listen 》CD-A6

□ 0089
attachment
/ətǽtʃmənt/
ビジネス問題

🔲❶(電子メールの)**添付ファイル**　❷(〜への)愛着、愛情(to [for] 〜)(≒love)　❸付属品
動 attach：(attach A to Bで)AをBに添付する、貼りつける

□ 0090
coincidence
/kouínsidəns/
Part 5, 6

🔲❶**偶然の一致**　❷(〜の)一致(of 〜)
動 coincide：(coincide withで)❶〜と同時に起こる　❷(意見などが)〜と一致する
形 coincident：(〜と)同時に起こる(with 〜)
形 coincidental：偶然の

□ 0091
plumber
/plʌ́mər/
❶発音注意
Part 1

🔲**配管工**、水道屋さん

□ 0092
flaw
/flɔ́ː/
Part 2, 3

🔲❶(〜の)**欠陥**、欠点(in 〜)(≒defect, fault)　❷(手続き・議論などの)不備、欠陥(in 〜)
形 flawed：欠点[欠陥]のある
形 flawless：欠点のない、非の打ちどころがない

□ 0093
reimbursement
/rìːimbə́ːrsmənt/
ビジネス問題

🔲**払い戻し**、返済(≒refund)
動 reimburse：(reimburse A for Bで)AにB(経費など)を返済する

□ 0094
courier
/kə́ːriər/
Part 2, 3

🔲**宅配便業者**；(小包などの)配達人

□ 0095
shareholder
/ʃéərhòuldər/
ビジネス問題

🔲**株主**(≒stockholder)
名 share：❶(〜s)株、株式　❷市場占有率　❸分け前
動 share：〜を(…と)共有する(with ...)

□ 0096
epidemic
/èpədémik/
Part 5, 6

🔲❶(病気などの)**流行**、蔓延　❷伝染病(≒plague)
⊕ endemicは「風土病」、pandemicは「全国[世界]的流行病」
形 (病気が)流行[伝染]性の

Day 5 》CD-A5
Quick Review
答えは右ページ下

- □ 受取人
- □ 掲示
- □ 従業員名簿
- □ 乱気流
- □ 偏見
- □ 修正
- □ 補給剤
- □ 誠実
- □ 卸売り
- □ 住所録
- □ 薬剤師
- □ 分譲マンション
- □ 指標
- □ 不慮の事故
- □ 学期
- □ 放射線

Check 2 Phrase

- send ~ as an attachment(~を添付ファイルで送る)
- form an attachment to [for] ~(~が好きになる)

- by pure [sheer] coincidence(全くの偶然の一致で)
- a coincidence of opinion(意見の一致)

- call a plumber(配管工を呼ぶ)

- a character flaw(性格上の欠点)
- a fatal flaw(致命的な欠陥)

- reimbursement for travel expenses(交通費の払い戻し)

- a motorcycle courier(バイク便)

- a shareholders' meeting(株主総会)

- a cholera epidemic(コレラの流行)
- prevent epidemics(伝染病を防ぐ)

Check 3 Sentence

- Don't open any suspicious e-mails or attachments.(怪しい電子メールや添付ファイルは開かないでください)

- It was a coincidence that I met an old friend of mine in Australia.(オーストラリアで旧友に会ったのは偶然の一致だった)

- The plumber is fixing a sink.(配管工は流しを修理している)

- The home inspector found serious flaws in the house.(家屋調査士はその家に深刻な欠陥があるのを見つけた)

- Employees can receive reimbursement for work-related expenses.(従業員は仕事に関連した経費の払い戻しを受けることができる)

- He sent the documents by courier.(彼はその書類を宅配便で送った)

- A majority of shareholders approved a proposed takeover of the company.(株主の過半数がその会社の買収案を承認した)

- The school has been closed due to a flu epidemic.(その学校はインフルエンザが流行しているため閉鎖されている)

Day 5))CD-A5
Quick Review
答えは左ページ下

- recipient
- bulletin
- payroll
- turbulence
- bias
- revision
- supplement
- integrity
- wholesale
- directory
- pharmacist
- condominium
- indicator
- contingency
- semester
- radiation

Day 7 名詞7

Check 1 Listen 》CD-A7

□ 0097
mileage
/máilidʒ/
Part 7

名 ❶**燃費** ❷総マイル数

□ 0098
rebate
/ríːbeit/
ビジネス問題

名 (支払金の一部の)**払い戻し** ❶refundとreimbursementは「(全額の)払い戻し」

□ 0099
fluctuation
/flʌ̀ktʃuéiʃən/
ビジネス問題

名 (〜の)**変動**(in [of] 〜)(≒change)
動 fluctuate：変動する

□ 0100
bribery
/bráibəri/
ビジネス問題

名 **賄賂行為**、贈賄、収賄(≒payoff)
名 bribe：賄賂
動 bribe：〜に賄賂を贈る

□ 0101
paycheck
/péitʃək/
ビジネス問題

名 **給料**(≒salary, wage)；給料支払小切手

□ 0102
tendency
/téndənsi/
Part 5, 6

名 (〜への／…する)**傾向**；性向(to [toward] 〜/to do)(≒trend, inclination)
動 tend：(tend to doで)〜しがちである、〜する傾向がある

□ 0103
disorder
/disɔ́ːrdər/
Part 7

名 ❶**病気**、疾患(≒disease, illness) ❷(社会的)無秩序、混乱(≒unrest) ❸乱雑(≒confusion)
形 disordered：❶乱雑な、乱れた ❷病気の、不調な
形 disorderly：❶無法な、乱暴な ❷無秩序の、混乱した

□ 0104
commerce
/kámərːs/
❗アクセント注意
ビジネス問題

名 **商業**(≒business)；通商、貿易(≒trade)
名 commercial：コマーシャル
形 commercial：商業の；通商[貿易]の

continued
▼

今日で『キクタンTOEIC Test Score 990』は1週間が終了！ 残りはまだまだ長いけど、急がず焦らず学習を進めていこう。

☐ 聞くだけモード　Check 1
☐ しっかりモード　Check 1 ▶ 2
☐ かんぺきモード　Check 1 ▶ 2 ▶ 3

Check 2　Phrase

☐ get good [poor] mileage（燃費がいい[悪い]）
☐ a car with low mileage（走行マイル数が少ない車）

☐ a tax [rent] rebate（税金[家賃]の払い戻し）

☐ fluctuations in temperature [stock prices]（気温[株価]の変動）

☐ be vulnerable to bribery（賄賂に弱い）
☐ a bribery scandal（贈収賄事件）

☐ a weekly paycheck（週給）
☐ deposit one's paycheck（給料を預金する）

☐ have a tendency to do ～（～する傾向がある）
☐ the downward [upward] tendency of prices（物価下降[上昇]の傾向）

☐ a stomach disorder（胃病）
☐ be in a state of disorder（混乱状態にある）

☐ commerce and industry（商工業）
☐ foreign commerce（外国貿易）

Check 3　Sentence

☐ Hybrid cars get good mileage.（ハイブリッドカーは燃費がいい）

☐ Eighty percent of those who received a tax rebate saved the money.（税金の払い戻しを受けた人の80パーセントは、その金を貯金した）

☐ This study analyzes the nature and causes of business fluctuations.（この研究は景気変動の特質と原因を分析している）

☐ The CEO has denied the bribery accusations.（そのCEOは贈収賄の罪状を否認している）

☐ His paycheck is around $50,000 a year.（彼の給料は年間約5万ドルだ）

☐ There is a tendency for the economy to slow down.（景気は減速傾向にある）

☐ The patient suffers from a serious heart disorder.（その患者は重い心臓病を患っている）

☐ The government should take immediate steps to promote domestic commerce.（政府は国内の商業を促進する措置をすぐに取るべきだ）

CHAPTER 1
CHAPTER 2
CHAPTER 3
CHAPTER 4
CHAPTER 5
CHAPTER 6
CHAPTER 7
CHAPTER 8
CHAPTER 9

continued
▼

Day 7

Check 1　Listen 》CD-A7

0105 outfit /áutfit/ Part 1
- 名 **服装**[衣装]（一そろい）（≒clothes, clothing, attire, apparel）
- 動 ～に（…を）装備させる（with ...）

0106 tag /tǽg/ Part 1
- 名 （つけ・下げ）**札**（ふだ）
- 動 ～に札をつける

0107 retailer /rí:teilər/ ビジネス問題
- 名 **小売業者**（⇔wholesaler：卸売業者）
- 名 retail：小売り
- 動 retail：（～の値で）小売りされる（for [at] ～）
- 副 retail：小売（価格）で

0108 extinction /ikstíŋkʃən/ Part 5, 6
- 名 **絶滅**
- 形 extinct：絶滅した

0109 cubicle /kjú:bikl/ Part 1
- 名 （オフィスなどの仕切られた）**小部屋**

0110 installation /ìnstəléiʃən/ Part 7
- 名 ❶（機械などの）**取りつけ**、設置　❷就任[任命]（式）
- ＋installmentは「分割払い」
- 動 install：❶～を取りつける　❷～を（…に）任命する（as ...）　❸～をインストールする

0111 undergraduate /ʌ̀ndərgrǽdʒuət/ Part 7
- 名 **大学生**、（大学の）学部学生（⇔postgraduate：大学院生）　＋graduateは「卒業生」
- 形 学部学生の

0112 patronage /péitrənidʒ/ ビジネス問題
- 名 （店などへの）**ひいき**、引き立て、愛顧
- 名 patron：❶顧客、ひいき客　❷後援者

Day 6　》CD-A6　Quick Review　答えは右ページ下

- □ サイン
- □ 補助金
- □ 専門的知識
- □ 仲裁
- □ 直販店
- □ お代わり
- □ 複製
- □ 得意料理
- □ 添付ファイル
- □ 偶然の一致
- □ 配管工
- □ 欠陥
- □ 払い戻し
- □ 宅配便業者
- □ 株主
- □ 流行

Check 2 Phrase

- a bride's outfit(花嫁衣装)
- a name tag(名札)
- a clothing retailer(衣料品小売業者)
- be in danger of extinction(絶滅の危機に瀕している)
- the extinction of the dinosaurs(恐竜の絶滅)
- cubicles separated by partitions(仕切り壁で分けられた小部屋)
- a shower cubicle(シャワー室)
- the installation of an air conditioner(エアコンの取りつけ)
- the installation of the new president(新大統領の就任式)
- an economics undergraduate(経済学部の学生)
- give ~ one's patronage(~をひいきにする)

Check 3 Sentence

- The man is in a cowboy outfit.(男性はカウボーイの装いをしている)
- The price tags are on the store's shelves.(店の棚に値札がついている)
- The company is the second largest retailer of electronics in the US.(その会社はアメリカで2番目に大きい電子機器の小売業者だ)
- One third of the world's amphibian species are in danger of extinction.(世界の両生類種の3分の1は絶滅の危機に瀕している)
- The man is working in a cubicle.(男性は小部屋で仕事をしている)
- The installation of electrical cables must be done by experts.(電気ケーブルの取りつけは専門の人によって行われなければならない)
- She is an undergraduate at Columbia University.(彼女はコロンビア大学の学生だ)
- We would like to thank you for your patronage over the years.(長年にわたりお引き立ていただき感謝申し上げます)

Day 6 CD-A6
Quick Review
答えは左ページ下

- autograph
- subsidy
- expertise
- arbitration
- outlet
- refill
- duplicate
- specialty
- attachment
- coincidence
- plumber
- flaw
- reimbursement
- courier
- shareholder
- epidemic

CHAPTER 1
CHAPTER 2
CHAPTER 3
CHAPTER 4
CHAPTER 5
CHAPTER 6
CHAPTER 7
CHAPTER 8
CHAPTER 9

Day 8　名詞8

Check 1　Listen 》CD-A8

□ 0113
aptitude
/ǽptətjùːd/
Part 5, 6

名 (〜の)**才能**、能力、素質(for [in] 〜)(≒talent)；適性
⊕attitude(態度)と混同しないように注意

□ 0114
emission
/imíʃən/
ビジネス問題

名 ❶(熱・光・ガスなどの)**放出**　❷排気；放出物
動 emit：(熱・光・ガスなど)を放出[放射]する、放つ

□ 0115
freight
/fréit/
❶発音注意
Part 1

名 ❶**運送貨物**(≒cargo)　❷運送料、運賃
動 〜を運送する

□ 0116
setback
/sétbæk/
Part 7

名 (進歩などの)**後退**、妨げ、挫折
動 set back：(計画など)を妨げる、遅らせる

□ 0117
friction
/fríkʃən/
Part 5, 6

名 ❶(〜の間の)**あつれき**、いさかい、不和(between 〜)
❷(〜に対する)摩擦(on [against] 〜)

□ 0118
ballot
/bǽlət/
Part 7

名 ❶**投票**(≒voting)　❷投票用紙　❸投票数
動 ❶投票する　❷〜を投票で決める

□ 0119
accuracy
/ǽkjurəsi/
Part 5, 6

名 **正確さ**、精密さ(≒precision)(⇔inaccuracy)
形 accurate：❶正確な　❷精密な
副 accurately：正確[精密]に

□ 0120
prototype
/próutətàip/
ビジネス問題

名 (〜の)**試作品**(of [for] 〜)

continued

同意語・類義語(≒)や反意語・反対語(⇔)もチェックしてる？ 余裕があれば確認して、語彙の数を積極的に増やしていこう。

- ☐ 聞くだけモード　Check 1
- ☐ しっかりモード　Check 1 ▶ 2
- ☐ かんぺきモード　Check 1 ▶ 2 ▶ 3

Check 2　Phrase

- ☐ have an aptitude for ～(～の才能がある)
- ☐ an aptitude test(適性検査)

- ☐ the emission of carbon dioxide(二酸化炭素の放出)
- ☐ an emission control(排気ガス規制)

- ☐ freight trains(貨物列車)
- ☐ freight paid(運賃支払い済み)

- ☐ suffer [experience] a setback(妨げに遭う；挫折する；[病気が]ぶり返す)

- ☐ friction between labor and management(労使間のあつれき)
- ☐ minimize friction(摩擦を最小限に抑える)

- ☐ elect ～ by ballot(～を投票で選ぶ)
- ☐ cast a ballot(投票する)

- ☐ with accuracy(正確に)

- ☐ a prototype of a new electric car(新しい電気自動車の試作車)

Check 3　Sentence

- ☐ She has a wonderful aptitude for music.(彼女には素晴らしい音楽の才能がある)

- ☐ It is said that the emission of greenhouse gases is linked to global warming.(温室効果ガスの放出と地球温暖化は関連していると言われている)

- ☐ They are loading freight onto an aircraft.(彼らは飛行機に貨物を積み込んでいる)

- ☐ The world is facing a serious economic setback.(世界は深刻な景気後退に直面している)

- ☐ Trade conflicts have generated friction between the two countries.(貿易摩擦が両国間のあつれきを生んでいる)

- ☐ All elections must be conducted by secret ballot.(すべての選挙は無記名投票で行われなければならない)

- ☐ Speed and accuracy are essential to the media industry.(スピードと正確さはメディア産業にとって不可欠だ)

- ☐ A prototype of a new aircraft will be test-flown by the company's own test pilots.(新しい飛行機の試作機はその会社のテストパイロットたちによって飛行テストされる予定だ)

continued ▼

Day 8

Check 1　Listen)) CD-A8

□ 0121
tariff
/tǽrif/
ビジネス問題

名 (〜にかかる)**関税**(率)(on 〜)

□ 0122
auditorium
/ɔ̀ːdit́ɔ́ːriəm/
❶アクセント注意
Part 1

名 **講堂**

□ 0123
divorce
/divɔ́ːrs/
Part 2, 3

名 **離婚**(⇔marriage)
動 〜と離婚する

□ 0124
subscriber
/səbskráibər/
Part 4

名 (〜の)**定期購読者**(to 〜); (電話などの)加入者
名 subscription: (〜の)定期購読(料)(to 〜)
動 subscribe: (subscribe toで)❶〜を定期購読する　❷(通例疑問・否定文で)〜に同意する

□ 0125
fitness
/fítnis/
Part 4

名 ❶**健康**(状態)(≒health)　❷(〜に対する)適合性(for 〜)
動 fit: (衣服などが)〜に(大きさ・型が)合う
形 fit: ❶(〜に)適した(for 〜)　❷健康[元気]な

□ 0126
allergy
/ǽlərdʒi/
❶発音注意
Part 2, 3

名 (〜に対する)**アレルギー**(to 〜)
形 allergic: (be allergic toで)❶〜に対してアレルギーがある　❷〜が大嫌いである

□ 0127
immigration
/ìməgréiʃən/
Part 5, 6

名 ❶**移住**、移民　❷入国管理[審査]
名 immigrant: (外国からの)移民、移住者
動 immigrate: (〜から/…へ)移住する(from 〜/to …)

□ 0128
commuter
/kəmjúːtər/
Part 1

名 **通勤者**
名 commute: 通勤
動 commute: (〜から/…へ)通勤する(from 〜/to …)

Day 7)) CD-A7 Quick Review 答えは右ページ下			
□ 燃費	□ 給料	□ 服装	□ 小部屋
□ 払い戻し	□ 傾向	□ 札	□ 取りつけ
□ 変動	□ 病気	□ 小売業者	□ 大学生
□ 賄賂行為	□ 商業	□ 絶滅	□ ひいき

Check 2 Phrase

- ☐ tariffs on imported goods（輸入品にかかる関税）

- ☐ the school auditorium（学校の講堂）

- ☐ get a divorce（離婚する）
- ☐ file for divorce（離婚を申請する）

- ☐ a subscriber to the magazine（その雑誌の定期購読者）

- ☐ a fitness boom（健康ブーム）
- ☐ one's fitness for a job（仕事に対する適性）

- ☐ an allergy to eggs = an egg allergy（卵アレルギー）

- ☐ illegal immigration（不法移住）
- ☐ an immigration officer（入国審査官）

- ☐ rush-hour commuters（ラッシュアワーの通勤者）
- ☐ a commuter train（通勤電車）

Check 3 Sentence

- ☐ The United States lowered tariffs on Australian beef.（アメリカはオーストラリア産牛肉にかかる関税を下げた）

- ☐ The auditorium is full of people.（講堂は人々でいっぱいになっている）

- ☐ Divorce is on the increase.（離婚は増加傾向にある）

- ☐ The publisher is trying to increase the number of subscribers.（その出版社は定期購読者の数を増やそうと努力している）

- ☐ Regular exercise is good for both mental and physical fitness.（定期的な運動は心と体の両方の健康にとってよい）

- ☐ I have an allergy to cedar pollen.（私はスギ花粉アレルギーだ）

- ☐ Japan has strict controls on immigration.（日本には移住に対する厳しい規制がある）

- ☐ The train is packed with commuters.（列車は通勤者ですし詰めになっている）

Day 7))CD-A7
Quick Review
答えは左ページ下

- ☐ mileage
- ☐ rebate
- ☐ fluctuation
- ☐ bribery
- ☐ paycheck
- ☐ tendency
- ☐ disorder
- ☐ commerce
- ☐ outfit
- ☐ tag
- ☐ retailer
- ☐ extinction
- ☐ cubicle
- ☐ installation
- ☐ undergraduate
- ☐ patronage

CHAPTER 1
CHAPTER 2
CHAPTER 3
CHAPTER 4
CHAPTER 5
CHAPTER 6
CHAPTER 7
CHAPTER 8
CHAPTER 9

Day 9　名詞9

Check 1　Listen 》CD-A9

☐ 0129
photocopier
/fóutoukàpiər/
Part 1

名 コピー機、写真複写機
名 photocopy：コピー
動 photocopy：〜をコピーする

☐ 0130
waste
/wéist/
ビジネス問題

名 ❶廃棄物　❷(〜の)浪費(of 〜)
動 (金・時間など)を(…で)浪費する、無駄にする(on …)
形 wasteful：無駄遣いの多い、浪費的な

☐ 0131
intermission
/ìntərmíʃən/
Part 2, 3

名 ❶(劇場などの)**休憩時間**、幕間(≒ interval)　❷休止、合間(≒ pause, break)

☐ 0132
acknowledgment
/æknálidʒmənt/
Part 5, 6

名 ❶(〜を)**認めること**、(〜の)自白、白状、承認(of 〜)
❷感謝　❸(〜s)謝辞　❹受取通知書
動 acknowledge：❶(過失など)を認める　❷(手紙など)を受け取ったことを知らせる

☐ 0133
gadget
/gǽdʒit/
Part 7

名 ちょっとした道具[装置]

☐ 0134
congestion
/kəndʒéstʃən/
Part 7

名 ❶(交通などの)**混雑**　❷うっ血
形 congested：❶混雑した　❷鼻が詰まった

☐ 0135
attire
/ətáiər/
Part 7

名 服装、衣装(≒ clothes, clothing, outfit, apparel)

☐ 0136
reminder
/rimáindər/
Part 5, 6

名 (〜を)**思い出させるもの**、(〜の)思い出(of 〜)；督促状　✚remainder(残り)と混同しないように注意
動 remind：(remind A of [about] B で)AにBを思い出させる、気づかせる

continued
▼

単語上のチェックボックスを使ってる？ 確実に押さえた単語にはチェックマーク、自信のないものには?マークをつけて復習に役立てよう。

☐ 聞くだけモード　Check 1
☐ しっかりモード　Check 1 ▶ 2
☐ かんぺきモード　Check 1 ▶ 2 ▶ 3

Check 2　Phrase

☐ a color photocopier（カラーコピー機）

☐ nuclear waste（核廃棄物）
☐ a waste of time [money, energy]（時間［金、エネルギー］の浪費）

☐ the intermission of a concert（コンサートの休憩時間）
☐ without intermission（絶え間なく、ひっきりなしに）

☐ acknowledgment of an error（誤りを認めること）
☐ in acknowledgment of ～（～に感謝して）

☐ kitchen gadgets（台所用小道具）
⊕皮むき器など

☐ traffic congestion（交通渋滞）
☐ nasal congestion（鼻詰まり）

☐ business attire（ビジネススーツ）

☐ serve as a reminder that ～（［主語が］～ということを思い出させる）
☐ a reminder of childhood（子どものころの思い出）

Check 3　Sentence

☐ The man is fixing a photocopier.（男性はコピー機を修理している）

☐ The factory generates more than 1,000 tons of industrial waste each year.（その工場は毎年1000トンを超える産業廃棄物を出している）

☐ We will now have a 10-minute intermission.（ただ今から10分間の休憩となります）⊕劇場などのアナウンス

☐ Acknowledgment of wrongdoing is the first step toward reconciliation.（罪を認めることが和解への第一歩だ）

☐ The store carries a wide variety of gadgets.（その店はさまざまな小道具を扱っている）

☐ Traffic congestion during rush hour is terrible in Los Angeles.（ラッシュアワーの交通渋滞はロサンゼルスではひどい）

☐ Guests attending the party are required to wear formal attire.（そのパーティーに出席する客は正装を求められている）

☐ A mark on the calendar served as a reminder that it was my wife's birthday.（その日が妻の誕生日であることをカレンダーの印を見て思い出した）

continued
▼

CHAPTER 1
CHAPTER 2
CHAPTER 3
CHAPTER 4
CHAPTER 5
CHAPTER 6
CHAPTER 7
CHAPTER 8
CHAPTER 9

Day 9

Check 1　Listen))) CD-A9

□ 0137
takeover
/téikòuvər/
ビジネス問題

名 **企業買収**、乗っ取り(≒buyout)；(支配・管理権などの)奪取
動 take over：❶(職務など)を(…から)引き継ぐ(from . . .) ❷(会社など)を買収する、乗っ取る

□ 0138
reunion
/rì:jú:njən/
Part 4

名 ❶ **同窓会**　❷(〜との)再会(with 〜)

□ 0139
fabric
/fǽbrik/
Part 5, 6

名 ❶ **織物**、布地(≒cloth, textile)　❷(建物・社会などの)構造、骨組み(≒structure)

□ 0140
delegate
/déligət/
Part 7

名 (政治的会議などの)**代表者**、使節
動 (/déligèit/) ❶(任務など)を(…に)委任する(to . . .)　❷〜を(…するように)代表に立てる(to do)
名 delegation：(集合的に)代表[派遣]団

□ 0141
suite
/swí:t/
❶発音注意
Part 7

名 ❶(ホテルなどの)**スイートルーム**、特別室　❷(物の)一組、一そろい

□ 0142
vacancy
/véikənsi/
Part 2, 3

名 ❶ **空室**、空き家　❷(職などの)欠員、空位(≒opening)
形 vacant：❶(家・座席などが)空いている　❷(職などが)欠員[空位]の

□ 0143
contractor
/kántræktər/
ビジネス問題

名 **建設業者**、請負業者[人]

□ 0144
resignation
/rèzignéiʃən/
ビジネス問題

名 ❶ **辞職**、辞任　❷辞表
動 resign：❶(地位などを)辞任[辞職]する(from 〜)　❷(地位など)を辞める

Day 8))) CD-A8
Quick Review
答えは右ページ下

- □ 才能
- □ 放出
- □ 運送貨物
- □ 後退
- □ あつれき
- □ 投票
- □ 正確さ
- □ 試作品
- □ 関税
- □ 講堂
- □ 離婚
- □ 定期購読者
- □ 健康
- □ アレルギー
- □ 移住
- □ 通勤者

Check 2 Phrase

- a hostile takeover（敵対的買収）
- a takeover bid（[買収のための]株式公開買い付け）⊕TOB

- a class reunion（クラス会）
- have a reunion with ~（~と再会する）

- cotton [silk] fabrics（綿[絹]織物）
- the fabric of society（社会構造）

- a US delegate to the UN（アメリカの国連代表）

- stay in a suite（スイートルームに泊まる）
- a suite of furniture（家具一式）

- a vacancy rate（空室率）
- fill the vacancy for ~（~の欠員を補充する）

- a general contractor（総合建設請負業者、ゼネコン）

- the resignation of a cabinet（内閣総辞職）
- hand in one's resignation（辞表を提出する）

Check 3 Sentence

- The company managed to avoid a foreign takeover.（その会社は外国企業による買収を回避することができた）

- I attended my 20-year high school reunion yesterday.（私は昨日、20周年の高校の同窓会に出席した）

- She made a quilt with scraps of fabric.（彼女は布の切れ端を使ってキルトを作った）

- Delegates from 187 countries met to begin framing a new global warming treaty.（新しい地球温暖化条約の立案を始めるために、187カ国の代表者たちが集まった）

- The hotel has 25 luxury suites with an ocean view.（そのホテルには海が見える豪華なスイートルームが25部屋ある）

- I tried to reserve a hotel room but there were no vacancies.（私はホテルの部屋を予約しようとしたが、空室がなかった）

- Seven contractors bid for the project.（建設業者7社がそのプロジェクトに入札した）

- The prime minister rejected calls for his resignation.（首相は辞任要求を退けた）

Day 8))CD-A8
Quick Review
答えは左ページ下

- aptitude
- emission
- freight
- setback
- friction
- ballot
- accuracy
- prototype
- tariff
- auditorium
- divorce
- subscriber
- fitness
- allergy
- immigration
- commuter

Day 10　名詞10

Check 1　Listen 》CD-A10

□ 0145
drought
/dráut/
Part 7

名 **干ばつ**、日照り

□ 0146
diploma
/diplóumə/
Part 7

名 **卒業**[修了]**証書**(≒certificate)

□ 0147
fraud
/frɔ́ːd/
Part 7

名 **詐欺**：詐欺事件
形 fraudulent：詐欺的な、不正な

□ 0148
partition
/pɑːrtíʃən/
Part 1

名 ❶(部屋などの)**仕切り壁**、間仕切り　❷分割；分配(≒division)
動 ❶(土地など)を分割[分配]する　❷(部屋など)を仕切る

□ 0149
trainee
/treiníː/
ビジネス問題

名 **研修**[実習、訓練]**生**(≒intern)
名 training：(〜の)訓練、教育、養成(in 〜)
動 train：❶〜を(…するように)訓練[教育]する(to do)　❷訓練[教育]を受ける

□ 0150
disposal
/dispóuzəl/
Part 7

名 (〜の)**処分**、処理(of 〜)
動 dispose：(dispose ofで)〜を処分[処理]する
形 disposable：使い捨ての

□ 0151
civilization
/sìvəlizéiʃən/
Part 4

名 **文明**
動 civilize：〜を文明化する
形 civilized：❶文明化した、文化の発達した　❷礼儀正しい

□ 0152
lumber
/lʌ́mbər/
Part 1

名 **材木**、木材(≒timber)
動 材木を切り出す

continued
▼

音と意味がつながるまでは「使える」ようになったとは言えない。チャンツの最初の「英語」部分で意味がすぐに浮かぶか試してみよう。

☐ 聞くだけモード　Check 1
☐ しっかりモード　Check 1 ▶ 2
☐ かんぺきモード　Check 1 ▶ 2 ▶ 3

Check 2　Phrase

☐ a severe drought（深刻な干ばつ）

☐ a high school diploma（高校の卒業証書）

☐ credit card fraud（クレジットカード詐欺）
☐ be sued for fraud（詐欺で訴えられる）

☐ a partition between two rooms（2つの部屋の間の仕切り壁）
☐ the partition of Yugoslavia（ユーゴスラビアの分割）

☐ a trainee nurse（看護師研修生）

☐ disposal of industrial waste（産業廃棄物の処分）

☐ ancient Egyptian civilization（古代エジプト文明）

☐ cut lumber from a log（丸太から材木を切り出す）
☐ a lumber mill（製材所）

Check 3　Sentence

☐ The country is suffering from prolonged drought and famine.（その国は長引く干ばつと飢饉に苦しんでいる）

☐ He holds an MBA diploma from Harvard University.（彼はハーバード大学のMBAの卒業証書を持っている）

☐ Frauds targeting senior citizens are widespread in Japan.（高齢者を狙った詐欺が日本では広まっている）

☐ The office space is divided by partitions.（オフィススペースは仕切り壁で分けられている）

☐ She was employed as a legal trainee with the law firm.（彼女はその法律事務所に司法修習生として採用された）

☐ Disposal of hazardous waste is strictly regulated.（有害廃棄物の処分は厳しく規制されている）

☐ The height of the Mayan civilization was over a 1,000 years ago.（マヤ文明の絶頂期は1000年前に終わった）

☐ The lumber is stacked in layers.（材木が何層にも積み重ねられている）

continued
▼

Day 10

Check 1　Listen))) CD-A10

☐ 0153
staple
/stéipl/
Part 5, 6

图 ❶**主食**、基本[必需]食品　❷ホチキスの針
動 ～をホチキスで留める
形 主要な
图 stapler：ホチキス

☐ 0154
enclosure
/inklóuʒər/
ビジネス問題

图 ❶**同封物**；同封　❷囲われた土地、構内
動 enclose：❶～を(…に)同封する(with [in] . . .)　❷～を取り囲む

☐ 0155
craft
/kræft/
Part 7

图 ❶(小型)**船舶**(≒boat, ship)；飛行機(≒aircraft, airplane, plane)　⊕この意味では単複同形　❷技術(≒skill)
動 ～を精巧[念入り]に作る
图 craftsman：職人
图 craftsmanship：職人の技能

☐ 0156
intuition
/ìntjuːíʃən/
Part 5, 6

图 **直感**(力)(≒instinct)

☐ 0157
attorney
/ətə́ːrni/
Part 4

图 **弁護士**(≒lawyer)

☐ 0158
quota
/kwóutə/
ビジネス問題

图 (仕事などの)**割当量**、ノルマ

☐ 0159
suspension
/səspénʃən/
Part 7

图 ❶(活動などの)**一時停止**、中止(of ～)　❷(～の理由での)停職、停学(for ～)
動 suspend：❶～を一時停止[中止]にする　❷～を(…から)停学[停職、出場停止]にする(from . . .)　❸～をつるす

☐ 0160
get-together
/géttəgèðər/
Part 4

图 (非公式の)**集まり**、パーティー、会合、親睦[懇親]会(≒meeting, gathering)
動 get together：集まる、(～と)会う(with ～)

| Day 9))) CD-A9
Quick Review
答えは右ページ下 | ☐ コピー機
☐ 廃棄物
☐ 休憩時間
☐ 認めること | ☐ ちょっとした道具
☐ 混雑
☐ 服装
☐ 思い出させるもの | ☐ 企業買収
☐ 同窓会
☐ 織物
☐ 代表者 | ☐ スイートルーム
☐ 空室
☐ 建設業者
☐ 辞職 |

Check 2 Phrase

- [ ] eat ~ as one's staple(~を主食として食べる)
- [ ] refill staples(ホチキスの替え針)

- [ ] a letter and its enclosures(手紙とその同封物)
- [ ] sheep in the enclosure(囲い地の中のヒツジ)

- [ ] a fishing craft(漁船)
- [ ] the craft of knitting(編み物の技術)

- [ ] women's intuition(女性の直感)

- [ ] a defense attorney(被告側弁護士)

- [ ] fishing quota(漁獲割当量)
- [ ] meet [fill] a quota(ノルマを果たす; 割当量を満たす)

- [ ] a suspension of military activities(軍事行動の一時停止)
- [ ] receive a one-month suspension(1カ月の停学[停職]を受ける)

- [ ] a family get-together(家族の集まり[団らん])

Check 3 Sentence

- [ ] Noodles are a staple of Italian and Chinese cooking.(めん類はイタリア料理と中国料理の主食だ)

- [ ] Please make sure that the following enclosures are included.(以下の同封物が含まれているか確認してください)

- [ ] Several rescue craft were sent to the scene of the crash.(数隻の救助艇が衝突現場へと送られた)

- [ ] His decision was based on intuition rather than on logic.(彼の決断は論理ではなく直感によるものだった)

- [ ] She is an attorney by profession.(彼女の職業は弁護士だ)

- [ ] Bonuses are available for those who meet their quotas.(ノルマを果たした者にはボーナスが与えられる)

- [ ] The president announced a suspension of US troop withdrawals from Iraq.(大統領はイラクからの米軍の撤退の一時停止を発表した)

- [ ] The annual Christmas get-together will be held on December 17 at the Village Club at 6 p.m.(毎年恒例のクリスマス会が12月17日の午後6時からヴィレッジクラブで開催される)

Day 9 》CD-A9
Quick Review
答えは左ページ下

- [ ] photocopier
- [ ] waste
- [ ] intermission
- [ ] acknowledgment
- [ ] gadget
- [ ] congestion
- [ ] attire
- [ ] reminder
- [ ] takeover
- [ ] reunion
- [ ] fabric
- [ ] delegate
- [ ] suite
- [ ] vacancy
- [ ] contractor
- [ ] resignation

Day 11　名詞11

Check 1　Listen 》CD-A11

☐ 0161
compartment
/kəmpá:rtmənt/
Part 4

名 ❶ **小物入れ**　❷(列車などの)仕切り客室、コンパートメント

☐ 0162
alteration
/ɔ̀:ltəréiʃən/
Part 5, 6

名 **変更**、修正、手直し
動 alter：❶〜を変える、改める　❷変わる

☐ 0163
nutrition
/nju:tríʃən/
Part 5, 6

名 **栄養**；栄養補給[摂取]
名 nutrient：栄養物、栄養素
形 nutritious：栄養のある、栄養に富んだ

☐ 0164
scrutiny
/skrú:təni/
Part 5, 6

名 **綿密**[精密]**な調査**[検査](≒examination)
動 scrutinize：〜を綿密に調べる、吟味する

☐ 0165
diagnosis
/dàiəgnóusis/
Part 2, 3

名 **診断**　➕ 複数形は diagnoses
動 diagnose：(diagnose A with [as] Bで)AをBと診断する

☐ 0166
amenity
/əménəti/
Part 7

名 (通例〜ies)**便利な設備**[施設]

☐ 0167
downturn
/dáuntə̀:rn/
ビジネス問題

名 (景気・物価などの)**下落**、沈滞(in 〜)(≒downswing)
(⇔upturn：好転)

☐ 0168
remittance
/rimítəns/
ビジネス問題

名 **送金**；送金額
動 remit：(金銭)を(…へ)送る(to . . .)

continued

余裕があるときは、派生語・関連語も覚えておこう。そうすれば、1つの語彙から、2倍、3倍と語彙が増えていくよ！

- ☐ 聞くだけモード　Check 1
- ☐ しっかりモード　Check 1 ▶ 2
- ☐ かんぺきモード　Check 1 ▶ 2 ▶ 3

Check 2　Phrase

☐ a freezer compartment（[冷蔵庫の]冷凍室）
☐ a first-class compartment（[列車などの]1等室）

☐ make alterations to ~（~に変更を加える）
☐ alterations to the initial plan（当初の計画の修正）

☐ deficiency of nutrition（栄養不足）
☐ good nutrition（十分な栄養補給）

☐ come under scrutiny（綿密な調査を受ける）
☐ close scrutiny（徹底的な調査[検査]）

☐ a diagnosis of diabetes（糖尿病の診断）
☐ make a diagnosis（診断する）

☐ shopping amenities（ショッピング施設）

☐ the economic downturn（経済の沈滞）
☐ a downturn in the housing market（住宅市場の低迷）

☐ remittance advice（送金通知書）
☐ make remittance（送金する）

Check 3　Sentence

☐ Please stow your luggage in the overhead compartments.（手荷物は上部の手荷物入れにおしまいください）⊕機内アナウンス

☐ The house needs a lot of alterations.（その家は多くの手直しが必要だ）

☐ Good nutrition and exercise are keys to staying healthy.（十分な栄養補給と運動は健康でいることの秘けつだ）

☐ The NASA budget will come under scrutiny on Capitol Hill.（NASAの予算案は米国議会で綿密な調査を受ける予定だ）

☐ What was the diagnosis from your doctor?（医者の診断はどうでしたか？）

☐ The hotel has numerous amenities including a heated indoor pool and fitness center.（そのホテルには、屋内温水プールやフィットネスセンターを含む多くの便利な設備がある）

☐ There has been a downturn in the stock market.（株式市場の下落が続いている）

☐ Remittance should be made by either a personal check, bank draft, or money order.（送金は個人小切手、銀行為替手形、または郵便為替のいずれかで行われなければならない）

CHAPTER 1
CHAPTER 2
CHAPTER 3
CHAPTER 4
CHAPTER 5
CHAPTER 6
CHAPTER 7
CHAPTER 8
CHAPTER 9

continued ▼

Day 11

Check 1 Listen 》CD-A11

□ 0169
implication
/ìmplikéiʃən/
Part 7

名 ❶**言外の意味**、含み　❷(通例〜s)(予想される)(〜の)影響、結果(of 〜)
動imply：〜をほのめかす、暗示する

□ 0170
conglomerate
/kənglɑ́mərət/
ビジネス問題

名**複合企業**(体)、コングロマリット

□ 0171
memorandum
/mèmərǽndəm/
ビジネス問題

名**社内連絡メモ**、社内伝言；メモ(≒memo)　●複数形はmemorandaとmemorandumsの2つある

□ 0172
cancellation
/kæ̀nsəléiʃən/
Part 7

名**取り消し**、キャンセル
動cancel：(取り決め・注文など)を取り消す、中止する、撤回する

□ 0173
turnover
/tə́ːrnòuvər/
ビジネス問題

名 ❶**離職率**；労働移動率　❷(商品などの)回転率

□ 0174
negligence
/néglidʒəns/
Part 5, 6

名 ❶**怠慢**　❷過失
名neglect：❶無視、軽視　❷怠慢
動neglect：❶〜を無視[軽視]する　❷(仕事など)を怠る
形negligent：怠慢な

□ 0175
dismissal
/dismísəl/
ビジネス問題

名(〜からの)**解雇**、免職(from 〜)
動dismiss：❶〜を解雇する　❷(dismiss A as Bで)A(提案など)をBだとして退ける、忘れてしまう

□ 0176
auditor
/ɔ́ːdətər/
ビジネス問題

名**会計検査官**、監査役
名audit：会計検査、監査
動audit：(会計・帳簿)を検査[監査]する

Day 10 》CD-A10
Quick Review
答えは右ページ下

□ 干ばつ　□ 研修生　□ 主食　□ 弁護士
□ 卒業証書　□ 処分　□ 同封物　□ 割当量
□ 詐欺　□ 文明　□ 船舶　□ 一時停止
□ 仕切り壁　□ 材木　□ 直感　□ 集まり

Check 2 Phrase

- by implication(暗に、それとなく)
- have implications for ~(~に影響を及ぼす)

- a financial conglomerate(金融複合企業)
- a multinational conglomerate(多国籍複合企業)

- circulate a memorandum(社内伝言を回覧する)
- make a memorandum of ~(~をメモしておく)

- cancellation of an appointment(面会の約束の取り消し)
- a cancellation charge [fee](キャンセル料)

- reduce staff turnover(社員の離職率を下げる)
- merchandise [capital] turnover(商品[資本]回転率)

- accuse him of negligence(彼の怠慢ぶりを非難する)
- medical negligence(医療過失)

- unfair [wrongful] dismissal(不当解雇)
- dismissal from the post of ~(~の地位からの解雇)

- an external [internal] auditor(外部[内部]監査役)

Check 3 Sentence

- I considered the implications of what he had said.(私は彼が言ったことの言外の意味を考えてみた)

- Disney is the largest media conglomerate in the world.(ディズニーは世界最大のメディア複合企業だ)

- Did you read the memorandum about our company's restructuring plan?(会社のリストラ計画に関する連絡メモを読みましたか?)

- Cancellation of the reservation, without any charge, is possible 48 hours prior to the arrival day.(到着日より48時間前であれば予約の取り消しは無料ですることができる)

- The company's staff turnover is below the industry average.(その会社の社員の離職率は業界の平均よりも低い)

- He was fired for repeated negligence of his duties.(彼は度重なる職務怠慢のかどで首になった)

- The factory employees were notified of their dismissal.(その工場の従業員は解雇の通知を受けた)

- The previous auditor was dismissed because of a disagreement with the company.(前任の会計検査官はその会社との意見の不一致のため解雇された)

Day 10 CD-A10
Quick Review
答えは左ページ下

- drought
- diploma
- fraud
- partition
- trainee
- disposal
- civilization
- lumber
- staple
- enclosure
- craft
- intuition
- attorney
- quota
- suspension
- get-together

Day 12　名詞12

Check 1　Listen)) CD-A12

0177
humidity
/hjuːmídəti/
Part 5, 6

名 **湿度**；湿気
形 humid：湿気の多い、蒸し蒸しする

0178
textile
/tékstail/
Part 5, 6

名 **織物**、布地(≒ cloth, fabric)

0179
leaflet
/líːflit/
Part 1

名 **ちらし**、ビラ(≒ flier)
動 ～にちらしを配る

0180
correspondence
/kɔ̀ːrəspάndəns/
Part 5, 6

名 (～との)**通信**、文通(with ～)；(集合的に)通信文、往復書簡(≒ communication)
名 correspondent：(新聞などの)特派員；通信員
動 correspond：❶(correspond to で)～に一致する；～に相当する　❷(correspond with で)～と文通する

0181
hemisphere
/hémisfìər/
Part 7

名 ❶(地球の)**半球**　❷脳半球
名 sphere：球

0182
remuneration
/rimjùːnəréiʃən/
ビジネス問題

名 (～に対する)**報酬**(≒ reward)；給料(≒ salary, wage, pay)(for ～)
動 remunerate：～に(…に対して)報酬を与える(for …)
形 remunerative：割に合う、もうかる

0183
gauge
/géidʒ/
❗定義注意
Part 5, 6

名 ❶(評価などの)**基準**、尺度(of ～)(≒ standard)　❷計器　❸標準寸法、規格　➕gage とつづることもある
動 ❶～を判断[評価]する　❷～を正確に計る

0184
prerequisite
/prìːrékwəzit/
Part 7

名 (～の)**必要[前提]条件**(for [to, of] ～)(≒ requirement, requisite)
形 前もって必要な、不可欠な

---

continued
▼

1つの単語には1つの品詞の用法しかないとは限らない。複数の品詞の用法がある場合には、その意味もなるべく確認しておこう。

- ☐ 聞くだけモード　Check 1
- ☐ しっかりモード　Check 1 ▶ 2
- ☐ かんぺきモード　Check 1 ▶ 2 ▶ 3

Check 2　Phrase

☐ high [low] humidity（高い[低い]湿度）

☐ woolen textile（毛織物）
☐ the textile industry（織物工業、繊維産業）

☐ hand out [pass] leaflets（ちらしを配る）
☐ advertising leaflets（広告ちらし）

☐ study by correspondence（通信教育で勉強する）
☐ commercial correspondence（商業通信文）

☐ the Northern [Southern] hemisphere（北[南]半球）
☐ the left [right] hemisphere（[脳の]左[右]半球）

☐ remuneration for the work（その仕事に対する報酬）

☐ a gauge of success（成功の基準）
☐ a fuel [rain] gauge（燃料[雨量]計）

☐ prerequisites for economic recovery（景気回復の必要条件）

Check 3　Sentence

☐ The summer humidity in Japan is very high.（日本の夏の湿度は非常に高い）

☐ The city is well known for its handwoven textiles.（その街は手織物でよく知られている）

☐ The woman is handing out leaflets to passersby.（女性は通行人にちらしを配っている）

☐ I have been keeping a regular correspondence with him for several years.（私は彼との定期的な文通を数年間続けている）

☐ About 90 percent of the world's population is concentrated in the northern hemisphere.（地球の人口の約90パーセントは北半球に集中している）

☐ Each participant received $100 as remuneration for participating in the study.（その研究に参加した報酬として各参加者は100ドルを受け取った）

☐ Health is one of the most important gauges of happiness.（健康は幸福の最も重要な尺度の1つだ）

☐ A Ph.D. degree in economics is a prerequisite for a career in economic research.（経済学の博士号は経済調査職の必要条件だ）

continued ▼

Day 12

Check 1　Listen))) CD-A12

□ 0185
segment
/ségmənt/
Part 5, 6

名 **部分**、区分(≒part)
動 (/ségmént/)～を(…に)分割[区分]する(into ...)

□ 0186
dose
/dóus/
Part 7

名 (1回分の薬の)**服用量**(of ～)(≒dosage)
動 ～に(…を)服用させる、投薬する(with ...)

□ 0187
apparel
/əpǽrəl/
❶アクセント注意
Part 5, 6

名 **衣服**、服装(≒clothes, clothing, attire, outfit)

□ 0188
inhabitant
/inhǽbətənt/
Part 5, 6

名 **住民**、居住者(≒resident)
動 inhabit:～に住む、生息する

□ 0189
coworker
/kóuwə̀ːrkər/
ビジネス問題

名 **同僚**、仕事仲間(≒colleague, associate, fellow worker)

□ 0190
amendment
/əméndmənt/
Part 5, 6

名 (～の)**修正**[改正](案)(to ～)
動 amend:(憲法など)を修正[改正]する

□ 0191
projection
/prədʒékʃən/
ビジネス問題

名 (将来の)**予測**、見積もり
名 project:❶(～する)計画(to do)　❷(大規模な)事業、プロジェクト
動 project:❶～を予想する　❷(be projected to doで)～すると予測されている　❸～を見積もる　❹～を計画する

□ 0192
voucher
/váutʃər/
ビジネス問題

名 **商品引換券**；割引券、クーポン券

Day 11))) CD-A11
Quick Review
答えは右ページ下

□ 小物入れ
□ 変更
□ 栄養
□ 綿密な調査

□ 診断
□ 便利な設備
□ 下落
□ 送金

□ 言外の意味
□ 複合企業
□ 社内連絡メモ
□ 取り消し

□ 離職率
□ 怠慢
□ 解雇
□ 会計検査官

Check 2 Phrase	Check 3 Sentence
☐ a large segment of the population (人口の大部分)	☐ People over the age of 60 are the fastest growing segment of the world population. (60歳以上の人々は世界の人口で最も急速に増えている部分だ)
☐ a lethal dose (致死量) ☐ a dose of penicillin (一服のペニシリン)	☐ Take one dose three times a day until symptoms improve. (症状が改善されるまで、1日3回服用すること) ❶薬のラベルの表現
☐ children's [men's, ladies'] apparel (子ども[紳士、婦人]服)	☐ The local apparel industry is facing increasingly fierce competition from abroad. (地方の衣料産業は海外からの激しい競争にますます直面するようになっている)
☐ a city of 100,000 inhabitants (住民数10万の街)	☐ Oslo is the capital city of Norway, and has about 500,000 inhabitants. (オスロはノルウェーの首都で、約50万人の住民がいる)
☐ one's coworkers in the office (職場の同僚)	☐ I went to the wedding of one of my coworkers yesterday. (私は昨日、同僚の1人の結婚式に行った)
☐ make amendments to ~ (~に修正を加える) ☐ a constitutional amendment (憲法改正)	☐ The government has made some amendments to its anti-terrorism bill. (政府は反テロ法案にいくつか修正を加えた)
☐ this year's sales projections (今年の売上予測)	☐ The company's revenues fell nearly 10 percent below projections. (その会社の収益は予測よりも10パーセント近く下がった)
☐ a breakfast [gift] voucher (朝食[ギフト]券)	☐ The voucher is only valid for six months from the date of issue. (その商品引換券は発行日から6カ月のみ有効だ)

Day 11))) CD-A11
Quick Review
答えは左ページ下

☐ compartment ☐ diagnosis ☐ implication ☐ turnover
☐ alteration ☐ amenity ☐ conglomerate ☐ negligence
☐ nutrition ☐ downturn ☐ memorandum ☐ dismissal
☐ scrutiny ☐ remittance ☐ cancellation ☐ auditor

Day 13　名詞13

Check 1　Listen 》CD-A13

☐ 0193
demonstration
/dèmənstréiʃən/
ビジネス問題

名❶(商品の)**実物宣伝**、実演　❷(〜に反対の)デモ、示威運動(against 〜)　❸証明；証拠
名demonstrator：❶デモ参加者　❷実演する人
動demonstrate：❶〜を証明[実証]する　❷(商品)を実演する　❸(〜に反対の)デモをする(against 〜)

☐ 0194
collaboration
/kəlǽbəréiʃən/
Part 5, 6

名(〜との／…の間の)**協力**；共同制作[研究](with 〜/between ...)
名collaborator：協力者；共同制作[研究]者
動collaborate：❶共同で行う；共同制作[研究]する　❷(collaborate to doで)共同で〜する

☐ 0195
quotation
/kwoutéiʃən/
ビジネス問題

名❶(〜の)**見積もり**(額)(for 〜)(≒estimate)　❷(〜からの)引用；引用文[句、語](from 〜)(≒citation)
名quote：❶見積額　❷引用文[句]
動quote：❶〜を見積もる　❷〜を引用する

☐ 0196
confirmation
/kànfərméiʃən/
Part 5, 6

名(〜の)**確認**(of 〜)；確認書
動confirm：❶〜を確認[確証]する　❷(決意など)を強める

☐ 0197
logistics
/loudʒístiks/
ビジネス問題

名**物流**
形logistic/logistical：物流の

☐ 0198
seniority
/si:njɔ́:rəti/
Part 4

名**年功**(序列)
名senior：❶(大学・高校の)最上級生　❷年長者
形senior：❶(役職・地位が)(〜より)上位[上級、先任]の(to 〜)　❷(〜より)年上[年長]の(to 〜)

☐ 0199
exemption
/igzémpʃən/
Part 7

名❶(課税対象からの)**控除**(額)(≒deduction)　❷(〜の)免除(from 〜)(≒excuse)
動exempt：(exempt A from Bで)AのB(義務など)を免除する
形exempt：(be exempt fromで)〜を免除されている

☐ 0200
custody
/kʌ́stədi/
Part 5, 6

名❶(〜の)**養育権**、親権(of 〜)　❷拘留、監禁
名custodian：❶(公共物の)管理人　❷後見人、保護者

continued
▼

「声を出しながら」CDを聞いてる？ えっ、恥ずかしい?! 恥ずかしがっていては「話せる」ようにはならないよ！ ガンバって！

☐ 聞くだけモード　Check 1
☐ しっかりモード　Check 1 ▶ 2
☐ かんぺきモード　Check 1 ▶ 2 ▶ 3

Check 2　Phrase

☐ give a demonstration of a new product（新製品の実物宣伝をする）
☐ hold a demonstration against war（戦争反対のデモを行う）

☐ a collaboration between the two companies（両社間の協力）
☐ in collaboration with ～（～と協力して、～と共同で）

☐ a quotation for the project（そのプロジェクトの見積額）
☐ a quotation from the Bible（聖書からの引用文）

☐ hotel reservation confirmation（ホテルの予約の確認）

☐ a logistics center（物流センター）

☐ a seniority system（年功序列制度）

☐ a tax exemption（税額控除）
☐ exemption from military service（兵役免除）

☐ have [grant] custody of ～（～の養育権を持っている[与える]）
☐ be in custody（拘留されている）

Check 3　Sentence

☐ He gave a demonstration on how to use the vacuum cleaner.（彼はその掃除機の使い方を実演した）

☐ Nissan has developed the car in collaboration with Renault.（日産はルノーと共同でその車を開発した）

☐ I asked five builders to give me a quotation for our new house.（私は新居の見積もりをするよう5つの建築業者に依頼した）

☐ The confirmation of your flight booking will be sent to your e-mail address.（飛行便の予約の確認はあなたの電子メールアドレスに送られます）

☐ Logistics costs account for 13-15 percent of the country's GDP.（物流費はその国のGDPの13～15パーセントを占めている）

☐ Promotion should be based on merit, not seniority.（昇進は年功ではなく、功績に基づくべきだ）

☐ Some congressmen are calling for the government to double the tax exemption for dependents.（何人かの議員は扶養家族への税額控除を倍にするよう政府に求めている）

☐ She got custody of her daughter after the divorce.（離婚後、彼女は娘の養育権を得た）

CHAPTER 1
CHAPTER 2
CHAPTER 3
CHAPTER 4
CHAPTER 5
CHAPTER 6
CHAPTER 7
CHAPTER 8
CHAPTER 9

continued ▼

Day 13

Check 1　Listen))) CD-A13

□ 0201
hesitation
/hézətéiʃən/
Part 5, 6

名 (〜することの)**ためらい**、躊躇(in doing)
動 hesitate：❶ためらう　❷(hesitate to doで)〜するのをためらう
形 hesitant：❶ためらいがちの　❷(be hesitant to doで)〜するのをためらっている

□ 0202
enterprise
/éntərpràiz/
❶アクセント注意
ビジネス問題

名 ❶**企業**、会社(≒company, business)　❷事業

□ 0203
transcript
/trænskript/
Part 7

名 ❶(手書き・タイプによる)(〜の)**写し**、コピー(of 〜) (≒transcription)　❷成績証明書
動 transcribe：〜を書き写す

□ 0204
periodical
/pìəriádikəl/
Part 7

名 **定期刊行物**、雑誌(≒magazine)
形 定期刊行(物)の
名 period：❶期間、時期　❷時代
形 periodic：周期的な；定期的な
副 periodically：定期的に；周期的に

□ 0205
compliance
/kəmpláiəns/
ビジネス問題

名 (法令)**順守**、(命令などに)従うこと(with 〜)(≒obedience, observance)
動 comply：(comply withで)(規則など)に従う、応じる

□ 0206
adoption
/ədápʃən/
Part 5, 6

名 ❶(〜の)**採用**、採択(of 〜)　❷養子縁組
動 adopt：❶(技術など)を採用[採択]する　❷〜を可決する　❸〜を養子にする

□ 0207
stake
/stéik/
ビジネス問題

名 ❶**投資**[出資](額)　❷(通例〜s)賭け金、賞金
動 (命・金など)を(…に)賭ける(on ...)

□ 0208
disturbance
/distə́:rbəns/
Part 7

名 ❶**妨害**[邪魔](物)(≒interruption)　❷(社会の)騒動、混乱
動 disturb：❶(平静など)を乱す、妨げる　❷〜に迷惑をかける
形 disturbing：平静を乱す、不安にさせる

Day 12))) CD-A12
Quick Review
答えは右ページ下

□ 湿度　□ 半球　□ 部分　□ 同僚
□ 織物　□ 報酬　□ 服用量　□ 修正
□ ちらし　□ 基準　□ 衣服　□ 予測
□ 通信　□ 必要条件　□ 住民　□ 商品引換券

Check 2 Phrase

- ☐ have no hesitation in doing 〜(〜するのをためらわない)
- ☐ without hesitation (躊躇なく)

- ☐ a private enterprise (私企業)
- ☐ embark on a new enterprise (新しい事業に着手する)

- ☐ the transcript of the witness's testimony (目撃者の証言の写し)
- ☐ a high school transcript (高校の成績証明書)

- ☐ a monthly [quarterly] periodical (月刊[季刊]の定期刊行物、月刊[季刊]誌)

- ☐ a compliance officer ([企業内での]法令順守担当責任者)
- ☐ in compliance with 〜 ([命令などに]従って、応じて)

- ☐ the adoption of the plan (その計画の採用)
- ☐ an adoption agency (養子縁組あっせん所)

- ☐ have a stake in 〜 (〜に投資[出資]している)
- ☐ win the stakes (賞金を得る)

- ☐ disturbance of law and order (治安の妨害)
- ☐ cause [create] a disturbance (騒動を起こす)

Check 3 Sentence

- ☐ He had no hesitation in accepting the job offer. (彼はためらうことなくその仕事の申し出を受けた)

- ☐ Small enterprises are the most sensitive to changes in the business environment. (小企業はビジネス環境の変化の影響を最も受けやすい)

- ☐ The jury was given a transcript of recorded telephone calls between the kidnappers and the victim's family. (陪審員団は誘拐犯と犠牲者の家族間の通話録音の写しを与えられた)

- ☐ The library subscribes to approximately 200 periodicals. (その図書館はおよそ200の定期刊行物を購入している)

- ☐ Compliance with the law is mandatory for all employees. (法律の順守は全従業員の義務だ)

- ☐ Adoption of new technology is often delayed because of cost considerations. (新しい技術の採用は経費を考慮して遅らされることが多い)

- ☐ He has a 10 percent stake in the company. (彼はその会社に10パーセント出資している)

- ☐ Residents have complained about the disturbances caused by aircraft. (住民たちは飛行機の騒音について苦情を述べている)

Day 12)) CD-A12
Quick Review
答えは左ページ下

- ☐ humidity
- ☐ textile
- ☐ leaflet
- ☐ correspondence
- ☐ hemisphere
- ☐ remuneration
- ☐ gauge
- ☐ prerequisite
- ☐ segment
- ☐ dose
- ☐ apparel
- ☐ inhabitant
- ☐ coworker
- ☐ amendment
- ☐ projection
- ☐ voucher

CHAPTER 1
CHAPTER 2
CHAPTER 3
CHAPTER 4
CHAPTER 5
CHAPTER 6
CHAPTER 7
CHAPTER 8
CHAPTER 9

Day 14　名詞14

Check 1　Listen)) CD-A14

☐ 0209
catering
/kéitəriŋ/
Part 4

名仕出し
名caterer：(宴会などの)仕出し屋、配膳業者
動cater：(cater to [for]で)〜に必要な物を提供する、〜の要求を満たす

☐ 0210
observance
/əbzə́:rvəns/
Part 5, 6

名❶(法律などの)**順守**(of 〜)(≒obedience, compliance)　❷(祝祭日を)祝うこと(of 〜)
名observation：観察；観察力
名observatory：観測所、天文台
動observe：❶〜を観察する　❷(法律など)を守る

☐ 0211
upheaval
/ʌphí:vəl/
Part 5, 6

名(社会状態などの)**大変動**、激変

☐ 0212
precedent
/présədənt/
Part 5, 6

名(〜に対する)**前例**、先例(for 〜)
動precede：〜に先立つ、〜より先に起こる
形preceding：(通例the 〜)前の、先の
形unprecedented：前例[先例]のない、空前の

☐ 0213
endorsement
/indɔ́:rsmənt/
Part 5, 6

名❶**承認**、是認　❷(小切手などの)裏書き
動endorse：❶〜を承認[是認、支持]する　❷(小切手など)に裏書きする

☐ 0214
layout
/léiàut/
Part 4

名❶**配置**、設計　❷(雑誌などの)割りつけ、レイアウト
動lay out：❶(建物など)を設計する　❷(ページなど)を割りつける

☐ 0215
credential
/kridénʃəl/
Part 7

名(通例〜s)**証明書**、資格

☐ 0216
allegation
/æligéiʃən/
Part 7

名(特に証拠のない)**申し立て**、主張
動allege：(証拠なしに)〜だと断言[主張]する
形alleged：❶申し立てられた　❷疑わしい
副allegedly：伝えられるところでは、申し立てによると

continued
▼

今日で『キクタンTOEIC Test Score 990』はようやく5分の1が終了。先はまだまだ長いけど、このペースで頑張っていこう！

- ☐ 聞くだけモード　Check 1
- ☐ しっかりモード　Check 1 ▶ 2
- ☐ かんぺきモード　Check 1 ▶ 2 ▶ 3

Check 2　Phrase

☐ a catering meal（仕出し弁当）

☐ the observance of copyright（著作権の順守）
☐ in observance of ~（~を祝って）

☐ economic upheaval（経済的大変動）

☐ set [create] a precedent for ~（~に前例を作る）
☐ without precedent（前例のない）

☐ the endorsement of a project（プロジェクトの承認）
☐ an endorsement of a check（小切手の裏書き）

☐ the layout of a city（都市計画）
☐ change the layout of a page（ページのレイアウトを変える）

☐ a teaching credential（教員資格）

☐ make allegations of ~（~の申し立てをする）
☐ the allegation that he stole the money（彼が金を盗んだという申し立て）

Check 3　Sentence

☐ My uncle runs a catering company.（私のおじは仕出し会社を経営している）

☐ Observance of human rights is a precondition of democracy.（人権の順守は民主主義の前提条件だ）

☐ Many nations experienced political upheaval and revolution in the 19th and 20th centuries.（多くの国は19世紀と20世紀に政変と革命を経験した）

☐ There are no precedents for this type of lawsuit.（この種の訴訟は前例がない）

☐ The project implementation requires government endorsement.（そのプロジェクトの実施には政府の承認が必要だ）

☐ I like the layout of my house.（私は自宅の間取りを気に入っている）

☐ The job applicant had excellent academic credentials.（その求職者は優秀な成績証明書を持っていた）

☐ She made allegations of sexual harassment against her supervisor.（彼女は上司を相手取ってセクハラの申し立てをした）

continued
▼

Day 14

Check 1　Listen)) CD-A14

□ 0217
expanse
/ikspǽns/
Part 4

名(〜の)**広がり**(of 〜)
名expansion：拡大、拡張
動expand：❶〜を拡大[拡張]する　❷拡大[拡張]する

□ 0218
intern
/íntəːrn/
ビジネス問題

名**研修[実習]生**(≒trainee)
名internship：実習訓練期間

□ 0219
surge
/sə́ːrdʒ/
ビジネス問題

名❶(価格などの)**急上昇**、高騰(in 〜)　❷(感情などの)高まり(of 〜)
動❶(群衆などが)押し寄せる　❷(物価などが)急騰する

□ 0220
debtor
/détər/
❶発音注意
ビジネス問題

名**債務者**、借り主(⇔creditor：債権者)
名debt：借金、負債；借金状態

□ 0221
clearance
/klíərəns/
ビジネス問題

名❶**在庫一掃セール**(≒clearance sale)　❷(公式の)許可　❸(2物間の)間隔　❹除去
動clear：❶〜を片づける　❷〜を通過する　❸〜をはっきりさせる
形clear：❶澄んだ　❷晴れた　❸明らかな

□ 0222
injection
/indʒékʃən/
Part 2, 3

名❶**注射**、注入(≒shot)　❷(資金などの)投入
動inject：(inject A into Bで)❶AをBに注射する　❷A(資金)をBにつぎ込む

□ 0223
predicament
/pridíkəmənt/
Part 7

名**苦境**、窮地(≒plight)

□ 0224
digit
/dídʒit/
Part 7

名(数字の)**けた**：アラビア数字
形digital：デジタル(式)の

Day 13)) CD-A13
Quick Review
答えは右ページ下

- □ 実物宣伝
- □ 協力
- □ 見積もり
- □ 確認
- □ 物流
- □ 年功
- □ 控除
- □ 養育権
- □ ためらい
- □ 企業
- □ 写し
- □ 定期刊行物
- □ 順守
- □ 採用
- □ 投資
- □ 妨害

Check 2　Phrase

- ☐ the vast expanse of the desert（広大な砂漠）

- ☐ work in ~ as an intern（~で研修生として働く）

- ☐ a surge in oil prices（原油価格の高騰）
- ☐ a surge of anger（こみ上げてくる怒り）

- ☐ a joint debtor（連帯債務者）
- ☐ a debtor nation（債務国）

- ☐ clearance price（在庫一掃セール価格）
- ☐ security clearance（秘密情報[文書]の取り扱い許可）

- ☐ give ~ an injection（~に注射を打つ）
- ☐ an injection of public funds（公的資金の投入）

- ☐ be placed in a predicament（苦境に置かれている）

- ☐ an eight-digit phone number（8けたの電話番号）

Check 3　Sentence

- ☐ From the hotel windows you can see the vast expanse of the sea.（ホテルの窓からは、広大な海を見渡すことができる）

- ☐ The company hires 10 interns every summer and about a quarter of its employees are former interns.（その会社は毎年夏に10名の研修生を雇っており、従業員の約4分の1は元研修生だ）

- ☐ There has been a surge in food prices over the past few years.（ここ数年で食品価格が急上昇している）

- ☐ Creditors have better memories than debtors.（貸し手は借り手よりもよく覚えている）➕ことわざ

- ☐ Our annual spring clearance will be held this weekend.（当店の毎年恒例の春の在庫一掃セールが今週末に開催されます）

- ☐ The doctor gave me an injection to reduce my temperature.（その医者は体温を下げるため私に注射を打った）

- ☐ Many companies are in a financial predicament.（多くの企業が財政的窮地にある）

- ☐ Please enter your seven-digit account number.（7けたの口座番号を入力してください）

Day 13))) CD-A13
Quick Review
答えは左ページ下

- ☐ demonstration
- ☐ collaboration
- ☐ quotation
- ☐ confirmation
- ☐ logistics
- ☐ seniority
- ☐ exemption
- ☐ custody
- ☐ hesitation
- ☐ enterprise
- ☐ transcript
- ☐ periodical
- ☐ compliance
- ☐ adoption
- ☐ stake
- ☐ disturbance

Day 15　名詞15

Check 1　Listen 》CD-A15

□ 0225
ally
/ǽlai/
Part 7

名 ❶協力者、味方　❷同盟国
動(/əlái/)(ally oneself to [with] ～で)～と同盟[提携]している
名 alliance：(国家間の)同盟；提携、協調
形 allied：❶同盟した　❷(～と)関連した(to [with] ～)

□ 0226
flier
/fláiər/
Part 7

名 ちらし、ビラ(≒leaflet)　◆flyerとつづることもある

□ 0227
orientation
/ɔ̀ːriəntéiʃən/
ビジネス問題

名 職業[入門、進路]**指導**、オリエンテーション
動 orient：(orient oneself to [toward]で)～に適応[順応]する

□ 0228
token
/tóukən/
Part 4

名 ❶印　❷代用硬貨、トークン

□ 0229
evacuation
/ivæ̀kjuéiʃən/
Part 7

名 避難
動 evacuate：❶～を(…から)避難させる(from …)　❷避難する

□ 0230
creditor
/kréditər/
ビジネス問題

名 債権者、貸し主(⇔debtor：債務者)
名 credit：❶信用貸し、クレジット　❷信用、信頼
動 credit：❶～を信用する　❷(be credited with [for]で)～の功績があると思われている

□ 0231
collision
/kəlíʒən/
Part 4

名 (～との／…の間の)**衝突**(with ～/between …)　◆比喩的な意味でも用いられる
動 collide：(collide withで)～と衝突する、ぶつかる

□ 0232
encouragement
/inkə́ːridʒmənt/
Part 4

名 激励、奨励
動 encourage：(encourage A to doで)Aに～するよう励ます
形 encouraging：激励の、励みとなる

continued
▼

今日でChapter 1は最後！ 時間に余裕があったら、章末のReviewにも挑戦しておこう。忘れてしまった単語も結構あるのでは?!

☐ 聞くだけモード　Check 1
☐ しっかりモード　Check 1 ▶ 2
☐ かんぺきモード　Check 1 ▶ 2 ▶ 3

Check 2　　Phrase

☐ one's closest ally（緊密な協力者）
☐ an ally of the US（アメリカの同盟国）

☐ a flier for the concert（そのコンサートのちらし）
☐ an election flier（選挙ちらし）

☐ orientation for new students（新入生向けのオリエンテーション）

☐ as a token of ~（~の印として）
☐ a subway token（地下鉄の代用硬貨）

☐ (an) emergency evacuation（緊急避難）

☐ a creditor nation（債権国）

☐ a head-on collision（正面衝突）
☐ a collision of opinions（意見の衝突）

☐ words of encouragement（激励の言葉）

Check 3　　Sentence

☐ The industry has strong allies in Congress.（その業界には国会に力強い協力者がいる）

☐ The flier says the sale is from May 27 to 31.（そのちらしには、セールは5月27日から31日までと書かれている）

☐ All new employees receive a two-week orientation.（全新入社員は2週間の職業指導を受ける）

☐ Please accept this gift as a token of my appreciation for your support.（あなたのご支援への感謝の印として、この贈り物をお受け取りください）

☐ Please follow the instructions of the staff in case of an evacuation.（避難の際は従業員の指示に従ってください）

☐ The company went bankrupt and couldn't pay its creditors.（その会社は倒産して、債権者への支払いができなかった）

☐ Four cars were involved in the collision.（4台の車がその衝突事故に巻き込まれた）

☐ I could never have succeeded without your help, advice and encouragement.（あなたの支援、助言、そして激励がなかったら、私は成功できなかっただろう）

continued ▼

Day 15

Check 1   Listen)) CD-A15

☐ 0233
restructuring
/rìːstrʌ́ktʃəriŋ/
ビジネス問題

名 **リストラ**、事業再構築、再編成
動 restructure：(組織・制度を)改革する、再構成[再編成]する

☐ 0234
cuisine
/kwizíːn/
Part 7

名 (ある地方・ホテルなどに特有の)**料理**(法)(≒cooking)

☐ 0235
enrollment
/inróulmənt/
Part 7

名 ❶**入学**[登録]**者数** ❷入学、入会
動 enroll：(enroll in [at, for]で)～に入学[入会]する

☐ 0236
ordinance
/ɔ́ːrdənəns/
Part 7

名 (地方自治体の)**条例**

☐ 0237
submission
/səbmíʃən/
Part 4

名 ❶(報告書などの)**提出**(of ～) ❷(～への)服従、屈服(to ～)(≒obedience)
動 submit：❶～を(…に)提出する(to . . .) ❷(submit toで)～に従う

☐ 0238
habitat
/hǽbitæt/
Part 7

名 (動植物の)**生息地**

☐ 0239
script
/skrípt/
Part 7

名 ❶**原稿** ❷脚本、台本 ❸文字

☐ 0240
intake
/ínteik/
Part 7

名 ❶**摂取量**、吸い込み量 ❷(空気・ガスなどの)取り入れ口、吸い込み口(⇔outlet)

Day 14)) CD-A14
Quick Review
答えは右ページ下

☐ 仕出し ☐ 承認 ☐ 広がり ☐ 在庫一掃セール
☐ 順守 ☐ 配置 ☐ 研修生 ☐ 注射
☐ 大変動 ☐ 証明書 ☐ 急上昇 ☐ 苦境
☐ 前例 ☐ 申し立て ☐ 債務者 ☐ けた

Check 2 Phrase

☐ **restructuring** under new management(新しい経営陣の下でのリストラ)

☐ Italian **cuisine**(イタリア料理)

☐ a drop in **enrollment**(入学者数の減少)
☐ an **enrollment** fee(入学金)

☐ a building **ordinance**(建築条例)

☐ the **submission** of the application form(申込用紙の提出)
☐ in **submission** to ~(~に服従[屈服]して)

☐ the natural **habitat** of ~(~の自然生息地)

☐ a **script** for a speech(スピーチの原稿)
☐ the **script** for the film(その映画の台本)

☐ an adequate **intake** of calcium(カルシウムの適量摂取)
☐ an air **intake**(空気取り入れ口)

Check 3 Sentence

☐ The company announced **restructuring** plans that would lay off 2,000 of its employees.(その会社は従業員2000人を解雇するリストラ計画を発表した)

☐ The restaurant is famous for its Mediterranean **cuisine**.(そのレストランは地中海料理で有名だ)

☐ The university intends to increase its **enrollment** of international students.(その大学は外国人留学生の入学者数を増やすつもりだ)

☐ The **ordinance** prohibits smoking in public areas.(その条例は公共の場所での喫煙を禁止している)

☐ The deadline for the **submission** of essays is May 31.(小論文の提出締め切り日は5月31日だ)

☐ The natural **habitat** of Asian elephants has been considerably reduced.(アジアゾウの自然生息地は著しく減少してきている)

☐ The examiner read instructions from a prepared **script**.(その試験官は用意された原稿の指示を読んだ)

☐ The recommended daily **intake** of water is approximately two liters.(1日の水分の推奨摂取量は約2リットルだ)

Day 14 》CD-A14
Quick Review
答えは左ページ下

☐ catering
☐ observance
☐ upheaval
☐ precedent
☐ endorsement
☐ layout
☐ credential
☐ allegation
☐ expanse
☐ intern
☐ surge
☐ debtor
☐ clearance
☐ injection
☐ predicament
☐ digit

Chapter 1 Review

左ページの(1)〜(20)の名詞の同意・類義語（≒）、反意・反対語（⇔）を右ページのA〜Tから選び、カッコの中に答えを書き込もう。意味が分からないときは、見出し番号を参照して復習しておこう（答えは右ページ下）。

- ☐ (1) brochure (0005) ≒は? (　　)
- ☐ (2) detour (0016) ⇔は? (　　)
- ☐ (3) altitude (0034) ≒は? (　　)
- ☐ (4) incentive (0046) ≒は? (　　)
- ☐ (5) surplus (0049) ⇔は? (　　)
- ☐ (6) integrity (0072) ≒は? (　　)
- ☐ (7) arbitration (0084) ≒は? (　　)
- ☐ (8) flaw (0092) ≒は? (　　)
- ☐ (9) paycheck (0101) ≒は? (　　)
- ☐ (10) freight (0115) ≒は? (　　)
- ☐ (11) intermission (0131) ≒は? (　　)
- ☐ (12) attire (0135) ≒は? (　　)
- ☐ (13) trainee (0149) ≒は? (　　)
- ☐ (14) attorney (0157) ≒は? (　　)
- ☐ (15) scrutiny (0164) ≒は? (　　)
- ☐ (16) leaflet (0179) ≒は? (　　)
- ☐ (17) quotation (0195) ≒は? (　　)
- ☐ (18) compliance (0205) ≒は? (　　)
- ☐ (19) debtor (0220) ⇔は? (　　)
- ☐ (20) predicament (0223) ≒は? (　　)

A. mediation
B. flier
C. cargo
D. elevation
E. interval
F. creditor
G. defect
H. booklet
I. lawyer
J. deficit
K. obedience
L. salary
M. intern
N. shortcut
O. plight
P. honesty
Q. examination
R. clothes
S. motivation
T. estimate

【解答】 (1) H (2) N (3) D (4) S (5) J (6) P (7) A (8) G (9) L (10) C
(11) E (12) R (13) M (14) I (15) Q (16) B (17) T (18) K (19) F (20) O

CHAPTER 2

動詞：超必修112

Chapter 2では、TOEIC「超必修」の動詞112を身につけていきます。Chapter 1を終え、学習のペースもだいぶつかめてきたのでは？「990点攻略」を目指して、このペースをキープしていきましょう。

Day 16【動詞1】
▶ 78
Day 17【動詞2】
▶ 82
Day 18【動詞3】
▶ 86
Day 19【動詞4】
▶ 90
Day 20【動詞5】
▶ 94
Day 21【動詞6】
▶ 98
Day 22【動詞7】
▶ 102
Chapter 2 Review
▶ 106

TOEIC的格言

Listen twice before you speak once.

念には念を入れよ。
[直訳] 1回話す前に2回聞け。

Day 16 動詞1

Check 1　Listen 》CD-A16

☐ 0241
expire
/ikspáiər/
Part 5, 6

動 **期限が切れる**、満了になる(≒end)
名 expiration：(期限の)満了、満期

☐ 0242
endorse
/indɔ́:rs/
Part 5, 6

動 ❶ **〜を承認**[是認、支持]**する**　❷(小切手など)に裏書きする
名 endorsement：❶承認、是認　❷(小切手などの)裏書き

☐ 0243
commute
/kəmjú:t/
Part 2, 3

動 (〜から／…へ) **通勤する**(from 〜/to ...)
名 通勤
名 commuter：通勤者

☐ 0244
evacuate
/ivǽkjuèit/
Part 4

動 ❶ **〜を**(…から) **避難させる**(from ...)　❷避難する
名 evacuation：避難

☐ 0245
facilitate
/fəsílətèit/
ビジネス頻出

動 ❶ **〜を促進**[助成]**する**(≒hasten, accelerate, expedite)　❷〜を容易にする

☐ 0246
update
/ʌ̀pdéit/
Part 2, 3

動 ❶ **〜を更新**[改訂]**する**、〜を最新のものにする　❷〜に(…の)最新情報を与える(on ...)
名 ❶(/ʌ́pdèit/)(〜に関する)最新情報(on 〜)　❷最新版
形 up-to-date：❶最新(式)の　❷現代的な

☐ 0247
verify
/vérəfài/
Part 5, 6

動 **〜が正しい**[事実である]**ことを証明**[立証、確認]**する**(≒check, confirm)
名 verification：証明、立証、確認

☐ 0248
surpass
/sərpǽs/
Part 7

動 (技量・能力などで) **〜より勝る**、〜をしのぐ(in [at] ...)(≒excel)

continued
▼

Chapter 2では、7日をかけて「超必修」の動詞112をチェック。まずはCDでチャンツを聞いて、単語を「耳」からインプット!

- ☐ 聞くだけモード　Check 1
- ☐ しっかりモード　Check 1 ▶ 2
- ☐ かんぺきモード　Check 1 ▶ 2 ▶ 3

Check 2　Phrase

☐ **expire** on March 31(3月31日に期限が切れる)
☐ **expire** with the next issue ([定期購読が]次号で切れる)

☐ **endorse** the proposal(その提案を承認する)
☐ **endorse** a check(小切手に裏書きする)

☐ **commute** from Yokohama to Tokyo(横浜から東京へ通勤する)
☐ **commute** by car(自動車で通勤する)

☐ **evacuate** refugees from the fighting zone(難民たちを戦闘地帯から避難させる)

☐ **facilitate** corporate activities(企業活動を促進する)
☐ **facilitate** communication(コミュニケーションを円滑にする)

☐ **update** a dictionary(辞書を改訂する)
☐ **update** him on the situation(彼に状況の最新情報を与える)

☐ **verify** the calculation(計算が正しいことを確認する)
☐ **verify** his statement(彼の言葉が事実であることを証明する)

☐ **surpass** one's colleagues in ability(能力で同僚より勝る)
☐ **surpass** expectations(期待を上回る)

Check 3　Sentence

☐ My driver's license **expires** next month.(私の運転免許証は来月で期限が切れる)

☐ The board of directors **endorsed** the new budget.(取締役会は新しい予算案を承認した)

☐ She **commutes** from Kobe to Osaka every day.(彼女は毎日、神戸から大阪へ通勤している)

☐ About 1,000 people were **evacuated** from their homes due to the threat of flooding.(洪水の恐れがあるため、約1000人が自宅から避難させられた)

☐ The economic stimulus package will **facilitate** economic recovery.(その経済刺激策は景気の回復を促進するだろう)

☐ We **update** our Web site on a regular basis.(当社はホームページを定期的に更新している)

☐ The results were **verified** by several experiments.(その結果が正しいことが何回かの実験で証明された)

☐ China will **surpass** the US in GNP in 20 to 30 years.(中国は2、30年後にはGNPでアメリカを超えるだろう)

continued
▼

Day 16

Check 1　Listen))) CD-A16

☐ 0249
disperse
/dispə́ːrs/
Part 7

動 ❶**～を分散させる**、四方に散らす　❷分散する、散らばる

☐ 0250
withhold
/wiðhóuld/
Part 7

動 **～を**(…に)**与えずにおく**(from ...)、～を保留する

☐ 0251
arise
/əráiz/
Part 5, 6

動 (問題などが)(～から)**生じる**、起こる(from [out of] ～)　⊕arouse(～をかき立てる)と混同しないように注意

☐ 0252
enhance
/inhǽns/
ビジネス問題

動 (力・価値など)**を高める**、強める
名 enhancement：増進、増大、強化

☐ 0253
certify
/sə́ːrtəfài/
Part 7

動 ❶**～を証明**[保証]**する**　❷～に免許状[証明書]を与える
名 certificate：❶証明書　❷修了証；免許状
動 certificate：～に証明書[免許状]を与える
形 certified：❶免許を持っている　❷保証された

☐ 0254
incur
/inkə́ːr/
Part 7

動 (負債など)**を負う**、被る、招く

☐ 0255
deduct
/didʌ́kt/
Part 5, 6

動 **～を**(…から)**差し引く**、控除する(from ...)(≒ subtract)(⇔add：～を加える)
名 deduction：❶(～からの)控除(from ～)　❷(～という)推論(that節 ～)
形 deductible：控除可能の

☐ 0256
retrieve
/ritríːv/
Part 7

動 ❶**～を**(…から)**回収する**、取り戻す(from ...)　❷(情報)を検索する
名 retrieval：❶(コンピューターの)(情報)検索　❷取り返し、回復

Day 15))) CD-A15
Quick Review
答えは右ページ下

☐ 協力者　☐ 避難　☐ リストラ　☐ 提出
☐ ちらし　☐ 債権者　☐ 料理　☐ 生息地
☐ 職業指導　☐ 衝突　☐ 入学者数　☐ 原稿
☐ 印　☐ 激励　☐ 条例　☐ 摂取量

Check 2 Phrase

- ☐ **disperse** the demonstrators（デモ参加者たちを追い散らす）
- ☐ **disperse** in all directions（四方八方に散らばる）

- ☐ **withhold** information from him（情報を彼に与えずにおく）
- ☐ **withhold** payment（支払いを保留する）

- ☐ **arise** from hard work（［成功などが］勤勉から生まれる）
- ☐ when the opportunity **arises**（機会があれば）

- ☐ **enhance** productivity（生産性を高める）
- ☐ **enhance** one's reputation（評判を高める）

- ☐ **certify** the quality of products（製品の品質を保証する）
- ☐ be **certified** as a teacher（教員免許を与えられる）

- ☐ **incur** debts（負債を負う）
- ☐ **incur** his anger [wrath]（彼の怒りを招く）

- ☐ **deduct** income tax from employee salaries（従業員の給料から所得税を差し引く）

- ☐ **retrieve** a malfunctioning satellite（故障した人工衛星を回収する）
- ☐ **retrieve** information on the Internet（インターネットで情報を検索する）

Check 3 Sentence

- ☐ Police **dispersed** the protesters with tear gas.（警察は催涙ガスを使って抗議者たちを追い散らした）

- ☐ Some people think that the US should **withhold** economic aid to Israel.（アメリカはイスラエルへの経済支援を見合わせるべきだと考える人もいる）

- ☐ The Cold War **arose** from Soviet aggression in Eastern Europe.（冷戦はソビエトの東欧侵攻から起こった）

- ☐ Our company needs to **enhance** its publicity.（我が社は知名度を高める必要がある）

- ☐ New vehicles must be **certified** to meet low-emission standards.（新車は低排気基準を満たしていることを証明されていなければならない）

- ☐ The auto manufacturer **incurred** a $10 million loss in the previous quarter.（その自動車メーカーは前四半期に1000万ドルの赤字を負った）

- ☐ Self-employed business owners can **deduct** health insurance costs from gross income.（自営業者は総収入から健康保険料を控除することができる）

- ☐ It is extremely expensive to **retrieve** data from a crashed hard disk.（クラッシュしたハードディスクからデータを回収するのは非常に費用がかかる）

Day 15))) CD-A15
Quick Review
答えは左ページ下

- ☐ ally
- ☐ flier
- ☐ orientation
- ☐ token
- ☐ evacuation
- ☐ creditor
- ☐ collision
- ☐ encouragement
- ☐ restructuring
- ☐ cuisine
- ☐ enrollment
- ☐ ordinance
- ☐ submission
- ☐ habitat
- ☐ script
- ☐ intake

Day 17 動詞2

Check 1　Listen 》CD-A17

☐ 0257
amend
/əménd/
Part 4

動 (憲法など)**を修正[改正]する**
名 amendment：(〜の)修正[改正](案)(to 〜)

☐ 0258
deteriorate
/ditíəriərèit/
ビジネス問題

動 (〜という状態に)**悪化する**(into 〜)(≒worsen)
(⇔improve：よくなる)
名 deterioration：悪化

☐ 0259
collaborate
/kəlǽbərèit/
Part 7

動 ❶ (〜を／…と)**共同で行う**；共同制作[研究]する(on [in] 〜/with . . .)(≒work together)　❷ (collaborate to do で)共同で〜する
名 collaboration：協力；共同制作[研究]
名 collaborator：協力者；共同制作[研究]者

☐ 0260
terminate
/tə́ːrmənèit/
Part 4

動 ❶ **〜を終わらせる**　❷ 終わる(≒end)
名 termination：終了、終結

☐ 0261
curb
/kə́ːrb/
Part 5, 6

動 (活動など)**を抑制[制限]する**(≒restrain, limit)
名 ❶ (歩道の)縁石　⊕この意味ではPart 1で頻出　❷ (〜に対する)抑制、制限(on 〜)(≒restraint)

☐ 0262
renovate
/rénəvèit/
Part 1

動 **〜を改装する**；〜を修理[復元]する
名 renovation：❶ 改装；修理　❷ 刷新、革新

☐ 0263
complement
/kámpləmènt/
Part 5, 6

動 **〜を補完[補足]する**；〜のよさを引き立てる
⊕compliment(褒め言葉)と混同しないように注意
名 (/kámpləmənt/)(〜の)補完物(to 〜)；(〜のよさを)引き立てる物(to 〜)
形 complementary：補足的な

☐ 0264
discontinue
/dìskəntínjuː/
ビジネス問題

動 (継続していたことなど)**を中止[中断]する**；(製品)を生産中止する
名 discontinuation：中断

continued
▼

見出し語下の「Part 1」マークの単語には、Check 3でPart 1型の例文を用意している。情景を頭に浮かべながら、音読してみよう！

☐ 聞くだけモード　Check 1
☐ しっかりモード　Check 1 ▶ 2
☐ かんぺきモード　Check 1 ▶ 2 ▶ 3

Check 2　Phrase

☐ amend the Constitution（憲法を改正する）

☐ deteriorating economy（悪化する経済）
☐ deteriorate into war（[事態などが]悪化して戦争になる）

☐ collaborate on a book with ~（~と本を共同執筆する）
☐ collaborate to produce a film（映画を共同制作する）

☐ terminate negotiations（交渉を終わらせる）
☐ terminate at the next stop（[列車などが]次の駅で終点となる）

☐ curb food prices [inflation]（食品価格［インフレ］を抑制する）

☐ renovate an old house（古い家を改装する）

☐ complement each other（互いを補完し合う）

☐ discontinue the project due to a tight budget（そのプロジェクトを予算不足のため中止する）

Check 3　Sentence

☐ The government should amend the pension law.（政府は年金法を修正するべきだ）

☐ The economic situation has been deteriorating worldwide.（経済状況は世界中で悪化している）

☐ The two companies are collaborating on the development of electric cars.（その2社は電気自動車の開発を共同で行っている）

☐ The electronics company announced plans to terminate television production.（その電機メーカーはテレビの生産を終了する計画を発表した）

☐ The government should curb its expenditure.（政府は支出を抑えるべきだ）

☐ The building is being renovated.（その建物は改修中だ）

☐ The music complements the movie perfectly.（音楽がその映画を見事に引き立てている）

☐ The airline decided to discontinue flights between New York and London.（その航空会社はニューヨークとロンドン間の便を中止することを決定した）

continued
▼

Day 17

Check 1　　Listen))) CD-A17

0265
scrub
/skrʌ́b/
Part 1

動 ～をごしごし磨く [洗う]

0266
compile
/kəmpáil/
Part 5, 6

動 ❶～を編集 [編さん] する　❷(資料など)を集める、まとめる
名 compilation：❶(本などの)編集　❷(資料などの)収集

0267
reinforce
/rìːinfɔ́ːrs/
Part 7

動 ～を(…で)補強 [強化] する (with . . .) (≒strengthen)
名 reinforcement：補強、強化

0268
violate
/váiəlèit/
Part 7

動 ❶(法律など)に違反する (≒disobey)　❷(権利など)を侵害する
名 violation：❶(法律などの)違反 (of ～)　❷(権利などの)侵害 (of ～)
名 violator：違反者

0269
alleviate
/əlíːvièit/
Part 7

動 (苦痛など)を緩和 [軽減] する (≒relieve)
名 alleviation：緩和、軽減

0270
emphasize
/émfəsàiz/
Part 5, 6

動 ～を強調 [力説] する、重要視する (≒stress, highlight, underline, underscore)
名 emphasis：(～の)強調、力説、重要視 (on [upon] ～)
形 emphatic：❶強調された、語気の強い　❷明らかな

0271
browse
/bráuz/
Part 5, 6

動 ❶(新聞などに)ざっと目を通す (through ～)　❷(インターネットで)～を閲覧する
名 browser：ブラウザ

0272
remit
/rimít/
Part 7

動 (金銭)を(…へ)送る (to . . .)　⊕emit([熱など]を放出する)と混同しないように注意
名 remittance：送金；送金額

Day 16))) CD-A16
Quick Review
答えは右ページ下

- □ 期限が切れる
- □ ～を承認する
- □ 通勤する
- □ ～を避難させる
- □ ～を促進する
- □ ～を更新する
- □ ～が正しいことを証明する
- □ ～より勝る
- □ ～を分散させる
- □ ～を与えずにおく
- □ 生じる
- □ ～を高める
- □ ～を証明する
- □ ～を負う
- □ ～を差し引く
- □ ～を回収する

Check 2 Phrase

- □ scrub the car（車をごしごし洗う）

- □ compile an encyclopedia（百科事典を編集する）
- □ compile data（データをまとめる）

- □ reinforce the river banks with sandbags（川の土手を砂袋で補強する）
- □ reinforce troops（軍隊を強化する）

- □ violate the law（法律に違反する）
- □ violate her privacy（彼女の私生活を侵害する）

- □ alleviate her sorrow（彼女の悲しみを和らげる）

- □ emphasize the importance [necessity] of ～（～の重要性[必要性]を強調する）

- □ browse through the newspaper（新聞にざっと目を通す）
- □ browse shopping sites（ショッピングサイトを閲覧する）

- □ remit a check（小切手を送る）

Check 3 Sentence

- □ The man is scrubbing the floor.（男性は床をごしごし磨いている）

- □ It took five years to compile the dictionary.（その辞書の編さんは5年かかった）

- □ The school building was reinforced with steel beams.（その校舎は鋼鉄の梁で補強された）

- □ The developer was charged with violating the building code.（その開発業者は建築基準法に違反したかどで告発された）

- □ The medicine will alleviate your pain if you take it every day.（毎日服用すれば、その薬であなたの痛みは和らぐだろう）

- □ The prime minister emphasized the importance of tax system reform.（首相は税制改革の重要性を強調した）

- □ She browsed through a few travel books to decide where to go on holiday.（彼女はどこへ旅行に行くかを決めるため、数冊の旅行本に目を通した）

- □ Please remit the tuition and admission fees no later than March 31.（3月31日までに授業料と入学金をご送金ください）

Day 16 ♪ CD-A16
Quick Review
答えは左ページ下

- □ expire
- □ endorse
- □ commute
- □ evacuate
- □ facilitate
- □ update
- □ verify
- □ surpass
- □ disperse
- □ withhold
- □ arise
- □ enhance
- □ certify
- □ incur
- □ deduct
- □ retrieve

Day 18 動詞3

Check 1　Listen 》CD-A18

□ 0273
discard
/diskɑ́ːrd/
Part 5, 6

動 (不用品・習慣など)**を捨てる**(≒ throw away, get rid of)
名 (/dískɑːrd/)捨てられた物

□ 0274
upgrade
/ʌ̀pgréid/
Part 2, 3

動 ❶〜の等級[格]**を上げる**、〜をグレードアップする ❶「グレードアップ」は和製英語 ❷(ソフト[ハード]ウエア)をアップグレードする
名 (/ʌ́pgrèid/)❶グレードアップ ❷アップグレード

□ 0275
enforce
/infɔ́ːrs/
Part 5, 6

動 ❶(法律など)**を守らせる**、施行[実施]する ❷(行為など)を(…に)強要する(on …)
名 enforcement：(法律などの)施行、実施

□ 0276
clarify
/klǽrəfài/
Part 7

動 (意味など)**を明らかにする**、明確にする

□ 0277
supervise
/súːpərvàiz/
Part 4

動 〜を監督[管理、指揮]**する**(≒ oversee, watch over)
名 supervisor：監督者、管理者
名 supervision：監督、管理、指揮
形 supervisory：監督[管理](上)の

□ 0278
vary
/véəri/
Part 5, 6

動 ❶(〜の点で)**異なる**、さまざまである(in 〜) ❷変わる ❸〜を変える(≒ change)
名 variation：変化、変動
形 various：さまざまな、いろいろな
形 variable：❶変わりやすい ❷変えられる

□ 0279
enlarge
/inlɑ́ːrdʒ/
Part 5, 6

動 ❶〜を拡大[拡張]**する** ❷(写真)を引き伸ばす ❸大きくなる
名 enlargement：❶(写真の)引き伸ばし ❷拡大、拡張

□ 0280
undertake
/ʌ̀ndərtéik/
ビジネス問題

動 ❶**〜に着手する**、取りかかる ❷(undertake to doで)〜することを約束する(≒ promise to do)
名 undertaking：事業、仕事

continued
▼

Quick Reviewは使ってる？ 昨日覚えた単語でも、記憶に残っているとは限らない。学習の合間に軽くチェックするだけでも効果は抜群！

- ☐ 聞くだけモード　Check 1
- ☐ しっかりモード　Check 1 ▶ 2
- ☐ かんぺきモード　Check 1 ▶ 2 ▶ 3

Check 2　Phrase

☐ discard an old computer（古いコンピューターを処分する）

☐ upgrade living standards（生活水準を上げる）
☐ upgrade the software to the latest version（そのソフトウエアを最新バージョンにアップグレードする）

☐ enforce speed limits（制限速度を守らせる）
☐ enforce obedience（服従を強いる）

☐ clarify the meaning of ～（～の意味を明らかにする）
☐ clarify one's position（自分の立場を明確にする）

☐ supervise the project（そのプロジェクトを監督する）
☐ supervise employees（従業員を指揮する）

☐ vary in size（大きさが異なる）
☐ vary according to ～（～に従って変わる）

☐ enlarge the hotel（そのホテルを増築する）
☐ have pictures enlarged（写真を引き伸ばしてもらう）

☐ undertake an investigation（調査に着手する）
☐ undertake to protect the environment（自然環境を守ることを約束する）

Check 3　Sentence

☐ The average household discards half a ton of paper and cardboard each year.（平均的な世帯は1年間に0.5トンの紙と段ボールを捨てている）

☐ I had my seat upgraded to business class.（私は座席をビジネスクラスに格上げしてもらった）

☐ Management has a responsibility to all employees to enforce safety rules.（経営陣は全従業員に対して安全規則を守らせる責任がある）

☐ It is important to clarify what the term "cost-effective" means.（「費用効率が高い」という用語が何を意味するかを明らかにすることが重要だ）

☐ He supervises 10 salespeople.（彼は10人の外交員を指揮している）

☐ DVD players vary in price from $50 to over $1,000.（DVDプレーヤーの価格は50ドルから1000ドルを超えるものまでさまざまである）

☐ The bank will enlarge its housing finance business.（その銀行は住宅金融ビジネスを拡大する予定だ）

☐ The company needs to undertake major restructuring of its operations.（その会社は事業の大リストラに着手する必要がある）

continued ▼

Day 18

Check 1 Listen))) CD-A18

☐ 0281
cease
/síːs/
❶発音注意
Part 5, 6

動 ❶ **〜を中止する**、やめる(≒stop)　❷(cease to do [doing]で)〜しなくなる、〜することをやめる　❸終わる
名 終止　➕通例、without cease(絶え間なく)の形で使われる

☐ 0282
presume
/prizúːm/
Part 5, 6

動 ❶(恐らく)**〜だと考える**、思う(≒suppose, assume)　❷(be presumed to doで)〜すると考えられている　➕resume(〜を再開する)と混同しないように注意
名 presumption:推定、推測、仮定
副 presumably:恐らく、多分

☐ 0283
emit
/imít/
Part 5, 6

動 (熱・光・ガスなど)**を放出[放射]する**、放つ
➕remit([金銭]を送る)と混同しないように注意
名 emission:❶(熱・光・ガスなどの)放出　❷排気;放出物

☐ 0284
delete
/dilíːt/
Part 5, 6

動 **〜を(…から)削除する**、消す(from ...)(≒erase)
名 deletion:削除;削除部分

☐ 0285
overcharge
/òuvərtʃáːrdʒ/
ビジネス問題

動 **〜に(…に対して)過剰請求をする**、法外な値を要求する(for ...)(⇔undercharge:〜に料金以下の金額を請求する)

☐ 0286
dine
/dáin/
Part 5, 6

動 (〜と)**食事をする**(with 〜)
名 dinner:ディナー、食事
名 diner:❶食事客　❷簡易食堂、小食堂

☐ 0287
speculate
/spékjulèit/
Part 5, 6

動 ❶**〜だと推測する**　❷(speculate on [about]で)〜について推測する　❸(speculate inで)(株など)に投機する、〜を思惑買い[売り]する
名 speculation:❶推測、推量　❷投機、思惑買い
名 speculator:投機[投資]家

☐ 0288
maximize
/mǽksəmàiz/
ビジネス問題

動 **〜を最大にする**(⇔minimize)
名 maximum:最大限、最高
形 maximum:最大限の、最高の
形 maximal:最大限の、最高の

Day 17))) CD-A17
Quick Review
答えは右ページ下

☐ 〜を修正する　☐ 〜を抑制する　☐ 〜をごしごし磨く　☐ 〜を緩和する
☐ 悪化する　☐ 〜を改装する　☐ 〜を編集する　☐ 〜を強調する
☐ 共同で行う　☐ 〜を補完する　☐ 〜を補強する　☐ ざっと目を通す
☐ 〜を終わらせる　☐ 〜を中止する　☐ 〜に違反する　☐ 〜を送る

Check 2　Phrase

- ☐ cease production（生産を中止する）
- ☐ cease to exist（なくなる、廃止される）

- ☐ presume that he is innocent（彼は無実だと考える）
- ☐ be presumed to have fled（逃亡したと考えられている）

- ☐ emit toxic chemicals（有毒化学物質を放出する）
- ☐ emit fragrances（よい香りを放つ）

- ☐ delete her name from the list（彼女の名前をリストから削除する）

- ☐ overcharge him by $10 for ～（彼に～に対して10ドル多く請求する）

- ☐ dine with her at the restaurant（そのレストランで彼女と食事をする）
- ☐ dine out（外食する）

- ☐ speculate that the company will go bankrupt（その会社は破産するだろうと推測する）
- ☐ speculate on the meaning of ～（～の意味を推測する）

- ☐ maximize profits（利益を最大にする）

Check 3　Sentence

- ☐ The company decided to cease the publication of its product catalog.（その会社は製品カタログの発行を中止することを決めた）

- ☐ I presume she is coming to the party.（彼女はパーティーに来ると思う）

- ☐ If we continue emitting greenhouse gases, global warming will continue.（私たちが温室効果ガスを排出し続ければ、地球温暖化は続くだろう）

- ☐ I have deleted important files by mistake.（私は重要なファイルを誤って削除してしまった）

- ☐ I was overcharged by $30 for shipping.（私は送料を30ドル多く請求された）

- ☐ She hates dining alone.（彼女は1人で食事をするのが嫌いだ）

- ☐ Some scientists speculate that global warming may lead to droughts, forest fires, and famines.（地球温暖化は干ばつ、森林火災、そして飢饉につながるだろうと推測する科学者もいる）

- ☐ Our key objective is to maximize productivity.（私たちの重要な目標は生産性を最大にすることだ）

Day 17 》CD-A17
Quick Review
答えは左ページ下

- ☐ amend
- ☐ deteriorate
- ☐ collaborate
- ☐ terminate
- ☐ curb
- ☐ renovate
- ☐ complement
- ☐ discontinue
- ☐ scrub
- ☐ compile
- ☐ reinforce
- ☐ violate
- ☐ alleviate
- ☐ emphasize
- ☐ browse
- ☐ remit

Day 19　動詞4

Check 1　Listen 》CD-A19

☐ 0289
diversify
/divə́ːrsəfài/
ビジネス問題

動 ❶(～に)**事業[投資]を広げる**(into ～)　❷(投資)を多角的にする　❸～を多角化する
名 diversity：多様性；相違
形 diverse：多様な、さまざまの

☐ 0290
relieve
/rilíːv/
Part 2, 3

動 ❶(苦痛など)**を和らげる**、軽減する(≒alleviate)　❷(relieve A of Bで)AからB(責任など)を取り除く；AをB(職)から解任[解雇]する
名 relief：❶安心　❷(苦痛などの)緩和　❸救済
形 relieved：(be relieved to doで)～して安心している

☐ 0291
induce
/indjúːs/
Part 5, 6

動 ❶**～を引き起こす**、誘発する(≒cause)　❷(induce A to doで)Aを説いて～する気にさせる
名 induction：❶誘発、誘導　❷帰納　❸就任
名 inducement：(行動へ)促すもの、誘因、刺激(to ～)

☐ 0292
consolidate
/kənsɑ́lədèit/
ビジネス問題

動 ❶(会社など)**を合併する**、整理統合する　❷合併する(≒merge)　❸～を強化する(≒strengthen)
名 consolidation：❶(会社などの)合併、整理統合　❷強化

☐ 0293
enact
/inǽkt/
Part 7

動 (法律・条例)**を制定する**、(法案)を成立させる

☐ 0294
summarize
/sʌ́məràiz/
Part 5, 6

動 **～を要約する**(≒sum up)
名 summary：(～の)要約、概略(of ～)

☐ 0295
discriminate
/diskrímənèit/
Part 5, 6

動 ❶(～を)**区別[識別]する**(between ～)　❷～を(…と)区別[識別]する(from ...)(≒distinguish)　❸(discriminate againstで)～を差別する
名 discrimination：(～に対する)差別(待遇)(against ～)

☐ 0296
minimize
/mínəmàiz/
Part 5, 6

動 ❶**～を最小にする**(⇔maximize)　❷～を最小限に評価する、軽視する
名 minimum：最低[最小]限
形 minimum：最低[最小]限の
形 minimal：最小(限度)の

continued
▼

見出し語の下にある「❶アクセント注意」や「❶発音注意」を見てる? 少しの違いで相手に伝わらないこともあるので要チェック!

- ☐ 聞くだけモード　Check 1
- ☐ しっかりモード　Check 1 ▶ 2
- ☐ かんぺきモード　Check 1 ▶ 2 ▶ 3

Check 2　Phrase

☐ diversify into the real estate business(不動産業に事業を広げる)
☐ diversify investments(投資を多角的にする)

☐ relieve anxiety(不安を和らげる)
☐ be relieved of the post of mayor(市長職から解任される)

☐ induce drowsiness([薬などが]眠気を引き起こす)
☐ induce him to take the job(彼を説いてその仕事をする気にさせる)

☐ consolidate a subsidiary(子会社を合併する)
☐ consolidate to form a single company([複数の会社が]合併して1つの会社になる)

☐ enact a law(法律を制定する)
☐ enact a bill(法案を成立させる)

☐ summarize the contents of the book(その本の内容を要約する)

☐ discriminate between good and bad = discriminate good from bad(善悪を区別する)

☐ minimize loss(損失を最小限にする)
☐ minimize the importance of ～(～の重要性を軽視する)

Check 3　Sentence

☐ The company is planning to diversify into the entertainment business.(その会社は娯楽産業に事業を広げることを計画している)

☐ Regular exercise will help relieve your stress.(定期的な運動はストレスを和らげるのに役立つだろう)

☐ This drug can induce side effects including nausea and dizziness.(この薬は吐き気や目まいなどの副作用を起こすことがある)

☐ The pharmaceutical company has consolidated its two manufacturing locations in Chicago.(その製薬会社は2つの生産拠点をシカゴに統合した)

☐ The city enacted an ordinance that bans the disposal of recyclable items.(その市はリサイクル可能な製品の廃棄を禁止する条例を制定した)

☐ Could you summarize the main points of the meeting?(その会議の要点を要約してくれますか?)

☐ A one-day-old baby can discriminate between the voice of its mother and that of another.(生後1日の赤ん坊は母親の声と別の人の声を聞き分けられる)

☐ Tamiflu can minimize the effects of the flu.(タミフルはインフルエンザの影響を最小限に抑えることができる)

continued
▼

Day 19

Check 1　Listen 》CD-A19

0297 detain /ditéin/ Part 5, 6
動 ❶〜を拘留[留置]する　❷〜を引き留める、待たせる
名 detention：拘留、留置

0298 jeopardize /dʒépərdàiz/ ❶発音注意 Part 7
動 〜を危険にさらす（≒ risk, endanger）
名 jeopardy：危険（にさらされること）　❶通例、in jeopardy（危険にさらされて）の形で使う

0299 tow /tóu/ Part 1
動 （車・船など）を牽引する、引く
名 引かれる[引く]こと、牽引

0300 conserve /kənsə́ːrv/ Part 5, 6
動 ❶〜を保護[保存]する（≒ preserve）　❷（エネルギーなど）を節約して使う
名 conservation：（自然環境などの）保護、保存

0301 embrace /imbréis/ ❶定義注意 Part 5, 6
動 ❶（考えなど）を受け入れる、採用する；（機会）を捕らえる、利用する　❷〜を抱き締める、抱擁する　❸〜を含む（≒ include）
名 抱擁

0302 penetrate /pénətrèit/ ビジネス問題
動 ❶（市場）に浸透する、進出する　❷〜を貫通する
名 penetration：進出、普及；浸透

0303 constitute /kánstətjùːt/ ❶アクセント注意 Part 5, 6
動 〜を構成する、〜の一部を成す（≒ make up, comprise）
名 constitution：❶憲法　❷体質　❸構造、構成、組織
形 constitutional：❶憲法（上）の、合憲の　❷体質の　❸構成上の

0304 dispatch /dispǽtʃ/ Part 5, 6
動 ❶〜を（…に）派遣する(to ...)　❷〜を（…に）発送する(to ...)
名 ❶派遣　❷発送

Day 18 》CD-A18　Quick Review　答えは右ページ下

- □ 〜を捨てる
- □ 〜の等級を上げる
- □ 〜を守らせる
- □ 〜を明らかにする
- □ 〜を監督する
- □ 異なる
- □ 〜を拡大する
- □ 〜に着手する
- □ 〜を中止する
- □ 〜だと考える
- □ 〜を放出する
- □ 〜を削除する
- □ 〜に過剰請求をする
- □ 食事をする
- □ 〜だと推測する
- □ 〜を最大にする

Check 2　Phrase

- ☐ detain a suspect（容疑者を拘留する）
- ☐ be detained by a traffic jam（交通渋滞で足止めされる）

- ☐ jeopardize one's life（命を危険にさらす）

- ☐ tow a ship（船を牽引する）

- ☐ conserve the habitat of rare animals（希少動物の生息地を保護する）
- ☐ conserve electricity [water]（電気［水］を節約して使う）

- ☐ embrace his opinion（彼の意見を受け入れる）
- ☐ embrace one's child（子どもを抱き締める）

- ☐ penetrate the European market（ヨーロッパ市場に浸透する）
- ☐ penetrate the wall（［弾丸などが］壁を貫通する）

- ☐ constitute 30 percent of the population（［人種などが］人口の30パーセントを構成している）

- ☐ dispatch a delegation to ~（~に代表団を派遣する）
- ☐ dispatch products to ~（~に製品を発送する）

Check 3　Sentence

- ☐ Police detained the suspect for three days for interrogation.（警察はその容疑者を取り調べのため3日間拘留した）

- ☐ Don't jeopardize your future by having an unreasonable amount of debt.（法外な借金を抱えて将来を危うくしてはならない）

- ☐ The wrecker is towing a car.（レッカー車が車を牽引している）

- ☐ We must conserve the environment.（私たちは自然環境を保護しなければならない）

- ☐ You should embrace this opportunity.（あなたはこの機会を利用するべきだ）

- ☐ Our company has successfully penetrated the Chinese market.（我が社は中国市場にうまく進出した）

- ☐ Women constitute 16 percent of the US Congress.（女性は米国連邦議会の16パーセントを構成している）

- ☐ An investigation team was dispatched to the crime scene.（調査班が犯罪現場へ派遣された）

Day 18))) CD-A18
Quick Review
答えは左ページ下

- ☐ discard
- ☐ upgrade
- ☐ enforce
- ☐ clarify
- ☐ supervise
- ☐ vary
- ☐ enlarge
- ☐ undertake
- ☐ cease
- ☐ presume
- ☐ emit
- ☐ delete
- ☐ overcharge
- ☐ dine
- ☐ speculate
- ☐ maximize

CHAPTER 1
CHAPTER 2
CHAPTER 3
CHAPTER 4
CHAPTER 5
CHAPTER 6
CHAPTER 7
CHAPTER 8
CHAPTER 9

Day 20　動詞5

Check 1　Listen)) CD-A20

0305 mow /móu/ Part 1
- 動 (草など)**を刈る**、刈り取る
- 名 mower：草刈り機、芝刈り機

0306 confiscate /kánfəskèit/ Part 7
- 動 **〜を**(…から)**没収[押収]する**(from ...)　⊕forfeitは「〜を没収される」
- 名 confiscation：没収[押収](品)

0307 restrain /ristréin/ Part 5, 6
- 動 ❶**〜を抑制する**、抑える(≒curb, limit)　❷(restrain oneself from doingで)〜するのを我慢[自制]する
- 名 restraint：❶自制、慎み　❷(〜への)抑制(力)(on 〜)
- 形 restrained：❶控えめな、節度のある　❷抑制された、抑えた

0308 exaggerate /igzǽdʒərèit/ Part 5, 6
- 動 **〜を誇張する**、大げさに言う
- 名 exaggeration：誇張
- 形 exaggerated：誇張した、大げさな

0309 proofread /prú:fri:d/ Part 2, 3
- 動 **〜を校正する**
- 名 proofreading：校正
- 名 proofreader：校正係

0310 deter /ditə́:r/ Part 5, 6
- 動 ❶**〜を防止する**、防ぐ　❷(deter A from doingで)Aに〜するのをやめさせる、思いとどまらせる　⊕defer(〜を延期する)と混同しないように注意
- 名 deterrent：抑止するもの、戦争抑止力
- 形 deterrent：妨げる、抑止する

0311 incorporate /inkɔ́:rpərèit/ Part 5, 6
- 動 ❶**〜を**(…に)**組み[取り]入れる**(into [in] ...)　❷〜を含む、包含する(≒include)
- 名 incorporation：(〜への)混入、混合(into 〜)

0312 soar /sɔ́:r/ ビジネス問題
- 動 ❶(物価・温度などが)**急上昇する**、急騰する　❷(空高く)舞い上がる

continued
▼

勉強する気分になれないときは、CDを「聞き流す」だけでもOK。家で、車内で、いつでもどこでも語彙に「触れる」時間を作ってみよう。

- ☐ 聞くだけモード　Check 1
- ☐ しっかりモード　Check 1 ▶ 2
- ☐ かんぺきモード　Check 1 ▶ 2 ▶ 3

Check 2　Phrase

☐ mow weeds（雑草を刈る）

☐ confiscate illegal drugs（違法薬物を押収する）

☐ restrain inflation（インフレを抑制する）
☐ restrain oneself from buying new clothes（新しい服を買うのを我慢する）

☐ exaggerate the threat of global warming（地球温暖化の脅威を誇張する）

☐ proofread a manuscript（原稿を校正する）

☐ deter enemy attacks（敵の攻撃を防ぐ）
☐ deter him from resigning（彼に辞職するのを思いとどまらせる）

☐ incorporate his ideas into the plan（彼の考えを計画に取り入れる）
☐ incorporate many features（[製品などが]多くの特徴を含んでいる）

☐ soar to 40 degrees Celsius（[気温が]セ氏40度に急上昇する）
☐ a plane soaring in the sky（空高く舞い上がる飛行機）

Check 3　Sentence

☐ The man is mowing the lawn.（男性は芝生を刈っている）

☐ He received a speeding ticket and his driver's license was confiscated.（彼はスピード違反切符を切られて、運転免許証を没収された）

☐ Higher oil prices will restrain economic growth.（原油価格が高くなると経済成長は抑制されるだろう）

☐ Politicians tend to exaggerate their talents and achievements.（政治家は自分の才能と業績を誇張する傾向がある）

☐ You should proofread the report before submitting it.（提出する前にその報告書を校正したほうがいい）

☐ Do you think the death penalty deters crime?（死刑は犯罪を防止すると思いますか？）

☐ Her suggestions were incorporated into the final design of the building.（彼女の提案はそのビルの最終デザインに取り入れられた）

☐ Stock prices soared nearly 8 percent today.（株価は今日、8パーセント近く急騰した）

continued ▼

Day 20

Check 1　Listen 》CD-A20

□ 0313 **bother**
/bάðər/
Part 2, 3

動 ❶〜に(…で)**迷惑**[面倒]**をかける**(with . . .)(≒ annoy)　❷(bother to do [doing]で)(通例否定文で)わざわざ〜する
名 悩みの種、厄介(者)

□ 0314 **infer**
/infə́ːr/
Part 5, 6

動 〜を(事実などから)**推測**[推論]**する**(from . . .)
名 inference：推測、推論

□ 0315 **downsize**
/dάunsàiz/
ビジネス問題

動 (人員など)**を削減**[縮小]**する**(≒ reduce, decrease, lower, curtail)
名 downsizing：人員削減、リストラ

□ 0316 **regulate**
/régjulèit/
Part 7

動 ❶〜を規制[統制、管理]**する**(≒ control)　❷〜を調節[調整]する(≒ adjust)
名 regulation：❶(〜に関しての)規則、条例(on [about] 〜)　❷規制
動 deregulate：〜の規制を緩和[撤廃]する

□ 0317 **dip**
/díp/
❶定義注意
ビジネス問題

動 ❶(価格などが)**減少する**、下がる　❷〜を(液体などに)ちょっと浸す[つける](in [into] . . .)　➕soakは「(一定の間)〜を浸す」
名 ❶ちょっと浸すこと；一泳ぎ　❷(価格などの)下落

□ 0318 **outline**
/άutlàin/
Part 5, 6

動 ❶〜**の要点を述べる**　❷〜の輪郭を描く
名 ❶概要、概略　❷輪郭

□ 0319 **defer**
/difə́ːr/
Part 5, 6

動 〜を(…まで)**延期する**(until [to] . . .)(≒ delay, postpone, put off)　➕deter(〜を防止する)と混同しないように注意

□ 0320 **fluctuate**
/flʌ́ktʃuèit/
ビジネス問題

動 **変動する**(≒ change)
名 fluctuation：(〜の)変動(in [of] 〜)

Day 19 》CD-A19
Quick Review
答えは右ページ下

□ 事業を広げる　□ 〜を制定する　□ 〜を拘留する　□ 〜を受け入れる
□ 〜を和らげる　□ 〜を要約する　□ 〜を危険にさらす　□ 〜に浸透する
□ 〜を引き起こす　□ 区別する　□ 〜を牽引する　□ 〜を構成する
□ 〜を合併する　□ 〜を最小にする　□ 〜を保護する　□ 〜を派遣する

Check 2 — Phrase

- □ bother her with trivial matters(ささいなことで彼女に迷惑をかける)
- □ bother to visit him(わざわざ彼を訪ねる)

- □ infer his intention from his behavior(彼の行動から彼の意図を推測する)

- □ downsize the work force(人員を削減する)

- □ regulate working conditions(労働条件を規制する)
- □ regulate the temperature(温度を調節する)

- □ dip to minus 10 degrees Celsius([気温が]セ氏マイナス10度に下がる)
- □ dip one's hand in water(水に手をちょっとつける)

- □ outline the purpose of the conference(会議の目的の要点を述べる)
- □ outline a map of Australia(オーストラリアの地図の輪郭を描く)

- □ defer the payment of ~(~の支払いを延期する)
- □ defer doing ~(~することを延期する)

- □ fluctuate between ~(~の間で変動する)
- □ fluctuate widely [greatly, wildly](大きく変動する)

Check 3 — Sentence

- □ I'm sorry to bother you, but could you give me a hand?(ご面倒ですが、手伝っていただけますか?)

- □ I inferred from his tone that he didn't like my proposal.(彼は私の提案を気に入っていないことが彼の口調からうかがえた)

- □ The company downsized its operations in Europe and the US.(その会社はヨーロッパとアメリカでの事業を縮小した)

- □ Emissions of carbon dioxide should be regulated.(二酸化炭素の排出は規制されるべきだ)

- □ New car sales dipped 23.7 percent last month.(先月は新車販売台数が23.7パーセント減少した)

- □ The CEO outlined a three-year business plan.(そのCEOは3カ年事業計画の概要を発表した)

- □ The board has deferred making a decision on the issue until next week.(役員会はその問題に関して決定を下すのを来週まで延期した)

- □ Tax revenues fluctuate with the economy.(税収は経済状態とともに変動する)

Day 19))) CD-A19
Quick Review
答えは左ページ下

- □ diversify
- □ relieve
- □ induce
- □ consolidate
- □ enact
- □ summarize
- □ discriminate
- □ minimize
- □ detain
- □ jeopardize
- □ tow
- □ conserve
- □ embrace
- □ penetrate
- □ constitute
- □ dispatch

Day 21 動詞6

Check 1　Listen))) CD-A21

0321 trigger /trígər/ Part 7
- 動 (事件など)**を引き起こす**、誘発する
- 名 ❶引き金　❷(〜の)きっかけ、誘因(for 〜)

0322 encounter /inkáuntər/ Part 7
- 動 ❶(困難など)**に直面する**　❷〜に偶然出会う
- 名 (〜との)(偶然の)出会い、遭遇(with 〜)

0323 safeguard /séifgɑ̀ːrd/ Part 5, 6
- 動 〜を(…から)**保護する**、守る(against [from] …)(≒protect)
- 名 (〜に対する)予防手段[措置](against 〜)(≒precaution)

0324 concede /kənsíːd/ Part 5, 6
- 動 〜を(正しいと)(渋々)**認める**
- 名 concession：(〜への)譲歩(to 〜)

0325 disrupt /disrʌ́pt/ Part 5, 6
- 動 **〜を混乱**[中断]**させる**
- 名 disruption：混乱、中断
- 形 disruptive：(行動などが)破壊的な、妨害する、邪魔をする

0326 arouse /əráuz/ ❶発音注意 Part 5, 6
- 動 (関心など)**をかき立てる**、喚起する、刺激する、誘発する　❶arise(生じる)と混同しないように注意

0327 soak /sóuk/ Part 7
- 動 ❶〜を(…に)**浸す**(in …)　❶dipは「〜をちょっと浸す」　❷(〜に)つかる、浸る(in 〜)　❸〜をびしょぬれにする
- 名 ❶浸すこと　❷入浴
- 形 soaking：ずぶぬれの

0328 curtail /kərtéil/ ビジネス問題
- 動 ❶**〜を削減する**、切り詰める(≒reduce, decrease, lower, downsize)　❷〜を短縮する(≒shorten)

continued
▼

今日で本書は3割の学習が終了。先を見ると道のりは長いけれど、1日1日着実に進めていこう。ゴールは確実に近づいている！

- ☐ 聞くだけモード　Check 1
- ☐ しっかりモード　Check 1 ▶ 2
- ☐ かんぺきモード　Check 1 ▶ 2 ▶ 3

Check 2　Phrase

☐ trigger a civil war（内戦を引き起こす）

☐ encounter difficulties（苦境に直面する）
☐ encounter an old friend（旧友に偶然出会う）

☐ safeguard the interests of ～（～の利益を守る）
☐ safeguard endangered species against extinction（絶滅危惧種を絶滅から守る）

☐ concede one's error（誤りを認める）
☐ concede defeat（敗北を認める）

☐ disrupt a computer system（コンピューターシステムを混乱させる）

☐ arouse her interest [suspicion]（彼女の興味[疑念]をかき立てる）

☐ soak beans overnight in water（豆を水に一晩浸す）
☐ soak in a hot bath（熱い風呂につかる）

☐ curtail expenditure [spending]（支出を削減する）
☐ curtail one's vacation（休暇を短縮する）

Check 3　Sentence

☐ A series of explosions triggered the fire.（一連の爆発でその火災は起きた）

☐ The world is now encountering a global financial crisis.（世界は今、地球規模の金融危機に直面している）

☐ All necessary steps must be taken to safeguard the interests of domestic industry.（国内産業の利益を守るために、すべての必要な策が講じられなければならない）

☐ The president conceded that the war in Iraq is not going as well as he had hoped.（大統領はイラク戦争が望んでいたほどうまく進んでいないことを認めた）

☐ Heavy snow disrupted air and rail travel in Europe.（豪雪によってヨーロッパの飛行機と列車の交通が混乱した）

☐ The science fiction novel aroused his interest in astronomy.（そのSF小説は天文学への彼の興味をかき立てた）

☐ To remove wine stains, soak the fabric in salted water for two hours, then rinse, and launder as usual.（ワインの染みを取るには、布地を塩水に2時間浸し、その後にゆすぎ、通常通り洗濯してください）

☐ The government should not curtail spending on health care.（政府は医療に対する支出を削減すべきではない）

continued
▼

Day 21

Check 1　Listen 》CD-A21

0329 inaugurate /inɔ́ːgjurèit/ Part 7
- 動 ❶〜の就任式を行う　❷〜の落成[開所]式を行う　❸〜を(正式に)開始する　❹(新時代)を新しく開く
- 名 inauguration：❶就任(式)　❷開業、開所　❸(新時代などの)開始

0330 demolish /dimáliʃ/ Part 1
- 動 (建物)を取り壊す、破壊する(≒destroy)
- 名 demolition：取り壊し、破壊

0331 thrive /θráiv/ ビジネス問題
- 動 成功する(≒succeed)、栄える、繁栄する(≒prosper, flourish)
- 形 thriving：繁栄している

0332 ease /íːz/ Part 7
- 動 ❶〜を緩和する　❷(痛みなど)を和らげる(≒relieve)　❸(痛み・緊張などが)和らぐ
- 名 ❶気楽さ　❷容易さ
- 形 easy：❶容易な　❷安楽な
- 副 easily：❶容易に　❷気楽に

0333 bet /bét/ Part 2, 3
- 動 ❶〜だと確信する、きっと〜だ　❷(金など)を(…に)賭ける(on ...)
- 名 ❶賭け　❷賭け金
- 名 betting：賭け、賭け事

0334 dictate /díkteit/ ❶定義注意 Part 5, 6
- 動 ❶(物・事が)〜に影響する、〜を決定[左右]する(≒determine)　❷〜を(…に)書き取らせる、口述する(to ...)　❸〜を(…に)命令する(to ...)
- 名 命令
- 名 dictation：❶書き取り、ディクテーション　❷命令

0335 oversee /òuvərsíː/ ビジネス問題
- 動 (仕事・作業員など)を監督[監視]する(≒watch over, supervise)

0336 adjourn /ədʒə́ːrn/ Part 7
- 動 ❶(会議・裁判など)を(…まで)延期する、休会にする(≒put off, postpone)(until ...)　❹通例、会議や裁判について用い、それ以外については用いられない　❷(〜まで)延期[休会]になる(until ...)
- 名 adjournment：延期、休会

Day 20 》CD-A20 Quick Review　答えは右ページ下
- □ 〜を刈る
- □ 〜を没収する
- □ 〜を抑制する
- □ 〜を誇張する
- □ 〜を校正する
- □ 〜を防止する
- □ 〜を組み入れる
- □ 急上昇する
- □ 〜に迷惑をかける
- □ 〜を推測する
- □ 〜を削減する
- □ 〜を規制する
- □ 減少する
- □ 〜の要点を述べる
- □ 〜を延期する
- □ 変動する

Check 2 Phrase

- ☐ inaugurate a president(大統領の就任式を行う)
- ☐ inaugurate a new library(新しい図書館の落成式を行う)

- ☐ demolish an old school(古い学校を取り壊す)

- ☐ thrive in business(事業に成功する)

- ☐ ease sanctions on ～(～に対する制裁措置を緩和する)
- ☐ ease a pain(痛みを和らげる)

- ☐ You can bet (that) ～.(～であるのは間違いない、必ず～だ)
- ☐ bet $100 on the horse(100ドルをその馬に賭ける)

- ☐ dictate the outcome of ～(～の結果に影響を及ぼす)
- ☐ dictate a letter to a secretary(手紙を秘書に書き取らせる)

- ☐ oversee the construction site(建築現場を監督する)

- ☐ adjourn the meeting until Friday(会議を金曜日まで延期する)
- ☐ adjourn until next week(来週まで延期になる)

Check 3 Sentence

- ☐ Barack Obama was inaugurated on January 20, 2009 as the 44th President of the United States.(バラク・オバマは2009年1月20日に第44代アメリカ大統領に就任した)

- ☐ The house is being demolished.(その家は解体中だ)

- ☐ The company is thriving under the leadership of its current CEO.(現在のCEOの指揮の下、その会社は繁栄している)

- ☐ Japan eased import restrictions on US beef.(日本はアメリカ産牛肉に対する輸入制限を緩和した)

- ☐ I bet he's lying.(きっと彼はうそをついている)

- ☐ Weather conditions will dictate whether or not we hold the barbecue.(天候によってバーベキューをするかどうかが決まる)

- ☐ As a sales manager, he oversees more than 100 employees.(営業部長として、彼は100人を超える従業員を監督している)

- ☐ The trial was adjourned until next month.(その裁判は来月まで延期になった)

Day 20))) CD-A20
Quick Review
答えは左ページ下

- ☐ mow
- ☐ confiscate
- ☐ restrain
- ☐ exaggerate
- ☐ proofread
- ☐ deter
- ☐ incorporate
- ☐ soar
- ☐ bother
- ☐ infer
- ☐ downsize
- ☐ regulate
- ☐ dip
- ☐ outline
- ☐ defer
- ☐ fluctuate

CHAPTER 1
CHAPTER 2
CHAPTER 3
CHAPTER 4
CHAPTER 5
CHAPTER 6
CHAPTER 7
CHAPTER 8
CHAPTER 9

Day 22　動詞7

Check 1　　Listen))) CD-A22

□ 0337
exert
/iɡzə́:rt/
❶発音注意
Part 5, 6

動 ❶(権力・影響力など)**を**(…に)**行使する**、使う(on ...) (≒ exercise)　❷(exert oneselfで)努力する(≒ make efforts)
名 exertion：❶(権力などの)行使　❷努力、尽力

□ 0338
await
/əwéit/
Part 5, 6

動 **～を待つ**、待ち受ける(≒ wait for)

□ 0339
disregard
/dìsriɡɑ́:rd/
Part 5, 6

動 **～を無視**[軽視]**する**(≒ ignore)
名 (～の)無視(for [of] ～)

□ 0340
streamline
/strí:mlàin/
ビジネス問題

動 ❶(仕事など)**を合理化**[能率化、簡素化]**する**　❷～を流線形にする

□ 0341
broaden
/brɔ́:dn/
Part 5, 6

動 ❶(視野・範囲など)**を広げる**[深める]　❷広がる
形 broad：幅の広い

□ 0342
mature
/mətjúər/
❶定義注意
ビジネス問題

動 ❶(保険などが)**満期になる**　❷成熟する
形 ❶(人が)分別のある(⇔ immature)　❷(生物が)十分に成長した　❸熟した
名 maturity：❶成熟(期)　❷満期(日)

□ 0343
denounce
/dináuns/
Part 5, 6

動 ❶～**を**(…だと)**公然と非難する**(as ...)　❷～を(…に)告発する(to ...)
名 denunciation：❶(公然の)非難　❷告発

□ 0344
escort
/iskɔ́:rt/
Part 7

動 ❶**～を護衛する**　❷(人)を案内する　❸～につき添う
名 (/éskɔ:rt/) ❶護衛者[団]　❷つき添い、同伴者

continued
▼

今日でChapter 2は最後！ 時間に余裕があったら、章末のReviewにも挑戦しておこう。忘れてしまった単語も結構あるのでは?!

- □ 聞くだけモード　Check 1
- □ しっかりモード　Check 1 ▶ 2
- □ かんぺきモード　Check 1 ▶ 2 ▶ 3

Check 2　Phrase

- □ exert one's influence（影響力を行使する）
- □ exert oneself to do ～（～するために努力する）

- □ await the result（結果を待つ）
- □ the long awaited sequel（待ちに待った続編）

- □ disregard school rules（校則を無視する）

- □ streamline management（経営を合理化する）
- □ streamline a car（車を流線形にする）

- □ broaden one's experience [horizons]（経験[視野]を広げる）
- □ broaden one's understanding（理解を深める）

- □ mature in 20 years（20年で満期になる）
- □ mature mentally（精神的に成熟する）

- □ denounce injustice（不正を非難する）
- □ denounce him to the police（彼を警察に告発する）

- □ escort a merchant ship（商船を護衛する）
- □ escort him on a tour of the factory（工場視察で彼を案内して回る）

Check 3　Sentence

- □ The US exerted pressure on Japan to open the home market to US products.（アメリカ製品に対して国内市場を開放するようアメリカは日本に圧力をかけた）

- □ Harsh conditions awaited immigrants to the country.（過酷な状況がその国への移民たちを待ち受けていた）

- □ He was fired for disregarding the rules and regulations of the company.（彼は会社の規則を無視したため解雇された）

- □ We need to streamline operations and maximize productivity.（私たちは生産過程を合理化して生産性を最大限にする必要がある）

- □ My trip to Europe broadened my cultural horizons.（ヨーロッパ旅行は私の文化的な視野を広げた）

- □ The bond matures in 10 years.（その社債は10年で満期になる）

- □ Many religious leaders denounced the movie as blasphemous.（多くの宗教指導者たちはその映画を冒とく的だと非難した）

- □ Five police cars escorted the presidential car to the White House.（5台の警察車両が大統領が乗った車をホワイトハウスまで護衛した）

continued
▼

Day 22

Check 1　Listen))) CD-A22

☐ 0345
aggravate
/ǽgrəvèit/
Part 5, 6

動 ～を悪化させる(≒ worsen)
名 aggravation：悪化

☐ 0346
reconcile
/rékənsàil/
❶アクセント注意
Part 5, 6

動 ❶～を(…と)**一致[調和、両立]させる**(with ...)　❷(be reconciled with で)～と和解[仲直り]する
名 reconciliation：(～の間の／…との)和解、調和(between ～/with ...)

☐ 0347
accelerate
/æksélərèit/
Part 5, 6

動 ❶～を加速[促進]する(≒ hasten, facilitate, expedite)　❷加速する(⇔ decelerate)
名 acceleration：加速、促進
名 accelerator：アクセル、加速装置

☐ 0348
transact
/trænzǽkt/
ビジネス問題

動 ❶(取引・業務など)**を行う**　❷(～と)取引[業務]を行う(with ～)
名 transaction：❶取引　❷(業務の)処理

☐ 0349
distract
/distrǽkt/
Part 5, 6

動 (人)**の気を**(…から)**散らす**、(注意など)を(…から)散らす、そらす(from ...)(⇔ attract)
名 distraction：❶気を散らす[散らされる]こと　❷気晴らし、娯楽
形 distracting：気が散る、集中できない

☐ 0350
waive
/wéiv/
ビジネス問題

動 (権利など)**を放棄する**、撤回する
名 waiver：権利放棄(証書)

☐ 0351
deem
/dí:m/
Part 5, 6

動 ～を(…だと)**考える**(as [to be] ...)　❶このas、to beは省略され、第5文型を取ることが多い

☐ 0352
underline
/ʌ̀ndərláin/
Part 5, 6

動 ❶～を強調する(≒ stress, emphasize, highlight, underscore)　❷～に下線を引く

Day 21))) CD-A21
Quick Review
答えは右ページ下

- ☐ ～を引き起こす
- ☐ ～に直面する
- ☐ ～を保護する
- ☐ ～を認める
- ☐ ～を混乱させる
- ☐ ～をかき立てる
- ☐ ～を浸す
- ☐ ～を削減する
- ☐ ～の就任式を行う
- ☐ ～を取り壊す
- ☐ 成功する
- ☐ ～を緩和する
- ☐ ～だと確信する
- ☐ ～に影響する
- ☐ ～を監督する
- ☐ ～を延期する

Check 2 — Phrase

- ☐ **aggravate** the economic crisis(経済危機を悪化させる)

- ☐ **reconcile** different opinions(異なる意見を一致させる)
- ☐ be **reconciled** with one's wife(妻と仲直りする)

- ☐ **accelerate** economic growth(経済成長を加速させる)
- ☐ **accelerate** from 0 to 60 mph in less than four seconds(時速0マイルから60マイルまで4秒未満で加速する)

- ☐ **transact** business with ~(~と取引をする)
- ☐ **transact** with suppliers(供給業者と取引を行う)

- ☐ Don't **distract** me.(私の気を散らさないでください)
- ☐ **distract** attention from ~(~から注意をそらす)

- ☐ **waive** one's right(権利を放棄する)
- ☐ **waive** one's objection(異議を撤回する)

- ☐ **deem** ~ (as [to be]) appropriate(~を適切であると考える)

- ☐ **underline** the necessity of ~(~の必要性を強調する)
- ☐ **underline** an important sentence(重要な文に下線を引く)

Check 3 — Sentence

- ☐ Consumption of a huge amount of fossil fuels has **aggravated** global warming.(大量の化石燃料の消費が地球温暖化を悪化させてきた)

- ☐ It is very difficult to **reconcile** ideals with reality.(理想と現実の折り合いをつけるのは非常に難しい)

- ☐ The automaker is **accelerating** its restructuring plans.(その自動車メーカーはリストラ計画を加速させている)

- ☐ There are a lot of reasons to open a website to **transact** business on the Internet.(インターネット上で取引をするためにウェブサイトを開く多くの理由がある)

- ☐ Don't **distract** him while he's studying.(勉強中は彼の気を散らさないでください)

- ☐ He **waived** his right to inherit property left by his father.(彼は父親から遺贈された財産を相続する権利を放棄した)

- ☐ As soon as the area is **deemed** safe, residents can return home.(その地域が安全だと見なされ次第、住民たちは帰宅することができる)

- ☐ The economist **underlined** the seriousness of the global recession.(その経済学者は世界的景気後退の深刻さを強調した)

Day 21))) CD-A21
Quick Review
答えは左ページ下

- ☐ trigger
- ☐ encounter
- ☐ safeguard
- ☐ concede
- ☐ disrupt
- ☐ arouse
- ☐ soak
- ☐ curtail
- ☐ inaugurate
- ☐ demolish
- ☐ thrive
- ☐ ease
- ☐ bet
- ☐ dictate
- ☐ oversee
- ☐ adjourn

CHAPTER 1
CHAPTER 2
CHAPTER 3
CHAPTER 4
CHAPTER 5
CHAPTER 6
CHAPTER 7
CHAPTER 8
CHAPTER 9

Chapter 2 Review

左ページの(1)～(20)の動詞の同意・類義語（≒）、反意・反対語（⇔）を右ページのA～Tから選び、カッコの中に答えを書き込もう。意味が分からないときは、見出し番号を参照して復習しておこう（答えは右ページ下）。

- ☐ (1) facilitate (0245) ≒は? (   )
- ☐ (2) surpass (0248) ≒は? (   )
- ☐ (3) deduct (0255) ⇔は? (   )
- ☐ (4) deteriorate (0258) ≒は? (   )
- ☐ (5) terminate (0260) ≒は? (   )
- ☐ (6) reinforce (0267) ≒は? (   )
- ☐ (7) supervise (0277) ≒は? (   )
- ☐ (8) presume (0282) ≒は? (   )
- ☐ (9) delete (0284) ≒は? (   )
- ☐ (10) relieve (0290) ≒は? (   )
- ☐ (11) minimize (0296) ⇔は? (   )
- ☐ (12) conserve (0300) ≒は? (   )
- ☐ (13) restrain (0307) ≒は? (   )
- ☐ (14) bother (0313) ≒は? (   )
- ☐ (15) regulate (0316) ≒は? (   )
- ☐ (16) safeguard (0323) ≒は? (   )
- ☐ (17) demolish (0330) ≒は? (   )
- ☐ (18) thrive (0331) ≒は? (   )
- ☐ (19) disregard (0339) ≒は? (   )
- ☐ (20) underline (0352) ≒は? (   )

A. strengthen
B. destroy
C. excel
D. control
E. erase
F. suppose
G. emphasize
H. hasten
I. limit
J. maximize
K. oversee
L. flourish
M. worsen
N. annoy
O. preserve
P. add
Q. ignore
R. alleviate
S. protect
T. end

【解答】(1) H (2) C (3) P (4) M (5) T (6) A (7) K (8) F (9) E (10) R
(11) J (12) O (13) I (14) N (15) D (16) S (17) B (18) L (19) Q (20) G

CHAPTER 3

形容詞：超必修112

Chapter 3では、TOEIC「超必修」の形容詞112を押さえていきます。このChapterが終われば、本書も4割が終了。そして、「超必修」の名詞・動詞・形容詞464が身についたことになります。

Day 23【形容詞1】
▶110
Day 24【形容詞2】
▶114
Day 25【形容詞3】
▶118
Day 26【形容詞4】
▶122
Day 27【形容詞5】
▶126
Day 28【形容詞6】
▶130
Day 29【形容詞7】
▶134
Chapter 3 Review
▶138

TOEIC的格言

It is better to have too much than too little.

大は小を兼ねる。
[直訳] 少な過ぎるより多過ぎるほうがいい。

Day 23　形容詞1

Check 1　Listen 》CD-A23

0353 intensive
/inténsiv/
Part 5, 6

形 ❶**集中的な**、徹底的な　❷(農業が)集約的な
名 intensity：激しさ、強烈さ
動 intensify：❶強まる　❷〜を強める
形 intense：激しい、強烈[猛烈]な
副 intensively：集中的に

0354 complimentary
/kàmpləméntəri/
Part 4

形 ❶**無料の**(≒free)　❷好意的な、称賛[敬意]を表す
⊕ complementary(補足的な)と混同しないように注意
名 compliment：(〜についての)褒め言葉、賛辞；お世辞(on 〜)
動 compliment：〜に賛辞を述べる；〜の(…を)褒める(on …)

0355 consecutive
/kənsékjutiv/
Part 5, 6

形 **連続した**(≒straight, successive)
副 consecutively：連続して

0356 mandatory
/mǽndətò:ri/
Part 5, 6

形 **義務[強制]的な**(≒compulsory, obligatory)(⇔voluntary：自発的な)
名 mandate：❶権限　❷(公式の)命令、指示
動 mandate：❶〜に(…するように)命令する(to do)
❷〜に(…する)権限を与える(to do)

0357 confidential
/kànfədénʃəl/
Part 5, 6

形 **秘密[内密]の**
名 confidence：❶信頼　❷自信　❸秘密
名 confidentiality：機密[秘密]性[保持]
副 confidentially：内密に

0358 adjacent
/ədʒéisnt/
Part 5, 6

形 (〜に)**隣接した**(to 〜)(≒next)；近隣の(≒nearby, neighboring)

0359 municipal
/mju:nísəpəl/
❶アクセント注意
Part 7

形 **市[町]の**；市営[町営]の；地方自治の
名 municipality：地方自治体

0360 hazardous
/hǽzərdəs/
Part 7

形 (〜にとって)**危険な**(≒dangerous)；有害な(to 〜)
名 hazard：危険；(〜への)危険要素(to 〜)
動 hazard：〜を危険にさらす

continued
▼

Chapter 3では、7日をかけて「超必修」の形容詞112をチェック。まずはCDでチャンツを聞いて、単語を「耳」からインプット！

☐ 聞くだけモード　Check 1
☐ しっかりモード　Check 1 ▶ 2
☐ かんぺきモード　Check 1 ▶ 2 ▶ 3

Check 2　Phrase

☐ intensive care（集中治療）
☐ intensive agriculture [farming]（集約農業）

☐ a complimentary ticket（無料招待券）
☐ a complimentary remark（褒め言葉、賛辞）

☐ for three consecutive days（3日間連続して）
☐ win [lose] five consecutive games（5連勝［連敗］する）

☐ mandatory education（義務教育）

☐ strictly confidential（極秘の）
☐ keep ~ confidential（~を秘密にしておく）

☐ a library adjacent to a school（学校に隣接した図書館）
☐ adjacent countries（近隣諸国）

☐ municipal authorities（市当局）
☐ a municipal zoo（市営動物園）

☐ a hazardous occupation（危険な職業）
☐ hazardous waste（有害廃棄物）

Check 3　Sentence

☐ I took a three-week intensive course in English.（私は3週間の英語集中コースを受講した）

☐ Following the meeting, a complimentary dinner will be served at 6 p.m.（会議の後に、無料の食事が午後6時に出される）

☐ It has been raining for five consecutive days.（5日間連続して雨が降っている）

☐ Wearing seat belts in the front and back seats is mandatory in Japan.（日本では前部と後部座席のシートベルト着用は義務だ）

☐ Confidential documents were stolen from headquarters.（機密文書が本社ビルから盗まれた）

☐ A parking lot is adjacent to the hotel.（駐車場はそのホテルの隣にある）

☐ Municipal elections will be held on July 17.（地方議会選挙が7月17日に行われる）

☐ Smoking is hazardous to your health.（喫煙は健康を害する）

continued ▼

Day 23

Check 1　Listen 》CD-A23

□ 0361
fiscal
/fískəl/
ビジネス問題

形 **会計の**、財政上の

□ 0362
qualified
/kwáləfàid/
ビジネス問題

形 (〜の／…する) **資格[免許]のある**(for 〜/to do)
名 qualification：❶(〜する)資格(to do)　❷(〜の)適性、資質(for 〜)
動 qualify：(qualify as [for])〜の資格を取る

□ 0363
alternate
/ɔ́ːltərnət/
Part 1

形 ❶**交互の**　❷1つおきの　❸代わりの(≒alternative)
名 代理人(≒substitute)
動 (/ɔ́ltərnèit/)❶(〜の間を)行きつ戻りつする(between 〜)　❷(alternate A with Bで)AをBと交互にする

□ 0364
fragile
/frǽdʒəl/
Part 7

形 ❶**壊れやすい**、もろい(≒delicate, frail)　❷虚弱な

□ 0365
prior
/práiər/
Part 5, 6

形 ❶**前の**、先の(≒earlier, previous)；(prior toで)(前置詞的に)〜より前に　❷(〜に)優先する、(〜より)重要な(to 〜)
名 priority：❶優先事項　❷優先(権)

□ 0366
comprehensive
/kàmprihénsiv/
Part 5, 6

形 **包括的な**(≒inclusive)；広範囲な　❶comprehensible(分かりやすい)と混同しないように注意

□ 0367
prospective
/prəspéktiv/
Part 5, 6

形 ❶**見込みのある**、期待される　❷予想される、将来の
名 prospect：(通例〜s)(成功などの)見込み、可能性(of [for] 〜)

□ 0368
overdue
/òuvərdjúː/
Part 7

形 (支払いなどが)**未払いの**、期限の過ぎた
形 due：支払期日の来た、満期の

Day 22 》CD-A22
Quick Review
答えは右ページ下

- □ 〜を行使する
- □ 〜を待つ
- □ 〜を無視する
- □ 〜を合理化する
- □ 〜を広げる
- □ 満期になる
- □ 〜を公然と非難する
- □ 〜を護衛する
- □ 〜を悪化させる
- □ 〜を一致させる
- □ 〜を加速する
- □ 〜を行う
- □ 〜の気を散らす
- □ 〜を放棄する
- □ 〜を考える
- □ 〜を強調する

Check 2 Phrase

- ☐ the fiscal year（会計年度）
- ☐ a fiscal policy（財政政策）

- ☐ a qualified architect（資格を持った建築士）
- ☐ be qualified to teach mathematics（数学を教える資格を持っている）

- ☐ alternate stripes of red and white（赤と白の交互のしま模様）
- ☐ work (on) alternate days（1日おきに働く）

- ☐ a fragile vase（壊れやすい花瓶）
- ☐ feel fragile（体がだるく感じる）

- ☐ a prior engagement（先約）
- ☐ have a prior claim on ～（～に優先権がある）

- ☐ a comprehensive report（包括的な報告書）
- ☐ comprehensive insurance（総合保険）

- ☐ a prospective customer（見込み客）
- ☐ prospective costs（予想される経費）

- ☐ overdue mortgage payments（住宅ローンの未払い分）

Check 3 Sentence

- ☐ Most companies' fiscal year starts in April in Japan.（日本ではほとんどの企業の会計年度は4月に始まる）

- ☐ A sufficient number of qualified applicants have applied for the position.（資格を持った十分な数の志願者がその職に応募してきた）

- ☐ The men and women are sitting in alternate seats.（男性と女性は交互に席に座っている）

- ☐ Handle fragile items with care.（壊れやすい物は注意して扱ってください）

- ☐ Applicants must have prior experience in system development.（応募者は以前にシステム開発の経験がなければならない）⊕求人広告の表現

- ☐ The two countries have entered into comprehensive peace talks.（両国は包括的な和平会談を開始した）

- ☐ The high school held an open house for prospective students and their families.（その高校は入学希望者とその家族のために一般公開を開催した）

- ☐ The fine for an overdue library book is 10 cents per book, per day.（返却期限が過ぎた図書館の本に対する罰金は1冊につき1日10セントだ）

Day 22))) CD-A22
Quick Review
答えは左ページ下

- ☐ exert
- ☐ await
- ☐ disregard
- ☐ streamline
- ☐ broaden
- ☐ mature
- ☐ denounce
- ☐ escort
- ☐ aggravate
- ☐ reconcile
- ☐ accelerate
- ☐ transact
- ☐ distract
- ☐ waive
- ☐ deem
- ☐ underline

CHAPTER 1
CHAPTER 2
CHAPTER 3
CHAPTER 4
CHAPTER 5
CHAPTER 6
CHAPTER 7
CHAPTER 8
CHAPTER 9

Day 24　形容詞2

Check 1　Listen 》CD-A24

☐ 0369
spacious
/spéiʃəs/
Part 7

形 (家・部屋などが)**広々とした**、広い
名 space：❶空間　❷場所　❸間隔　❹宇宙
動 space：❶〜を間隔を置いて配置する　❷(文字・行など)の間を空ける

☐ 0370
flawless
/flɔ́ːlis/
Part 5, 6

形 **欠点のない**、非の打ちどころがない
名 flaw：❶(〜の)欠陥、欠点(in 〜)　❷(手続き・議論などの)不備、欠陥(in 〜)
形 flawed：欠点[欠陥]のある

☐ 0371
unanimous
/juːnǽnəməs/
❶発音注意
Part 5, 6

形 ❶満場[全員]**一致の**　❷(〜で)意見が一致して(in 〜)　⊕anonymous(匿名の)と混同しないように注意
副 unanimously：満場一致で

☐ 0372
toll-free
/tóulfriː/
Part 4

形 **フリーダイヤルの**
副 フリーダイヤルで
名 toll：❶使用料；長距離通話料　❷死傷者数

☐ 0373
lucrative
/lúːkrətiv/
❶発音注意
ビジネス問題

形 **もうかる**、利益の上がる(≒profitable)

☐ 0374
defective
/diféktiv/
Part 5, 6

形 **欠陥[欠点]のある**(≒faulty)
名 defect：(〜の)欠陥、欠点(in 〜)

☐ 0375
respective
/rispéktiv/
Part 5, 6

形 **それぞれの**、各自の　⊕respectful(礼儀正しい)と混同しないように注意
副 respectively：それぞれ、各自

☐ 0376
adverse
/ædvə́ːrs/
Part 5, 6

形 ❶**不都合[不利]な**；(効果などが)マイナスの　❷敵意に満ちた
名 adversary：敵；(試合などの)相手

continued
▼

形容詞の役割は、名詞を修飾する「限定用法」と、文中で補語になる「叙述用法」の2つ。それぞれの使われ方をCheck 2, 3で押さえよう。

- ☐ 聞くだけモード　Check 1
- ☐ しっかりモード　Check 1 ▶ 2
- ☐ かんぺきモード　Check 1 ▶ 2 ▶ 3

Check 2　Phrase

☐ a spacious living room（広々とした居間）

☐ a flawless performance（欠点のない演奏）

☐ a unanimous verdict（全員一致の評決）
☐ be unanimous in supporting him（彼を支持することで意見が一致している）

☐ a toll-free line（フリーダイヤル回線）

☐ a lucrative business（もうかる商売）

☐ a defective car（欠陥車）

☐ carry out respective duties（それぞれの職務を果たす）

☐ adverse conditions（不利な条件）
☐ adverse criticism（酷評）

Check 3　Sentence

☐ This 3-bedroom, 2-bathroom condominium is spacious and bright with mountain views.（寝室3部屋、バスルーム2つのこの分譲マンションは広々としていて、山が見渡せて明るい）

☐ She speaks flawless French.（彼女は非の打ちどころのないフランス語を話す）

☐ She was elected chairperson by a unanimous vote.（彼女は満場一致の票決で議長に選ばれた）

☐ For further details call our toll-free number.（詳細については、当社のフリーダイヤル番号にお電話ください）

☐ This partnership will be very lucrative for both companies.（この提携は両社にとって非常に利益が高いだろう）

☐ Defective merchandise will be replaced free of charge within 30 days of purchase.（購入後30日以内であれば、欠陥商品は無料で取り換えられる）

☐ They exchanged their respective views on the issue.（彼らはその問題に関する各自の意見を取り交わした）

☐ The game was called off due to adverse weather conditions.（その試合は悪天候のため中止になった）

continued ▼

Day 24

Check 1　Listen 》CD-A24

□ 0377
luxurious
/lʌɡʒúəriəs/
❶アクセント注意
Part 4

形 **豪華な**、ぜいたくな
名 luxury：❶ぜいたくさ、豪華さ、快適さ；(形容詞的に)ぜいたく[豪華]な　❷ぜいたく品

□ 0378
considerate
/kənsídərət/
Part 5, 6

形 **思いやりがある**、理解がある(⇔inconsiderate)
✚ considerable(かなりの)と混同しないように注意
名 consideration：考慮、考察
動 consider：❶〜をよく考える、熟慮[熟考]する　❷(consider doingで)〜することをよく考える

□ 0379
quarterly
/kwɔ́ːrtərli/
Part 5, 6

形 **年4回の**、四半期ごとの
副 年4回、四半期ごとに
名 季刊誌
名 quarter：❶四半期　❷15分　❸4分の1

□ 0380
discreet
/diskríːt/
Part 5, 6

形 **慎重な**(≒careful)；(〜について)口が堅い(about 〜)
名 discretion：❶自由裁量、判断[行動、選択]の自由　❷思慮深さ、慎重さ、分別

□ 0381
round-trip
/ráundtríp/
Part 4

形 (切符が)**往復の**(⇔one-way：片道の)

□ 0382
chronic
/kránik/
Part 5, 6

形 ❶(病気が)**慢性の**(⇔acute：急性の)　❷(悪い状態が)長期にわたる

□ 0383
messy
/mési/
Part 2, 3

形 **散らかった**、乱雑な(≒untidy)(⇔tidy, neat)
名 mess：めちゃくちゃな状態[様子]、乱雑、混乱
動 mess：(mess upで)❶〜を台無しにする　❷〜を散らかす

□ 0384
durable
/djúərəbl/
Part 5, 6

形 **耐久性[力]のある**；永続性のある(≒lasting)
名 durability：耐久性[力]；永続性

| Day 23 》CD-A23
Quick Review
答えは右ページ下 | □ 集中的な
□ 無料の
□ 連続した
□ 義務的な | □ 秘密の
□ 隣接した
□ 市の
□ 危険な | □ 会計の
□ 資格のある
□ 交互の
□ 壊れやすい | □ 前の
□ 包括的な
□ 見込みのある
□ 未払いの |

Check 2　Phrase

- ☐ a luxurious hotel（豪華なホテル）

- ☐ considerate words（思いやりのある言葉）
- ☐ It is considerate of ~ to do ...（…するとは~は思いやりがある）

- ☐ a quarterly magazine（季刊誌）
- ☐ a quarterly fiscal report（四半期ごとの会計報告書）

- ☐ a discreet inquiry（慎重な調査）
- ☐ be discreet about the project（そのプロジェクトについて口外しないでいる）

- ☐ a round-trip ticket（往復切符）

- ☐ a chronic disease（慢性病）
- ☐ a chronic shortage of ~（長期にわたる~の不足）

- ☐ a messy kitchen（散らかった台所）

- ☐ durable goods（耐久消費財）
- ☐ a durable peace（永続的平和）

Check 3　Sentence

- ☐ All the rooms are equipped with luxurious furniture and air conditioning.（すべての部屋には豪華な家具とエアコンが備えつけられている）

- ☐ Be courteous and considerate to others.（人には礼儀正しく思いやりを持ちなさい）

- ☐ The newsletter is issued on a quarterly basis.（その会報誌は年に4回発行される）

- ☐ He is a discreet man who does not talk much.（彼はあまり多くを語らない慎重な人だ）

- ☐ A round-trip air ticket between Paris and London costs about $500.（パリ・ロンドン間の往復航空券の値段は約500ドルだ）

- ☐ He has been suffering from chronic asthma.（彼は慢性ぜん息を患っている）

- ☐ Why is your room always so messy?（どうしてあなたの部屋はいつもこんなに散らかっているの？）

- ☐ Toys must be made of durable materials.（玩具は耐久性のある材料で作られていなければならない）

Day 23))) CD-A23
Quick Review
答えは左ページ下

- ☐ intensive
- ☐ complimentary
- ☐ consecutive
- ☐ mandatory
- ☐ confidential
- ☐ adjacent
- ☐ municipal
- ☐ hazardous
- ☐ fiscal
- ☐ qualified
- ☐ alternate
- ☐ fragile
- ☐ prior
- ☐ comprehensive
- ☐ prospective
- ☐ overdue

Day 25　形容詞3

Check 1　Listen 》CD-A25

0385
clerical
/klérikəl/
ビジネス問題

形 **事務(職)の**
名 clerk：❶(会社・ホテルなどの)事務員　❷店員

0386
authentic
/ɔːθéntik/
Part 7

形 **本物の**、本当の(≒ real, genuine)(⇔ fake：偽の)
名 authenticity：本物であること
動 authenticate：〜が本物であることを証明する

0387
tentative
/téntətiv/
❶発音注意
Part 5, 6

形 **仮の**、試験的な、一時的な
副 tentatively：仮に、試験的に

0388
ambiguous
/æmbígjuəs/
Part 5, 6

形 **あいまいな**：2つ以上の意味に取れる
名 ambiguity：(意味などの)あいまいさ；多義性
副 ambiguously：あいまいに

0389
unprecedented
/ʌnprésədəntid/
Part 7

形 **前例[先例]のない**、空前の
名 precedent：(〜に対する)前例、先例(for 〜)
動 precede：〜に先立つ、〜より先に起こる
形 preceding：(通例the 〜)前の、先の

0390
brisk
/brísk/
ビジネス問題

形 ❶(商売が)**活況の**、繁盛して　❷活発な、きびきびした

0391
incredible
/inkrédəbl/
Part 2, 3

形 ❶**信じられない**(ほどの)(≒ unbelievable)(⇔ credible)　❷驚くべき(≒ amazing)、素晴らしい(≒ wonderful)
副 incredibly：信じられないほど；非常に

0392
endangered
/indéindʒərd/
Part 7

形 (動植物が)**絶滅寸前の**、絶滅の危機に瀕した
＋extinctは「絶滅した」
動 endanger：〜を危険にさらす

continued
▼

「声に出す」練習は続けている？ えっ、周りに人がいてできない?! そんなときは「口パク」でもOK。「耳+口」の練習を忘れずに！

□ 聞くだけモード　Check 1
□ しっかりモード　Check 1 ▶ 2
□ かんぺきモード　Check 1 ▶ 2 ▶ 3

Check 2　Phrase

□ a clerical job（事務職）

□ an authentic signature（本物のサイン）
□ authentic Italian food（本格的なイタリア料理）

□ reach a tentative agreement with ~（~と仮合意に達する）
□ a tentative plan（試案）

□ an ambiguous reply（あいまいな[どちらとも取れる]返事）

□ on an unprecedented scale（前例のない規模で）
□ an unprecedented victory（空前の勝利）

□ brisk sales（好調な売れ行き）
□ a brisk walk（きびきびとした歩み）

□ an incredible story（信じられない話）
□ an incredible invention（驚くべき発明）

□ endangered species（絶滅危惧種）

Check 3　Sentence

□ The company cut costs by reducing the number of clerical staff.（その会社は事務職員の数を減らすことで経費を削減した）

□ The store offers authentic antiques from 100 to 400 years old.（その店は100年から400年前の本物の骨董品を売っている）

□ Both countries have agreed to a tentative cease-fire.（両国は暫定休戦に合意した）

□ The government has been ambiguous on the issue of gun control.（政府は銃規制の問題に関してあいまいな態度を取り続けている）

□ The country is experiencing unprecedented economic growth.（その国は前例のない経済成長を経験している）

□ When the economy is brisk, everyone feels confident about his or her prospects for the future.（経済が活況な時は、誰もが将来の見通しに自信を感じる）

□ The Internet has expanded at an incredible rate over the last 10 years or so.（インターネットはここ10年ほどで信じられないほどの速さで拡大した）

□ The giant panda is an endangered animal.（ジャイアント・パンダは絶滅の危機に瀕している動物だ）

continued
▼

Day 25

Check 1　Listen 🔊 CD-A25

☐ 0393 **mutual**
/mjúːtʃuəl/
Part 5, 6

形 ❶**相互の**、互いの　❷共通の(≒common)
副 mutually：互いに、相互に

☐ 0394 **inexpensive**
/ìnikspénsiv/
Part 2, 3

形 **安い**、割安の、費用のかからない(≒cheap)(⇔expensive)　➕質の割には「安い」というニュアンス

☐ 0395 **sluggish**
/slʌ́giʃ/
ビジネス問題

形 ❶(商売などが)**停滞した**、不景気な　❷(動きが)のろい　➕「slug(ナメクジ)のような」が原意

☐ 0396 **prestigious**
/prestídʒəs/
Part 7

形 **一流の**、名声のある
名 prestige：(地位・業績などによる)名声、威信

☐ 0397 **crude**
/krúːd/
Part 7

形 ❶**天然のままの**、未加工の(≒raw)(⇔refined：精製された)　❷無礼な、不作法な(≒rude, impolite)

☐ 0398 **mobile**
/móubəl/
Part 1

形 **移動式の**、可動性の
名 (/móubiːl/)携帯電話(≒cellphone)

☐ 0399 **upright**
/ʌ́prait/
Part 4

形 ❶**まっすぐな**、垂直の、直立した(≒vertical)(⇔horizontal)　❷正直[高潔]な(≒honest)
副 まっすぐに、直立して

☐ 0400 **distinct**
/distíŋkt/
Part 5, 6

形 ❶**はっきりした**、明瞭な(≒clear)　❷(〜と)(まるで)異なった、別個の(from 〜)(≒different)
動 distinguish：(distinguish A from Bで)AをBと区別する
名 distinction：(〜の間の)区別、差別(between 〜)

Day 24 🔊 CD-A24
Quick Review
答えは右ページ下

☐ 広々とした
☐ 欠点のない
☐ 満場一致の
☐ フリーダイヤルの

☐ もうかる
☐ 欠陥のある
☐ それぞれの
☐ 不都合な

☐ 豪華な
☐ 思いやりがある
☐ 年4回の
☐ 慎重な

☐ 往復の
☐ 慢性の
☐ 散らかった
☐ 耐久性のある

Check 2 Phrase

- by mutual consent [agreement]（双方合意の上で）
- a mutual friend（共通の友人）

- inexpensive medicine（安い薬）

- a sluggish economy（停滞した経済）
- a sluggish speed（のろい速度）

- a prestigious hotel（一流ホテル）
- a prestigious award（名誉ある賞）

- crude rubber（生ゴム）
- a crude remark（無礼な発言）

- a mobile library（移動図書館）
- a mobile phone（携帯電話）

- stand in an upright position（まっすぐな姿勢で立つ）
- an upright citizen（高潔な市民）

- have a distinct memory of ～（～をはっきり覚えている）
- be distinct from each other（互いに異なっている）

Check 3 Sentence

- Married life should be based on mutual understanding and respect.（結婚生活は相互理解と尊重に基づいていなければならない）

- The food at the restaurant was excellent and inexpensive.（そのレストランの料理は素晴らしくて安かった）

- Home sales were sluggish last year.（昨年、住宅販売は停滞していた）

- Oxford University is one of the most prestigious universities in the world.（オックスフォード大学は世界で最も名声のある大学の1つだ）

- Crude oil prices have been on a downward trend for the past several weeks.（この数週間、原油価格は下降傾向にある）

- The woman is talking on a mobile phone.（女性は携帯電話で話をしている）

- Please return your seat to an upright position and fasten your seat belt.（座席をまっすぐに戻し、シートベルトを着用してください）●機内アナウンス

- There is a distinct difference between males and females in terms of muscular strength.（筋力の点では男女の間にははっきりとした違いがある）

Day 24))) CD-A24
Quick Review
答えは左ページ下

- spacious
- flawless
- unanimous
- toll-free
- lucrative
- defective
- respective
- adverse
- luxurious
- considerate
- quarterly
- discreet
- round-trip
- chronic
- messy
- durable

CHAPTER 1
CHAPTER 2
CHAPTER 3
CHAPTER 4
CHAPTER 5
CHAPTER 6
CHAPTER 7
CHAPTER 8
CHAPTER 9

Day 26　形容詞4

Check 1　Listen 》CD-A26

□ 0401
legitimate
/lidʒítəmət/
Part 7

形 **合法[適法]の**(≒legal, lawful)；正当[公正]な
名 legitimacy：合法(性)、正当(性)

□ 0402
obscure
/əbskjúər/
Part 5, 6

形 **あいまいな**、分かりにくい、不明瞭な(≒unclear, vague)(⇔clear)
動 ～をあいまいにする、分かりにくくする、不明瞭にする(⇔clarify)
名 obscurity：あいまいさ、不明瞭

□ 0403
deductible
/didʌ́ktəbl/
ビジネス問題

形 **控除可能の**
名 deduction：❶(～からの)控除(from ～)　❷(～という)推論(that節 ～)
動 deduct：～を(…から)差し引く、控除する(from ...)

□ 0404
obligatory
/əblígətɔ̀ːri/
Part 5, 6

形 (～にとって)**義務[強制]的な**(for [on] ～)(≒compulsory, mandatory)(⇔voluntary：自発的な)
名 obligation：(～に対する／…する)(道徳的・法律的な)義務、責任(to ～/to do)
動 oblige：(be obliged to doで)～せざるを得ない

□ 0405
up-to-date
/ʌ́ptədéit/
Part 7

形 **最新[最近]の**(⇔out-of-date：時代遅れの)　●叙述用法の場合はハイフンなしでup to dateとつづることもある

□ 0406
affluent
/ǽfluənt/
●アクセント注意
Part 5, 6

形 **裕福な**、豊かな(≒rich, wealthy)(⇔poor)
名 affluence：豊かさ、裕福

□ 0407
preceding
/prisíːdiŋ/
Part 5, 6

形 (通例the ～)**前の**、先の(⇔following, subsequent)
名 precedent：(～に対する)前例、先例(for ～)
動 precede：～に先立つ、～より先に起こる
形 unprecedented：前例[先例]のない、空前の

□ 0408
inclement
/inklémənt/
●アクセント注意
Part 4

形 (天候が)**荒れ模様の**　●increment(増加)と混同しないように注意

continued
▼

「分散学習」も効果的。朝起きたらCheck 1、昼食後にCheck 2、寝る前にCheck 3といった具合に、学習時間を作る工夫をしてみよう。

- ☐ 聞くだけモード　Check 1
- ☐ しっかりモード　Check 1 ▶ 2
- ☐ かんぺきモード　Check 1 ▶ 2 ▶ 3

Check 2　Phrase

- ☐ legitimate ownership(合法的な所有権)
- ☐ a legitimate reason(正当な理由)

- ☐ an obscure explanation [answer](あいまいな説明[回答])

- ☐ tax deductible(課税控除の)

- ☐ an obligatory subject(必修科目)

- ☐ an up-to-date hairstyle(最新のヘアスタイル)
- ☐ keep ~ up-to-date(~を最新の状態にしておく)

- ☐ an affluent neighborhood(裕福な地域)

- ☐ the preceding page [paragraph](前ページ[段落])

- ☐ inclement weather(悪天候)

Check 3　Sentence

- ☐ Most countries do not recognize the Taliban as the legitimate government of Afghanistan.(ほとんどの国はタリバンをアフガニスタンの合法政府として認めていない)

- ☐ The cause of the disease remains obscure.(その病気の原因はいまだに分かっていない)

- ☐ All donations are tax deductible in the US.(すべての寄付はアメリカでは課税控除である)

- ☐ Education is obligatory for children aged 6 to 15.(6歳から15歳までの子どもたちにとって教育は義務だ)

- ☐ The travel guide provides up-to-date information on attractions, hotels, and restaurants.(その旅行ガイドにはアトラクション、ホテル、そしてレストランの最新情報が載っている)

- ☐ Switzerland is one of the most affluent countries in the world.(スイスは世界で最も豊かな国の1つだ)

- ☐ The population growth in the region was 3.7 percent in the preceding decade.(先の10年間でのその地域の人口増加は3.7パーセントだった)

- ☐ The flight was canceled due to inclement weather.(悪天候のため、その便は欠航になった)

continued ▼

Day 26

Check 1 Listen)) CD-A26

□ 0409
multinational
/mʌltinǽʃənl/
ビジネス問題

形 **多国籍の**
名 多国籍企業

□ 0410
pharmaceutical
/fɑːrməsúːtikəl/
ビジネス問題

形 **製薬の**；薬学の；薬剤の
名 (〜s) ❶(集合的に)医薬 ❷製薬会社
名 pharmacist：薬剤師
名 pharmacy：薬局

□ 0411
genetic
/dʒənétik/
Part 7

形 **遺伝子の**；遺伝(学)の
名 genetics：遺伝学
副 genetically：遺伝子上、遺伝学的に

□ 0412
scenic
/síːnik/
Part 4

形 ❶**景色のよい**、眺めのよい ❷景色の、風景の
名 scenery：(集合的に)(通例美しい)景色、風景

□ 0413
intact
/intǽkt/
Part 5, 6

形 **無傷の**、損なわれていない ❶叙述用法のみ

□ 0414
toxic
/táksik/
Part 7

形 **有毒な**、毒性の
名 toxin：毒素

□ 0415
rational
/rǽʃənl/
❶発音注意
Part 5, 6

形 ❶**合理的な**、道理にかなった(⇔irrational) ❷理性的な、分別のある(≒reasonable)
名 rationale：(〜の)根本的理由；理論的根拠 (for 〜)

□ 0416
brand-new
/brǽndnjúː/
Part 4

形 **新品の**、真新しい

Day 25)) CD-A25
Quick Review
答えは右ページ下

□ 事務の
□ 本物の
□ 仮の
□ あいまいな

□ 前例のない
□ 活況の
□ 信じられない
□ 絶滅寸前の

□ 相互の
□ 安い
□ 停滞した
□ 一流の

□ 天然のままの
□ 移動式の
□ まっすぐな
□ はっきりした

Check 2 Phrase

- a multinational peacekeeping force(多国籍平和維持軍)

- the pharmaceutical industry(製薬産業)
- pharmaceutical education(薬学教育)

- genetic engineering(遺伝子工学)
- a genetic disease(遺伝病)

- a scenic route(景色のよい路線)
- scenic beauty(景色の美しさ)

- remain intact(無傷のままでいる)
- keep [leave] ~ intact(~に手をつけないでおく、~をそのままにしておく)

- toxic waste(有毒廃棄物)

- a rational explanation(合理的な説明)
- a rational person(理性的な人)

- a brand-new car(新車)

Check 3 Sentence

- Sony is a leading multinational electronics manufacturer.(ソニーは一流の多国籍電機メーカーだ)

- She works for a pharmaceutical company as a researcher.(彼女は製薬会社に研究員として勤務している)

- Dr. Smith emphasized the significance of genetic research.(スミス博士は遺伝子研究の重要性を強調した)

- The hotel offers scenic views of the Rocky Mountains.(そのホテルからはロッキー山脈の素晴らしい眺めが望める)

- The order arrived intact on time.(注文品は時間通りに無傷で届いた)

- The company was charged with dumping toxic chemicals.(その会社は有毒化学物質を廃棄したかどで告発された)

- All important decisions must be made through rational arguments.(すべての重要な決定は合理的な議論を通じてなされるべきだ)

- I bought a brand-new computer with Windows Vista yesterday.(私は昨日、ウィンドウズビスタ搭載の新品のコンピューターを買った)

Day 25))) CD-A25
Quick Review
答えは左ページ下

- clerical
- authentic
- tentative
- ambiguous

- unprecedented
- brisk
- incredible
- endangered

- mutual
- inexpensive
- sluggish
- prestigious

- crude
- mobile
- upright
- distinct

CHAPTER 1
CHAPTER 2
CHAPTER 3
CHAPTER 4
CHAPTER 5
CHAPTER 6
CHAPTER 7
CHAPTER 8
CHAPTER 9

Day 27　形容詞5

Check 1　Listen)) CD-A27

☐ 0417
hectic
/héktik/
Part 2, 3

形 **大変忙しい**、てんてこ舞いの

☐ 0418
serial
/síəriəl/
Part 5, 6

形 ❶**連続的な**、通しの　❷続き[シリーズ]物の
名 (テレビの)連続番組、(新聞などの)連載物

☐ 0419
verbal
/vɚːrbəl/
Part 5, 6

形 **言葉による**、言葉での(≒spoken, oral)(⇔written)

☐ 0420
profound
/prəfáund/
Part 5, 6

形 ❶(影響などが)**重大[重要]な**；意味深い　❷(悲しみなどが)深い(≒deep)
副 profoundly：深く；大いに

☐ 0421
extinct
/ikstíŋkt/
Part 5, 6

形 **絶滅した**　⊕endangeredは「絶滅寸前の」
名 extinction：絶滅

☐ 0422
tolerant
/tɑ́lərənt/
Part 5, 6

形 ❶(~に対して)**寛大[寛容]な**(of ~)　❷(~に)抵抗力がある(of ~)
名 tolerance：❶寛大、寛容　❷耐性
動 tolerate：~を許容[黙認]する、大目に見る
形 tolerable：❶耐えられる　❷まあまあの

☐ 0423
memorable
/mémərəbl/
Part 4

形 (~で)**記憶[注目]すべき**、忘れられない(for ~)

☐ 0424
vertical
/vɚːrtikəl/
Part 1

形 **垂直の**；縦の(≒upright)(⇔horizontal)
名 (the ~)垂直線[面]

continued

定義が分かっていても、その単語を「使える」とは限らない。Check 2と3の和訳を見て、英語がすぐに出てくれば「使える」レベルは目前！

- □ 聞くだけモード　Check 1
- □ しっかりモード　Check 1 ▶ 2
- □ かんぺきモード　Check 1 ▶ 2 ▶ 3

Check 2　Phrase

- □ a hectic schedule（大変忙しいスケジュール）

- □ a serial number（通し番号、製造番号）
- □ serial murders（連続殺人）

- □ a verbal explanation（口頭説明）

- □ have a profound effect [influence, impact] on ～（～に重大な影響を与える）
- □ profound sadness（深い悲しみ）

- □ become extinct（絶滅する）
- □ extinct species（絶滅種）

- □ a tolerant society（寛容な社会）
- □ be tolerant of cold [heat]（[動植物が] 寒さ [暑さ] に強い）

- □ a memorable event（記憶すべき出来事）

- □ a vertical line（垂直線）
- □ a vertical cliff（垂直な絶壁）

Check 3　Sentence

- □ I had a pretty hectic day at the office today.（今日は職場でとても忙しい1日を過ごした）

- □ You must enter a serial number to use the software.（そのソフトウエアを使うには通し番号を入力しなければならない）

- □ Verbal abuse is the most common form of violence.（言葉による虐待は最も一般的な暴力の形だ）

- □ The experience of war had a profound effect on him.（戦争の経験は彼に重大な影響を与えた）

- □ Dinosaurs became extinct about 65 million years ago.（恐竜は約6500万年前に絶滅した）

- □ We should be tolerant of others.（私たちは他者に対して寛大であるべきだ）

- □ In 1963, Martin Luther King, Jr. delivered a memorable speech known as "I have a dream."（1963年にマーチン・ルーサー・キングは「I have a dream」として知られている忘れられない演説をした）

- □ The man is wearing a shirt with vertical stripes.（男性は縦じまの入ったシャツを着ている）

continued ▼

Day 27

Check 1　Listen))) CD-A27

□ 0425
costly
/kɔ́:stli/
Part 7

形 ❶**費用のかかる**、高価な(≒expensive)　❷犠牲[損失]の大きい
名cost：❶(しばしば~s)(必要)経費、費用；値段、代価　❷(時間などの)犠牲
動cost：(時間・費用・労力)がかかる

□ 0426
renowned
/rináund/
Part 7

形 (~で/…として)**有名な**、名高い(for ~/as …)(≒famous, well-known, distinguished, eminent, prominent)
名renown：有名、高名

□ 0427
customary
/kʌ́stəmèri/
Part 5, 6

形 **習慣的な**、慣習の(≒habitual)
名custom：❶(社会の)習慣、風習　❷(~s)税関；関税
形custom：オーダーメードの、あつらえの

□ 0428
informative
/infɔ́:rmətiv/
Part 2, 3

形 **有益な**、教えられるところの大きい、教育的な
名information：(~に関する)情報(about [on] ~)
名informant：情報提供者
動inform：(inform A of Bで)AにBについて知らせる、通知する

□ 0429
strategic
/strətí:dʒik/
ビジネス問題

形 **戦略**(上)**の**；戦略的な
名strategy：(~の/…するための)戦略、戦術(for ~/to do)
名strategist：戦略家、策士
副strategically：戦略上

□ 0430
gross
/gróus/
❶発音注意
ビジネス問題

形 **総計[全体]の**、総~(≒total)(⇔net：[諸費用を差し引いた]正味の)
動~の総収益を上げる
副税込みで

□ 0431
outrageous
/autréidʒəs/
Part 2, 3

形 **とんでもない**、法外な、常軌を逸した
名outrage：(~に対する)激怒(at [over] ~)
動outrage：~を慣慨させる、怒らせる
形outraged：激怒した

□ 0432
multiple
/mʌ́ltəpl/
Part 5, 6

形 **多数の**；多種多様な(≒many, various)
名 (~の)倍数(of ~)
名multiplication：❶増加　❷掛け算
動multiply：❶~を増やす　❷増える　❸(multiply A by Bで)AにBを掛ける

Day 26))) CD-A26
Quick Review
答えは右ページ下

- □ 合法の
- □ あいまいな
- □ 控除可能の
- □ 義務的な
- □ 最新の
- □ 裕福な
- □ 前の
- □ 荒れ模様の
- □ 多国籍の
- □ 製薬の
- □ 遺伝子の
- □ 景色のよい
- □ 無傷の
- □ 有毒な
- □ 合理的な
- □ 新品の

Check 2 Phrase

- ☐ a costly lawsuit（費用のかかる訴訟）
- ☐ a costly victory（犠牲の大きい勝利）

- ☐ a renowned scientist（有名な科学者）
- ☐ a city renowned for its cultural heritage（文化遺産で有名な都市）

- ☐ a customary practice（慣行）
- ☐ It is customary for ~ to do ...（…するのが~の習慣だ）

- ☐ an informative book（有益な本）

- ☐ a strategic plan（戦略計画）
- ☐ a strategic alliance（戦略的提携）

- ☐ gross income [weight]（総収入 [重量]）

- ☐ It is outrageous that ~.（~とはとんでもないことだ）
- ☐ an outrageous price（法外な値段）

- ☐ make multiple errors（多数の間違いをする）

Check 3 Sentence

- ☐ Without health insurance, medical care is very costly.（健康保険がなければ、医療は非常に費用がかかる）

- ☐ Paris is renowned as the fashion capital of the world.（パリは世界のファッションの中心地として有名だ）

- ☐ It is customary for Japanese people to say *itadakimasu* just before eating a meal.（料理を食べる直前に「いただきます」と言うのが日本人の習慣だ）

- ☐ The program was entertaining and informative.（その番組は面白くて有益だった）

- ☐ The CEO announced a strategic plan to streamline operations.（そのCEOは事業を合理化するための戦略計画を発表した）

- ☐ The company's gross profit in the fourth quarter was $4.4 million.（その会社の第4四半期の総利益は440万ドルだった）

- ☐ It is outrageous that Wall Street executives got more than $18 billion in bonuses last year.（米国金融界の経営幹部らが180億ドルを超えるボーナスを昨年得ていたとはとんでもないことだ）

- ☐ He received multiple job offers.（彼は多くの仕事の申し出を受けた）

Day 26))) CD-A26
Quick Review
答えは左ページ下

- ☐ legitimate
- ☐ obscure
- ☐ deductible
- ☐ obligatory
- ☐ up-to-date
- ☐ affluent
- ☐ preceding
- ☐ inclement
- ☐ multinational
- ☐ pharmaceutical
- ☐ genetic
- ☐ scenic
- ☐ intact
- ☐ toxic
- ☐ rational
- ☐ brand-new

CHAPTER 1
CHAPTER 2
CHAPTER 3
CHAPTER 4
CHAPTER 5
CHAPTER 6
CHAPTER 7
CHAPTER 8
CHAPTER 9

Day 28 形容詞6

Check 1　Listen 》CD-A28

0433 upcoming
/ʌ́pkʌ̀miŋ/
Part 2, 3

形 **今度の**、間近に迫った、近づく

0434 congested
/kəndʒéstid/
Part 1

形 ❶**混雑した**　❷鼻が詰まった
名 congestion：❶（交通などの）混雑　❷うっ血

0435 miscellaneous
/mìsəléiniəs/
Part 7

形 **種々雑多な**（ものから成る）

0436 feasible
/fí:zəbl/
Part 5, 6

形 **実現可能な**、実行できる（≒ viable）
名 feasibility：実現可能性

0437 nominal
/nάmənl/
Part 7

形 ❶（価格などが）**ごくわずかの**　❷名ばかりの、名目上の

0438 synthetic
/sinθétik/
Part 5, 6

形 **合成の**、人造の

0439 counterfeit
/káuntərfit/
❶発音注意
Part 7

形 **偽造[模造]の**、偽の（≒ fake, bogus）
動 ～を偽造する

0440 rectangular
/rektǽŋgjulər/
Part 1

形 **長方形の**　❶「正方形の」は square
名 rectangle：長方形

---

continued
▼

Quick Reviewは使ってる？ 昨日覚えた単語でも、記憶に残っているとは限らない。学習の合間に軽くチェックするだけでも効果は抜群！

- □ 聞くだけモード　Check 1
- □ しっかりモード　Check 1 ▶ 2
- □ かんぺきモード　Check 1 ▶ 2 ▶ 3

Check 2　Phrase

- □ preparations for the upcoming exams（間近に迫った試験への準備）

- □ a congested area（[人口などの]密集地域）
- □ a congested nose（鼻詰まり）

- □ miscellaneous information（種々雑多な情報）
- □ miscellaneous expenses（雑費）

- □ a feasible plan（実現可能な計画）

- □ a nominal amount of money（ごくわずかな金）
- □ a nominal leader（名ばかりの指導者）

- □ synthetic detergent [resin]（合成洗剤[樹脂]）

- □ counterfeit coins [bills]（偽造硬貨[紙幣]）

- □ a rectangular box（長方形の箱）

Check 3　Sentence

- □ The politician has decided not to run in the upcoming general election.（その政治家は次の総選挙に立候補しないことを決めた）

- □ The street is congested with pedestrians.（通りは歩行者で混雑している）

- □ The store sells miscellaneous household items.（その店はさまざまな家庭用品を売っている）

- □ New technology will make electric cars economically feasible.（新しい技術が電気自動車を経済的に実現可能にするだろう）

- □ We can deliver your order for a nominal fee.（当店ではごくわずかな料金でご注文品をお届けできます）

- □ Most carpets are made of synthetic fibers.（ほとんどのじゅうたんは合成繊維で作られている）

- □ Five men were arrested for manufacturing counterfeit passports.（偽造パスポートを作った容疑で男5人が逮捕された）

- □ The table is rectangular in shape.（そのテーブルの形は長方形だ）

continued ▼

Day 28

Check 1　Listen))) CD-A28

□ 0441
contagious
/kəntéidʒəs/
Part 5, 6

形 ❶**伝染しやすい**、人から人へ広がりやすい　❷(接触)伝染性の　➕「(間接)伝染性の」はinfectious
名contagion：❶接触伝染　❷接触伝染病

□ 0442
irrelevant
/iréləvənt/
Part 5, 6

形 (〜と)**無関係の**(to 〜)(≒unrelated)；不適切な、見当違いの(⇔relevant)

□ 0443
ultimate
/ʌ́ltəmət/
Part 5, 6

形 ❶**究極の**、最終[最後]の　❷最高の
名(the 〜)(〜において)究極のもの(in 〜)
副ultimately：最終的に、結局、最後に

□ 0444
hands-on
/hǽndzɔ́n/
ビジネス問題

形 **実地の**、実践の、現場での(≒on-the-job)

□ 0445
in-house
/ínhàus/
ビジネス問題

形 **社内の**
副 社内で

□ 0446
predictable
/pridíktəbl/
Part 5, 6

形 **予測できる**(⇔unpredictable)
名prediction：(〜についての)予測、予報、予言、予想(about [of] 〜)
動predict：〜を予測[予言、予想]する

□ 0447
biased
/báiəst/
Part 7

形 (意見などが)(〜に)**偏った**、偏見を持った(against [toward, in favor of] 〜)
名bias：(〜に対する)偏見；先入観(against 〜)
動bias：〜に偏見[先入観]を抱かせる

□ 0448
humid
/hjú:mid/
Part 4

形 **湿気の多い**、蒸し蒸しする　➕「(寒くて)湿気のある」はdamp、「(ほどよく)湿気のある」はmoist
名humidity：湿度；湿気

| Day 27))) CD-A27
Quick Review
答えは右ページ下 | □ 大変忙しい
□ 連続的な
□ 言葉による
□ 重大な | □ 絶滅した
□ 寛大な
□ 記憶すべき
□ 垂直の | □ 費用のかかる
□ 有名な
□ 習慣的な
□ 有益な | □ 戦略の
□ 総計の
□ とんでもない
□ 多数の |

Check 2 Phrase

- ☐ contagious laughter（人から人へとうつる笑い）
- ☐ a contagious disease（接触伝染病）

- ☐ irrelevant information（無関係の情報）
- ☐ ask an irrelevant question（見当違いの質問をする）

- ☐ the ultimate goal [aim, objective]（究極の目標）
- ☐ the ultimate power（最高権力）

- ☐ hands-on training（実地訓練）
- ☐ hands-on experience（現場での経験）

- ☐ in-house research（社内調査）

- ☐ a predictable effect（予測できる結果[影響]）
- ☐ It is predictable that ~.（~ということが予測できる）

- ☐ one's biased opinion（偏った意見）
- ☐ be biased against the defendant（被告人に偏見を持っている）

- ☐ humid weather（蒸し暑い天気）

Check 3 Sentence

- ☐ Yawning is contagious among people.（あくびは人々の間でうつりやすい）

- ☐ Young people tend to view politics as irrelevant to their lives.（若者は政治を自分たちの生活と無関係だと見なしがちだ）

- ☐ The ultimate goal for companies is to increase profits.（企業にとって究極の目標は利益を増やすことだ）

- ☐ Nothing is more valuable than hands-on experience.（現場での経験ほど価値のあるものはない）

- ☐ Most companies understand the importance of in-house training.（ほとんどの企業は社内教育の重要性を理解している）

- ☐ The ending of the novel was pretty predictable.（その小説の結末は簡単に予想がついた）

- ☐ Reports should not be biased by personal perceptions or opinions.（報道は個人的な認識や意見によって偏ってはならない）

- ☐ Japan is hot and humid in summer.（日本の夏は暑くて湿気が多い）

Day 27 ♪)) CD-A27
Quick Review
答えは左ページ下

- ☐ hectic
- ☐ serial
- ☐ verbal
- ☐ profound
- ☐ extinct
- ☐ tolerant
- ☐ memorable
- ☐ vertical
- ☐ costly
- ☐ renowned
- ☐ customary
- ☐ informative
- ☐ strategic
- ☐ gross
- ☐ outrageous
- ☐ multiple

Day 29　形容詞7

Check 1　Listen ») CD-A29

□ 0449
gourmet
/ɡuərméi/
❶発音注意
Part 7

形 **グルメ**(向き)**の**、美食家の
名 グルメ、美食家

□ 0450
sustainable
/səstéinəbl/
Part 7

形 **持続可能な**、環境を破壊しない、環境にやさしい
名 sustainability：持続可能性
動 sustain：❶～を維持する、持続する　❷(損失など)を被る　❸～を養う

□ 0451
notorious
/noutɔ́:riəs/
Part 5, 6

形 (～で／…として)**悪名高い**(for ～/as …)(≒infamous)
名 notoriety：悪名、悪評
副 notoriously：悪名高く

□ 0452
metropolitan
/mètrəpálitən/
Part 7

形 **大都市の**、都会の
名 metropolis：主要都市、大都市

□ 0453
dependable
/dipéndəbl/
Part 5, 6

形 **信頼できる**、当てになる(≒reliable)
名 dependence：❶(～への)依存(on [upon] ～)　❷(～への)信頼、信用(on [upon] ～)
動 depend：(depend onで)❶～に頼る　❷～によって決まる

□ 0454
bilateral
/bailǽtərəl/
Part 5, 6

形 **二国**[二者]**間の**　●unilateralは「一方[片側]だけの」、multilateralは「多数国(参加)の」

□ 0455
variable
/véəriəbl/
Part 5, 6

形 ❶**変わりやすい**(≒changeable)　❷変えられる
名 ❶変化する[変わりやすい]もの　❷変数
動 vary：❶(～の点で)異なる、さまざまである(in ～)　❷変わる　❸～を変える
形 varied：さまざまな、多様な、変化に富む

□ 0456
marketable
/má:rkitəbl/
ビジネス問題

形 (商品が)**よく**[すぐ]**売れる**；市場向きの
名 market：❶市場　❷スーパーマーケット
動 market：～を市場に出す、売り込む

continued
▼

今日でChapter 3は最後！ 時間に余裕があったら、章末のReviewにも挑戦しておこう。忘れてしまった単語も結構あるのでは?!

- □ 聞くだけモード　Check 1
- □ しっかりモード　Check 1 ▶ 2
- □ かんぺきモード　Check 1 ▶ 2 ▶ 3

Check 2　Phrase

□ a gourmet magazine（グルメ雑誌）

□ sustainable development（持続可能な[環境を破壊しない]開発）

□ a notorious figure（悪名高い人物）

□ a metropolitan area（大都市圏、首都圏）

□ a dependable man [car]（信頼できる人[車]）

□ a bilateral treaty（二国間条約）

□ variable winds（変わりやすい風向き）
□ a variable interest rate（変動利率）

□ a marketable product（よく売れる製品）
□ a marketable skill（売り物になる技術）

Check 3　Sentence

□ The hotel has six gourmet restaurants including Asian and French.（そのホテルにはアジア料理とフランス料理を含む6つのグルメ向きのレストランがある）

□ Sustainable economic growth is essential to poverty reduction.（持続可能な経済成長は貧困の減少のために不可欠である）

□ The city is notorious for its traffic jams.（その都市は交通渋滞で悪名高い）

□ Cairo's metropolitan population is about 15 million.（カイロの都市部の人口は約1500万人だ）

□ I doubt that the information is dependable.（その情報は信頼できないと思う）

□ The US and Singapore signed a bilateral free trade agreement in 2003.（アメリカとシンガポールは二国間自由貿易協定を2003年に結んだ）

□ Mountain weather is variable.（山の天気は変わりやすい）

□ This product is very marketable all over the world.（この製品は世界中で非常によく売れている）

continued ▼

Day 29

Check 1　Listen ») CD-A29

0457 preventive
/privéntiv/
Part 5, 6

形 **予防の**
名 prevention: (〜の)予防、防止(of 〜); (〜の)予防[防止]策(against 〜)
動 prevent: ❶(事故など)を防ぐ ❷(prevent A from doingで)Aが〜するのを妨げる

0458 generic
/dʒenérik/
ビジネス問題

形 ❶**ノーブランドの**、無印商品の ❷一般的な

0459 phenomenal
/finámənl/
Part 7

形 **驚くべき**、並外れた
名 phenomenon: 現象、事象

0460 approximate
/əpráksəmət/
Part 7

形 **おおよその**
動 (/əpráksəmèit/)おおよそ〜になる、〜に近い
副 approximately: おおよそ、約

0461 talented
/tǽləntid/
Part 7

形 **才能のある**、有能な(≒gifted)
名 talent: ❶(〜の)才能、素質(for 〜) ❷才能のある人 ❸(集合的に)才能のある人々

0462 constructive
/kənstrʌ́ktiv/
Part 5, 6

形 (考えなどが)**建設的な**(⇔destructive)
名 construction: ❶建設; 建築工事 ❷構造
動 construct: 〜を(…で)建設する(of [from] ...)

0463 nationwide
/néiʃənwàid/
Part 7

形 **全国的な**、全国的規模の ❶「世界的な」はworldwide
副 全国的に、全国的規模で

0464 subsequent
/sʌ́bsikwənt/
❶アクセント注意
Part 5, 6

形 (〜の)**後[次]の**、後に起こる(to 〜)(≒following)(⇔preceding)
副 subsequently: 後で

Day 28 ») CD-A28
Quick Review
答えは右ページ下

□ 今度の　　　□ ごくわずかの　　□ 伝染しやすい　　□ 社内の
□ 混雑した　　□ 合成の　　　　　□ 無関係の　　　　□ 予測できる
□ 種々雑多な　□ 偽造の　　　　　□ 究極の　　　　　□ 偏った
□ 実現可能な　□ 長方形の　　　　□ 実地の　　　　　□ 湿気の多い

Check 2　Phrase

- preventive medicine(予防薬；予防医学)

- a generic drug(ノーブランド薬、ジェネリック医薬品) ● 特許の切れた医薬品
- a generic term(一般名称、総称)

- a phenomenal talent(驚くべき才能)

- approximate time of arrival(おおよその到着時間)

- a talented pianist(才能のあるピアニスト)

- constructive criticism(建設的な批評)

- a nationwide network(全国放送、全国放送網)
- get nationwide attention(全国的な注目を集める)

- a subsequent chapter(次の章)
- subsequent to ~(~の後[次]に)

Check 3　Sentence

- The government is taking preventive measures against influenza.(政府はインフルエンザに対する予防策を講じている)

- A generic product is one that is not sold under a brand name.(ノーブランド商品とは商標名で売られていない商品のことだ)

- Internet advertising is growing at a phenomenal rate.(インターネット広告は驚くべき速さで拡大している)

- The approximate cost of the project is $300 million.(そのプロジェクトのおおよその経費は3億ドルだ)

- Stephen King is one of the most talented living authors.(スティーヴン・キングは最も才能のある存命の作家の1人だ)

- We had a constructive discussion on this issue.(私たちはこの問題に関して建設的な討論をした)

- The company runs a nationwide supermarket chain.(その会社は全国的なスーパーマーケットチェーンを経営している)

- Subsequent to Mr. Brown's resignation, Mr. Harrison was appointed to the position of CEO.(ブラウン氏の辞職の後に、ハリソン氏がCEOの職に任命された)

Day 28)) CD-A28
Quick Review
答えは左ページ下

- upcoming
- congested
- miscellaneous
- feasible
- nominal
- synthetic
- counterfeit
- rectangular
- contagious
- irrelevant
- ultimate
- hands-on
- in-house
- predictable
- biased
- humid

CHAPTER 1
CHAPTER 2
CHAPTER 3
CHAPTER 4
CHAPTER 5
CHAPTER 6
CHAPTER 7
CHAPTER 8
CHAPTER 9

Chapter 3 Review

左ページの(1)〜(20)の形容詞の同意・類義語（≒）、反意・反対語（⇔）を右ページのA〜Tから選び、カッコの中に答えを書き込もう。意味が分からないときは、見出し番号を参照して復習しておこう（答えは右ページ下）。

- [ ] (1) complimentary (0354) ≒は? (　　　)
- [ ] (2) mandatory (0356) ⇔は? (　　　)
- [ ] (3) hazardous (0360) ≒は? (　　　)
- [ ] (4) lucrative (0373) ≒は? (　　　)
- [ ] (5) chronic (0382) ⇔は? (　　　)
- [ ] (6) messy (0383) ⇔は? (　　　)
- [ ] (7) authentic (0386) ⇔は? (　　　)
- [ ] (8) incredible (0391) ≒は? (　　　)
- [ ] (9) upright (0399) ≒は? (　　　)
- [ ] (10) obscure (0402) ≒は? (　　　)
- [ ] (11) affluent (0406) ≒は? (　　　)
- [ ] (12) preceding (0407) ⇔は? (　　　)
- [ ] (13) verbal (0419) ≒は? (　　　)
- [ ] (14) costly (0425) ≒は? (　　　)
- [ ] (15) gross (0430) ≒は? (　　　)
- [ ] (16) feasible (0436) ≒は? (　　　)
- [ ] (17) irrelevant (0442) ≒は? (　　　)
- [ ] (18) notorious (0451) ≒は? (　　　)
- [ ] (19) dependable (0453) ≒は? (　　　)
- [ ] (20) talented (0461) ≒は? (　　　)

A. acute
B. unbelievable
C. viable
D. wealthy
E. voluntary
F. reliable
G. unclear
H. profitable
I. total
J. fake
K. gifted
L. free
M. expensive
N. tidy
O. unrelated
P. vertical
Q. infamous
R. dangerous
S. spoken
T. following

【解答】(1) L (2) E (3) R (4) H (5) A (6) N (7) J (8) B (9) P (10) G (11) D (12) T (13) S (14) M (15) I (16) C (17) O (18) Q (19) F (20) K

CHAPTER 4

名詞：必修240

Chapter 4では、TOEIC「必修」の名詞240をマスターします。「超」が抜けても、どれも重要な単語ばかり。本テストで慌てることがないよう、1語1語を着実に身につけていきましょう。

TOEIC的格言

One of these days is none of these days.

思い立つ日が吉日。
[直訳] いずれそのうちという日はない。

Day 30 【名詞16】
▶142
Day 31 【名詞17】
▶146
Day 32 【名詞18】
▶150
Day 33 【名詞19】
▶154
Day 34 【名詞20】
▶158
Day 35 【名詞21】
▶162
Day 36 【名詞22】
▶166
Day 37 【名詞23】
▶170
Day 38 【名詞24】
▶174
Day 39 【名詞25】
▶178
Day 40 【名詞26】
▶182
Day 41 【名詞27】
▶186
Day 42 【名詞28】
▶190
Day 43 【名詞29】
▶194
Day 44 【名詞30】
▶198
Chapter 4 Review
▶202

Day 30 名詞16

Check 1 Listen)) CD-A30

☐ 0465
discrepancy
/dɪskrépənsi/
Part 5, 6

名 (〜の間の)**相違**、不一致(between 〜)(≒difference)

☐ 0466
petroleum
/pətróuliəm/
❶アクセント注意
ビジネス問題

名 **石油**(≒oil)

☐ 0467
concession
/kənséʃən/
Part 5, 6

名 (〜への)**譲歩**(to 〜)(≒compromise)
動 concede：〜を(正しいと)(渋々)認める

☐ 0468
validity
/vəlídəti/
Part 5, 6

名 **妥当**[有効、正当]**性**
名 validation：検証、実証、確証
動 validate：〜が正しいことを証明する
形 valid：❶(契約などが)(法的に)有効な ❷(理由などが)妥当な

☐ 0469
acclaim
/əkléim/
Part 5, 6

名 **称賛**(≒praise) ⊕claim(〜だと主張する)と混同しないように注意
動 〜を称賛する

☐ 0470
expiration
/èkspəréiʃən/
ビジネス問題

名 (期限の)**満期**、満了
動 expire：期限が切れる、満期になる

☐ 0471
dimension
/diménʃən/
Part 5, 6

名 ❶(通例〜s)**寸法**(≒measurement)；大きさ(≒size)
❷局面、側面(≒aspect) ❸(〜s)規模；重要性 ❹次元

☐ 0472
outing
/áutiŋ/
Part 7

名 **遠足**、遠出、ピクニック(≒excursion, picnic)

continued
▼

Chapter 4では、15日をかけて頻出名詞240をチェック。まずはCDでチャンツを聞いて、単語を「耳」からインプット!

- □ 聞くだけモード　Check 1
- □ しっかりモード　Check 1 ▶ 2
- □ かんぺきモード　Check 1 ▶ 2 ▶ 3

Check 2　Phrase

□ a discrepancy between the two accounts（2つの計算の食い違い）
□ a discrepancy of opinions（意見の不一致）

□ crude [raw] petroleum（原油）
□ a petroleum company（石油会社）

□ make a concession to him on [about] ~（~に関して彼に譲歩する）

□ the validity of opinion polls（世論調査の妥当性）
□ give [lend] validity to ~（~を妥当とする）

□ win [receive] acclaim（称賛を浴びる）
□ critical acclaim（評論家の称賛）

□ the expiration of an insurance policy（保険契約の満期）
□ expiration date（満期［満了］日；有効［使用、正味］期限）

□ take the dimensions of ~（~の寸法を測る）
□ a new dimension of ~（~の新たな局面）

□ go on an outing to ~（~に遠足に行く）

Check 3　Sentence

□ There was a significant discrepancy between simulation results and measured data.（シミュレーションの結果と測定データの間にはかなりの違いがあった）

□ It is said that petroleum will be exhausted in about 40 years.（石油は約40年で枯渇すると言われている）

□ No concessions must be made to terrorists.（テロリストに対してはいかなる譲歩もしてはならない）

□ The validity of the experiment's results is in question.（その実験結果の妥当性が問題になっている）

□ The movie won worldwide acclaim.（その映画は世界中で称賛された）

□ What is the expiration date of your passport?（あなたのパスポートの有効期限はいつですか?）

□ I was overwhelmed by the dimensions of the cathedral.（私はその大聖堂の大きさに圧倒された）

□ Our whole-school outing will be held this Friday.（当校の全校遠足が今週の金曜日に行われる予定だ）

continued
▼

Day 30

Check 1　Listen)) CD-A30

☐ 0473
census
/sénsəs/
Part 7

名 **国勢調査**、人口調査

☐ 0474
viewpoint
/vjú:pɔ̀int/
Part 5, 6

名 **観点**、立場、見地(≒point of view, perspective, standpoint)

☐ 0475
interference
/ìntərfíərəns/
Part 7

名 ❶(〜に対する)**干渉**、介入(in 〜)　❷(〜に対する)妨害、邪魔(with 〜)
動interfere：❶(interfere withで)〜を邪魔する　❷(interfere inで)〜に干渉する

☐ 0476
stapler
/stéiplər/
Part 2, 3

名 **ホチキス**
名staple：❶主食、基本[必需]食品　❷ホチキスの針
動staple：〜をホチキスで留める

☐ 0477
bin
/bín/
Part 1

名 **ごみ箱**(≒can)；容器

☐ 0478
deduction
/didʌ́kʃən/
Part 7

名 ❶(〜からの)**控除**(from 〜)(≒exemption)　❷(〜という)推論(that節 〜)
動deduct：〜を(…から)差し引く、控除する(from …)
形deductible：控除可能の

☐ 0479
rejection
/ridʒékʃən/
❶定義注意
Part 5, 6

名 ❶**不採用**[不合格]**通知**　❷(〜の)拒絶、拒否、却下(of 〜)(⇔acceptance)
動reject：〜を拒絶する、断る

☐ 0480
disclosure
/disklóuʒər/
Part 5, 6

名 (〜の)**発覚**、暴露；発表(of 〜)
動disclose：(秘密など)を明らかにする、暴露する、暴く

Day 29)) CD-A29
Quick Review
答えは右ページ下

☐ グルメの
☐ 持続可能な
☐ 悪名高い
☐ 大都市の

☐ 信頼できる
☐ 二国間の
☐ 変わりやすい
☐ よく売れる

☐ 予防の
☐ ノーブランドの
☐ 驚くべき
☐ おおよその

☐ 才能のある
☐ 建設的な
☐ 全国的な
☐ 後の

Check 2 Phrase

- □ take a census（国勢調査をする）

- □ from a historical [religious] viewpoint（歴史的［宗教的］観点から見ると）

- □ the government's interference in the market（市場への政府の介入）
- □ cause interference with ~（~を妨害する）

- □ bind papers with a stapler（書類をホチキスでとじる）

- □ throw garbage [litter, trash, rubbish] in the bin（ごみをごみ箱に捨てる）
- □ a bread bin（パン入れ）

- □ a tax deduction（税額控除）
- □ draw deductions from ~（~から推論する）

- □ a rejection letter（不採用［不合格］通知書）
- □ rejection of war（戦争の拒否）

- □ the disclosure of the truth（事実の発覚）

Check 3 Sentence

- □ A census is taken every five years in Japan.（日本では国勢調査は5年ごとに行われる）

- □ From an environmental viewpoint, human activities change the global climate.（環境的観点から見ると、人間の活動は地球環境に変化をもたらしている）

- □ The country opposes any foreign interference in its internal affairs.（その国は国内問題に対する外国からのいかなる干渉にも抵抗している）

- □ Can I borrow your stapler?（あなたのホチキスを借りてもいいですか?）

- □ There are recycling bins in front of the store.（店の前にリサイクル用の容器がある）

- □ My taxable income after deductions was about $40,000.（控除後の私の課税所得は約4万ドルだった）

- □ She applied for several jobs, but received rejection letters from all of them.（彼女はいくつかの仕事に応募したが、そのすべてから不採用通知書をもらった）

- □ Companies must prevent the disclosure of personal information.（企業は個人情報の漏えいを防がなくてはならない）

Day 29 » CD-A29
Quick Review
答えは左ページ下

- □ gourmet
- □ sustainable
- □ notorious
- □ metropolitan
- □ dependable
- □ bilateral
- □ variable
- □ marketable
- □ preventive
- □ generic
- □ phenomenal
- □ approximate
- □ talented
- □ constructive
- □ nationwide
- □ subsequent

Day 31　名詞17

Check 1　Listen 》CD-A31

□ 0481
blizzard
/blízərd/
Part 4

名 猛吹雪　● 「吹雪」はsnowstorm

□ 0482
occurrence
/əkə́:rəns/
Part 5, 6

名 ❶出来事、事件(≒event, incident, accident)　❷発生、出現(≒incidence)
動 occur：❶(事件などが)起こる、生じる　❷(occur toで)(考えなどが)〜の心に(ふと)浮かぶ

□ 0483
wholesaler
/hóulsèilər/
ビジネス問題

名 卸売業者(⇔retailer：小売業者)
名 wholesale：卸売り
形 wholesale：卸売りの

□ 0484
gathering
/gǽðəriŋ/
Part 5, 6

名 集会、集まり、会合(≒meeting, get-together)
動 gather：❶集まる　❷〜を集める　❸〜だと推測する

□ 0485
closure
/klóuʒər/
ビジネス問題

名 閉鎖；閉店
動 close：❶〜を閉める　❷閉まる　❸〜を終える　❹終わる
形 closed：閉鎖した
形 closing：終わり[結び]の、締めくくりの

□ 0486
stopover
/stápòuvər/
Part 4

名 (旅行の途中での)短期[一時]滞在

□ 0487
default
/difɔ́:lt/
ビジネス問題

名 ❶(〜の)債務不履行、滞納(on 〜)　❷デフォルト、初期設定
動 (〜の)債務の履行を怠る(on 〜)

□ 0488
booking
/búkiŋ/
Part 4

名 予約(≒reservation)
動 book：〜を予約する

continued
▼

英字紙・英字雑誌などを使って、語彙との出合いを増やそう。学習した語彙ともきっと遭遇するはず。出合いの数と定着度は正比例する！

- □ 聞くだけモード　Check 1
- □ しっかりモード　Check 1 ▶ 2
- □ かんぺきモード　Check 1 ▶ 2 ▶ 3

Check 2　　Phrase

□ be stuck in a blizzard（猛吹雪の中で立ち往生する）

□ a rare [an unexpected] occurrence（まれな[思いがけない]出来事）
□ the occurrence of an earthquake（地震の発生）

□ a furniture wholesaler（家具卸売業者）

□ a social gathering（懇親会、親睦会）

□ the closure of the supermarket（そのスーパーマーケットの閉店）

□ a one-day stopover in London（[旅の途中での]ロンドンでの1日の滞在）

□ a default on a loan（ローンの債務不履行）
□ default settings（初期設定値）

□ make [cancel] a booking（予約をする[取り消す]）

Check 3　　Sentence

□ The airport was closed due to a blizzard.（猛吹雪のため空港は閉鎖された）

□ Sports injuries are a common occurrence among children.（スポーツでのけがは子どもたちの間ではよくあることだ）

□ A cheaper way is to buy bulk quantities from a wholesaler online.（安上がりな方法は卸売業者からオンラインで大量に買うことだ）

□ There was a gathering of business leaders in Tokyo.（財界首脳らの会合が東京であった）

□ The closure of the factory will result in the loss of 500 jobs.（その工場の閉鎖で500人が仕事を失うことになるだろう）

□ I had a two-day stopover in Los Angeles on the way to New York.（ニューヨークへ行く途中に私は2日間ロサンゼルスに滞在した）

□ Many homeowners are now in default on their mortgage payments in the US.（アメリカでは現在、多くの自宅所有者が住宅ローンの支払いを滞納している）

□ Online booking is available on our website.（当社のウェブサイトでオンライン予約ができる）

continued ▼

Day 31

Check 1　Listen 》CD-A31

□ 0489
sightseeing
/sáitsì:iŋ/
Part 4

名 **観光**、見物
名sightseer：観光客

□ 0490
conductor
/kəndʌ́ktər/
Part 1

名 ❶ **車掌**　❷(オーケストラの)指揮者
名conduct：❶行い　❷実施、遂行
動conduct：(業務など)を行う、管理する

□ 0491
publication
/pʌ̀bləkéiʃən/
Part 5, 6

名 ❶ **出版**、発行　❷刊行[出版]物　❸発表、公表
名publisher：出版社
動publish：❶〜を出版[発行]する　❷〜を発表[公表]する

□ 0492
duration
/djuréiʃən/
Part 5, 6

名 **継続**[存続、持続]**期間**
前during：〜の間中(ずっと)

□ 0493
turnout
/tə́:rnàut/
Part 2, 3

名 ❶ (会などへの)**人出**、出席者数　❷投票者数；投票率
動turn out：❶〜であることが判明する、結局は〜になる　❷(〜に)出席する、出かける(for 〜)

□ 0494
workforce
/wə́:rkfɔ̀:rs/
ビジネス問題

名 **全従業員**(≒labor force)　⊕work forceと2語に分ける場合もある

□ 0495
aviation
/èiviéiʃən/
ビジネス問題

名 ❶ **航空**(学)、飛行(術)　❷航空機産業

□ 0496
limitation
/lìmətéiʃən/
Part 5, 6

名 ❶ **制限**　❷(〜s)(能力などの)限界
名limit：❶限度、制限　❷(通例〜s)範囲、区域
動limit：〜を(…に)制限する(to ...)

Day 30 》CD-A30
Quick Review
答えは右ページ下

□ 相違	□ 称賛	□ 国勢調査	□ ごみ箱
□ 石油	□ 満期	□ 観点	□ 控除
□ 譲歩	□ 寸法	□ 干渉	□ 不採用通知
□ 妥当性	□ 遠足	□ ホチキス	□ 発覚

Check 2 Phrase

- ☐ do [go] sightseeing(観光をする[に出かける])

- ☐ a bus [train] conductor(バス[列車]の車掌)
- ☐ a guest conductor(客演指揮者)

- ☐ the publication date(発行日)
- ☐ a monthly publication(月刊の刊行物、月刊誌)

- ☐ the duration of life(生存期間)
- ☐ for the duration of ～(～の期間中)

- ☐ the turnout for the event(その行事への人出)
- ☐ a low [high] turnout(低い[高い]投票率)

- ☐ a company with a workforce of more than 1,000(全従業員1000人以上の会社)

- ☐ civil aviation(民間航空)
- ☐ an aviation company(航空会社)

- ☐ the limitation of nuclear weapons(核兵器の制限)
- ☐ have one's limitations(限界がある)

Check 3 Sentence

- ☐ I'm planning to do a lot of sightseeing in Rome.(私はローマでたくさん観光をするつもりだ)

- ☐ The conductor is checking a passenger's ticket.(車掌は乗客の切符を確認している)

- ☐ "Newsweek" began publication in 1933.(『ニューズウィーク』は1933年に出版が始まった)

- ☐ I stayed at my friend's house for the duration of my holiday in Hong Kong.(私は香港での休暇の間、友人の家に滞在した)

- ☐ The turnout for the conference was about 200.(その会議への出席者数は約200人だった)

- ☐ The automaker will reduce its workforce by 10 percent.(その自動車メーカーは従業員を10パーセント削減する予定だ)

- ☐ The aviation industry is facing a shortage of pilots.(航空業界はパイロット不足に直面している)

- ☐ The ordinance raised the height limitation from 30 to 35 feet in all residential districts.(その条例によって全住宅区域の高さ制限が30フィートから35フィートに引き上げられた)

Day 30))) CD-A30
Quick Review
答えは左ページ下

- ☐ discrepancy
- ☐ petroleum
- ☐ concession
- ☐ validity
- ☐ acclaim
- ☐ expiration
- ☐ dimension
- ☐ outing
- ☐ census
- ☐ viewpoint
- ☐ interference
- ☐ stapler
- ☐ bin
- ☐ deduction
- ☐ rejection
- ☐ disclosure

Day 32　名詞18

Check 1　Listen))) CD-A32

☐ 0497
stimulation
/stìmjuléiʃən/
Part 5, 6

名 **刺激**、興奮
名 stimulus：刺激(するもの)
動 stimulate：〜を刺激する、活気づける

☐ 0498
investigator
/invéstigèitər/
Part 4

名 **調査員**；(犯罪の)調査官、捜査官
名 investigation：(〜の)調査；捜査(into [of] 〜)
動 investigate：〜を(詳細に)調査する、取り調べる

☐ 0499
boundary
/báundəri/
Part 5, 6

名 ❶(〜の間の)**境界線**(between 〜)(≒border)　❷(通例〜ies)限界(≒limitation)

☐ 0500
repetition
/rèpətíʃən/
Part 5, 6

名 **繰り返し**、反復
動 repeat：❶〜を繰り返して言う　❷〜を繰り返す
形 repeated：繰り返された、度々の
形 repetitive：繰り返しの多い
副 repeatedly：繰り返して、再三再四

☐ 0501
diabetes
/dàiəbí:ti:z/
Part 7

名 **糖尿病**
名 diabetic：糖尿病患者
形 diabetic：糖尿病の

☐ 0502
optimism
/áptəmìzm/
Part 7

名 **楽観**(論)、楽観[楽天]主義(⇔pessimism：悲観主義)
名 optimist：楽天家；楽天主義者
形 optimistic：(be optimistic about)〜について楽観[楽天]的である

☐ 0503
accountability
/əkàuntəbíləti/
Part 5, 6

名 (説明)**責任**(≒responsibility)
動 account：(account forで)❶(ある割合)を占める　❷〜(の理由・原因)を説明する

☐ 0504
wheelbarrow
/hwí:lbærou/
Part 1

名 (通例一輪の)**手押し車**(≒barrow)

continued
▼

「書いて覚える」のも効果的。「聞く＋音読する」に加えて、「書く」学習もしてみよう。そう、語彙学習は「あの手この手」が大切！

- ☐ 聞くだけモード　Check 1
- ☐ しっかりモード　Check 1 ▶ 2
- ☐ かんぺきモード　Check 1 ▶ 2 ▶ 3

Check 2　Phrase

☐ intellectual stimulation（知的刺激）

☐ an accident investigator（事故調査員）
☐ a private investigator（私立探偵）

☐ the boundary between the US and Mexico（アメリカとメキシコ間の境界線）
☐ beyond the boundaries of ～（～の限界を超えて）

☐ avoid a repetition of ～（～の繰り返しを避ける）

☐ suffer from diabetes（糖尿病を患う）

☐ cautious optimism（慎重な楽観論）

☐ accountability for results（結果に対する説明責任）
☐ assume accountability for ～（～に対する責任を負う）

☐ carry sand in a wheelbarrow（手押し車で砂を運ぶ）

Check 3　Sentence

☐ Children need stimulation in order for the brain to develop.（脳が発達するために子どもには刺激が必要だ）

☐ Investigators believe that the fire was arson.（捜査官たちはその火事は放火だったと考えている）

☐ The Andes mountains form the boundary between Chile and Argentina.（アンデス山脈はチリとアルゼンチン間の境界線を形成している）

☐ Constant repetition is the best way to learn something.（何度も繰り返すことが何かを覚えるための最善の方法だ）

☐ Diabetes is one of the most common chronic diseases.（糖尿病は最も一般的な慢性病の1つだ）

☐ There is little reason for optimism on the current US economy.（現在のアメリカ経済を楽観する理由はほとんどない）

☐ The registered nurse assumes accountability for the nursing care of a patient.（正看護師は患者の看護に対する責任を負っている）

☐ The man is pushing a wheelbarrow.（男性は手押し車を押している）

continued
▼

Day 32

Check 1　Listen))) CD-A32

0505
contradiction
/kɑ̀ntrədíkʃən/
Part 7

- 名 (〜の間の)**矛盾**(between 〜)
- 動 contradict：〜と矛盾する
- 形 contradictory：(〜と)矛盾した(to 〜)

0506
handout
/hǽndàut/
Part 4

- 名 (講演などの)**配付資料**、プリント
- 動 hand out：〜を(…に)配る、分配する(to …)

0507
cardboard
/kɑ́ːrdbɔ̀ːrd/
Part 1

- 名 **段ボール**、ボール紙

0508
debris
/dəbríː/
❶発音注意
Part 5, 6

- 名 **残骸**、破片、がれき(≒ rubble)

0509
hallway
/hɔ́ːlwèi/
Part 1

- 名 **廊下**、通路(≒ corridor)；玄関(の広間)

0510
raft
/rǽft/
Part 1

- 名 **ゴムボート**；いかだ
- 動 ❶いかだに乗って行く　❷〜をいかだで運ぶ
- 名 rafting：(いかだ・ゴムボートによる)川下り

0511
validation
/væ̀lədéiʃən/
Part 7

- 名 **検証**、実証、確証
- 名 validity：妥当[有効、正当]性
- 動 validate：〜が正しいことを証明する
- 形 valid：❶(契約などが)(法的に)有効な　❷(理由などが)妥当な

0512
liaison
/líːeizən/
Part 5, 6

- 名 ❶(〜の間の)**連絡係**[担当者、窓口](between 〜)　❷(〜の間の)連絡(between 〜)

Day 31))) CD-A31
Quick Review
答えは右ページ下

- □ 猛吹雪
- □ 出来事
- □ 卸売業者
- □ 集会
- □ 閉鎖
- □ 短期滞在
- □ 債務不履行
- □ 予約
- □ 観光
- □ 車掌
- □ 出版
- □ 継続期間
- □ 人出
- □ 全従業員
- □ 航空
- □ 制限

Check 2 Phrase

- a contradiction in terms（言葉の矛盾）
- a contradiction between the two policies（その2つの政策間の矛盾）

- the handouts for the meeting（その会議のための配付資料）

- a cardboard box（段ボール箱）
- a sheet of cardboard（1枚のボール紙）

- the debris of the crashed airplane（墜落した飛行機の残骸）

- an empty hallway（人がいない廊下）

- a life raft（救命ゴムボート）

- a validation method（検証方法）

- a liaison between the two sides（両者間の連絡係）
- liaison between departments（部署間の連絡）

Check 3 Sentence

- There is a contradiction between his words and deeds.（彼が言っていることと行っていることの間には矛盾がある）

- You will find a list of recommended books on the last page of your handout.（配付資料の最後のページに推薦図書の一覧表がある）

- Cardboard boxes are stacked against the wall.（壁際に段ボール箱が積み重ねられている）

- Four people were rescued from the debris of a collapsed building.（倒壊したビルのがれきの中から4人が救助された）

- There are rooms on both sides of the hallway.（廊下の両側に部屋がある）

- They are going down the river on a raft.（彼らはゴムボートに乗って川を下っている）

- The validation process is essential for gaining scientific credibility.（検証プロセスは科学的信頼性を得るために不可欠だ）

- He serves as a liaison between labor and management.（彼は労使間の連絡窓口の役割を果たしている）

Day 31 》CD-A31
Quick Review
答えは左ページ下

- blizzard
- occurrence
- wholesaler
- gathering
- closure
- stopover
- default
- booking
- sightseeing
- conductor
- publication
- duration
- turnout
- workforce
- aviation
- limitation

Day 33　名詞19

Check 1　Listen 》CD-A33

□ 0513
distraction
/distrǽkʃən/
Part 2, 3

名 ❶**気を散らす**[散らされる]**こと**　❷気晴らし、娯楽
動distract：(人)の気を(…から)散らす、(注意など)を(…から)散らす、そらす(from . . .)
形distracting：気が散る、集中できない

□ 0514
competence
/kάmpətəns/
Part 5, 6

名 (～の)**能力**、適性(in [for] ～)(⇔incompetence)
形competent：❶(仕事などに)有能な(at [in] ～)；(～する)能力のある(to do)；(～するのに)適格な(to do)　❷(仕事が)満足のいく

□ 0515
allocation
/æləkéiʃən/
Part 7

名 **割り当て**、配分；割当量[額]
動allocate：❶(allocate A for Bで)AをBのために取っておく、充てる、計上する　❷(allocate A to Bで)AをBに割り当てる、配分する

□ 0516
gear
/gíər/
Part 2, 3

名 ❶(集合的に)**道具**、用具一式　❷(車の)ギア、歯車
動 ～を(…に)適合させる(to . . .)

□ 0517
beep
/bíːp/
Part 4

名 (ビーッという)**発信音**、信号音(≒tone)
動 ❶ビーッという音を出す　❷(警笛など)を鳴らす

□ 0518
copyright
/kάpiràit/
ビジネス問題

名 (～の)**著作権**、版権(on [to, for] ～)　❶記号は©
動 ～の著作権を取る
形 著作権のある

□ 0519
prospectus
/prəspéktəs/
Part 7

名 (大学・会社などの)**案内書**、事業紹介

□ 0520
implementation
/ìmpləməntéiʃən/
Part 5, 6

名 **実行**、実施、履行
名implement：道具、用具
動implement：(計画・約束など)を実行[履行]する

continued
▼

本を持ち歩かなくても、語彙学習はできる！
特に復習はCDを「聞き流す」だけでもOK。
通勤・通学時などの「細切れ時間」を活用しよう。

☐ 聞くだけモード　Check 1
☐ しっかりモード　Check 1 ▶ 2
☐ かんぺきモード　Check 1 ▶ 2 ▶ 3

CHAPTER 1
CHAPTER 2
CHAPTER 3
CHAPTER 4
CHAPTER 5
CHAPTER 6
CHAPTER 7
CHAPTER 8
CHAPTER 9

Check 2　Phrase

☐ reduce driver distraction（運転手の注意散漫を低減させる）
☐ a pleasant distraction（楽しい気晴らし）

☐ competence in English（英語の能力）
☐ competence as a teacher（教師としての適性）

☐ the allocation of funds（資金の割り当て）

☐ fishing [rain] gear（釣り[雨]具）
☐ a car with five gears（5段ギアの車）

☐ a warning beep（警告音）

☐ own [hold] the copyright on ～（～の著作権を持っている）
☐ a violation of copyright laws（著作権法違反）

☐ a college [business] prospectus（大学[事業]案内書）

☐ implementation of a plan（計画の実行）

Check 3　Sentence

☐ Talking on a cellphone can be a distraction from driving.（携帯電話での通話は運転から気が散ることもある）

☐ Applicants must demonstrate competence in programming using a high-level program language.（志願者は高度なプログラム言語を使ったプログラムの能力を証明しなければならない）➕求人広告の表現

☐ A fairer allocation of wealth is crucial to reducing the gap between the rich and poor.（より公平な富の配分は貧富の格差を減らすために極めて重要だ）

☐ I loaded camping gear into my car.（私は車にキャンプ用具を積み込んだ）

☐ Please leave your name and message after the beep.（発信音の後に、お名前とメッセージを残してください）➕留守番電話の表現

☐ Copyright lasts 70 years after the author's death.（著者の死後、著作権は70年間継続する）

☐ Please read the prospectus carefully before you invest.（投資をする前に事業紹介を丁寧にお読みください）➕投資パンフレットなどの表現

☐ The implementation of the project was delayed due to a lack of funds.（そのプロジェクトの実施は資金不足のため延期された）

continued
▼

Day 33

Check 1　Listen))) CD-A33

☐ 0521
momentum
/mouméntəm/
Part 7

名 **勢い**、弾み

☐ 0522
tenant
/ténənt/
ビジネス問題

名 **借家**[借地]**人**、テナント(≒lessee)(⇔landlord：地主、家主)
名 tenancy：❶借用(権)　❷借用期間

☐ 0523
mandate
/mǽndeit/
Part 5, 6

名 ❶**権限**(≒authority)　❷(公式の)命令、指令(≒order, command)
動 ❶〜に(…するように)命令する(to do)　❷〜に(…する)権限を与える(to do)
形 mandatory：義務[強制]的な

☐ 0524
shuttle
/ʃʌ́tl/
Part 2, 3

名 **定期往復便**
動 (〜の間を)(定期的に)往復する(between 〜)(≒ply)

☐ 0525
farewell
/fèərwél/
Part 4

名 ❶**別れ**　❷別れの言葉[あいさつ]

☐ 0526
vicinity
/vɪsínəti/
Part 5, 6

名 (〜の)**付近**、周辺(of 〜)(≒neighborhood)

☐ 0527
beneficiary
/bènəfíʃièri/
❶アクセント注意
Part 7

名 (遺産・年金などの)**受取人**、受給者

☐ 0528
aging
/éidʒiŋ/
Part 5, 6

名 **老化**、高齢化
形 年老いた、高齢の；老朽化した
名 age：年齢、歳
動 age：年を取る
形 aged：(数詞の前に置いて)〜歳の

Day 32))) CD-A32　Quick Review
答えは右ページ下

☐ 刺激　☐ 糖尿病　☐ 矛盾　☐ 廊下
☐ 調査員　☐ 楽観　☐ 配付資料　☐ ゴムボート
☐ 境界線　☐ 責任　☐ 段ボール　☐ 検証
☐ 繰り返し　☐ 手押し車　☐ 残骸　☐ 連絡係

Check 2 Phrase

- ☐ lose momentum(勢いを失う)
- ☐ gain [gather] momentum(弾みをつける、加速する)

- ☐ the tenant of the house(その家の借家人)

- ☐ have a mandate to do ~(~する権限を持っている)
- ☐ a royal mandate(王の命令)

- ☐ take the shuttle from the airport to the city center(空港から都心まで定期往復便に乗る)

- ☐ a farewell speech(別れの言葉)
- ☐ bid [say] farewell to her(彼女に別れを告げる)

- ☐ in the vicinity of ~(~の近くに[で])

- ☐ pension beneficiaries(年金受給者)

- ☐ prevent aging(老化を防ぐ)

Check 3 Sentence

- ☐ The global economy is losing momentum.(世界経済は勢いを失いつつある)

- ☐ The office building has very few tenants.(そのオフィスビルにはテナントがほとんど入っていない)

- ☐ The government has a mandate to govern the country.(政府は国を統治する権限を持っている)

- ☐ The hotel has a free shuttle bus between the airport and the hotel.(そのホテルには空港とホテル間の無料往復バスがある)

- ☐ A farewell party for Mr. Tanaka will be held this Friday.(タナカさんの送別会が今週の金曜日に行われる)

- ☐ There was a fire in the immediate vicinity of my house.(私の家のすぐ近くで火事があった)

- ☐ She was the sole beneficiary of her father's inheritance.(彼女は父親の遺産の唯一の受取人だった)

- ☐ Memory loss is a normal part of aging.(物忘れは老化の普通の現象だ)

Day 32))) CD-A32
Quick Review
答えは左ページ下

- ☐ stimulation
- ☐ investigator
- ☐ boundary
- ☐ repetition
- ☐ diabetes
- ☐ optimism
- ☐ accountability
- ☐ wheelbarrow
- ☐ contradiction
- ☐ handout
- ☐ cardboard
- ☐ debris
- ☐ hallway
- ☐ raft
- ☐ validation
- ☐ liaison

Day 34　名詞20

Check 1　Listen)) CD-A34

0529
clutter
/klʌ́tər/
Part 2, 3

名 **散らかり**(の山)、乱雑、混乱(≒mess)
動 ❶(物が)(場所)に散らかる　❷(場所)を(…で)散らかす (with ...)

0530
awning
/ɔ́ːniŋ/
Part 1

名 (店先などの)**日よけ**、雨よけ

0531
grandeur
/grǽndʒər/
Part 5, 6

名 **雄大さ**、壮大さ(≒magnificence)
形 grand：❶壮大[雄大]な　❷偉大[崇高]な

0532
plaque
/plǽk/
❶発音注意
Part 1

名 ❶**記念額**；飾り額　❷歯垢　●イギリス英語では❷は /plɑ́ːk/ と発音することもある

0533
turnaround
/tə́ːrnəràund/
ビジネス問題

名 (企業業績などの)**好転**、(黒字への)転換
動 turn around：(経済など)を好転させる

0534
hypothesis
/haipɑ́θəsis/
❶アクセント注意
Part 5, 6

名 **仮説**　●複数形はhypotheses
形 hypothetical：仮説[仮定](上)の

0535
diligence
/dílədʒəns/
Part 5, 6

名 **勤勉**、不断の努力
形 diligent：(〜に)勤勉な(in [about] 〜)
副 diligently：勤勉に、こつこつと

0536
consolidation
/kənsɑ̀lədéiʃən/
ビジネス問題

名 ❶(会社などの)**合併**、整理統合　❷強化
動 consolidate：❶(会社など)を合併する、整理統合する　❷合併する　❸〜を強化する

continued ▼

1日の「サボり」が挫折につながる。語彙習得論的にも、2日(=32語)を1日で覚えるのは難しい。1日1日の「積み重ね」を大切に！

☐ 聞くだけモード　Check 1
☐ しっかりモード　Check 1 ▶ 2
☐ かんぺきモード　Check 1 ▶ 2 ▶ 3

Check 2　　Phrase

☐ clutter in the kitchen（台所の散らかり）
☐ be in a clutter（散らかっている）

☐ a striped awning（しま模様の日よけ）

☐ the grandeur of Beethoven's 9th symphony（ベートーベンの交響曲第9番の壮大さ）

☐ a bronze plaque（ブロンズの記念額）
☐ remove plaque（歯垢を取り除く）

☐ the turnaround of the Japanese economy（日本経済の好転）

☐ support [establish] a hypothesis（仮説を裏づける[証明する]）

☐ work with diligence（勤勉に働く）

☐ the consolidation of two insurance companies（2つの保険会社の合併）
☐ the consolidation of the domestic industry（国内産業の強化）

Check 3　　Sentence

☐ Keep your room free of clutter.（部屋を散らかさないでおきなさい）

☐ The awning covers the entrance of the store.（日よけが店の入り口を覆っている）

☐ I was overwhelmed by the grandeur of the Rocky Mountains.（私はロッキー山脈の雄大さに圧倒された）

☐ Several plaques are installed on the wall.（壁にいくつかの記念額が据えつけられている）

☐ The company made a miraculous performance turnaround.（その会社は奇跡的な業績好転を果たした）

☐ The widely accepted hypothesis is that birds evolved from dinosaurs.（広く受け入れられている仮説は、鳥類は恐竜から進化したということだ）

☐ Diligence and persistence are the key to success.（勤勉と粘り強さが成功への鍵だ）

☐ The automaker announced the consolidation of its three factories into one.（その自動車メーカーは3つの工場を1つに統合することを発表した）

continued ▼

Day 34

Check 1　Listen)) CD-A34

□ 0537
appraisal
/əpréizəl/
ビジネス問題

名 (〜の)**評価**、鑑定、査定 (of 〜) (≒ assessment, evaluation)
動 appraise：〜を(…と)評価[鑑定、査定]する (at …)

□ 0538
criterion
/kraitíəriən/
Part 5, 6

名 (判断・評価などのための)**基準**、尺度 (for 〜) ● 複数形は criteria だが、criteria を単数で用いる場合も多い

□ 0539
rubble
/rʌ́bl/
Part 7

名 **残骸**、破片、がれき (≒ debris)

□ 0540
usage
/júːsidʒ/
Part 4

名 ❶ **使用**(法、量)　❷ (言語の)語法、慣用法

□ 0541
insurer
/inʃúərər/
ビジネス問題

名 **保険会社**[業者]
名 insurance：保険
動 insure：〜に(…に備えて)保険をかける (against …)

□ 0542
dormitory
/dɔ́ːrmətɔ̀ːri/
Part 7

名 (大学などの)**寮**、寄宿舎

□ 0543
bidder
/bídər/
ビジネス問題

名 **入札者**、競り手
名 bid：❶ (工事などの)入札 (for 〜)　❷ (〜のための)企て、試み (for 〜)
動 bid：❶ (bid for で)〜に入札する　❷ (bid A for B で)(競売などで) A(値)を B(物)につける

□ 0544
collateral
/kəlǽtərəl/
ビジネス問題

名 **担保** (≒ security)
形 ❶ (〜に)付随する (with 〜)　❷ 傍系の

Day 33)) CD-A33
Quick Review
答えは右ページ下

- □ 気を散らすこと
- □ 能力
- □ 割り当て
- □ 道具
- □ 発信音
- □ 著作権
- □ 案内書
- □ 実行
- □ 勢い
- □ 借家人
- □ 権限
- □ 定期往復便
- □ 別れ
- □ 付近
- □ 受取人
- □ 老化

Check 2 Phrase

- a job [performance] appraisal（勤務評価）
- make an appraisal of ~（~を評価する）

- the criterion of judgment（判断の基準）

- the rubble of the broken wall（崩れた壁の残骸）
- reduce ~ to rubble（~をがれきに帰す）

- a usage rate（使用率）
- modern English usage（現代英語用法）

- the second-biggest insurer in the world（世界第2位の保険会社）

- a student [company] dormitory（学生[社員]寮）

- the highest bidder（最高入札者）
- a rival bidder（競争入札者）

- put up ~ as collateral for ...（~を…の担保とする）

Check 3 Sentence

- Most companies conduct performance appraisals annually.（ほとんどの会社は1年に1度勤務評価を行っている）

- The criteria for choosing a college are different for every student.（大学を選ぶ基準は生徒ごとに異なる）

- Rescue workers searched the rubble for survivors.（レスキュー隊員たちががれきの中を生存者がいないか探した）

- Electricity usage goes up in summer and down in winter.（電気の使用量は夏は増え、冬は減る）

- If you need to make an insurance claim, please contact your insurer directly.（保険金を請求する必要がある場合は、保険会社に直接連絡してください）

- The university has both men's and women's dormitories.（その大学には男性寮と女性寮の両方がある）

- The painting will go to the highest bidder.（その絵画は最高入札者の手に渡る予定だ）

- He put up his house as collateral for the loan.（彼は自宅をそのローンの担保とした）

Day 33)) CD-A33
Quick Review
答えは左ページ下

- distraction
- competence
- allocation
- gear
- beep
- copyright
- prospectus
- implementation
- momentum
- tenant
- mandate
- shuttle
- farewell
- vicinity
- beneficiary
- aging

Day 35　名詞21

Check 1　Listen)) CD-A35

0545
dignity
/dígnəti/
Part 5, 6

名 **威厳**、尊厳
動 dignify：〜に（…で）威厳をつける（with [by] ...）

0546
pathway
/pǽθwèi/
Part 1

名 **小道**、細道（≒ path, lane）

0547
testimonial
/tèstəmóuniəl/
Part 7

名 **感謝の印**、感謝状、表彰状

0548
medium
/míːdiəm/
Part 5, 6

名 ❶（伝達などの）**手段**（≒ means）　❷媒体［媒介］（物）
＋複数形は media と mediums の2つある
形 ❶中間の、中位の　❷（ステーキが）ミディアムの

0549
standstill
/stǽndstìl/
Part 7

名 （a 〜）**停止**、休止；行き詰まり

0550
boarding
/bɔ́ːrdiŋ/
Part 4

名 **搭乗**、乗車、乗船
動 board：（飛行機など）に乗り込む

0551
avoidance
/əvɔ́idns/
Part 5, 6

名 （〜を）**回避**（すること）（of 〜）
動 avoid：❶〜を避ける　❷（avoid doing で）〜することを避ける；〜しないようにする

0552
delegation
/dèligéiʃən/
Part 7

名 （集合的に）**代表**［派遣］**団**
名 delegate：（政治的会議などの）代表者、使節
動 delegate：❶（任務など）を（…に）委任する（to ...）　❷〜を（…するように）代表に立てる（to do）

continued
▼

今日で『キクタンTOEIC Test Score 990』は前半戦が終了！ ここまで一緒に学習を続けてくれてありがとう！ あと5週間、頑張ろう！

- ☐ 聞くだけモード　Check 1
- ☐ しっかりモード　Check 1 ▶ 2
- ☐ かんぺきモード　Check 1 ▶ 2 ▶ 3

Check 2　Phrase

☐ a man of dignity（威厳のある人）
☐ human dignity（人間の尊厳）

☐ a pedestrian pathway（歩道）

☐ give a testimonial to ～（～に感謝の意を伝える）
☐ a testimonial letter（感謝状）

☐ a medium of transportation（交通手段）
☐ the medium of television（テレビ媒体）

☐ come [grind] to a standstill（停止する、行き詰まる）
☐ be at a standstill（行き詰まっている）

☐ a boarding pass（搭乗券）

☐ the avoidance of danger（危険の回避）
☐ tax avoidance（[合法的な]節税、税金逃れ）● 「脱税」はtax evasion

☐ send a delegation to ～（～に代表団を派遣する）

Check 3　Sentence

☐ She is a woman of grace and dignity.（彼女は気品と威厳のある女性だ）

☐ The pathway leads through the woods.（森の中に小道が通っている）

☐ I would like to give you a testimonial for your efforts.（あなたのご尽力に感謝申し上げます）

☐ E-mail has become a primary medium of communication in business.（電子メールはビジネスでの主要な伝達の手段となった）

☐ Heavy snow brought traffic to a standstill.（大雪で交通は麻痺した）

☐ Ladies and gentlemen, boarding will start in 10 minutes.（皆さま、搭乗は10分後に始まります）● 空港のアナウンス

☐ The avoidance of overtraining is important for injury reduction.（過度な練習を避けるのはけがを減らすために重要だ）

☐ A US delegation arrived in Tokyo to discuss trade issues.（貿易問題について協議するためにアメリカの代表団が東京に到着した）

continued
▼

Day 35

Check 1 Listen)) CD-A35

□ 0553 incidence
/ínsədəns/
Part 5, 6

名 (病気・事件などの)**発生**(率) (≒ occurrence)
名 incident：出来事、事件、事故
形 incident：(〜に)ありがちな、起こりがちな(to 〜)

□ 0554 respondent
/rispándənt/
Part 5, 6

名 **回答**[応答]**者**
名 response：(〜への)返答、応答(to 〜)
動 respond：(respond toで)❶〜に応答[返答]する ❷〜に反応する

□ 0555 housekeeping
/háuskì:piŋ/
Part 2, 3

名 **家事**；家計費
形 housekeeper：家政婦

□ 0556 pundit
/pʌ́ndit/
Part 7

名 **評論**[批評]**家**(≒ critic, reviewer)、専門家(≒ expert)

□ 0557 vocation
/voukéiʃən/
ビジネス問題

名 ❶**天職** ❷職業(≒ job, occupation, profession, career)
形 vocational：職業(上)の

□ 0558 cultivation
/kʌ̀ltəvéiʃən/
Part 5, 6

名 ❶**栽培** ❷耕作 ❸教養、修養
動 cultivate：❶〜を耕す ❷〜を栽培する ❸(才能など)を養う
形 cultivated：❶教養のある、洗練された ❷栽培された ❸耕作された

□ 0559 benchmark
/béntʃmà:rk/
Part 7

名 (価値判断などの)**基準**、尺度(≒ standard)

□ 0560 constraint
/kənstréint/
Part 7

名 ❶(〜に対する)**制約**(on 〜)(≒ restriction) ❷強制
動 constrain：〜を抑制[抑止]する

Day 34)) CD-A34 Quick Review
答えは右ページ下

□ 散らかり □ 好転 □ 評価 □ 保険会社
□ 日よけ □ 仮説 □ 基準 □ 寮
□ 雄大さ □ 勤勉 □ 残骸 □ 入札者
□ 記念額 □ 合併 □ 使用 □ 担保

Check 2 Phrase

- ☐ the incidence of traffic accidents (交通事故の発生率)

- ☐ a questionnaire [poll] respondent (アンケート[世論調査]の回答者)

- ☐ be good at housekeeping (家事が上手である)

- ☐ a sports pundit (スポーツ評論家)

- ☐ regard one's profession as a vocation (自分の職業を天職と考える)
- ☐ one's vocation as a teacher (教師としての仕事)

- ☐ the cultivation of rice (米の栽培)
- ☐ land under cultivation (耕作中の土地)

- ☐ a benchmark of evaluation (評価の基準)

- ☐ financial constraints (財政的制約)
- ☐ under constraint (やむを得ずに、強いられて)

Check 3 Sentence

- ☐ Residents in the area are concerned about the increasing incidence of crime. (その地域の住民は犯罪の発生の増加を心配している)

- ☐ The survey showed that nearly 70 percent of respondents disapproved of the cabinet. (その調査では回答者の70パーセント近くは内閣を支持していないことが明らかになった)

- ☐ Doing the laundry is one of the most important parts of housekeeping. (洗濯は家事の最も大切な部分の1つだ)

- ☐ He is one of the most influential political pundits. (彼は最も影響力のある政治評論家の1人だ)

- ☐ He found his vocation as a composer after some years spent as a pianist. (彼は何年かピアニストとして過ごした後、作曲家としての天職を見つけた)

- ☐ The cultivation of marijuana is a criminal offense in many countries. (マリファナの栽培は多くの国で犯罪である)

- ☐ The prime rate is a benchmark for setting interest rates on many types of loans. (プライムレートとは多くの種類のローンの利率を設定する際に基準となるものだ)

- ☐ The construction of the bridge was canceled due to budget constraints. (その橋の建設は予算の制約のため取り消された)

Day 34))) CD-A34
Quick Review
答えは左ページ下

- ☐ clutter
- ☐ awning
- ☐ grandeur
- ☐ plaque
- ☐ turnaround
- ☐ hypothesis
- ☐ diligence
- ☐ consolidation
- ☐ appraisal
- ☐ criterion
- ☐ rubble
- ☐ usage
- ☐ insurer
- ☐ dormitory
- ☐ bidder
- ☐ collateral

Day 36　名詞22

Check 1　Listen 》CD-B1

0561 grain /gréin/ Part 7
名 ❶(集合的に)**穀物**(≒cereal)　❷(穀物の)粒

0562 specimen /spésəmən/ Part 1
名 ❶**標本**　❷見本

0563 commentary /kάməntèri/ Part 4
名 (〜の)(実況)**解説**；論評(on 〜)
名 comment：(〜についての)論評、コメント(about [on] 〜)
動 comment：(comment onで)〜について論評[コメント]する

0564 administrator /ædmínəstrèitər/ Part 7
名 **管理者**、経営者
名 administration：❶管理、経営　❷行政；(しばしばthe A〜)政府、内閣
動 administer：❶〜を管理[経営]する　❷〜を治める
形 administrative：❶管理の、経営上の　❷行政上の

0565 gymnasium /dʒimnéiziəm/ ❶アクセント注意 Part 1
名 **体育館**、ジム　➕短縮形はgym

0566 trustee /trʌstíː/ Part 4
名 ❶(会社・学校などの)**理事**、役員、評議員　❷(他人の財産の)管財[保管]人

0567 literacy /lítərəsi/ Part 7
名 ❶(コンピューターなどの)**使用能力**；(特定分野の)知識、能力　❷識字能力、読み書きの能力
形 literate：❶読み書きができる　❷(特定分野の)知識[技能]がある

0568 diner /dáinər/ Part 1
名 ❶**食事客**　❷簡易食堂、小食堂
名 dinner：ディナー、食事
動 dine：(〜と)食事をする(with 〜)

continued ▼

つらくて挫折しそうになったら、Check 1の「聞くだけモード」だけでもOK。少しずつでもいいので、「継続する」ことを大切にしよう！

☐ 聞くだけモード　Check 1
☐ しっかりモード　Check 1 ▶ 2
☐ かんぺきモード　Check 1 ▶ 2 ▶ 3

Check 2　Phrase

☐ a field of grain（穀物畑）
☐ a grain of wheat（小麦の粒）

☐ a fossil specimen（化石の標本）
☐ a fine specimen of ～（～の好見本）

☐ a basketball commentary（バスケットボールの解説）

☐ a system administrator（システム管理者）
☐ a business administrator（企業経営者）

☐ a school gymnasium（学校の体育館）

☐ the board of trustees（理事会）
☐ a trustee in bankruptcy（破産管財人）

☐ computer literacy（コンピューターの使用能力）
☐ the literacy rate（識字率）

☐ restaurant diners（レストランの食客）
☐ a diner along the road（道路沿いの簡易食堂）

Check 3　Sentence

☐ Rice is the staple grain of North East and South East Asia.（米は北東アジアと東南アジアの主要な穀物だ）

☐ The man is examining a specimen.（男性は標本を調べている）

☐ He writes political commentary for "The Washington Post."（彼は『ワシントンポスト』紙に政治解説を書いている）

☐ He works as a school administrator.（彼は学校管理者として勤務している）

☐ They are exercising in the gymnasium.（彼らは体育館で運動をしている）

☐ She is a member of the university board of trustees.（彼女はその大学の理事会のメンバーだ）

☐ Computer literacy is essential for this position.（コンピューターの使用能力はこの仕事に必須である）➕求人広告の表現

☐ The restaurant is almost full of diners.（レストランは食客でほぼ満席である）

continued
▼

Day 36

Check 1　Listen 》CD-B1

□ 0569
breadth
/brédθ/
Part 5, 6

名 ❶**幅**、横幅(≒ width)　❶「長さ」はlength、「奥行き」はdepth　❷(知識などの)広さ

□ 0570
crackdown
/krǽkdàun/
Part 7

名 (〜に対する)**厳重な取り締まり** (on 〜)
動 crack down on：〜を厳しく取り締まる

□ 0571
hub
/hʌ́b/
Part 5, 6

名 **中心**(地)、中核、中枢(≒ center)

□ 0572
screening
/skríːniŋ/
Part 7

名 ❶**選考**、選抜、審査　❷検診、医学検査
動 screen：❶〜を選別する　❷〜を(…から)守る；隠す(from ...)

□ 0573
patron
/péitrən/
❶発音注意
ビジネス問題

名 ❶**顧客**、ひいき客(≒ client, customer)　❷後援者(≒ supporter)
名 patronage：(店などへの)ひいき、引き立て、愛顧

□ 0574
citizenship
/sítəzənʃip/
Part 5, 6

名 **市民**[公民]**権**、国籍
名 citizen：❶市民　❷国民

□ 0575
affluence
/ǽfluəns/
Part 5, 6

名 **豊かさ**、裕福(≒ wealth)
形 affluent：裕福な、豊かな

□ 0576
fixture
/fíkstʃər/
Part 7

名 (通例〜s)(家屋内の)**設備**、備品

Day 35 》CD-A35
Quick Review
答えは右ページ下

- ☐ 威厳
- ☐ 小道
- ☐ 感謝の印
- ☐ 手段
- ☐ 停止
- ☐ 搭乗
- ☐ 回避
- ☐ 代表団
- ☐ 発生
- ☐ 回答者
- ☐ 家事
- ☐ 評論家
- ☐ 天職
- ☐ 栽培
- ☐ 基準
- ☐ 制約

Check 2 Phrase

- the breadth of the table（そのテーブルの幅）
- the breadth of his knowledge（彼の知識の広さ）

- a crackdown on speeding（スピード違反に対する厳重な取り締まり）

- the hub of the town（街の中心地）
- a hub airport（拠点空港、ハブ空港）❶航空ネットワークの中心になる空港

- a screening process（選考過程）
- cancer screening（がん検診）

- patrons of the store（その店のひいき客）
- a patron of charities（慈善団体の後援者）

- acquire [lose, grant] citizenship（市民権を得る[失う、与える]）
- dual citizenship（二重国籍）

- material [spiritual] affluence（物質的[精神的]な豊かさ）
- live in affluence（裕福に暮らす）

- lighting fixtures（照明設備）

Check 3 Sentence

- The length of the rectangle is twice its breadth.（その長方形の長さは幅の2倍だ）

- Police will begin an unprecedented crackdown on drunk driving.（警察は飲酒運転に対する前例のない厳重な取り締まりを始める予定だ）

- Wall Street is the hub of global financial markets.（ウォール街は世界の金融市場の中心だ）

- The initial screening of applicants is based on academic performance.（志願者の第1次選考は学業成績に基づいている）

- We need to maintain and develop a relationship with our patrons.（私たちは顧客との関係を維持し、発展させていく必要がある）

- She acquired US citizenship last year.（彼女は昨年、アメリカの市民権を得た）

- In the country, a very few enjoy affluence, while the majority of people live in poverty.（その国では、ごく少数の人々が豊かさを享受している一方で、人々の大多数は貧しい暮らしをしている）

- The price includes all furniture and fixtures.（価格にはすべての家具と設備が含まれている）❶住宅広告の表現

Day 35 》CD-A35
Quick Review
答えは左ページ下

- dignity
- pathway
- testimonial
- medium
- standstill
- boarding
- avoidance
- delegation
- incidence
- respondent
- housekeeping
- pundit
- vocation
- cultivation
- benchmark
- constraint

CHAPTER 1
CHAPTER 2
CHAPTER 3
CHAPTER 4
CHAPTER 5
CHAPTER 6
CHAPTER 7
CHAPTER 8
CHAPTER 9

Day 37　名詞23

Check 1　Listen)) CD-B2

☐ 0577
ventilation
/vèntəléiʃən/
Part 7

名 **換気**、風通し
動 ventilate：(部屋など)を換気する

☐ 0578
proximity
/prɑksíməti/
Part 5, 6

名 (～に)**近いこと**(to ～)、近接(≒nearness)

☐ 0579
diplomat
/dípləmæt/
Part 4

名 ❶**外交官** ❷外交家
名 diplomacy：❶外交 ❷外交的手腕
形 diplomatic：❶外交(上)の ❷外交的手腕のある

☐ 0580
confidentiality
/kɑ̀nfədenʃiǽləti/
Part 5, 6

名 **機密**[秘密]**性**[保持]
名 confidence：❶信頼 ❷自信 ❸秘密
形 confidential：秘密[内密]の
副 confidentially：内密に

☐ 0581
lag
/lǽg/
Part 5, 6

名 **遅れ**、遅延(≒delay)
動 遅れる；(～より)進み方が遅い(behind ～)

☐ 0582
shortcut
/ʃɔ́ːrtkʌ̀t/
Part 2, 3

名 (～への)**近道**(to ～)(⇔detour：迂回路) ❶比喩的な意味でも用いられる

☐ 0583
pointer
/pɔ́intər/
❶定義注意
Part 7

名 (～についての)**助言**、ヒント(on ～)(≒tip, hint)
動 point：❶(point atで)～を指し示す、指さす ❷～を(…に)向ける(at …)

☐ 0584
funding
/fʌ́ndiŋ/
ビジネス問題

名 (～のための)**財政的支援**、資金提供、財源(for ～)
名 fund：(しばしば～s)(～のための)資金、基金(for ～)
動 fund：～に資金を提供する

continued
▼

毎日繰り返しチャンツCDを聞いていれば、リスニング力もアップしているはず。英語ニュースなどを聞いて、効果を確認してみては？

☐ 聞くだけモード　Check 1
☐ しっかりモード　Check 1 ▶ 2
☐ かんぺきモード　Check 1 ▶ 2 ▶ 3

Check 2　　Phrase

☐ a ventilation system（換気システム）
☐ have good [poor] ventilation（[家などが]換気がいい[悪い]）

☐ in close proximity to ~（~のすぐ近くに[で]）

☐ a diplomat posted in France（フランス駐在の外交官）

☐ the confidentiality of votes（投票の秘密性）
☐ a breach of confidentiality（守秘義務の違反）

☐ a time lag（時間の遅れ[ずれ]）
☐ jet lag（時差ぼけ）

☐ take a shortcut（近道をする）

☐ give him pointers on ~（彼に~についての助言を与える）

☐ funding for the project（そのプロジェクトのための財政的支援）
☐ get [give] funding for ~（~のための財政的支援を得る[与える]）

Check 3　　Sentence

☐ Good ventilation is essential to both comfort and health.（十分な換気は快適さと健康の両方にとって必要だ）

☐ The best thing about the house is its proximity to the station.（その家の最もいいところは駅に近いことだ）

☐ My dream was to be a diplomat.（私の夢は外交官になることだった）

☐ The doctor-patient relationship is based on confidentiality.（医者と患者の関係は機密保持に基づいている）

☐ There is always a time lag between a financial market's crisis and its effect on the real economy.（金融市場の危機と実体経済へのその影響の間には常に時間のずれがある）

☐ There is no shortcut to success.（成功への近道はない）

☐ He gave me some pointers on how to write a term paper.（彼は期末リポートの書き方について私にいくつか助言してくれた）

☐ The bank received emergency funding from the government.（その銀行は政府から緊急財政支援を受けた）

continued ▼

Day 37

Check 1　Listen 》CD-B2

☐ 0585
regime
/rəʒíːm/
Part 5, 6

名 **政権**(≒ government)

☐ 0586
mentor
/méntɔːr/
Part 2, 3

名 (信頼のおける)**助言**[指導]**者**、教育役[係]

☐ 0587
synergy
/sínərdʒi/
ビジネス問題

名 **相乗効果**

☐ 0588
artisan
/ɑ́ːrtəzən/
ビジネス問題

名 **職人**(≒ craftsman)

☐ 0589
correction
/kərékʃən/
Part 5, 6

名 **修正**、訂正、校正　●collection(収集物)と混同しないように注意
動correct：(誤りなど)を訂正する
形correct：❶正しい、正確な　❷適切な、妥当な
副correctly：正しく、正確に

☐ 0590
adherence
/ædhíərəns/
Part 7

名 ❶(規則などの)**厳守**(to ~)　❷(~に対する)固執、執着(to ~)
名adherent：(~の)支持者(of ~)
動adhere：(adhere toで)❶(規則など)を厳守する　❷(考えなど)に固執する

☐ 0591
influx
/ínflʌks/
Part 7

名 (~の)**流入**、殺到、到来(of ~)

☐ 0592
saturation
/sætʃəréiʃən/
ビジネス問題

名 (市場の)**飽和**(状態)、過剰供給
動saturate：❶(市場)に商品を過剰供給する　❷~を(…で)満たす、いっぱいにする(with ...)

| Day 36 》CD-B1
Quick Review
答えは右ページ下 | ☐ 穀物
☐ 標本
☐ 解説
☐ 管理者 | ☐ 体育館
☐ 理事
☐ 使用能力
☐ 食事客 | ☐ 幅
☐ 厳重な取り締まり
☐ 中心
☐ 選考 | ☐ 顧客
☐ 市民権
☐ 豊かさ
☐ 設備 |

Check 2　Phrase

- [ ] the military regime（軍事政権）

- [ ] the ideal mentor（理想的な助言者）

- [ ] create [generate, produce] synergy（相乗効果を生み出す）

- [ ] a skilled artisan（熟練した職人、熟練工）

- [ ] make a correction（修正[訂正]する）
- [ ] correction marks（校正記号）

- [ ] adherence to laws（法律の厳守）
- [ ] adherence to old ideas（古い考えに対する固執）

- [ ] an influx of foreign capital（外国資本の流入）

- [ ] market saturation（市場の飽和状態）⊕供給が需要を上回っている状態
- [ ] saturation point（飽和点、飽和状態）

Check 3　Sentence

- [ ] Saddam Hussein's regime was overthrown by US forces.（サダム・フセイン政権は米軍によって倒された）

- [ ] My current boss is my best mentor.（私の現在の上司は私の最良の助言者だ）

- [ ] The partnership of the two companies will create synergy.（両社の提携は相乗効果を生み出すだろう）

- [ ] Small manufacturers are faced with an acute shortage of skilled artisans.（小規模メーカーは深刻な熟練工不足に直面している）

- [ ] My essay was returned with lots of corrections.（私の小論文はたくさん修正されて戻ってきた）

- [ ] Adherence to safety regulations is of the utmost importance.（安全規則の厳守が最も大切である）

- [ ] The country is faced with an influx of Iraqi refugees.（その国はイラク人難民の流入に直面している）

- [ ] The mobile phone market has almost reached saturation.（携帯電話市場は飽和状態にほぼ達している）

Day 36))) CD-B1
Quick Review
答えは左ページ下

- [ ] grain
- [ ] specimen
- [ ] commentary
- [ ] administrator
- [ ] gymnasium
- [ ] trustee
- [ ] literacy
- [ ] diner
- [ ] breadth
- [ ] crackdown
- [ ] hub
- [ ] screening
- [ ] patron
- [ ] citizenship
- [ ] affluence
- [ ] fixture

Day 38　名詞24

Check 1　Listen 》CD-B3

□ 0593
heredity
/hərédəti/
Part 7

名 **遺伝**(的形質)　❶「遺伝子」はgene
形 hereditary：❶遺伝(性)の　❷世襲の

□ 0594
brokerage
/bróukəridʒ/
ビジネス問題

名 ❶**証券会社**(≒brokerage house [firm])　❷仲買手数料

□ 0595
excellence
/éksələns/
Part 4

名 (〜における)**優秀さ**、卓越(in 〜)
動 excel：(excel in [at]で)〜に秀でている、ずば抜けている
形 excellent：素晴らしい、非常に優れた

□ 0596
perk
/pə́ːrk/
ビジネス問題

名 (通例〜s)(地位などに伴う)**特典**、特権、役得(≒perquisite)

□ 0597
contributor
/kəntríbjutər/
Part 5, 6

名 ❶(〜の)**一因**、誘因(to 〜)　❷(〜への)寄付者、貢献者(to 〜)　❸(〜への)寄稿者(to 〜)
名 contribution：❶貢献、寄与　❷寄付(金)
動 contribute：❶(contribute A to [toward] Bで)AをBに寄付する　❷(contribute toで)〜に貢献[寄与]する

□ 0598
probation
/proubéiʃən/
ビジネス問題

名 ❶**見習**[実習]**期間**　❷執行猶予、保護観察

□ 0599
annuity
/ənjúːəti/
Part 7

名 **年金**(≒pension)

□ 0600
depot
/díːpou/
❶発音注意
Part 5, 6

名 ❶**倉庫**、貯蔵所(≒warehouse, storehouse)　❷(鉄道の)駅、(バスなどの)発着所(≒station)

continued
▼

Quick Reviewは使ってる？ 昨日覚えた単語でも、記憶に残っているとは限らない。学習の合間に軽くチェックするだけでも効果は抜群！

☐ 聞くだけモード Check 1
☐ しっかりモード Check 1 ▶ 2
☐ かんぺきモード Check 1 ▶ 2 ▶ 3

Check 2　Phrase

☐ a disease due to heredity（遺伝による病気）

☐ a mid-sized brokerage（中堅の証券会社）

☐ excellence in studies（学業の優秀さ）

☐ give perks to ～（～に特典を与える）
☐ the perks of the job（その仕事の特典）

☐ a contributor to the current economic crisis（現在の経済危機の一因）
☐ a contributor to charities（慈善団体への寄付者）

☐ put [place] ～ on probation（～を仮採用にする）
☐ give ～ three years' probation（～を執行猶予3年にする）

☐ annuity insurance（年金保険）
☐ receive an annuity（年金を受け取る）

☐ a weapons depot（兵器庫）
☐ a bus depot（バス発着所）

Check 3　Sentence

☐ Heredity is the most common factor in hair loss.（遺伝は抜け毛の最も一般的な要因だ）

☐ Most brokerages suffered huge losses last year.（ほとんどの証券会社は昨年、大きな損失を被った）

☐ He was cited for his excellence in sales performance.（彼は営業成績の優秀さで表彰された）

☐ One of the perks of freelancing is the flexibility in your schedule.（フリーランスの特権の1つはスケジュールの柔軟性だ）

☐ Carbon dioxide is one of the main contributors to global warming.（二酸化炭素は地球温暖化の要因の1つだ）

☐ You will be on probation for three months before being considered a regular employee.（正社員と見なされる前に、あなたは3カ月の見習期間に就くことになる）

☐ Under this form of payment, you will receive an annuity of $5,000 each year for the rest of your life.（この支払い形式では、あなたは年間5000ドルの年金を生涯受け取ることになる）

☐ There was an explosion at the fuel depot yesterday.（昨日、その燃料貯蔵所で爆発があった）

continued
▼

Day 38

Check 1　Listen 》CD-B3

0601
plea
/plíː/
Part 5, 6

名 ❶(～に対する)**嘆願**、請願(for ～)(≒appeal, request)　❷(訴訟での事実の)申し立て　❸弁解、口実(≒excuse)
動plead：❶(plead forで)～を嘆願[懇願]する　❷(plead with A to doで)Aに～してくれと訴える

0602
transparency
/trænspéərənsi/
Part 5, 6

名 ❶(状況・過程などの)**透明性**、オープン度　❷透明(度)
形transparent：透明な、透き通った

0603
crease
/kríːs/
Part 5, 6

名 (布などの)**しわ**；(ズボンなどの)折り目(≒fold, wrinkle)
動 ❶～をしわくちゃにする；～に折り目をつける　❷しわになる；折り目がつく

0604
adversary
/ǽdvərsèri/
❶アクセント注意
Part 7

名 **敵**；(試合などの)相手、ライバル(≒enemy, opponent)
形adverse：❶不都合[不利益]な；(効果などが)マイナスの　❷敵意に満ちた

0605
carousel
/kærəsél/
❶アクセント注意
Part 1

名 ❶(空港などにある)**回転式**[手荷物受け渡し]**コンベアー**　❷回転木馬(≒merry-go-round)

0606
misunderstanding
/mìsʌndərstǽndiŋ/
Part 7

名 (～についての)**誤解**、考え違い(of [about] ～)
動misunderstand：～を誤解する
形misunderstood：誤解された

0607
semiconductor
/sémikəndʌ̀ktər/
ビジネス問題

名 **半導体**

0608
lecturer
/léktʃərər/
Part 1

名 **講演者**、講師
名lecture：(～についての)講義、講演(on [about] ～)
動lecture：❶～に(…について)講義[講演]する(on [about] ...)　❷～に(…のことで)説教する(on [about, for] ...)

Day 37 》CD-B2
Quick Review
答えは右ページ下

- ☐ 換気
- ☐ 近いこと
- ☐ 外交官
- ☐ 機密性
- ☐ 遅れ
- ☐ 近道
- ☐ 助言
- ☐ 財政的支援
- ☐ 政権
- ☐ 助言者
- ☐ 相乗効果
- ☐ 職人
- ☐ 修正
- ☐ 厳守
- ☐ 流入
- ☐ 飽和

Check 2 Phrase

- ☐ make a plea for ~(~を嘆願する)
- ☐ make [enter] a plea of not guilty(無罪の申し立てをする)

- ☐ the transparency of the electoral process(選挙過程の透明性)
- ☐ the transparency of the lake(その湖の透明度)

- ☐ iron creases [a crease](しわにアイロンをかける[アイロンで折り目をつける])

- ☐ a political adversary(政敵)

- ☐ pick up one's baggage from a carousel(回転式コンベアーから手荷物を拾い上げる)
- ☐ ride (on) a carousel(回転木馬に乗る)

- ☐ have a misunderstanding of [about] ~(~を誤解している)

- ☐ a semiconductor chip(半導体チップ)
- ☐ semiconductor business(半導体事業)

- ☐ a lecturer in economics(経済学の講師)

Check 3 Sentence

- ☐ She made a tearful plea for help.(彼女は涙ながらに助けを訴えた)

- ☐ The government should improve the transparency of its ODA program.(政府はODAプログラムの透明性を改善すべきだ)

- ☐ To remove creases from velvet, hang it in a steamy bathroom.(ビロードからしわを取るには、湯気の多い浴室に干してください)

- ☐ Hillary Clinton was Obama's adversary in the Democratic primaries.(ヒラリー・クリントンは民主党の予備選挙でオバマのライバルだった)

- ☐ They are waiting for their baggage by the carousel.(彼らは回転式コンベアーのそばで手荷物を待っている)

- ☐ Misunderstanding often leads to disagreement.(誤解はしばしばいさかいにつながる)

- ☐ Semiconductors are essential components of computers and many electrical devices.(半導体はコンピューターや多くの電子機器に欠かせない部品だ)

- ☐ They are listening to the lecturer.(彼らは講演者の話を聞いている)

Day 37 》CD-B2
Quick Review
答えは左ページ下

- ☐ ventilation
- ☐ proximity
- ☐ diplomat
- ☐ confidentiality
- ☐ lag
- ☐ shortcut
- ☐ pointer
- ☐ funding
- ☐ regime
- ☐ mentor
- ☐ synergy
- ☐ artisan
- ☐ correction
- ☐ adherence
- ☐ influx
- ☐ saturation

Day 39　名詞25

Check 1　Listen))CD-B4

☐ 0609
enhancement
/inhǽnsmənt/
Part 5, 6

名 **増進**、増大、強化
動 enhance：(力・価値など)を高める、強める

☐ 0610
reservoir
/rézərvwà:r/
Part 7

名 ❶ **貯水池**　❷(知識などの)蓄積、宝庫(of ～)

☐ 0611
confiscation
/kànfiskéiʃən/
Part 7

名 **没収**[押収](品)
動 confiscate：～を(…から)没収[押収]する(from ...)

☐ 0612
bachelor
/bǽtʃələr/
Part 7

名 ❶ **学士**　❶「修士」はmaster、「博士」はdoctor　❷ 未婚の男子

☐ 0613
discouragement
/diskə́:ridʒmənt/
Part 5, 6

名 **落胆**、がっかりさせること[もの]
動 discourage：❶～を落胆させる；～のやる気をなくさせる　❷(discourage A from doingで)Aに～するのをやめさせる、思いとどまらせる
形 discouraging：思わしくない、落胆させる

☐ 0614
installment
/instɔ́:lmənt/
ビジネス問題

名 **分割払い**(の1回分)　❶ installationは「(機械などの)取りつけ」

☐ 0615
quarantine
/kwɔ́:rənti:n/
Part 7

名 ❶(伝染病予防のための)**隔離**(期間)　❷ 検疫
動 ～を隔離する

☐ 0616
pledge
/plédʒ/
Part 7

名 (～するという)**誓約**、公約、堅い約束(to do) (≒ promise, vow)
動 ❶ ～を堅く約束する　❷(pledge to doで)～することを堅く約束する、誓う

continued
▼

「声に出す」練習もずいぶん慣れてきたのでは？次はチャンツの「単語」だけでなく、Check 2 の「フレーズ」の音読にも挑戦してみよう！

- ☐ 聞くだけモード Check 1
- ☐ しっかりモード Check 1 ▶ 2
- ☐ かんぺきモード Check 1 ▶ 2 ▶ 3

Check 2 Phrase

☐ enhancement of health（健康の増進）

☐ the water level of the reservoir（その貯水池の水位）
☐ a reservoir of information（情報の宝庫）

☐ the confiscation of private property（私有財産の没収）

☐ a Bachelor of Arts [Science]（文［理］学士）
☐ a confirmed bachelor（独身主義の男性）

☐ a feeling of discouragement（落胆感）

☐ buy ~ on installment（~を分割払いで買う）
☐ pay for ~ in installments（~を分割で支払う）

☐ put [place] ~ in [under] quarantine（~を隔離する）
☐ a quarantine officer（検疫官）

☐ make [take, give] a pledge to do ~（~することを誓う）
☐ fulfill one's pledge（誓約を守る）

Check 3 Sentence

☐ The enhancement of productivity is one of the company's top priorities.（生産性の強化がその会社の最優先事項の1つだ）

☐ The reservoir is nearly dry due to the drought.（その貯水池は干ばつのためほとんど干上がっている）

☐ Any use of a cellphone during class will result in confiscation of the phone.（授業中の携帯電話の使用は電話機の没収につながる）

☐ She holds a bachelor's degree from Harvard University.（彼女はハーバード大学の学士号を持っている）

☐ Don't let discouragement stop you.（落胆して立ち止まっていてはならない）

☐ You can pay for the car in monthly installments.（あなたはその車を月賦で支払うことができる）

☐ The poultry farm was placed under quarantine due to an outbreak of bird flu.（その養鶏場は鳥インフルエンザが発生したため隔離された）

☐ The government made a pledge not to raise consumption tax next year.（政府は消費税を来年引き上げないことを約束した）

continued ▼

Day 39

Check 1　Listen))) CD-B4

0617 broom /brú:m/ Part 1
名 ほうき　●bloom(花)と混同しないように注意。「ちり取り」はdustpan

0618 gratuity /grətjú:əti/ Part 2, 3
名 チップ、心づけ(≒tip)

0619 speculator /spékjulèitər/ ビジネス問題
名 投機[投資]家(≒investor)
名 speculation：❶推測、推量　❷投機、思惑買い
動 speculate：❶〜だと推測する　❷(speculate on [about]で)〜について推測する　❸(speculate inで)(株など)に投機する、〜を思惑買い[売り]する

0620 poultry /póultri/ Part 7
名 (集合的に)家禽　●ニワトリ、シチメンチョウ、アヒル、ガチョウなど

0621 bookkeeping /búkki:piŋ/ ビジネス問題
名 簿記
名 bookkeeper：簿記係

0622 descent /disént/ Part 4
名 ❶降下、下降(⇔ascent)　❷家系、血統　❸(状態などの)(〜への)低下、下落(into 〜)
動 descend：❶(〜から／…へ)降りる、下る(from 〜/to ...)　❷(be descended fromで)〜の子孫である、系統を引いている

0623 archive /á:rkaiv/ Part 5, 6
名 ❶公文書[記録]保管所　❷(コンピューターの)アーカイブ
動 〜を(公文書保管所などに)保管する

0624 consortium /kənsɔ́:rʃiəm/ ビジネス問題
名 共同事業[企業]体、合併企業、コンソーシアム　●複数形はconsortiaとconsortiumsの2つある

Day 38))) CD-B3　Quick Review　答えは右ページ下
□ 遺伝　□ 証券会社　□ 優秀さ　□ 特典
□ 一因　□ 見習期間　□ 年金　□ 倉庫
□ 嘆願　□ 透明性　□ しわ　□ 敵
□ 回転式コンベアー　□ 誤解　□ 半導体　□ 講演者

Check 2 Phrase	Check 3 Sentence
☐ a bamboo broom(竹ぼうき)	☐ The woman is sweeping the floor with a broom.(女性はほうきで床を掃いている)
☐ give a gratuity to ~(~にチップを渡す) ☐ receive a gratuity from ~(~からチップを受け取る)	☐ In the US, it is customary to give gratuities in recognition of service.(アメリカでは、サービスを評価してチップを与える習慣がある)
☐ foreign speculators(海外投機家)	☐ The government should prevent speculators from manipulating stock prices.(政府は投機家たちが株価を操作するのを防ぐべきだ)
☐ poultry products(家禽食品) ☐ a poultry farmer(養鶏業者)	☐ Poultry farmers are faced with increasing energy and feed costs.(養鶏業者はエネルギー代と飼料代の高騰に直面している)
☐ do bookkeeping(帳簿をつける) ☐ be good at bookkeeping(簿記が得意である)	☐ At least five years' experience in bookkeeping is required.(少なくとも5年間の簿記の経験が必須である)❶求人広告の表現
☐ make a steep descent(急降下する) ☐ people of Chinese descent(中国系の人々)	☐ Ladies and gentlemen, we're beginning our final descent into Narita International Airport.(皆さま、当機は成田国際空港への最終降下を始めています)❶飛行機のアナウンス
☐ archive material(公文書保管所の資料)	☐ Archives are useful in obtaining information about the past.(公文書保管所は過去に関する情報を得るのに役立つ)
☐ a consortium of three oil companies(石油会社3社の共同事業体)	☐ A consortium of four construction companies built the bridge.(建設会社4社の共同事業体がその橋を建設した)

Day 38)) CD-B3
Quick Review
答えは左ページ下

☐ heredity ☐ contributor ☐ plea ☐ carousel
☐ brokerage ☐ probation ☐ transparency ☐ misunderstanding
☐ excellence ☐ annuity ☐ crease ☐ semiconductor
☐ perk ☐ depot ☐ adversary ☐ lecturer

CHAPTER 1
CHAPTER 2
CHAPTER 3
CHAPTER 4
CHAPTER 5
CHAPTER 6
CHAPTER 7
CHAPTER 8
CHAPTER 9

Day 40　名詞26

Check 1　Listen)) CD-B5

0625 abbreviation /əbrìːviéiʃən/ Part 2, 3
名 (〜の)**省略形**、略語(of [for] 〜)
動 abbreviate : (abbreviate A as [to] Bで)AをBに短縮[省略]する

0626 strait /stréit/ Part 7
名 **海峡**

0627 litigation /lìtəgéiʃən/ Part 7
名 **訴訟**(≒ suit, lawsuit)
動 litigate : ❶訴訟を起こす　❷〜を訴訟に持ち込む

0628 feedback /fíːdbæk/ Part 2, 3
名 (〜についての)(利用者などの)**反応**、反響、感想(on [about] 〜)

0629 canteen /kæntíːn/ Part 1
名 ❶**水筒**　❷(工場・学校などの)食堂(≒ cafeteria)

0630 myriad /míriəd/ Part 5, 6
名 **無数**(の人、物)(of 〜)
形 無数の

0631 precipitation /prisìpətéiʃən/ Part 7
名 **降水**[降雨、降雪]**量**

0632 gateway /géitwèi/ Part 7
名 (the 〜)(〜への)**入り口**、通路(to 〜)　❶比喩的な意味でも用いられる

continued
▼

疲れているときは、「聞き流す」学習だけでもOK。大切なのは途中で挫折しないこと。でもテキストを使った復習も忘れずにね！

- ☐ 聞くだけモード　Check 1
- ☐ しっかりモード　Check 1 ▶ 2
- ☐ かんぺきモード　Check 1 ▶ 2 ▶ 3

Check 2　Phrase

☐ the abbreviation of "unidentified flying object"(「未確認飛行物体」の省略形)❶UFO

☐ the Straits of Dover(ドーバー海峡)

☐ the expense of litigation(訴訟費用)

☐ feedback from customers on the new product(新製品についての客の反応)

☐ a plastic canteen(プラスチック製の水筒)
☐ a school canteen(学校の食堂)

☐ a myriad of stars(無数の星)

☐ mean [average] annual precipitation(平均年間降水量)

☐ the gateway to the American West(アメリカ西部への入り口)❶セントルイス
☐ the gateway to victory(勝利への道)

Check 3　Sentence

☐ IOC is an abbreviation for the International Olympic Committee.(IOCは国際オリンピック委員会の省略形だ)

☐ A tunnel under the Straits of Gibraltar has been officially under consideration.(ジブラルタル海峡トンネルが公式に検討されている)

☐ The company agreed to the settlement to avoid litigation.(その会社は訴訟を避けるため和解に応じた)

☐ Feedback from the participants on the event was positive.(そのイベントに関する参加者たちの反応はよかった)

☐ The boy is drinking from a canteen.(少年は水筒から水を飲んでいる)

☐ American consumers have a myriad of choices on almost everything.(アメリカの消費者はほとんどすべての物において無数の選択肢がある)

☐ We had 120.2 millimeters of precipitation last month.(先月の降雨量は120.2ミリメートルだった)

☐ Knowledge is the gateway to success.(知識は成功への道だ)

continued ▼

Day 40

Check 1　Listen)) CD-B5

0633 additive /ǽdətiv/ Part 5, 6
名 **添加物**

0634 zeal /zíːl/ Part 5, 6
名 (〜に対する)**熱意**、熱中(for 〜)(≒enthusiasm, eagerness)
▶ zealous：熱心な、熱烈的な

0635 hygiene /háidʒiːn/ Part 5, 6
名 **衛生**(状態)；衛生学
▶ hygienic：衛生(上)の、衛生的な

0636 lapse /lǽps/ Part 7
名 ❶ **ちょっとした誤り**、過失　❷(時の)経過(of 〜)
動 ❶(契約などが)失効する、無効になる　❷終わる

0637 footing /fútiŋ/ Part 7
名 ❶(物事の)**基盤**、基礎　❷足元、足取り　❸土台(≒base)

0638 showdown /ʃóudàun/ Part 7
名 (〜との/…との間の)**決定的**[最後の]**対決**、土壇場 (with 〜/between ...)

0639 usher /ʌ́ʃər/ Part 4
名 (劇場などの)**案内係**
動 〜を(…へ)案内する(to [into] ...)

0640 overview /óuvərvjùː/ Part 7
名 **概観**、全体像

Day 39)) CD-B4 Quick Review
答えは右ページ下

- □ 増進
- □ 貯水池
- □ 没収
- □ 学士
- □ 落胆
- □ 分割払い
- □ 隔離
- □ 誓約
- □ ほうき
- □ チップ
- □ 投機家
- □ 家禽
- □ 簿記
- □ 降下
- □ 公文書保管所
- □ 共同事業体

Check 2　Phrase

- ☐ food additives（食品添加物）

- ☐ show zeal for ~（~に熱意を示す）
- ☐ with zeal（熱意を込めて、熱心に）

- ☐ public hygiene（公衆衛生）
- ☐ good [bad] hygiene（よい[悪い]衛生状態）

- ☐ a lapse of judgment（判断の誤り）
- ☐ the lapse of time（時の経過）

- ☐ a firm [solid] footing（堅固な[しっかりした]基盤）
- ☐ lose [miss] one's footing（足を滑らす）

- ☐ a showdown between the two parties（両者間の決定的対決）
- ☐ a courtroom showdown（法廷での対決）

- ☐ a theater usher（劇場の案内係）

- ☐ give him an overview of ~（彼に~の概観を伝える）

Check 3　Sentence

- ☐ Most processed foods contain additives.（ほとんどの加工食品には添加物が含まれている）

- ☐ The prime minister showed great zeal for addressing global warming.（首相は地球温暖化に取り組む強い熱意を示した）

- ☐ Tooth decay is caused by poor dental hygiene.（虫歯は歯の不衛生によって起こる）

- ☐ Anyone can have a lapse of memory.（誰でも度忘れをすることがある）

- ☐ The company is on a firm financial footing.（その会社は堅固な財政基盤に支えられている）

- ☐ There was a showdown between the top two teams in the American League.（アメリカン・リーグのトップ2チームの間の決戦があった）

- ☐ If you arrive late, an usher will lead you to your seat.（遅れて到着した場合は、案内係があなたを席へ案内する）

- ☐ He gave the board a brief overview of the plan.（彼は重役たちに計画の概要を簡潔に伝えた）

Day 39 》CD-B4
Quick Review
答えは左ページ下

- ☐ enhancement
- ☐ reservoir
- ☐ confiscation
- ☐ bachelor
- ☐ discouragement
- ☐ installment
- ☐ quarantine
- ☐ pledge
- ☐ broom
- ☐ gratuity
- ☐ speculator
- ☐ poultry
- ☐ bookkeeping
- ☐ descent
- ☐ archive
- ☐ consortium

Day 41　名詞27

Check 1　Listen)) CD-B6

☐ 0641
epicenter
/épəsèntər/
❶定義注意
Part 7

名 ❶(活動などの)**中心**、中核　❷震央；爆心地

☐ 0642
boulevard
/búləvàːrd/
Part 4

名 **大通り**(≒ avenue)

☐ 0643
helm
/hélm/
Part 5, 6

名 (the ～)**支配**、指揮(権)

☐ 0644
culprit
/kʌ́lprit/
Part 7

名 **犯人**、罪人(≒ offender, criminal)　❶「容疑者」は suspect

☐ 0645
prosecution
/pràsikjúːʃən/
Part 5, 6

名 ❶(the ～)(集合的に)**検察側**[当局](⇔ defense：被告側)　❷起訴[訴追](手続き)　❸実行、遂行
名 prosecutor：検察官
動 prosecute：❶～を(…で)起訴する(for . . .)　❷～を遂行する

☐ 0646
meltdown
/méltdàun/
❶定義注意
ビジネス問題

名 ❶(会社などの)**崩壊**；株価の大暴落　❷(原子炉の)炉心溶融

☐ 0647
confectionery
/kənfékʃənèri/
Part 7

名 (集合的に)**菓子類**、砂糖菓子(≒ sweets)

☐ 0648
glimmer
/glímər/
Part 7

名 ❶(希望などの)**わずかな兆し**、かすかな光　❷ちらちらする光
動 ちらちら光る

continued
▼

見出し語下の「⊕定義注意！」マークに気をつけてる？ このマークがついた単語の用法はTOEIC独特のもの。定義をしっかりチェック！

- ☐ 聞くだけモード Check 1
- ☐ しっかりモード Check 1 ▶ 2
- ☐ かんぺきモード Check 1 ▶ 2 ▶ 3

Check 2　Phrase

☐ the epicenter of fashion（ファッションの中心地）
☐ the epicenter of an earthquake（地震の震央）

☐ stroll along the boulevard（大通り沿いを散歩する）
☐ Sunset Boulevard（[ハリウッドの]サンセット大通り）

☐ take the helm of ~（~を支配する）
☐ be at the helm（指揮を執っている）

☐ the search for the culprit（その犯人の捜索）

☐ the prosecution witness（検察側証人）
☐ a criminal prosecution（刑事訴追）

☐ economic meltdown（経済崩壊）
☐ a meltdown accident（炉心溶融事故）

☐ a confectionery company（製菓会社）

☐ a glimmer of hope（わずかな希望の兆し）
☐ the glimmer of a candle（ろうそくのちらちらする光）

Check 3　Sentence

☐ New York is the epicenter of the global financial market.（ニューヨークは世界の金融市場の中心だ）

☐ There are many restaurants along the boulevard.（その大通り沿いには多くのレストランがある）

☐ He has been at the helm of the company for almost 20 years.（彼はほぼ20年間、その会社の指揮を執っている）

☐ Police have finally tracked down the culprit.（警察はついにその犯人を突き止めた）

☐ The prosecution demanded a three-year prison sentence for the accused.（検察側は被告人に懲役3年を求刑した）

☐ The whole world is facing global recession and financial meltdown.（全世界は世界的な景気後退と金融崩壊に直面している）

☐ Confectionery sales decreased 3 percent compared to the previous year.（菓子類の売り上げは前年と比較して3パーセント下がった）

☐ There is a glimmer of hope that the economy is recovering.（景気が回復しているわずかな希望の兆しがある）

continued
▼

Day 41

Check 1 Listen)) CD-B6

□ 0649
occupancy
/ákjupənsi/
Part 5, 6

名(土地・家屋などの)**居住**、占有；(ホテルの部屋の)使用
名occupant：(土地・家屋などの)占有者、居住者
動occupy：❶(場所など)を占める、占有する　❷(be occupied with)〜に従事している、〜で忙しい

□ 0650
tribute
/tríbju:t/
Part 4

名(〜への)**尊敬**[感謝、称賛]**の印**；賛辞(to 〜)

□ 0651
proponent
/prəpóunənt/
Part 5, 6

名(〜の)**支持者**、賛成者(of 〜)(⇔opponent：反対者)

□ 0652
inequality
/ìnikwáləti/
Part 5, 6

名**不平等**、不均衡(⇔equality)

□ 0653
detector
/ditéktər/
Part 5, 6

名**探知器**、検出器
名detection：探知；発見
名detective：刑事；探偵
動detect：〜を感知[探知]する；〜を見つける

□ 0654
acumen
/əkjú:mən/
Part 7

名**洞察力**、眼識、明敏

□ 0655
faction
/fǽkʃən/
Part 5, 6

名**派閥**、党派
形factional：派閥[党派]の；党派的な

□ 0656
repertoire
/répərtwà:r/
❶発音注意
Part 7

名**レパートリー**、演奏曲目、上演目録

Day 40)) CD-B5
Quick Review
答えは右ページ下

□ 省略形	□ 水筒	□ 添加物	□ 基盤
□ 海峡	□ 無数	□ 熱意	□ 決定的対決
□ 訴訟	□ 降水量	□ 衛生	□ 案内係
□ 反応	□ 入り口	□ ちょっとした誤り	□ 概観

Check 2　Phrase

- an occupancy rate（居住率；[ホテルの部屋の]利用率）
- take occupancy of ~（~を占有する；~に入居する）

- pay tribute to ~（~に敬意を表す、~に賛辞を贈る）
- as a tribute to ~（~への感謝の印として）

- a proponent of tax cuts（減税の支持者）

- prevent racial inequality（人種的不平等を防ぐ）
- inequality between men and women（男女間の不平等）

- a metal detector（金属探知器）
- a lie detector（うそ発見器）

- political acumen（政治的洞察力）
- business acumen（商才）

- the right-wing faction of the party（その政党の右派）

- have a large repertoire（レパートリーが広い）

Check 3　Sentence

- The occupancy rate of the condominium is about 60 percent.（その分譲マンションの居住率は約60パーセントだ）

- I would like to pay tribute to his remarkable contribution to the project.（プロジェクトへの彼の顕著な貢献に敬意を表したいと思います）

- She is one of the leading proponents of early childhood education.（彼女は早期幼児教育の主要な支持者の1人だ）

- In Japan, income inequality between the rich and the poor is increasing.（日本では、貧富の所得格差が増大している）

- The installation of smoke detectors is required by law.（煙探知器の設置が法律で義務づけられている）

- The entrepreneur has excellent business acumen.（その起業家は素晴らしい商才を持っている）

- He is the leader of the largest faction of the Liberal Democratic Party.（彼は自由民主党の最大派閥の領袖だ）

- The ballet company has more than 50 ballets in its repertoire.（そのバレエ団は50以上のバレエのレパートリーがある）

Day 40　CD-B5
Quick Review
答えは左ページ下

- abbreviation
- strait
- litigation
- feedback
- canteen
- myriad
- precipitation
- gateway
- additive
- zeal
- hygiene
- lapse
- footing
- showdown
- usher
- overview

Day 42　名詞28

Check 1　Listen 》CD-B7

☐ 0657
stratum
/strǽtəm/
Part 5, 6

名 ❶(社会的な)**階層**、階級　❷層；地層　❸複数形はstrataとstratumsの2つある

☐ 0658
dignitary
/dígnətèri/
Part 5, 6

名 **高官**、高位の人

☐ 0659
centerpiece
/séntərpìːs/
Part 7

名 (the ~)(政策などの)**目玉**、最も重要なもの(of ~)

☐ 0660
forefront
/fɔ́ːrfrʌ̀nt/
Part 7

名 (the ~)**最前線**；最先端

☐ 0661
fingerprint
/fíŋgərprìnt/
Part 5, 6

名 (通例~s)**指紋**
動 ~の指紋を採る

☐ 0662
novice
/nάvis/
Part 7

名 (~の)**初心者**、素人(at ~)(≒beginner)

☐ 0663
start-up
/stάːrtʌ̀p/
ビジネス問題

名 **新興[ベンチャー]企業**
形 新進の、活動を始めたばかりの
動 start up：❶現れる、生じる　❷~を始める、起こす

☐ 0664
keynote
/kíːnòut/
Part 4

名 (政策などの)**基本方針**、基調
動 (会議など)で基調演説を行う

continued
▼

なかなか覚えられないときこそ「音読」を！面倒くさがっていては、いつになっても語彙は身につかない。口を積極的に動かそう！

☐ 聞くだけモード　Check 1
☐ しっかりモード　Check 1 ▶ 2
☐ かんぺきモード　Check 1 ▶ 2 ▶ 3

Check 2　Phrase

☐ **strata** of American society（アメリカ社会の階層）
☐ a **stratum** of the Jurassic period（ジュラ紀の地層）

☐ a government **dignitary**（政府高官）

☐ the **centerpiece** of the economic stimulus package（経済刺激政策の目玉）

☐ be in [at] the **forefront** of ~（〜の最前線[最先端]にいる）

☐ take his **fingerprints**（彼の指紋を採る）

☐ a **novice** at golf ＝ a **novice** golfer（ゴルフの初心者）

☐ an Internet **start-up**（インターネット関連の新興企業）

☐ a **keynote** speech [address]（基本方針演説、基調演説）

Check 3　Sentence

☐ Domestic violence is a problem in every **stratum** of society.（家庭内暴力は社会のすべての階層で問題になっている）

☐ About 180 foreign **dignitaries** attended the inaugural ceremony.（約180カ国の高官がその就任式に出席した）

☐ Tax cuts are the **centerpiece** of the president's plan to revive the economy.（減税が大統領の経済復興計画の目玉だ）

☐ The university is at the **forefront** of nanotechnology research.（その大学はナノテクノロジー研究の最先端にいる）

☐ DNA can be extracted from **fingerprints**.（DNAは指紋から抽出できる）

☐ This motorcycle is too powerful for a **novice** to control.（このオートバイはパワーがあり過ぎて初心者には制御できない）

☐ Almost 60 percent of **start-ups** fail within their first three years.（新興企業のほぼ60パーセントは最初の3年以内に倒産する）

☐ Mr. Palmer will deliver a **keynote** address after the opening ceremony.（開会式の後でパーマー氏が基調演説をする予定だ）

continued ▼

Day 42

Check 1 Listen))) CD-B7

0665 reasoning /ríːzəniŋ/ Part 5, 6
- 名 論法；推論
- 名 reason：❶(〜の)理由、訳(for 〜) ❷道理、理屈
- 動 reason：〜だと判断[推測、推論]する
- 形 reasonable：❶理にかなった ❷(値段が)手ごろな

0666 philanthropy /filǽnθrəpi/ Part 7
- 名 **慈善活動**[事業] (≒ charity)

0667 oversight /óuvərsàit/ Part 7
- 名 ❶**見落とし**、ミス (≒ mistake) ❷監視、監督 (≒ supervision)

0668 turmoil /tə́ːrmɔil/ Part 5, 6
- 名 **混乱**、騒動 (≒ tumult)

0669 latitude /lǽtətjùːd/ Part 5, 6
- 名 **緯度** ◆「経度」は longitude

0670 fable /féibl/ Part 5, 6
- 名 ❶**寓話** ❷作り話

0671 asthma /ǽzmə/ ❶発音注意 Part 4
- 名 **ぜん息**

0672 degradation /dègrədéiʃən/ Part 7
- 名 (品質などの)**悪化**、低下、劣化
- 動 degrade：❶〜の体面を傷つける ❷(質など)を落とす、減らす

Day 41))) CD-B6
Quick Review
答えは右ページ下

- □ 中心
- □ 大通り
- □ 支配
- □ 犯人
- □ 検察側
- □ 崩壊
- □ 菓子類
- □ わずかな兆し
- □ 居住
- □ 尊敬の印
- □ 支持者
- □ 不平等
- □ 探知器
- □ 洞察力
- □ 派閥
- □ レパートリー

Check 2 Phrase

- the reasoning behind ~(〜の背後にある論法)
- logical reasoning(論理的な推論)

- corporate philanthropy(企業による慈善活動)

- a simple oversight(単純な見落とし)
- an oversight committee(監視委員会)

- be in turmoil(混乱状態にある)
- political turmoil(政治的混乱)

- latitude 40 degrees north [south] = north [south] latitude 40 degrees(北[南]緯40度)

- the fable of the rabbit and the turtle(ウサギとカメの寓話)
- a mere fable(単なる作り話)

- suffer from [have] asthma(ぜん息を患う)
- an asthma attack(ぜん息の発作)

- environmental degradation(環境の悪化)

Check 3 Sentence

- The reasoning behind the court's decision is very clear.(裁判所の判決の背後にある論法は非常に明快だ)

- The company has been actively involved in philanthropy.(その会社は慈善活動に積極的に参加してきている)

- A small oversight can lead to big problems.(小さなミスが大問題へとつながることもある)

- The world is in economic turmoil.(世界は経済的混乱状態にある)

- London is higher in latitude than Tokyo.(ロンドンは東京よりも高緯度に位置する)

- Aesop's Fables are among the most famous fables.(イソップ物語は最も有名な寓話の1つだ)

- Traffic exhaust can cause asthma.(車の排気ガスがぜん息を起こすこともある)

- The degradation of water quality is a major problem in the city.(水質の悪化がその街で大きな問題となっている)

Day 41 》CD-B6
Quick Review
答えは左ページ下

- epicenter
- boulevard
- helm
- culprit
- prosecution
- meltdown
- confectionery
- glimmer
- occupancy
- tribute
- proponent
- inequality
- detector
- acumen
- faction
- repertoire

Day 43　名詞29

Check 1　Listen 》CD-B8

☐ 0673
defiance
/difáiəns/
Part 7

名 (〜の)**無視**、軽蔑(of 〜)
動 defy：❶(物事が)(解決・理解など)を拒む、受け入れない　❷(人が)〜を無視する、物ともしない
形 defiant：挑戦[反抗]的な、けんか腰の

☐ 0674
proprietor
/prəpráiətər/
ビジネス問題

名 (企業などの)**経営者**、所有者(≒owner)

☐ 0675
tribunal
/traibjúːnl/
Part 5, 6

名 (特定の問題の裁定を行う)**裁判所**、法廷(≒court)

☐ 0676
proliferation
/prəlìfəréiʃən/
Part 7

名 (〜の)**急増**、拡散(of 〜)
動 proliferate：急増する

☐ 0677
stagnation
/stæɡnéiʃən/
ビジネス問題

名 **停滞**、沈滞；不景気、不況
動 stagnate：沈滞する
形 stagnant：停滞[沈滞]した

☐ 0678
moratorium
/mɔ̀ːrətɔ́ːriəm/
Part 5, 6

名 ❶(〜の)**一時停止**[延期](on 〜)　❷(〜の)支払い猶予(期間)(on 〜)　❸複数形はmoratoriaとmoratoriumsの2つある

☐ 0679
gala
/ɡéilə/
Part 4

名 **祝祭**、お祭り

☐ 0680
catastrophe
/kətǽstrəfi/
Part 7

名 ❶**大惨事**、大災害　❷破滅、破局
形 catastrophic：壊滅的な

continued
▼

語彙を見て、発音やアクセントが正確に分かる？自信がない人は「聞く・音読する」の練習をもっと増やしていこう。

☐ 聞くだけモード　Check 1
☐ しっかりモード　Check 1 ▶ 2
☐ かんぺきモード　Check 1 ▶ 2 ▶ 3

Check 2　Phrase

☐ in defiance of ～(～を無視して)
☐ a look of defiance(軽蔑のまなざし)

☐ a hotel proprietor(ホテル経営者)

☐ a war crimes tribunal(戦争犯罪裁判所)

☐ the proliferation of small businesses(小規模企業の急増)
☐ the proliferation of nuclear weapons(核兵器の拡散)

☐ economic stagnation(経済停滞)
☐ fall into stagnation(不況に陥る)

☐ a moratorium on commercial whaling(商業捕鯨の一時停止)
☐ a moratorium on interest payments(金利の支払い猶予)

☐ a gala day(祝日、祭日)
☐ a gala dress(晴れ着)

☐ the catastrophe of World War II(第2次世界大戦の大惨事)
☐ move toward catastrophe(破滅へと向かう)

Check 3　Sentence

☐ Many Mexicans cross the border in defiance of US law.(多くのメキシコ人がアメリカの法律を無視して国境を越えている)

☐ He is the proprietor of a real estate company.(彼は不動産会社の経営者だ)

☐ The Supreme Court is the highest tribunal in the nation.(最高裁判所は国内における最高位の法廷だ)

☐ The past few years have seen the proliferation of human rights NGOs.(この数年で人権NGOの急増が見られた)

☐ The stagnation of household consumption is due to increased uncertainty about the future.(家計消費の停滞は未来に関する不確実性が高まっているためだ)

☐ The government announced a moratorium on nuclear tests.(政府は核実験の一時停止を発表した)

☐ Nearly 400 guests enjoyed a gala dinner at the hotel.(400人近い来賓がそのホテルでの祝賀ディナーを楽しんだ)

☐ The Black Death was one of the most serious catastrophes in human history.(黒死病は人類史で最も深刻な惨事の1つだった)

CHAPTER 1
CHAPTER 2
CHAPTER 3
CHAPTER 4
CHAPTER 5
CHAPTER 6
CHAPTER 7
CHAPTER 8
CHAPTER 9

continued
▼

Day 43

Check 1　Listen))) CD-B8

0681
downpour
/dáunpɔ̀:r/
Part 7

名 **豪雨**、土砂降り

0682
landlord
/lǽndlɔ̀:rd/
Part 5, 6

名 **家主**、地主 (⇔tenant：借家[借地]人)

0683
overture
/óuvərtʃər/
❶定義注意
Part 7

名 ❶(通例～s)(交渉を始めるための) **申し入れ**、提案、打診　❷(オペラなどの)序曲 (to ～)

0684
reviewer
/rivjú:ər/
Part 7

名 **評論**[批評]**家** (≒ critic, pundit)
名 review：❶再調査　❷復習　❸批評
動 review：❶～を再調査[検討]する　❷～を復習する　❸～を批評する

0685
fate
/féit/
Part 5, 6

名 **運命**、運 (≒ destiny, doom)
名 fatality：❶不慮の死、死亡者(数)　❷致死性
形 fated：(～するように)運命づけられた (to do)
形 fateful：運命を決する、重大な
形 fatal：致命的な

0686
migration
/maigréiʃən/
Part 7

名 (人・動物の) **移動**　➕ 人の場合、通例国内での「移動、移住」を表す。immigrationは他国への「移住」
名 migrant：❶渡り鳥　❷出稼ぎ[季節]労働者
動 migrate：❶(動物が)移動する　❷(人が)移住する

0687
hassle
/hǽsl/
Part 4

名 **面倒**、煩わしいこと　➕ hustle(ハッスルする)と混同しないように注意
動 ❶～を悩ます、苦しめる　❷(hassle A to doで)Aに～するようにせがむ

0688
anecdote
/ǽnikdòut/
Part 5, 6

名 **逸話**、秘話

Day 42))) CD-B7
Quick Review
答えは右ページ下

□ 階層　　　□ 指紋　　　□ 論法　　　□ 緯度
□ 高官　　　□ 初心者　　□ 慈善活動　□ 寓話
□ 目玉　　　□ 新興企業　□ 見落とし　□ ぜん息
□ 最前線　　□ 基本方針　□ 混乱　　　□ 悪化

Check 2 Phrase

- [ ] a localized downpour（集中豪雨）

- [ ] pay rent to a landlord（家主に家賃を払う）

- [ ] make overtures to ～（～に交渉を申し入れる）
- [ ] the overture to "The Magic Flute"（『魔笛』の序曲）

- [ ] a book reviewer（書評家）

- [ ] suffer [meet] the same fate as ～（～と同じ運命に遭う）
- [ ] decide his fate（彼の運命を決める）

- [ ] seasonal migration（季節による移動）
- [ ] the migration of swans（ハクチョウの渡り）

- [ ] avoid the hassle of doing ～（～する面倒を避ける）

- [ ] an amusing anecdote about ～（～に関する面白い逸話）

Check 3 Sentence

- [ ] The downpour is expected to continue through tonight.（今晩中、豪雨が続く見込みだ）

- [ ] The landlord demanded three months security deposit.（家主は3カ月の敷金を要求した）

- [ ] Israel made peace overtures to the Arab states.（イスラエルはアラブ諸国に和平交渉を打診した）

- [ ] The film was received favorably by many reviewers.（その映画は多くの評論家から好評を得た）

- [ ] Everyone has the right to decide his or her own fate.（誰にも自分自身の運命を決める権利がある）

- [ ] There is a continuous migration of rural people into urban areas.（農村部の人々の都市部への移動が続いている）

- [ ] I don't want the hassle of moving to a new place anymore.（新しい所へ引っ越す面倒はもうごめんだ）

- [ ] He has numerous anecdotes about famous people.（彼は有名人に関する逸話をたくさん知っている）

Day 42 ≫ CD-B7
Quick Review
答えは左ページ下

- [ ] stratum
- [ ] dignitary
- [ ] centerpiece
- [ ] forefront
- [ ] fingerprint
- [ ] novice
- [ ] start-up
- [ ] keynote
- [ ] reasoning
- [ ] philanthropy
- [ ] oversight
- [ ] turmoil
- [ ] latitude
- [ ] fable
- [ ] asthma
- [ ] degradation

CHAPTER 1
CHAPTER 2
CHAPTER 3
CHAPTER 4
CHAPTER 5
CHAPTER 6
CHAPTER 7
CHAPTER 8
CHAPTER 9

Day 44　名詞30

Check 1　Listen))) CD-B9

☐ 0689
infringement
/infrínd͡ʒmənt/
Part 7

名 ❶(権利などの)**侵害**(of [on] ~)　❷(法律などの)違反(of ~)
動 infringe：❶(権利など)を侵害する、(法律など)に違反する　❷(infringe on [upon]で)~を侵害する

☐ 0690
credibility
/krèdəbíləti/
Part 5, 6

名 **信用**[信頼](性)(≒reliability)
形 credible：信用[信頼]できる

☐ 0691
liquidation
/lìkwidéiʃən/
ビジネス問題

名 ❶(会社などの)**破産**(≒bankruptcy)　❷(負債などの)清算、弁済
動 liquidate：❶(倒産会社など)を解散[整理]する　❷(負債など)を清算[弁済]する

☐ 0692
redundancy
/ridʌ́ndənsi/
ビジネス問題

名 ❶**解雇**(≒layoff)；余剰人員　❷余分
形 redundant：❶余分な　❷解雇された

☐ 0693
upside
/ʌ́psàid/
Part 2, 3

名 (通例悪い状況の中での)**よい面**、利点(⇔downside)

☐ 0694
fund-raising
/fʌ́ndrèiziŋ/
Part 4

名 (政治・慈善団体の)**資金集め**、資金調達、募金
名 fund-raiser：❶資金集めのパーティー　❷資金調達者
動 fund-raise：(資金)を調達する

☐ 0695
courtyard
/kɔ́ːrtjɑ̀ːrd/
Part 4

名 (塀・建物で囲まれた)**中庭**

☐ 0696
fabrication
/fæbrikéiʃən/
Part 5, 6

名 **うそ**、作り話(≒lie)
動 fabricate：(うそなど)を作り上げる、でっち上げる

continued
▼

今日でChapter 4は最後！ 時間に余裕があったら、章末のReviewにも挑戦しておこう。忘れてしまった単語も結構あるのでは?!

- ☐ 聞くだけモード　Check 1
- ☐ しっかりモード　Check 1 ▶ 2
- ☐ かんぺきモード　Check 1 ▶ 2 ▶ 3

Check 2　Phrase

☐ **infringement** of a patent（特許権の侵害）
☐ **infringement** of traffic regulations（交通規則の違反）

☐ gain [lose] **credibility**（信用を得る[失う]）
☐ the **credibility** of a witness's testimony（目撃者の証言の信頼性）

☐ go into **liquidation**（破産する）
☐ **liquidation** of debts（借金の清算）

☐ voluntary **redundancy**（希望退職）
☐ labor **redundancy**（過剰雇用）

☐ have **upsides** and downsides（よい面も悪い面もある）

☐ a **fund-raising** event（資金集めのためのイベント）

☐ a paved **courtyard**（舗装された中庭）

☐ a complete **fabrication**（全くの作り話）

Check 3　Sentence

☐ Copyright **infringement** is severely punished.（著作権の侵害は厳しく処罰される）

☐ The prime minister has lost **credibility** among the people.（首相は国民の信用を失ってしまっている）

☐ The insurance company went into **liquidation** with debts of $2 billion.（その保険会社は20億ドルの負債を抱えて破産した）

☐ The automaker announced the **redundancies** of 3,000 staff.（その自動車メーカーは3000人の社員の解雇を発表した）

☐ Is there any **upside** in starting a new business when the economy is shrinking?（経済が縮小しているのに新しい事業を始める利点などあるだろうか?）

☐ The annual **fund-raising** campaign will take place on December 1.（毎年恒例の募金運動が12月1日に行われる予定だ）

☐ All of the guest rooms face a **courtyard**.（すべての客室は中庭に面している）

☐ Her story turned out to be a **fabrication**.（彼女の話はうそであることが分かった）

continued ▼

Day 44

Check 1 Listen)) CD-B9

□ 0697 **outlay**
/áutlèi/
ビジネス問題

名 (〜への) **支出**、経費 (on [for] 〜) (≒ expenditure, spending, cost, expense)

□ 0698 **buffet**
/bəféi/
❶発音注意
Part 4

名 **立食**、ビュッフェ、バイキング

□ 0699 **flagship**
/flǽgʃìp/
❶定義注意
ビジネス問題

名 ❶(会社の) **主力製品**、最も重要なもの ❷旗艦

□ 0700 **stool**
/stúːl/
Part 1

名 ❶**腰掛け**、スツール ❶ひじ掛けや背もたれのないいすを指す ❷踏み台

□ 0701 **feat**
/fíːt/
Part 7

名 **偉業**、功績；離れ技、妙技

□ 0702 **goodwill**
/gúdwíl/
ビジネス問題

名 ❶(店などの) **信用**、評判、のれん ❷善意；親善

□ 0703 **debacle**
/deibáːkl/
❶発音注意
ビジネス問題

名 **完全な失敗**、大失敗

□ 0704 **rarity**
/réərəti/
Part 7

名 **まれな**[珍しい]**こと**[物]
形 rare：❶まれな、珍しい ❷(肉が)生焼け[レア]の
副 rarely：めったに[たまにしか]〜しない

Day 43)) CD-B8
Quick Review
答えは右ページ下

- □ 無視
- □ 経営者
- □ 裁判所
- □ 急増
- □ 停滞
- □ 一時停止
- □ 祝祭
- □ 大惨事
- □ 豪雨
- □ 家主
- □ 申し入れ
- □ 評論家
- □ 運命
- □ 移動
- □ 面倒
- □ 逸話

Check 2　Phrase

- ☐ initial outlay（当初支出、初期経費）
- ☐ outlay on [for] education（教育費）

- ☐ a buffet party（立食パーティー）
- ☐ an all-you-can-eat buffet（食べ放題のバイキング）

- ☐ the flagship of Apple's desktop computers（アップル社のデスクトップコンピューターの主力製品）
- ☐ the company's flagship store（その会社の旗艦店）

- ☐ a piano stool（ピアノ用のいす）
- ☐ a three-legged stool（脚が3つついている腰掛け）

- ☐ accomplish [achieve] a feat（偉業を達成する）
- ☐ circus feats（サーカスの離れ技）

- ☐ customer goodwill（顧客の信用）
- ☐ as a gesture of goodwill（善意を表して）

- ☐ end in a debacle（完全な失敗に終わる）
- ☐ an election debacle（選挙での大敗）

- ☐ be something of a rarity（かなり珍しい）
- ☐ rarity value（希少価値）

Check 3　Sentence

- ☐ With any business there is an initial outlay to get started.（いかなる事業でも、始めるには初期経費がある）

- ☐ The hotel offers a complimentary breakfast buffet.（そのホテルでは無料のセルフサービス式朝食を提供している）

- ☐ Prius is one of the flagships of Toyota's range.（プリウスはトヨタ社製品の主力車種の1つだ）

- ☐ The woman is sitting on a stool.（女性は腰掛けに座っている）

- ☐ The space station is a remarkable feat of engineering.（宇宙ステーションは工学技術の目覚ましい偉業だ）

- ☐ Customer goodwill is one of the business's greatest assets.（顧客の信用は企業の最も重要な財産の1つだ）

- ☐ The company's bankruptcy was one of the biggest business debacles in US history.（その会社の倒産はアメリカ史で最大の事業の失敗の1つだった）

- ☐ Snow is a rarity in London.（雪はロンドンではめったに降らない）

Day 43 》CD-B8
Quick Review
答えは左ページ下

- ☐ defiance
- ☐ proprietor
- ☐ tribunal
- ☐ proliferation
- ☐ stagnation
- ☐ moratorium
- ☐ gala
- ☐ catastrophe
- ☐ downpour
- ☐ landlord
- ☐ overture
- ☐ reviewer
- ☐ fate
- ☐ migration
- ☐ hassle
- ☐ anecdote

Chapter 4 Review

左ページの(1)～(20)の名詞の同意・類義語（≒）、反意・反対語（⇔）を右ページのA～Tから選び、カッコの中に答えを書き込もう。意味が分からないときは、見出し番号を参照して復習しておこう（答えは右ページ下）。

- □ (1) discrepancy (0465) ≒は？ (   )
- □ (2) outing (0472) ≒は？ (   )
- □ (3) wholesaler (0483) ⇔は？ (   )
- □ (4) accountability (0503) ≒は？ (   )
- □ (5) hallway (0509) ≒は？ (   )
- □ (6) mandate (0523) ≒は？ (   )
- □ (7) grandeur (0531) ≒は？ (   )
- □ (8) appraisal (0537) ≒は？ (   )
- □ (9) benchmark (0559) ≒は？ (   )
- □ (10) hub (0571) ≒は？ (   )
- □ (11) lag (0581) ≒は？ (   )
- □ (12) annuity (0599) ≒は？ (   )
- □ (13) adversary (0604) ≒は？ (   )
- □ (14) pledge (0616) ≒は？ (   )
- □ (15) litigation (0627) ≒は？ (   )
- □ (16) prosecution (0645) ⇔は？ (   )
- □ (17) novice (0662) ≒は？ (   )
- □ (18) philanthropy (0666) ≒は？ (   )
- □ (19) landlord (0682) ⇔は？ (   )
- □ (20) liquidation (0691) ≒は？ (   )

A. defense
B. difference
C. promise
D. standard
E. responsibility
F. tenant
G. delay
H. magnificence
I. opponent
J. retailer
K. bankruptcy
L. evaluation
M. corridor
N. beginner
O. center
P. pension
Q. excursion
R. charity
S. authority
T. lawsuit

【解答】 (1) B (2) Q (3) J (4) E (5) M (6) S (7) H (8) L (9) D (10) O (11) G (12) P (13) I (14) C (15) T (16) A (17) N (18) R (19) F (20) K

CHAPTER 5
動詞：必修112

Chapter 5 では、TOEIC 必修の動詞112を見ていきます。ところで、学習が単調になってきていませんか？「990点を攻略する！」日を目指して、着々と語彙力をつけていきましょう。

TOEIC的格言

Time and tide wait for no man.

歳月人を待たず。
[直訳] 時と潮は人を待たない。

Day 45【動詞8】
▶ 206
Day 46【動詞9】
▶ 210
Day 47【動詞10】
▶ 214
Day 48【動詞11】
▶ 218
Day 49【動詞12】
▶ 222
Day 50【動詞13】
▶ 226
Day 51【動詞14】
▶ 230
Chapter 5 Review
▶ 234

Day 45　動詞8

Check 1　Listen)) CD-B10

0705
scrutinize
/skrúːtənàiz/
Part 7

動 **〜を綿密に調べる**、吟味する(≒examine, inspect)
名scrutiny：綿密[精密]な調査[検査]

0706
disconnect
/dìskənékt/
Part 2, 3

動 ❶(ガス・電気など)**の供給を止める**　❷〜を(…から)分離する(from . . .)(⇔connect)

0707
prosper
/prάspər/
Part 7

動 **繁栄[繁盛]する**(≒thrive, flourish)；成功する(≒succeed)
名prosperity：(特に財政的な)繁栄、繁盛
形prosperous：繁栄している；(経済的に)成功している

0708
unfold
/ʌnfóuld/
Part 5, 6

動 ❶(折り畳んだ紙など)**を広げる**、開く(⇔fold：〜を折り畳む)　❷(物語などが)展開する(≒develop)

0709
bounce
/báuns/
Part 1

動 ❶**〜を弾ませる**、バウンドさせる　❷跳ね返る、バウンドする(≒rebound)
名 ❶バウンド、跳ね返り　❷活力、元気

0710
necessitate
/nəsésətèit/
Part 5, 6

動 ❶**〜を必要とする**　❷(necessitate doingで)〜することを必要とする
形necessary：(〜のために)必要な、なくてはならない(for 〜)
副necessarily：(否定文で)必ずしも〜ない

0711
undermine
/ʌ̀ndərmáin/
Part 5, 6

動 **〜を徐々に衰えさせる**、むしばむ

0712
offset
/ɔ̀fsét/
Part 5, 6

動 **〜を相殺する**、埋め合わせる(≒compensate for, make up for)

continued
▼

Chapter 5では、7日をかけて必修動詞112をチェック。まずはCDでチャンツを聞いて、単語を「耳」からインプット！

□ 聞くだけモード　Check 1
□ しっかりモード　Check 1 ▶ 2
□ かんぺきモード　Check 1 ▶ 2 ▶ 3

Check 2　Phrase

□ scrutinize the document（書類を綿密に調べる）

□ disconnect electricity [gas, water]（電気[ガス,水道]の供給を止める）
□ disconnect the hose from the faucet（ホースを蛇口から外す）

□ prosper in business（事業に成功する）

□ unfold a letter（手紙を開く）
□ as the story unfolds（物語が展開するにつれて）

□ bounce the ball against the wall（ボールを壁に当てて跳ね返らせる）
□ bounce off the wall（壁に当たって跳ね返る）

□ necessitate further investigation（さらなる調査を必要とする）
□ necessitate closing the road（[工事などが]道路の閉鎖を必要とする）

□ undermine the economy（経済を徐々に衰えさせる）
□ undermine physical health（体の健康をむしばむ）

□ offset the losses（[利益などが]損失を埋め合わせる）

Check 3　Sentence

□ Police scrutinized the crime scene.（警察は犯罪現場を綿密に調べた）

□ My cellphone was disconnected because I didn't pay the bill.（請求書の支払いをしなかったので、私の携帯電話は止められてしまった）

□ The video game industry is prospering despite the economic crisis.（経済危機にもかかわらず、テレビゲーム業界はうまくいっている）

□ He unfolded a map on the desk.（彼は机の上に地図を広げた）

□ The boy is bouncing a basketball.（男の子はバスケットボールをバウンドさせている）

□ An economic downturn necessitates budget cuts.（景気の低迷で予算の削減が必要になっている）

□ Bank nationalization would undermine confidence in the financial system.（銀行の国有化は金融システムへの信頼を損ねるだろう）

□ The decline in domestic production was offset by the increase in overseas production.（国内生産の減少は海外生産の増加によって相殺された）

continued
▼

Day 45

Check 1　Listen)) CD-B10

☐ 0713
commemorate
/kəmémərèit/
Part 4

動 **～を記念する**、祝う(≒celebrate)
名commemoration：❶記念(すること)　❷記念式[祭、式典]；記念物
形commemorative：記念の、記念となる

☐ 0714
simulate
/símjulèit/
Part 4

動 **～の模擬実験をする**、シミュレーションをする
名simulation：模擬実験、シミュレーション

☐ 0715
administer
/ædmínistər/
Part 5, 6

動 ❶**(会社・学校など)を管理[経営]する**　❷(国など)を治める　❸(処罰など)を執行する
名administration：❶管理、経営　❷行政
名administrator：管理者、経営者
形administrative：❶管理の、経営上の　❷行政上の

☐ 0716
weave
/wíːv/
Part 1

動 **～を編む**、織る
名 織り方、編み方

☐ 0717
hamper
/hæmpər/
Part 5, 6

動 **～を妨げる**、妨害する(≒prevent, hinder)
名 ❶洗濯かご　❷買い物かご

☐ 0718
shred
/ʃréd/
Part 7

動 **～を細かく切る[刻む]**、シュレッダーにかける
名 ❶切れ端、断片　❷(a shred of ～で)わずかな～

☐ 0719
convene
/kənvíːn/
Part 7

動 ❶**～を招集する**(≒summon)　❷招集される

☐ 0720
relinquish
/rilíŋkwiʃ/
Part 7

動 ❶**(権利など)を放棄する**、手放す　❷～を(…に)引き渡す、譲渡する(to ...)

Day 44)) CD-B9
Quick Review
答えは右ページ下

☐ 侵害　☐ よい面　☐ 支出　☐ 偉業
☐ 信用　☐ 資金集め　☐ 立食　☐ 信用
☐ 破産　☐ 中庭　☐ 主力製品　☐ 完全な失敗
☐ 解雇　☐ うそ　☐ 腰掛け　☐ まれなこと

Check 2　Phrase

- ☐ a stamp commemorating the landing on the moon（月面着陸を記念した切手）

- ☐ simulate an earthquake（地震の模擬実験をする）
- ☐ simulate an accident（事故のシミュレーションをする）

- ☐ administer a company（会社を経営する）
- ☐ administer a country（国を治める）

- ☐ weave a basket（かごを編む）
- ☐ weave a rug（じゅうたんを織る）

- ☐ hamper the progress of ～（～の進行を妨げる）

- ☐ shredded carrot（ニンジンのみじん切り）
- ☐ shred the document（その書類をシュレッダーにかける）

- ☐ convene a board（委員会を招集する）
- ☐ convene once a month（[委員会などが]月に1度招集される）

- ☐ relinquish a claim（要求を放棄する）
- ☐ relinquish custody to ～（養育権を～に譲る）

Check 3　Sentence

- ☐ In 2008, we commemorated the 60th anniversary of the Universal Declaration of Human Rights.（2008年に、私たちは世界人権宣言60周年を記念した）

- ☐ The machine can simulate different road conditions.（その機械はさまざまな道路状況のシミュレーションをすることができる）

- ☐ The personnel department administers benefit programs for employees.（人事部は従業員向けの福利プログラムを管理している）

- ☐ The woman is weaving cloth.（女性は布を織っている）

- ☐ The rescue operation was hampered by bad weather.（救出作業は悪天候に妨げられた）

- ☐ Shred the cheese and sprinkle it over the potatoes.（チーズを細かく刻んで、ジャガイモの上にふりかける）➕レシピの表現

- ☐ The meeting was convened to discuss the current economic crisis.（現在の経済危機について話し合うために会議が招集された）

- ☐ He was forced to relinquish his position as CEO due to illness.（彼は病気のためCEOの職を辞めざるを得なかった）

Day 44　CD-B9
Quick Review
答えは左ページ下

- ☐ infringement
- ☐ credibility
- ☐ liquidation
- ☐ redundancy
- ☐ upside
- ☐ fund-raising
- ☐ courtyard
- ☐ fabrication
- ☐ outlay
- ☐ buffet
- ☐ flagship
- ☐ stool
- ☐ feat
- ☐ goodwill
- ☐ debacle
- ☐ rarity

CHAPTER 1
CHAPTER 2
CHAPTER 3
CHAPTER 4
CHAPTER 5
CHAPTER 6
CHAPTER 7
CHAPTER 8
CHAPTER 9

Day 46 動詞9

Check 1　Listen 》CD-B11

□ 0721
abolish
/əbáliʃ/
Part 5, 6

動 (制度など)**を廃止**[撤廃]**する**
名 abolition：(制度などの)廃止、撤廃(of ～)

□ 0722
withstand
/wiðstǽnd/
Part 5, 6

動 **～によく耐える**、持ちこたえる、抵抗する(≒ bear)

□ 0723
nurture
/nə́ːrtʃər/
Part 5, 6

動 **～を育てる**、養育する
名 養育

□ 0724
hinder
/híndər/
Part 5, 6

動 **～を妨げる**(≒ prevent, hamper)
名 hindrance：❶(～の)妨害、邪魔(to ～)　❷(～の)邪魔になる物[人] (to ～)

□ 0725
confer
/kənfə́ːr/
Part 5, 6

動 ❶(～と／…について)**話し合う**、協議する(with ～/ about [on] …)　❷(資格・学位など)を(…に)与える、贈る(on [upon] …)

□ 0726
recollect
/rèkəlékt/
Part 7

動 ❶**～を思い出す**(≒ remember, recall)　❷(recollect doing で)～したことを思い出す
名 recollection：❶思い出　❷記憶(力)

□ 0727
subsidize
/sʌ́bsədàiz/
ビジネス問題

動 **～に補助**[助成]**金を与える**
名 subsidy：補助[助成]金

□ 0728
overhaul
/òuvərhɔ́ːl/
Part 5, 6

動 ❶**～を分解点検**[修理]**する**　❷～を徹底的に見直す、改める
名 (/óuvərhɔ̀ːl/)分解点検[修理]；総点検

continued
▼

同じ語でも、品詞によって発音やアクセントの違いがあるのは知ってる？ 発音記号にも注意しながら学習しよう。

☐ 聞くだけモード　Check 1
☐ しっかりモード　Check 1 ▶ 2
☐ かんぺきモード　Check 1 ▶ 2 ▶ 3

Check 2　　Phrase

☐ abolish racial discrimination（人種差別を廃止する）

☐ withstand storms（暴風に耐える）
☐ withstand the test of time（時の試練に耐える、長く記憶にとどまる）

☐ nurture one's child（子どもを養育する）

☐ hinder economic recovery（経済回復を妨げる）

☐ confer with him about the plan（彼とその計画について話し合う）
☐ confer degrees on graduates（学位を卒業生に与える）

☐ recollect his name（彼の名前を思い出す）
☐ recollect seeing her（彼女に会ったことを思い出す）

☐ subsidize solar panel installation（ソーラーパネルの設置に補助金を与える）

☐ overhaul the engine（エンジンを分解点検する）
☐ overhaul the healthcare system（医療制度を徹底的に見直す）

Check 3　　Sentence

☐ Slavery was abolished in the US in 1865.（奴隷制度はアメリカでは1865年に廃止された）

☐ The bridge is designed to withstand an earthquake of magnitude 8.（その橋はマグニチュード8の地震に耐えるように設計されている）

☐ Schools should nurture creativity and imagination in children.（学校は子どもの中の創造性と想像力を育てるべきだ）

☐ The high cost of gasoline hinders tourism.（ガソリン高が観光業の妨げとなっている）

☐ He conferred with his attorney about the case.（彼は弁護士とその訴訟について話し合った）

☐ Do you recollect what you said to me the last time we met?（この前会った時に私に何を言ったか覚えていますか？）

☐ Private schools are subsidized by the government.（私立学校は政府から補助金を与えられている）

☐ I had my computer overhauled.（私はコンピューターを分解修理してもらった）

continued
▼

Day 46

Check 1 Listen)) CD-B11

0729 affirm /əfə́ːrm/ Part 5, 6
- 動 ～だと**断言**[主張]**する**(⇔deny)
- 名 affirmation：断言
- 名 affirmative：肯定、賛成
- 形 affirmative：肯定的な、積極的な

0730 embezzle /imbézl/ Part 7
- 動 ～を(…から)**横領**[着服]**する**(from …)
- 名 embezzlement：横領、着服

0731 slump /slʌ́mp/ ❶定義注意 ビジネス問題
- 動 (物価などが)**急落**[暴落]**する**
- 名 (物価などの)暴落(in ～)

0732 testify /téstəfài/ Part 2, 3
- 動 ❶(～に有利に／…に不利に)**証言する**(for ～/against …) ❷～だと証言する
- 名 testimony：(宣誓)証言

0733 sag /sǽg/ ビジネス問題
- 動 ❶(価格などが)**下落する**(≒drop) ❷たわむ、沈下する(≒sink)
- 名 ❶(価格などの)下落(in ～) ❷たわみ、沈下

0734 dilute /dilúːt/ Part 7
- 動 ～を(…で)**薄める**(with …)
- 形 薄めた、希釈した
- 名 dilution：薄めること

0735 abate /əbéit/ Part 4
- 動 (勢い・激しさなどが)**和らぐ**、衰える

0736 rake /réik/ Part 1
- 動 ～を熊手で集める
- 名 熊手

Day 45)) CD-B10
Quick Review
答えは右ページ下

- □ ～を綿密に調べる
- □ ～の供給を止める
- □ 繁栄する
- □ ～を広げる
- □ ～を弾ませる
- □ ～を必要とする
- □ ～を徐々に衰えさせる
- □ ～を相殺する
- □ ～を記念する
- □ ～の模擬実験をする
- □ ～を管理する
- □ ～を編む
- □ ～を妨げる
- □ ～を細かく切る
- □ ～を招集する
- □ ～を放棄する

Check 2 Phrase

- affirm that it is true (それが真実であると断言する)

- embezzle $1 million from the company (会社から100万ドルを横領する)

- slump by half [two-thirds] (半分[3分の2]に急落する)

- testify in court (法廷で証言する)
- testify that the defendant was not involved in the crime (被告が犯罪に関与していなかったと証言する)

- the sagging housing market (下落する住宅市場)
- a sagging floor (たわんだ床)

- dilute soy sauce with water (しょうゆを水で薄める)

- abating winds (和らぎ始めた風)

- rake garbage (ごみを熊手で集める)

Check 3 Sentence

- The suspect affirmed that he was innocent. (容疑者は自分は無実だと主張した)

- He was charged with embezzling $20,000 from his employer over a three-year period. (彼は3年間にわたって雇用主から2万ドルを横領したかどで告訴された)

- Car sales slumped by nearly 25 percent compared to the previous year. (前年と比較して、車の販売台数は25パーセント近く急落した)

- The witness testified for the defendant. (証人は被告に有利な証言をした)

- Stock prices sagged yesterday. (株価は昨日、下落した)

- Dilute condensed milk with hot water. (コンデンスミルクを熱湯で薄めてください)

- The rain abated and the sun emerged. (雨が弱まって、太陽が現れた)

- The woman is raking the fallen leaves. (女性は落ち葉を熊手で集めている)

Day 45 CD-B10
Quick Review
答えは左ページ下

- scrutinize
- disconnect
- prosper
- unfold
- bounce
- necessitate
- undermine
- offset
- commemorate
- simulate
- administer
- weave
- hamper
- shred
- convene
- relinquish

Day 47　動詞10

Check 1　Listen 》CD-B12

0737 stabilize /stéibəlàiz/ ビジネス問題
動 ❶〜を安定させる　❷安定する
名 stability：安定(性)
形 stable：安定した

0738 misplace /mispléis/ Part 2, 3
動 〜を置き間違える；〜を置き忘れる

0739 skyrocket /skáirɑ̀kit/ ビジネス問題
動 (物価などが)急上昇する

0740 trim /trím/ Part 1
動 ❶〜を刈り込む　❷(予算など)を削減する(≒reduce)

0741 pollute /pəlú:t/ ビジネス問題
動 〜を汚染する、汚す(≒contaminate)
名 pollution：汚染；公害
名 pollutant：汚染物質

0742 avert /əvə́:rt/ Part 5, 6
動 ❶(危険など)を防ぐ、避ける(≒prevent)　❷(目など)を(…から)そらす、そむける(from ...)

0743 publicize /pʌ́bləsàiz/ Part 5, 6
動 〜を公表[広告、宣伝]する、公にする(≒announce, advertise)
名 publicity：❶周知、知名度、評判　❷宣伝、広報

0744 appraise /əpréiz/ ビジネス問題
動 〜を(…と)評価[鑑定、査定]する(at ...)(≒assess, evaluate)
名 appraisal：(〜の)評価、鑑定、査定(of 〜)

continued
▼

なかなか単語学習の時間が取れない?! もう1度、1日の生活を見直してみよう。寝る前の数分でも、語彙学習はできるはず！

- ☐ 聞くだけモード　Check 1
- ☐ しっかりモード　Check 1 ▶ 2
- ☐ かんぺきモード　Check 1 ▶ 2 ▶ 3

Check 2　　Phrase

☐ **stabilize** food prices（食品価格を安定させる）
☐ start **stabilizing**（安定し始める）

☐ **misplace** one's keys（鍵を置き間違える[置き忘れる]）

☐ **skyrocketing** oil prices（急上昇する原油価格）

☐ have one's hair **trimmed**（髪を刈りそろえてもらう）
☐ **trim** personnel costs（人件費を削減する）

☐ **pollute** the atmosphere（大気を汚染する）

☐ **avert** disaster（災害を防ぐ）
☐ **avert** one's eyes [gaze] from ～（～から目をそらす）

☐ **publicize** the results of ～（～の結果を公表する）
☐ highly [widely, well] **publicized**（広く知られた）

☐ **appraise** employees' performance（従業員の実績を評価する）
☐ **appraise** the house at $200,000（その家を20万ドルと評価する）

Check 3　　Sentence

☐ The government must **stabilize** the domestic economy.（政府は国内経済を安定させなければならない）

☐ I have **misplaced** my cellphone somewhere in my house.（私は家のどこかに携帯電話を置き忘れてしまった）

☐ Housing prices have **skyrocketed** over the past five years.（この5年間で住宅価格は急上昇した）

☐ The man is **trimming** the lawn.（男性は芝生を刈っている）

☐ Human beings have **polluted** the environment for many decades.（人類は何十年にもわたって自然環境を汚染してきた）

☐ Countries should take urgent measures to **avert** the ongoing financial crisis.（各国は進行中の金融危機を防ぐために緊急の措置を取るべきだ）

☐ Private information should not be **publicized** without permission.（個人情報は許可なく公表されてはならない）

☐ The building was **appraised** at $25 million.（そのビルは2500万ドルと評価された）

continued
▼

Day 47

Check 1　Listen)) CD-B12

□ 0745
foresee
/fɔːrsíː/
Part 5, 6

動 **〜を予見する**、見越す
形 foreseeable：予見[予知、予測]できる
形 unforeseen：予期しない、思いがけない、不測の

□ 0746
stir
/stə́ːr/
Part 1

動 **〜をかき混ぜる**、かき回す
名 かき混ぜる[回す]こと

□ 0747
rebound
/ribáund/
ビジネス問題

動 ❶(株価などが)**回復する**、立ち直る　❷(〜から)跳ね返る(off 〜)
名 (/ríːbaund/) ❶跳ね返り　❷回復、立ち直り

□ 0748
disseminate
/disémənèit/
Part 7

動 (情報・思想など)**を広める**、普及させる

□ 0749
insulate
/ínsəlèit/
Part 2, 3

動 **〜を**(…から)**断熱**[防音、絶縁]**する**(from [against] …)
名 insulation：❶断熱材、防音材、絶縁材[体]　❷(熱・音・電気などの)遮断、絶縁

□ 0750
slash
/slǽʃ/
❶定義注意
ビジネス問題

動 ❶(予算など)**を大幅に削減する**　❷〜に深く切りつける
名 ❶切りつけること；切り傷　❷一撃　❸スラッシュ、斜線

□ 0751
suppress
/səprés/
Part 5, 6

動 ❶(暴動など)**を鎮圧**[抑圧]**する**　❷(感情など)を抑える、我慢する(≒subdue)
名 suppression：❶(暴動などの)鎮圧、抑圧　❷(感情などの)抑制

□ 0752
interpret
/intə́ːrprit/
❶アクセント注意
Part 5, 6

動 ❶**〜を通訳する**　◯「〜を翻訳する」はtranslate
❷(interpret A as Bで)AをBだと解釈[理解]する
名 interpretation：❶解釈、説明　❷通訳
名 interpreter：通訳者

| Day 46)) CD-B11
Quick Review
答えは右ページ下 | □ 〜を廃止する
□ 〜によく耐える
□ 〜を育てる
□ 〜を妨げる | □ 話し合う
□ 〜を思い出す
□ 〜に補助金を与える
□ 〜を分解点検する | □ 〜だと断言する
□ 〜を横領する
□ 急落する
□ 証言する | □ 下落する
□ 〜を薄める
□ 和らぐ
□ 〜を熊手で集める |

Check 2 Phrase

- ☐ foresee what will happen in the future(将来何が起こるか予見する)

- ☐ stir one's coffee with a spoon(コーヒーをスプーンでかき混ぜる)

- ☐ rebound sharply([株価が]急反発する)
- ☐ rebound off the wall(壁に当たって跳ね返る)

- ☐ disseminate rumors(うわさを広める)

- ☐ insulate a house from heat [noise](家を熱[騒音]から断熱[防音]する)

- ☐ slash the budget(予算を大幅に削減する)
- ☐ a slashed tire(深く切りつけられたタイヤ)

- ☐ suppress a rebellion(暴動を鎮圧する)
- ☐ suppress one's anger(怒りを抑える)

- ☐ interpret the speech in Japanese(演説を日本語で通訳する)
- ☐ interpret silence as approval(沈黙を承認と解釈する)

Check 3 Sentence

- ☐ Few analysts foresaw the financial crisis.(金融危機を予見したアナリストはほとんどいなかった)

- ☐ The man is stirring the sauce.(男性はソースをかき混ぜている)

- ☐ Stock prices rebounded today after five successive days of losses.(5日連続で下落した後に株価は今日回復した)

- ☐ The Internet is the best medium to gather and disseminate information.(インターネットは情報を集めたり広めたりするのに最良の手段だ)

- ☐ My house is insulated with fiberglass insulation.(私の家はファイバーグラスの断熱材で断熱されている)

- ☐ All prices have been slashed by 60 percent!(価格はすべて60パーセント引き!)❶広告の表現

- ☐ The government sent troops to suppress demonstrators.(政府はデモ参加者たちを鎮圧するために軍隊を派遣した)

- ☐ The conference was simultaneously interpreted into five languages.(その会議は5カ国語に同時通訳された)

Day 46))) CD-B11
Quick Review
答えは左ページ下

- ☐ abolish
- ☐ withstand
- ☐ nurture
- ☐ hinder
- ☐ confer
- ☐ recollect
- ☐ subsidize
- ☐ overhaul
- ☐ affirm
- ☐ embezzle
- ☐ slump
- ☐ testify
- ☐ sag
- ☐ dilute
- ☐ abate
- ☐ rake

Day 48 動詞11

Check 1 Listen)) CD-B13

☐ 0753
subside
/səbsáid/
Part 5, 6

動 (嵐などが)**静まる**、治まる

☐ 0754
concur
/kənkə́ːr/
Part 5, 6

動 ❶(~と/…ということに)**同意見である**、一致する(with ~/that節 . . .)(≒agree) ❷同時に起こる(≒coincide)
形 concurrent：❶(~と)同時に発生[存在]する(with ~) ❷(~と)同一の、一致した(with ~)

☐ 0755
revolutionize
/rèvəlúːʃənàiz/
Part 5, 6

動 **~に革命をもたらす**、大変革を起こす
名 revolution：革命
形 revolutionary：革命の；革命的な

☐ 0756
contaminate
/kəntǽmənèit/
Part 7

動 **~を汚染する**、汚す(≒pollute)
名 contamination：汚染
名 contaminant：汚染物質

☐ 0757
sip
/síp/
Part 1

動 ❶**~をちびちび飲む** ❷(~を)ちびちび飲む(on [at] ~)
名 (飲み物の)一口(の量)

☐ 0758
dwindle
/dwíndl/
ビジネス問題

動 **次第に減少する**(≒decrease)

☐ 0759
forfeit
/fɔ́ːrfit/
❶発音注意
Part 5, 6

動 **~を没収される**、(罰として)失う ⊕confiscateは「~を没収する」
名 ❶没収、喪失 ❷没収物、罰金
形 (~に)没収された(to ~)

☐ 0760
activate
/ǽktəvèit/
ビジネス問題

動 ❶**~を活性化する**、活発にする ❷~を始動[起動、稼働]させる
名 activity：活動
形 active：❶活動的な ❷積極的な ❸活動中の

continued ▼

Quick Reviewは使ってる? 昨日覚えた単語でも、記憶に残っているとは限らない。学習の合間に軽くチェックするだけでも効果は抜群!

- □ 聞くだけモード　Check 1
- □ しっかりモード　Check 1 ▶ 2
- □ かんぺきモード　Check 1 ▶ 2 ▶ 3

Check 2　Phrase

□ subside as time passes（時がたつにつれて静まる）

□ concur with his view（彼の考え方に同意する）
□ Everything concurred to do ~.（あらゆることが相まって~した）

□ revolutionize science（[発見などが]科学に革命をもたらす）

□ contaminate drinking water（飲料水を汚染する）

□ sip (on [at]) wine（ワインをちびちび飲む）

□ dwindle to nothing [one, two]（次第に減ってなくなる[1つになる、2つになる]）

□ forfeit one's driver's license（運転免許証を没収される）
□ forfeit the right to do ~（~する権利を失う）

□ activate foreign investment（海外投資を活性化する）
□ activate an alarm（警報器を作動させる）

Check 3　Sentence

□ The doctor said the pain would subside in a few days.（痛みは数日で治まると医者は言った）

□ The results concurred with the experimental data.（結果は実験のデータと一致した）

□ The Internet has revolutionized the way we do business.（インターネットはビジネス方法に革命をもたらした）

□ The accident at the Chernobyl nuclear power plant contaminated large areas of Europe.（チェルノブイリ原子力発電所の事故はヨーロッパの広い地域を汚染した）

□ The woman is sipping a beverage.（女性は飲み物に口をつけている）

□ CD sales have dwindled since downloading music became popular.（音楽のダウンロードが一般的になって以来、CDの売り上げは次第に減少してきている）

□ If you cancel your reservation, you will forfeit your deposit.（予約を取り消す場合、前払い金は没収される）

□ The government is finding a way to activate the domestic economy.（政府は国内経済を活性化する方法を探っている）

continued
▼

Day 48

Check 1　Listen))) CD-B13

☐ 0761 solicit
/səlísit/
Part 7

動 ❶(援助・金銭など)を(…に)**求める**、懇願する(from …)(≒ask)　❷~を訪問販売する
名 solicitor：❶(町・市・州などの)法務官　❷外交[勧誘]員、セールスマン

☐ 0762 veto
/víːtou/
Part 7

動 ❶(法案など)を(拒否権を行使して)**拒否[否認]する**、~に対して拒否権を行使する　❷~を認めない、~に反対する
名 (~に対する)拒否権(on ~)

☐ 0763 overestimate
/òuvəréstəmèit/
Part 7

動 ❶~を過大評価する(⇔underestimate)　❷~を多く[高く]見積もり過ぎる
名 (/òuvəréstəmət/)過大評価；過大な見積もり
動 estimate：❶~を見積もる　❷を評価する

☐ 0764 empower
/impáuər/
Part 7

動 ❶**~の能力[地位]を向上させる**　❷~に(…する)権限を与える(to do)(≒authorize)

☐ 0765 revitalize
/rìváitəlaiz/
ビジネス問題

動 **~に再び活気を与える**
動 vitalize：~に活気[活力]を与える

☐ 0766 itemize
/áitəmàiz/
Part 7

動 **~を項目に分ける**、個条書きにする
名 item：品目、項目

☐ 0767 deduce
/didjúːs/
Part 5, 6

動 ❶**~だと推定[推論]する**　❷(deduce A from Bで)A(結論など)をBから推定[推論]する
名 deduction：❶(~からの)控除(from ~)　❷(~という)推論(that節 ~)

☐ 0768 unveil
/ʌnvéil/
Part 5, 6

動 ❶(秘密など)**を明らかにする**、公表する(≒reveal, disclose, uncover, expose)(⇔conceal：~を秘密にする)　❷~のベール[覆い]を取る；~の除幕式を行う

Day 47))) CD-B12　Quick Review　答えは右ページ下

- ☐ ~を安定させる
- ☐ ~を置き間違える
- ☐ 急上昇する
- ☐ ~を刈り込む
- ☐ ~を汚染する
- ☐ ~を防ぐ
- ☐ ~を公表する
- ☐ ~を評価する
- ☐ ~を予見する
- ☐ ~をかき混ぜる
- ☐ 回復する
- ☐ ~を広める
- ☐ ~を断熱する
- ☐ ~を大幅に削減する
- ☐ ~を鎮圧する
- ☐ ~を通訳する

Check 2 Phrase

- □ solicit donations（寄付を求める）
- □ solicit customers（顧客を訪問販売する）

- □ veto a bill（法案を拒否する）
- □ veto his plan to do ~（彼の~する計画を認めない）

- □ overestimate his abilities（彼の能力を過大評価する）
- □ overestimate construction costs（建設費を多く見積もり過ぎる）

- □ empower ethnic minority groups（少数民族の地位を向上させる）
- □ be empowered to do ~（~する権限を持っている）

- □ revitalize the economy（経済を再活性化する）

- □ itemize tax deductions（税控除を項目に分ける）
- □ an itemized bill（勘定の明細書）

- □ deduce that the suspect is innocent（容疑者は無実だと推定する）
- □ the conclusion deduced from the experiments（実験から推定される結論）

- □ unveil a secret（秘密を明かす）
- □ unveil a statue of ~（~の像の除幕式をする）

Check 3 Sentence

- □ It is illegal for legislators to solicit gifts from lobbyists.（国会議員がロビイストに贈与を求めることは違法だ）

- □ The US vetoed a UN Security Council resolution condemning Israel's attacks in Gaza.（アメリカはイスラエルのガザ攻撃を非難する国連安全保障理事会の決議に対して拒否権を行使した）

- □ In general, people tend to overestimate their skill level.（一般に、人々は自分の技能のレベルを過大評価する傾向がある）

- □ Companies need to empower employees with the necessary skills.（企業は従業員に必要な技術を身につけさせて能力を向上させる必要がある）

- □ The project will revitalize the local business district.（そのプロジェクトは地元の商業地域を再活性化するだろう）

- □ Itemize the budget in as much detail as possible.（できるだけ詳細に予算を項目別にしてください）

- □ Police deduced that a man who appeared to have committed suicide was actually murdered.（自殺したと思われていた男性は実は殺されていたと警察は推定した）

- □ Honda's new hybrid was unveiled at a press conference.（ホンダの新しいハイブリッド車が記者会見で公表された）

Day 47 》CD-B12
Quick Review
答えは左ページ下

- □ stabilize
- □ misplace
- □ skyrocket
- □ trim
- □ pollute
- □ avert
- □ publicize
- □ appraise
- □ foresee
- □ stir
- □ rebound
- □ disseminate
- □ insulate
- □ slash
- □ suppress
- □ interpret

Day 49 動詞12

Check 1　Listen))) CD-B14

☐ 0769
plummet
/plʌ́mit/
ビジネス問題

動 (物価などが)(~に)**急落する**(to ~)(≒ plunge, tumble)

☐ 0770
differentiate
/dìfərénʃièit/
Part 5, 6

動 ❶ ~を(…と)**区別する**、差別化[差異化]する(from …)　❷ (~の間の)差別[区別]をする(between ~)(≒ distinguish)
名 differentiation:区別;差異化

☐ 0771
outsource
/àutsɔ́ːrs/
ビジネス問題

動 (業務)を**外部委託する**;(部品など)を外部調達する
名 outsourcing:外部委託;外部調達

☐ 0772
procure
/proukjúər/
Part 7

動 ~を(努力[苦労]して)**手に入れる**、入手[獲得、調達]する(≒ obtain)

☐ 0773
vend
/vénd/
Part 1

動 (通例街頭などで)**~を売る**
名 vendor:露天商人、行商人

☐ 0774
infringe
/infríndʒ/
ビジネス問題

動 ❶ (権利など)**を侵害する**、(法律など)に違反する(≒ violate)　❷ (infringe on [upon]で)~を侵害する
名 infringement:❶ (権利などの)侵害(of [on] ~)　❷ (法律などの)違反(of ~)

☐ 0775
tumble
/tʌ́mbl/
ビジネス問題

動 ❶ (株価などが)**暴落する**(≒ plunge, plummet)　❷ 転ぶ
名 転倒、転落

☐ 0776
depict
/dipíkt/
Part 5, 6

動 ~を(…として)**描く**、描写する(as …)(≒ describe, represent, portray)
名 depiction:描写

continued
▼

チャンツを持ち歩いて復習を！　携帯プレーヤーにチャンツを録音して、通勤・通学時などに「聞き流し」の復習をしよう。

☐ 聞くだけモード　Check 1
☐ しっかりモード　Check 1 ▶ 2
☐ かんぺきモード　Check 1 ▶ 2 ▶ 3

Check 2　　Phrase

☐ **plummet** to a 10-year low（[株価などが]10年ぶりの安値に急落する）

☐ **differentiate** good from bad = **differentiate** between good and bad（善悪を区別する）

☐ **outsource** customer service（顧客サービスを外部委託する）

☐ **procure** evidence（証拠を入手する）

☐ a **vending** machine（自動販売機）

☐ **infringe** (on) copyright（著作権を侵害する）
☐ **infringe** a law（法律に違反する）

☐ **tumble** about 100 points（[株価が]100ポイントほど暴落する）
☐ **tumble** down the stairs（階段を転がり落ちる）

☐ **depict** him as a hero（彼を英雄として描く）

Check 3　　Sentence

☐ Oil prices have **plummeted** in recent months.（原油価格が最近の数カ月で急落した）

☐ We need to **differentiate** our products from our competitors'.（私たちは自社製品を競合他社の製品と差別化する必要がある）

☐ The company is planning to **outsource** a portion of its production.（その会社は生産の一部を外部委託することを計画している）

☐ I have managed to **procure** tickets to the concert.（私は何とかそのコンサートのチケットを手に入れた）

☐ The man is **vending** newspapers.（男性は新聞を売っている）

☐ The electronics manufacturer **infringed** four patents relating to digital cameras.（その電機メーカーはデジタルカメラに関連する4つの特許を侵害した）

☐ Stock prices **tumbled** to their lowest level in three years.（株価がこの3年で最低のレベルまで暴落した）

☐ "The Last Supper" **depicts** Christ and his 12 disciples.（『最後の晩餐』はキリストと彼の12人の弟子を描いている）

continued

Day 49

Check 1 Listen)) CD-B14

☐ 0777
privatize
/práivətàiz/
ビジネス問題

動 **〜を民営化する**(⇔nationalize:〜を国営[国有]化する)
名 privatization:民営化
形 private: ❶私有の;民営[私営]の ❷私的な

☐ 0778
mingle
/míŋgl/
Part 4

動 ❶(〜と)**歓談[交際]する**(with 〜) ❷(〜と)混ざる(with 〜) ❸〜を(…と)混ぜる(with ...)

☐ 0779
evoke
/ivóuk/
Part 5, 6

動 (感情など)**を呼び起こす**、喚起する
形 evocative: (感情などを)呼び起こす、喚起する、思い出させる(of 〜)

☐ 0780
shelve
/ʃélv/
Part 7

動 ❶(計画など)**を棚上げする**、延期する(≒put off, postpone, delay) ❷(本など)を棚に置く
名 shelf:棚

☐ 0781
lessen
/lésn/
Part 5, 6

動 ❶**〜を減らす**、小さくする ❷減る、小さくなる(≒decrease)
形 less:より少ない
副 less:より〜でなく
形 lesser:より劣った[重要でない]

☐ 0782
energize
/énərdʒàiz/
Part 7

動 ❶**〜を活気[元気]づける**(≒stimulate) ❷(機械など)を作動させる
名 energy:活力、エネルギー

☐ 0783
procrastinate
/proukrǽstənèit/
Part 7

動 (しなければならないことを)**ぐずぐずと引き延ばす**

☐ 0784
depose
/dipóuz/
Part 5, 6

動 (高官など)**を**(高位から)**免職にする**、退陣させる、退ける(from ...)
名 deposition: (高官などの)免職

Day 48)) CD-B13
Quick Review
答えは右ページ下

- ☐ 静まる
- ☐ 同意見である
- ☐ 〜に革命をもたらす
- ☐ 〜を汚染する
- ☐ 〜をちびちび飲む
- ☐ 次第に減少する
- ☐ 〜を没収される
- ☐ 〜を活性化する
- ☐ 〜を求める
- ☐ 〜を拒否する
- ☐ 〜を過大評価する
- ☐ 〜の能力を向上させる
- ☐ 〜に再び活気を与える
- ☐ 〜を項目に分ける
- ☐ 〜だと推定する
- ☐ 〜を明らかにする

Check 2 Phrase

- ☐ privatize government-run companies（国営企業を民営化する）

- ☐ mingle with guests（来客たちと歓談する）
- ☐ mingle with water（水と混ざる）

- ☐ evoke sorrow（悲しみを呼び起こす）

- ☐ shelve the bill（法案を棚上げにする）
- ☐ shelve books（本を棚に置く）

- ☐ lessen the risk of ～（～の危険性を減らす）
- ☐ considerably lessen（著しく減る）

- ☐ energize the civil rights movement（公民権運動を活気づける）
- ☐ be energized by solar power（太陽熱[光]で作動する）

- ☐ procrastinate until it is too late（手遅れになるまでぐずぐずと引き延ばす）

- ☐ depose the dictator（独裁者を退陣させる）

Check 3 Sentence

- ☐ Japan's postal system was privatized in 2007.（日本の郵政は2007年に民営化された）

- ☐ This event provides an opportunity to mingle with local people.（このイベントは地元の人々と触れ合う機会を提供する）

- ☐ The photo evoked memories of my childhood.（その写真は私の子どものころの記憶を呼び覚ました）

- ☐ The new airport project has been shelved due to the economic downturn.（新空港計画は景気低迷のため棚上げされたままになっている）

- ☐ Strengthening trade ties will lessen international tensions.（貿易関係を強化することで国際緊張は緩和するだろう）

- ☐ The development of the mall will energize the local economy.（そのショッピングセンターの開発は地元経済を活性化するだろう）

- ☐ Stop procrastinating and start acting.（ぐずぐずするのはやめて、行動を開始しましょう）

- ☐ The CEO was deposed due to poor leadership.（そのCEOは指導力不足のため免職になった）

Day 48))) CD-B13
Quick Review
答えは左ページ下

- ☐ subside
- ☐ concur
- ☐ revolutionize
- ☐ contaminate
- ☐ sip
- ☐ dwindle
- ☐ forfeit
- ☐ activate
- ☐ solicit
- ☐ veto
- ☐ overestimate
- ☐ empower
- ☐ revitalize
- ☐ itemize
- ☐ deduce
- ☐ unveil

CHAPTER 1
CHAPTER 2
CHAPTER 3
CHAPTER 4
CHAPTER 5
CHAPTER 6
CHAPTER 7
CHAPTER 8
CHAPTER 9

Day 50　動詞13

Check 1　Listen 》CD-B15

☐ 0785
weed
/wíːd/
Part 1

動 (庭など)の雑草を取る
名 雑草
名 seaweed：海草

☐ 0786
envision
/invíʒən/
Part 7

動 (将来のこと)を想像する、心に描く (≒ imagine, envisage)

☐ 0787
subdue
/səbdjúː/
Part 7

動 ❶(反乱など)を鎮圧[制圧]する　❷(感情など)を抑える、抑制する (≒ suppress)
形 subdued：❶(色・光・声などが)和らげられた　❷(人が)(いつもより)おとなしい

☐ 0788
flounder
/fláundər/
ビジネス問題

動 ❶(経済などが)低迷する　❷(混乱して)まごつく、口ごもる　❸もがく、あがく

☐ 0789
ameliorate
/əmíːljərèit/
Part 7

動 ～を改善[改良]する (≒ improve)
名 amelioration：改善、改良

☐ 0790
revamp
/riːvǽmp/
Part 4

動 ～を刷新[改造]する
名 刷新

☐ 0791
foretell
/fɔːrtél/
Part 5, 6

動 ～を予言[予告]する (≒ predict)

☐ 0792
modernize
/mádərnàiz/
ビジネス問題

動 ❶～を現代[近代]化する、最新式にする　❷現代[近代]的になる
名 modernization：近代[現代]化
形 modern：現代の、近代の

continued
▼

本書も残すところあと3週間＝21日！ TOEICで満点＝990点を獲得する日も少しずつ近づいている！ この調子で頑張っていこう。

☐ 聞くだけモード Check 1
☐ しっかりモード Check 1 ▶ 2
☐ かんぺきモード Check 1 ▶ 2 ▶ 3

Check 2　Phrase

☐ weed the lawn（芝生の雑草を取る）

☐ envision a better future（よりよい未来を想像する）
☐ It is hard to envision ～．（～を想像するのは難しい）

☐ subdue the enemy（敵を制圧する）
☐ subdue one's laughter（笑いをこらえる）

☐ the floundering economy（低迷する経済）
☐ flounder for something to say（何か言おうとして口ごもる）

☐ ameliorate the quality of life（生活の質を改善する）

☐ revamp the education system（教育制度を刷新する）
☐ revamp the cabinet（内閣を改造する）

☐ foretell the future（未来を予言する）

☐ modernize a country（国を近代化する）
☐ modernize a kitchen（台所を最新式にする）

Check 3　Sentence

☐ The man is weeding his garden.（男性は庭の雑草を取っている）

☐ I envision a day when all information is shared and more easily accessible.（すべての情報が共有され、より容易に入手できる日を私は想像する）

☐ It took four hours to subdue the fire.（その火事を鎮火するのに4時間かかった）

☐ The domestic car market is floundering due to lack of demand.（国内自動車市場は需要不足のため低迷している）

☐ The union has requested management to ameliorate working conditions.（その労働組合は経営陣に労働環境を改善するよう求めている）

☐ The automaker has revamped its marketing strategy.（その自動車メーカーは販売戦略を刷新した）

☐ It is extremely difficult to foretell when a recession will end.（いつ景気後退が終わるか予測するのは非常に難しい）

☐ It is imperative for manufacturers to modernize their production lines.（生産ラインを近代化することはメーカーにとって絶対に必要だ）

continued ▼

Day 50

Check 1　Listen))) CD-B15

□ 0793
dispel
/dispél/
Part 7

　動 (疑いなど)**を一掃する**、晴らす、追い払う

□ 0794
redress
/ridrés/
Part 5, 6

　動 **～を是正[矯正]する**
名(/ríːdres/)補償、賠償

□ 0795
underpin
/ʌ̀ndərpín/
Part 7

　動 ❶(議論など)**を支える**、支持する(≒support)　❷～を下から支える
名underpinning：❶支持　❷(建物の)土台

□ 0796
exemplify
/igzémpləfài/
Part 7

　動 ❶**～のよい例となる**　❷～を例証[実証]する
名exemplification：❶実例、好例　❷例証、実証

□ 0797
overshadow
/òuvərʃǽdou/
Part 7

　動 ❶(比喩的に)**～の影を薄くする**、～を見劣りさせる　❷～に影を投げかける

□ 0798
commend
/kəménd/
Part 4

　動 ❶**～を**(…のことで)**褒める**、称賛する(for ...)(≒praise)　❷～を(…に)推薦する(to ...)(≒recommend)
名commendation：❶称賛、推奨　❷推薦
形commendable：称賛に値する

□ 0799
spawn
/spɔ́ːn/
❶定義注意
Part 5, 6

　動 ❶**～を引き起こす**、生む(≒cause)　❷(魚・カエルなどが)卵を産む
名(魚・カエルなどの)卵

□ 0800
equalize
/íːkwəlàiz/
Part 5, 6

　動 **～を等しくする**、均一にする
名equality：等しいこと、平等
動equal：～と等しい
形equal：❶同量の、同等の　❷(be equal to で)～と等しい；～に匹敵する　❸平等な

Day 49))) CD-B14　Quick Review
答えは右ページ下

- □ 急落する
- □ ～を区別する
- □ ～を外部委託する
- □ ～を手に入れる
- □ ～を売る
- □ ～を侵害する
- □ 暴落する
- □ ～を描く
- □ ～を民営化する
- □ 歓談する
- □ ～を呼び起こす
- □ ～を棚上げする
- □ ～を減らす
- □ ～を活気づける
- □ ぐずぐずと引き延ばす
- □ ～を免職にする

Check 2 Phrase

- ☐ dispel the notion that ~(~という考えを一掃する)
- ☐ dispel her fears(彼女の不安を一掃する)

- ☐ redress wrongs(不正を正す)
- ☐ redress the imbalance(不均衡を是正する)

- ☐ underpin one's argument(論点を支える)
- ☐ underpin the foundation of the home(家の基礎を支える)

- ☐ exemplify the Romanesque style([芸術作品などが]ロマネスク様式の好例である)
- ☐ exemplify the importance of ~(~の重要性を実証する)

- ☐ feel overshadowed(見劣りを感じる)
- ☐ be overshadowed by skyscrapers(超高層ビルの影で覆われている)

- ☐ commend him for his hard work(彼の勤勉ぶりを褒める)
- ☐ commend the book to her(その本を彼女に推薦する)

- ☐ spawn environmental problems(環境問題を引き起こす)
- ☐ spawn in spring(春に卵を産む)

- ☐ equalize pay between men and women(男女間の賃金を等しくする)

Check 3 Sentence

- ☐ The minister dispelled rumors of his resignation.(その大臣は辞職のうわさを一掃した)

- ☐ The government should redress the unfair treatment of women in the workplace.(政府は職場での女性の不公平な待遇を是正すべきだ)

- ☐ Developments in the financial sector have underpinned the country's rapid economic growth.(金融部門の発展がその国の急速な経済成長を支えてきた)

- ☐ The painting exemplifies the characteristics of impressionism.(その絵画は印象主義の特徴をよく表している例だ)

- ☐ The state of the US economy has overshadowed the issue of the Iraq War.(アメリカの経済状況はイラク戦争の問題の影を薄くしている)

- ☐ I would like to commend her for her commitment to the company.(会社に対する彼女の貢献を称賛したいと思います)

- ☐ The US financial meltdown has spawned a global economic crisis.(アメリカの金融崩壊が世界的な経済危機を引き起こした)

- ☐ We should equalize educational opportunity for children.(私たちは子どもたちの教育の機会を均等にすべきだ)

Day 49))) CD-B14
Quick Review
答えは左ページ下

- ☐ plummet
- ☐ differentiate
- ☐ outsource
- ☐ procure
- ☐ vend
- ☐ infringe
- ☐ tumble
- ☐ depict
- ☐ privatize
- ☐ mingle
- ☐ evoke
- ☐ shelve
- ☐ lessen
- ☐ energize
- ☐ procrastinate
- ☐ depose

Day 51　動詞14

Check 1　Listen)) CD-B16

☐ 0801
redeem
/ridíːm/
Part 7

動❶(名誉など)**を**(苦労して)**回復**[挽回]**する**、取り[買い]戻す　❷(引換券など)を現金[商品]に換える
名redemption：❶買い[取り]戻し　❷償い、あがない

☐ 0802
worsen
/wə́ːrsn/
ビジネス問題

動❶**悪化する**、より悪くなる　❷~を悪化させる、より悪くする(≒aggravate)
名worse：一層悪いこと[物、状態]
形worse：より悪い、より劣った
副worse：より悪く

☐ 0803
expedite
/ékspədàit/
Part 7

動**~を早める**、促進する(≒hasten, facilitate, accelerate)

☐ 0804
detach
/ditǽtʃ/
Part 7

動**~を**(…から)**引き**[切り]**離す**、取り外す(from ...)(⇔attach)
名detachment：❶(~からの)分離(from ~)　❷超然、無関心
形detached：❶分離した　❷(人が)超然とした

☐ 0805
rearrange
/rìːəréindʒ/
Part 2, 3

動❶(会合など)**の日時を決め直す**、日程を変更する　❷~を配列し直す
動arrange：❶~をきちんと並べる、整頓する　❷~の準備[手配]をする

☐ 0806
underestimate
/ʌ̀ndəréstəmèit/
Part 7

動❶**~を過小評価する**(⇔overestimate)　❷~を安く[少なく]見積もり過ぎる
名(/ʌ̀ndəréstəmət/)過小評価；安過ぎる見積もり
動estimate：❶~を見積もる　❷~を評価する

☐ 0807
outnumber
/àutnʌ́mbər/
Part 7

動**~より数が多い**、~に数で勝る

☐ 0808
traverse
/trǽvəːrs/
Part 7

動(場所)**を横断する**、横切る、渡る

continued
▼

今日でChapter 5は最後！ 時間に余裕があったら、章末のReviewにも挑戦しておこう。忘れてしまった単語も結構あるのでは?!

☐ 聞くだけモード　Check 1
☐ しっかりモード　Check 1 ▶ 2
☐ かんぺきモード　Check 1 ▶ 2 ▶ 3

Check 2　Phrase

☐ redeem oneself（名誉を挽回する）
☐ redeem a voucher（商品引換券を商品に換える）

☐ the worsening economy（悪化する経済）
☐ worsen the situation（状況を悪化させる）

☐ expedite the construction process（建設工程を早める）

☐ detach the cable from the phone（ケーブルを電話から取り外す）

☐ rearrange the meeting for late August（会議の日時を8月下旬に変更する）
☐ rearrange the furniture（家具を並べ直す）

☐ underestimate the importance of ～（～の重要性を過小評価する）
☐ underestimate the total costs（総費用を安く見積もり過ぎる）

☐ outnumber ～ by three to one（3対1で～より数が多い）

☐ traverse the African continent（アフリカ大陸を横断する）

Check 3　Sentence

☐ He redeemed his watch from the pawnshop.（彼はその質屋から彼の時計を買い戻した）

☐ The company's financial troubles have worsened in the last six months.（その会社の財政難はこの半年でさらに悪くなっている）

☐ The government sought to expedite the passage of the bill.（政府はその法案の早期成立を図ろうとした）

☐ Detach the lower portion of this form and return it to the above address.（この申込用紙の下の部分を切り離して、上記の住所へ返送してください）

☐ Could we rearrange your appointment for next week?（面会の約束を来週にずらせるでしょうか?）

☐ Don't underestimate your opponent.（相手を見くびってはならない）

☐ In the high school, girls outnumber boys by almost two to one.（その高校では、女子がほぼ2対1で男子より数が多い）

☐ About 200,000 vehicles traverse the tollway daily.（約20万台の車がその有料道路を毎日通っている）

continued
▼

Day 51

Check 1　Listen 》CD-B16

0809 excavate
/ékskəvèit/
Part 4
- 動 ❶ 〜を発掘する　❷〜を掘る（≒dig）
- 名 excavation：発掘(物)

0810 entail
/intéil/
Part 7
- 動 〜を伴う、必要とする

0811 stroll
/stróul/
Part 1
- 動 散歩[散策]する、ぶらつく
- 名 散歩
- 名 stroller：散歩する人

0812 hatch
/hǽtʃ/
❗定義注意
Part 7
- 動 ❶ 〜を(ひそかに)企てる、謀る　❷孵化する　❸(卵)を孵化する；〜を卵からかえす
- 名 ❶孵化　❷(甲板の)ハッチ

0813 unpack
/ʌ̀npǽk/
Part 1
- 動 (包みなど)を開ける、解く；(中の物)を取り出す（⇔pack：〜を荷造りする）

0814 abound
/əbáund/
Part 5, 6
- 動 ❶(物・生物が)(〜に)たくさんある[いる] (in 〜)　❷(場所が)(〜に)満ちている (in [with] 〜)
- 名 abundance：豊富、多数、多量
- 形 abundant：豊富な

0815 reaffirm
/rì:əfə́:rm/
Part 5, 6
- 動 ❶ 〜だと再び断言[主張]する　❷〜を再確認する
- 名 reaffirmation：再確認

0816 ply
/plái/
Part 7
- 動 ❶(川など)を定期運航[運行]する、往復する　❷(〜の間を)定期的に往復する (between 〜)（≒shuttle）

Day 50 》CD-B15　Quick Review
答えは右ページ下

- □ 〜の雑草を取る
- □ 〜を想像する
- □ 〜を鎮圧する
- □ 低迷する
- □ 〜を改善する
- □ 〜を刷新する
- □ 〜を予言する
- □ 〜を現代化する
- □ 〜を一掃する
- □ 〜を是正する
- □ 〜を支える
- □ 〜のよい例となる
- □ 〜の影を薄くする
- □ 〜を褒める
- □ 〜を引き起こす
- □ 〜を等しくする

Check 2 Phrase

- excavate ruins（遺跡を発掘する）
- excavate a tunnel（トンネルを掘る）

- entail high risks（[投資などが]高いリスクを伴う）

- stroll in a park（公園内を散歩する）

- hatch a plot（陰謀を企てる）
- hatch an egg（卵を孵化する）

- unpack a cardboard box（段ボール箱を開ける）

- abound in Paris（[店などが]パリにたくさんある）
- abound in rare species（[場所が]希少種に満ちている）

- reaffirm that the suspect is innocent（その容疑者は無実だと再び主張する）

- ply the Nile（ナイル川を定期運航する）
- ply between Tokyo and Nagoya（東京・名古屋間を定期的に往復する）

Check 3 Sentence

- Mohenjo-Daro was excavated for the first time in 1922.（モヘンジョダロは1922年に初めて発掘された）

- Owning a car entails spending a lot of money on gas, insurance, maintenance and so on.（自動車を所有すると、ガソリン、保険、整備などたくさんの出費が必要となる）

- People are strolling along the beach.（人々は海岸沿いを散歩している）

- Three men were arrested for hatching a plot to kidnap the son of a wealthy banker.（裕福な銀行家の息子の誘拐を企てたかどで男3人が逮捕された）

- The woman is unpacking groceries.（女性は食料品を取り出している）

- Restaurants and shops abound in the area. ＝ The area abounds in restaurants and shops.（レストランと商店がその地域にはたくさんある）

- The government has reaffirmed that it will take steps to maintain law and order.（政府は治安を維持するための措置を講じることを再び断言した）

- Passenger ships ply the waters between the island and the mainland.（旅客船がその島と本土間の海域を定期運航している）

Day 50))CD-B15
Quick Review
答えは左ページ下

- [ ] weed
- [ ] envision
- [ ] subdue
- [ ] flounder
- [ ] ameliorate
- [ ] revamp
- [ ] foretell
- [ ] modernize
- [ ] dispel
- [ ] redress
- [ ] underpin
- [ ] exemplify
- [ ] overshadow
- [ ] commend
- [ ] spawn
- [ ] equalize

Chapter 5 Review

左ページの(1)～(20)の動詞の同意・類義語［熟語］（≒）、反意・反対語（⇔）を右ページのＡ～Ｔから選び、カッコの中に答えを書き込もう。意味が分からないときは、見出し番号を参照して復習しておこう（答えは右ページ下）。

- □ (1) scrutinize (0705) ≒は？（　　）
- □ (2) offset (0712) ≒は？（　　）
- □ (3) hamper (0717) ≒は？（　　）
- □ (4) recollect (0726) ≒は？（　　）
- □ (5) affirm (0729) ⇔は？（　　）
- □ (6) sag (0733) ≒は？（　　）
- □ (7) pollute (0741) ≒は？（　　）
- □ (8) publicize (0743) ≒は？（　　）
- □ (9) suppress (0751) ≒は？（　　）
- □ (10) concur (0754) ≒は？（　　）
- □ (11) dwindle (0758) ≒は？（　　）
- □ (12) procure (0772) ≒は？（　　）
- □ (13) infringe (0774) ≒は？（　　）
- □ (14) privatize (0777) ⇔は？（　　）
- □ (15) envision (0786) ≒は？（　　）
- □ (16) foretell (0791) ≒は？（　　）
- □ (17) underpin (0795) ≒は？（　　）
- □ (18) expedite (0803) ≒は？（　　）
- □ (19) detach (0804) ⇔は？（　　）
- □ (20) excavate (0809) ≒は？（　　）

A. subdue
B. nationalize
C. drop
D. dig
E. compensate for
F. obtain
G. predict
H. deny
I. agree
J. attach
K. prevent
L. decrease
M. imagine
N. remember
O. violate
P. announce
Q. facilitate
R. contaminate
S. support
T. examine

【解答】 (1) T (2) E (3) K (4) N (5) H (6) C (7) R (8) P (9) A (10) I (11) L (12) F (13) O (14) B (15) M (16) G (17) S (18) Q (19) J (20) D

CHAPTER 6
形容詞：必修112

Chapter 6 では、TOEIC 必修の形容詞112をマスターします。単語は「繰り返しの学習」で身につけるもの。目・耳・口をフル動員して、あきらめることなく学習を続けていきましょう！

Day 52【形容詞8】
▶ 238
Day 53【形容詞9】
▶ 242
Day 54【形容詞10】
▶ 246
Day 55【形容詞11】
▶ 250
Day 56【形容詞12】
▶ 254
Day 57【形容詞13】
▶ 258
Day 58【形容詞14】
▶ 262
Chapter 6 Review
▶ 266

TOEIC的格言

After rain comes fair weather.

雨降って地固まる。
［直訳］雨天の後に好天が来る。

Day 52　形容詞8

Check 1　Listen 》CD-B17

☐ 0817
prevailing
/privéiliŋ/
Part 7

形 **広く行き渡っている**、一般的な（≒prevalent）
名 prevalence：普及；流行
動 prevail：❶（prevail over [against]で）〜に勝つ、勝る　❷（prevail in [among]で）〜に普及している、広がっている

☐ 0818
eminent
/émənənt/
Part 5, 6

形 **著名**[高名、有名]**な**（≒famous, well-known, distinguished, renowned, prominent）　✚imminent（差し迫った）と混同しないように注意
名 eminence：名声、著名

☐ 0819
visionary
/víʒənèri/
Part 7

形 ❶**先見の明のある**、洞察力のある　❷想像[空想]上の、架空の
名 先見性のある人
名 vision：❶（〜の）理想像；想像（図）（of 〜）　❷視力　❸想像力　❹幻覚

☐ 0820
barren
/bǽrən/
Part 1

形 **不毛の**（⇔fertile：肥沃な）

☐ 0821
occupied
/ákjupàid/
Part 1

形 ❶**使用中の**（⇔unoccupied）　❷占領された
名 occupancy：居住、占有；（ホテルの部屋の）使用
名 occupant：（土地・家屋などの）占有者、居住者
動 occupy：❶（場所など）を占める、占有する　❷（be occupied withで）〜に従事している、〜で忙しい

☐ 0822
challenging
/tʃǽlindʒiŋ/
Part 2, 3

形 （難しいが）**やりがいのある**、やる気をそそる；難しい、骨の折れる
名 challenge：❶（やりがいのある）難問、課題　❷挑戦
動 challenge：〜に挑戦する

☐ 0823
unavailable
/ʌ̀nəvéiləbl/
Part 4

形 ❶（人が）**会うことができない**、要求に応じられない　❷利用[入手]できない（⇔available）

☐ 0824
introductory
/ìntrədʌ́ktəri/
Part 4

形 ❶**入門的な**　❷紹介の；前置きの
名 introduction：❶（〜への）導入（into [to] 〜）　❷（〜への）紹介（to 〜）
動 introduce：❶（商品など）を（市場などに）売り出す（to ...）　❷〜を（…に）紹介する（to ...）　❸〜を導入する

continued
▼

Chapter 6では、7日をかけて必修形容詞112をチェック。まずはCDでチャンツを聞いて、単語を「耳」からインプット！

- □ 聞くだけモード　Check 1
- □ しっかりモード　Check 1 ▶ 2
- □ かんぺきモード　Check 1 ▶ 2 ▶ 3

Check 2　Phrase

- □ prevailing superstitions（広く行き渡っている迷信）

- □ an eminent scientist（著名な科学者）

- □ a visionary author（先見の明のある作家）
- □ a visionary animal（想像上の動物）

- □ a barren land（不毛の砂漠）

- □ "occupied"（「使用中」）➕浴室・トイレの掲示
- □ an occupied land（占領地）

- □ a challenging job（やりがいのある仕事）

- □ be unavailable for comment（コメントに応じない）
- □ unavailable information（入手不可能な情報）

- □ an introductory book（入門書）
- □ an introductory chapter（序章）

Check 3　Sentence

- □ Fashion is a prevailing style of dress, hair and so on.（流行とは服や髪などの広く行き渡っているスタイルのことだ）

- □ Glazunov is one of the most eminent Russian composers.（グラズノフは最も著名なロシアの作曲家の1人だ）

- □ Our country needs a visionary leader who can move the country forward.（私たちの国には国を前進させることができる先見の明のある指導者が必要だ）

- □ The land is almost barren.（その土地には草木がほとんど生えていない）

- □ All the seats are occupied.（席はすべてふさがっている）

- □ The music was complex and difficult, but challenging and fun to play.（その音楽は複雑で難しかったが、演奏するやる気をそそって楽しかった）

- □ I am unavailable at the moment, so please leave a message after the beep.（ただ今留守にしていますので、発信音の後にメッセージを残してください）➕留守番電話の表現

- □ She enrolled in an introductory psychology course.（彼女は心理学入門講座に受講登録した）

continued
▼

Day 52

Check 1 Listen)) CD-B17

0825 ironic /airánik/ Part 5, 6
形 **皮肉な**(≒sarcastic)
名irony:皮肉(な言葉)
副ironically:皮肉にも、皮肉なことに

0826 ongoing /ángòuiŋ/ Part 7
形 **進行[継続]中の**
動go on:(活動などが)続く

0827 fierce /fíərs/ Part 5, 6
形 ❶(競争などが)**激しい** ❷(人・動物などが)どう猛な
副fiercely:❶激しく ❷どう猛に

0828 secondary /sékəndèri/ Part 5, 6
形 ❶(重要性などが)**第2(位)の**、2番目の;二次的な ❹「第1の」はprimary、「第3の」はtertiary ❷(学校・教育が)中等の

0829 derogatory /dirágətɔ̀:ri/ Part 7
形 **軽蔑的な**、見くびった

0830 minimal /mínəməl/ Part 5, 6
形 **最小(限度)の**(⇔maximal)
名minimum:最低[最小]限
形minimum:最低[最小]限の
動minimize:❶~を最小にする ❷~を最小限に評価する、軽視する

0831 provisional /prəvíʒənl/ Part 7
形 **暫定的な**、臨時の、仮の(≒temporary, interim)

0832 preparatory /pripǽrətɔ̀:ri/ Part 5, 6
形 **準備[予備]の**
名preparation:(~の)用意、準備(for [of] ~)
動prepare:❶~の用意[準備]をする ❷(prepare forで)~に備える ❸(prepare to doで)~する準備をする ❹(be prepared to doで)~する覚悟[用意]ができている

Day 51)) CD-B16 Quick Review 答えは右ページ下
- ~を回復する
- 悪化する
- ~を早める
- ~を引き離す
- ~の日時を決め直す
- ~を過小評価する
- ~より数が多い
- ~を横断する
- ~を発掘する
- ~を伴う
- 散歩する
- ~を企てる
- ~を開ける
- たくさんある
- ~だと再び断言する
- ~を定期運航する

Check 2 Phrase

- an ironic remark（皮肉な発言）
- It is ironic that ~.（皮肉にも~）

- an ongoing project（進行中のプロジェクト）

- face fierce resistance（激しい抵抗に遭う）
- a fierce animal（どう猛な動物）

- be of secondary importance（2番目に重要である、二の次である）
- secondary education（中等教育）

- a derogatory term（軽蔑的な言葉）

- minimal damage（最小限の損傷）

- a provisional government（暫定政府）
- a provisional contract（仮契約）

- preparatory work（準備作業）

Check 3 Sentence

- It is ironic that there was a "global warming" rally in the snow.（皮肉にも、「地球温暖化」集会が雪の中で行われた）

- The contract negotiations are still ongoing.（契約交渉はまだ継続中だ）

- There is fierce competition among international companies to increase market share.（市場占有率を増やそうとする国際企業間の激しい競争がある）

- If you desire the highest quality, price is a secondary issue.（最高品質を求めるならば、価格は二次的な問題だ）

- The politician made some derogatory remarks about women.（その政治家は女性に関して軽蔑的な発言をした）

- Cacti are easy to grow with minimal care.（サボテンはごくわずかの世話で簡単に育てることができる）

- We regret that we do not accept provisional bookings.（申し訳ありませんが、当店では仮予約は受け付けていません）

- Meaningful progress has been made to narrow differences during the preparatory meetings.（予備会談中に、意見の相違を狭める意味のある進展があった）

Day 51)) CD-B16
Quick Review
答えは左ページ下

- redeem
- worsen
- expedite
- detach
- rearrange
- underestimate
- outnumber
- traverse
- excavate
- entail
- stroll
- hatch
- unpack
- abound
- reaffirm
- ply

CHAPTER 1
CHAPTER 2
CHAPTER 3
CHAPTER 4
CHAPTER 5
CHAPTER 6
CHAPTER 7
CHAPTER 8
CHAPTER 9

Day 53　形容詞9

Check 1　Listen 》CD-B18

☐ 0833
varied
/véərid/
Part 5, 6

形 **さまざまな**、多様な、変化に富む
動 vary：❶（〜の点で）異なる、さまざまである（in 〜）　❷変わる　❸〜を変える
形 variable：❶変わりやすい　❷変えられる

☐ 0834
imperative
/impérətiv/
Part 5, 6

形 **絶対必要な**、重要な
名 緊急になすべきこと

☐ 0835
occupational
/àkjupéiʃənl/
ビジネス問題

形 **職業（上）の**、職業に関係のある（≒vocational）
名 occupation：❶職業、仕事　❷（土地・家屋などの）占有；占拠（of 〜）

☐ 0836
fabulous
/fǽbjuləs/
Part 2, 3

形 ❶（とても）**素晴らしい**　❷信じ難い

☐ 0837
invaluable
/invǽljuəbl/
Part 4

形 **非常に**［計り知れないほど］**貴重な**（≒valuable, precious）（⇔valueless）
名 value：❶価値　❷価格
動 value：〜を高く評価する、尊重する
名 valuable：（通例〜s）貴重品

☐ 0838
maternity
/mətə́:rnəti/
Part 7

形 ❶**出産**［妊娠］**の**　❷妊婦［産婦］の
名 母であること、母性（⇔paternity：父であること）

☐ 0839
sweeping
/swí:piŋ/
Part 7

形 ❶**全面的な**、広範な　❷大ざっぱな
動 sweep：〜を掃除する、掃く

☐ 0840
insolvent
/insálvənt/
ビジネス問題

形 **破産した**、破産（者）の（≒bankrupt）；支払い不能の（⇔solvent：支払い能力がある）
名 insolvency：破産（状態）

continued
▼

「固まり」の中で語彙を覚えている？ 特に形容詞は、ほかの品詞(特に名詞)との結びつきで覚えるのが効果的。Check 2を飛ばさずに！

☐ 聞くだけモード　Check 1
☐ しっかりモード　Check 1 ▶ 2
☐ かんぺきモード　Check 1 ▶ 2 ▶ 3

Check 2　Phrase

☐ varied hobbies(さまざまな趣味)
☐ a varied selection of ~(~の豊富な品ぞろえ)

☐ It is imperative that ~.(~ということが絶対に必要だ) ➕ 通例、that節の動詞は仮定法現在(＝原形)になる

☐ occupational training(職業訓練)
☐ an occupational hazard(職業上の危険)

☐ have a fabulous time(素晴らしい時を過ごす)
☐ a fabulous amount of money(信じ難いほど巨額の金)

☐ an invaluable asset(非常に貴重な資産)

☐ maternity leave(出産休暇、産休)
☐ a maternity dress(妊婦服)

☐ make sweeping changes(全面的な変更を行う)
☐ a sweeping generalization(大ざっぱな[十把ひとからげの]一般論)

☐ an insolvent company(破産した会社)

Check 3　Sentence

☐ She has gained varied experience in the field of accounting over 20 years.(彼女は20年にわたって会計分野での豊富な経験を身につけた)

☐ It is imperative that everyone attend the next meeting.(全員が次の会議に出席することが絶対に必要である)

☐ Hearing loss is the most common occupational disease for road construction workers.(難聴は道路建設作業員にとって最も一般的な職業病だ)

☐ We had a fabulous meal at the restaurant.(私たちはそのレストランで素晴らしい食事を食べた)

☐ I gained a lot of invaluable experience during my internship at the company.(私はその会社での実習訓練期間中に多くの貴重な経験を得た)

☐ She took a three-month maternity leave and then returned to work again full-time.(彼女は3カ月の産休を取った後、常勤の仕事に再び戻った)

☐ The governor announced sweeping cuts to the state's budget.(その知事は州予算の全面的な削減を発表した)

☐ About 30,000 European retailers became insolvent last year.(約3万のヨーロッパの小売業者が昨年倒産した)

continued
▼

Day 53

Check 1　Listen)) CD-B18

0841 delinquent
/dilíŋkwənt/
ビジネス問題

形 ❶(負債などが)**滞納**[延滞]**の** ❷非行の
名 非行少年
名 delinquency：❶非行　❷滞納金、未払い金

0842 latter
/lǽtər/
Part 5, 6

形 ❶(the 〜)**後者の**；(代名詞的に)後者(⇔former)　❷(the 〜)後の、後半の

0843 sanitary
/sǽnətèri/
Part 7

形 ❶**衛生的な**、清潔な(≒hygienic)　❷衛生(上)の
名 sanitation：公衆衛生

0844 irregular
/irégjulər/
Part 5, 6

形 ❶**不規則な**(≒erratic)(⇔regular)　❷不均整の、ふぞろいの　❸不法な
名 irregularity：❶不規則　❷ふぞろい
副 irregularly：❶不規則に　❷ふぞろいに

0845 statistical
/stətístikəl/
Part 5, 6

形 **統計**(上)**の**
名 statistics：統計；統計学
名 statistician：統計学者
副 statistically：統計的に

0846 operational
/ὰpəréiʃənl/
ビジネス問題

形 ❶**操業**[使用、運転]**できる**　❷営業[事業、操業]上の
名 operation：❶営業；操業；事業　❷(〜の)手術(on 〜)　❸(機械などの)操作
動 operate：❶〜を操作する　❷〜を経営する　❸作動する

0847 negotiable
/nigóuʃiəbl/
ビジネス問題

形 ❶**交渉の余地がある**
名 negotiation：(〜に関する)交渉、話し合い(on [over] 〜)
動 negotiate：❶(〜と)交渉する(with 〜)　❷(契約など)を(…と)取り決める(with ...)

0848 faulty
/fɔ́ːlti/
Part 5, 6

形 ❶**欠陥**[欠点]**のある**(≒defective)　❷(考えなどが)誤った
名 fault：❶(過失の)責任、罪；過失、誤り　❷故障　❸(性格などの)短所、欠点
動 fault：〜を批判[非難]する

Day 52)) CD-B17　Quick Review
答えは右ページ下

- 広く行き渡っている
- 著名な
- 先見の明のある
- 不毛の
- 使用中の
- やりがいのある
- 会うことができない
- 入門的な
- 皮肉な
- 進行中の
- 激しい
- 第2の
- 軽蔑的な
- 最小の
- 暫定的な
- 準備の

Check 2　Phrase

- delinquent taxes（滞納税）
- a delinquent boy（非行少年）

- the latter plan（[2つ提示されたうちの]後者の計画）
- the latter half of the previous year（前年の後半）

- a sanitary kitchen（清潔な台所）
- sanitary facilities（衛生施設）➕ トイレなどを指す

- an irregular heartbeat（不整脈）
- an irregular coastline（入り組んだ海岸線）

- statistical analysis [data]（統計分析［データ］）

- be fully operational（完全に使える状態にある）
- operational costs（営業費）

- be negotiable at this stage（現段階では交渉の余地がある）

- a faulty engine（欠陥エンジン）
- faulty reasoning（誤った論法）

Check 3　Sentence

- He is three months delinquent in paying his mortgage.（彼は住宅ローンの支払いを3カ月滞納している）

- Of the two methods, I prefer the latter.（その2つの方法のうち、私は後者のほうが気に入っている）

- To prevent food contamination, food must be prepared under sanitary conditions.（食品汚染を防ぐために、食品は清潔な状態の下で調理されなければならない）

- Working irregular hours can cause health problems such as insomnia.（不規則勤務は不眠症などの健康問題を引き起こすことがある）

- Statistical evidence shows that smoking is a risk factor of heart disease.（喫煙は心臓病の危険因子であることが統計的に証明されている）

- The power plant will be operational within three months.（その発電所は3カ月以内で操業可能になる予定だ）

- Salary is negotiable depending on experience.（給与は経験によって交渉の余地がある）➕求人広告の表現

- The car accident was caused by faulty brakes.（その自動車事故は欠陥ブレーキが原因で起きた）

Day 52 》CD-B17
Quick Review
答えは左ページ下

- prevailing
- eminent
- visionary
- barren
- occupied
- challenging
- unavailable
- introductory
- ironic
- ongoing
- fierce
- secondary
- derogatory
- minimal
- provisional
- preparatory

CHAPTER 1
CHAPTER 2
CHAPTER 3
CHAPTER 4
CHAPTER 5
CHAPTER 6
CHAPTER 7
CHAPTER 8
CHAPTER 9

Day 54　形容詞10

Check 1　Listen ») CD-B19

□ 0849
hygienic
/hàidʒénik/
Part 7

形 **衛生(上)の**、衛生的な(≒sanitary)
名 hygiene：衛生(状態)；衛生学

□ 0850
integrated
/íntəgrèitid/
Part 5, 6

形 **統合[一体化]された**
名 integration：統合
動 integrate：(integrate A with B で)AをBと統合する、結びつける

□ 0851
offshore
/ɔ́ːfʃɔ́ːr/
ビジネス問題

形 ❶**海外(で)の**　❷沖(合)の
副 ❶海外で　❷沖合で

□ 0852
imminent
/ímənənt/
Part 5, 6

形 **差し迫った**、今にも起こりそうな(≒impending)
⊕ eminent(著名な)と混同しないように注意
名 imminence：差し迫った状態、切迫

□ 0853
robust
/roubʌ́st/
❶アクセント注意
ビジネス問題

形 ❶(経済などが)**活気のある**、活発な　❷強い、強健な(≒strong)

□ 0854
interim
/íntərəm/
Part 7

形 **暫定[一時]的な**、仮の(≒temporary, provisional)；中間の
名 合間、しばらくの間　⊕通例、in the interim(その間に)の形で使う

□ 0855
depressed
/diprést/
ビジネス問題

形 ❶**不景気の**、不況の　❷気落ちした、憂うつな
名 depression：❶(長期の)不景気、不況　❷うつ病
動 depress：❶~を憂うつにさせる、意気消沈させる　❷(be depressed about [over]で)~で憂うつになっている、意気消沈している　❸(市場など)を不景気にする

□ 0856
noticeable
/nóutisəbl/
Part 5, 6

形 **目立つ**、人目を引く；著しい
名 notice：❶通知、通達　❷掲示、告示　❸注目
動 notice：~に気がつく；~に注意[注目]する
動 notify：(notify A of B で)AにBを知らせる、報告する
副 noticeably：目立って、著しく

continued

Check 2の「フレーズ」の音読をやってる？慣れてきたら、Check 3の「センテンス」にも挑戦してみよう。定着度がさらにアップするよ！

- ☐ 聞くだけモード　Check 1
- ☐ しっかりモード　Check 1 ▶ 2
- ☐ かんぺきモード　Check 1 ▶ 2 ▶ 3

Check 2　Phrase

☐ hygienic conditions（衛生状態）

☐ an integrated information system（統合情報システム）

☐ offshore investment（海外投資）
☐ offshore fishing（沖合漁業）

☐ imminent danger（差し迫った危険）

☐ a robust economy（好景気）
☐ a robust young man（たくましい若者）

☐ an interim government（暫定政府）
☐ an interim report（中間報告）

☐ a depressed area（不況地域）
☐ feel depressed（憂うつな気分になる）

☐ a noticeable stain（目立つ染み）
☐ a noticeable difference（顕著な違い）

Check 3　Sentence

☐ It is not hygienic to leave opened canned food in the refrigerator.（開けた缶詰食品を冷蔵庫に入れたままにしておくのは衛生的ではない）

☐ The modern buildings are well integrated with the old houses.（現代的なビルが古い家々とうまく一体化している）

☐ Offshore outsourcing has been blamed for the employment cutbacks.（海外への業務委託は雇用縮小の批判を受けている）

☐ Global warming is an imminent threat to the environment.（地球温暖化は自然環境に対する差し迫った脅威だ）

☐ With ongoing industrialization, China's economy will remain robust.（工業化が進行しているので、中国経済は活気を維持するだろう）

☐ An interim CEO will be appointed until a new CEO is selected.（新しいCEOが選出されるまで、暫定的なCEOが指名される予定だ）

☐ The current depressed market will continue for some time.（現在の市場の低迷はしばらく続くだろう）

☐ There has been a noticeable improvement in productivity over the past few months.（ここ数カ月で生産性の目立った改善があった）

continued ▼

Day 54

Check 1 Listen ») CD-B19

0857 viable
/vάiəbl/
Part 5, 6

形 **実行可能な**(≒feasible)
名 viability：実行可能性

0858 erratic
/irǽtik/
Part 5, 6

形 ❶**不規則な**、不安定な(≒irregular) ❷(行動などが)とっぴな、風変わりな

0859 binding
/báindiŋ/
ビジネス問題

形 (契約などが)**拘束力のある**
名 ❶表紙 ❷縛る物、ひも
名 bind：困難な状況[事態]
動 bind：❶~を縛る、結ぶ ❷(bind A to doで)Aに~することを義務づける

0860 overpriced
/òuvərpráist/
Part 2, 3

形 **値段が高過ぎる**
動 overprice：~に法外な値をつける

0861 inconsistent
/ìnkənsístənt/
Part 5, 6

形 ❶**一貫性のない**、矛盾した(⇔consistent) ❷(be inconsistent withで)~と一致[調和]しない(⇔be consistent with)
名 inconsistency：不一致、矛盾

0862 tolerable
/tάlərəbl/
Part 5, 6

形 ❶**耐えられる**、我慢できる(≒bearable) ❷まあまあの、悪くない
名 tolerance：❶寛大、寛容 ❷耐性
動 tolerate：~を許容[黙認]する、大目に見る
形 tolerant：❶寛大[寛容]な ❷抵抗力がある

0863 fraudulent
/frɔ́ːdʒulənt/
Part 7

形 **詐欺的な**、不正な
名 fraud：詐欺；詐欺事件

0864 neighboring
/néibəriŋ/
Part 5, 6

形 **近隣[近所]の**
名 neighbor：近所の人；隣国
名 neighborhood：❶(ある特定の)地域 ❷近所、近隣 ❸(集合的に)近所の人々 ❹(the ~)(~に)近いこと(of ~)

Day 53 ») CD-B18
Quick Review
答えは右ページ下

- □ さまざまな
- □ 絶対必要な
- □ 職業の
- □ 素晴らしい
- □ 非常に貴重な
- □ 出産の
- □ 全面的な
- □ 破産した
- □ 滞納の
- □ 後者の
- □ 衛生的な
- □ 不規則な
- □ 統計の
- □ 操業できる
- □ 交渉の余地がある
- □ 欠陥のある

Check 2 Phrase

- [ ] a viable alternative(実行可能な代替案)
- [ ] economically [commercially] viable(経済的[商業的]に実行可能な)

- [ ] erratic winds(不規則な風)
- [ ] erratic behavior(とっぴな行動)

- [ ] a binding contract(拘束力のある契約)
- [ ] be legally binding(法的に拘束力がある)

- [ ] an overpriced restaurant(値段が高過ぎるレストラン)

- [ ] an inconsistent policy(一貫性のない政策)
- [ ] be inconsistent with the facts([話などが]事実と一致しない)

- [ ] a tolerable situation(耐えられる状況)
- [ ] speak tolerable French(まあまあのフランス語を話す)

- [ ] a fraudulent practice(詐欺的行為)
- [ ] a fraudulent insurance claim(不正な保険請求)

- [ ] a neighboring town(隣町)

Check 3 Sentence

- [ ] I don't think that the project is financially viable.(そのプロジェクトが財政的に実行可能だと私は思わない)

- [ ] He is emotionally erratic.(彼は情緒が不安定だ)

- [ ] The agreement is legally binding.(その協定は法的に拘束力がある)

- [ ] The bag is very nice, but outrageously overpriced.(そのバッグはとても素敵だが、とんでもなく値段が高い)

- [ ] His ideas are logically inconsistent.(彼の意見は論理的に一貫していない)

- [ ] The weather was cold, but tolerable.(天気は寒かったが、我慢できるものだった)

- [ ] The man was arrested for fraudulent use of a credit card.(その男はクレジットカードの不正使用で逮捕された)

- [ ] The military force of the country is a threat to neighboring countries.(その国の軍事力は近隣諸国にとって脅威になっている)

Day 53)) CD-B18
Quick Review
答えは左ページ下

- [ ] varied
- [ ] imperative
- [ ] occupational
- [ ] fabulous
- [ ] invaluable
- [ ] maternity
- [ ] sweeping
- [ ] insolvent
- [ ] delinquent
- [ ] latter
- [ ] sanitary
- [ ] irregular
- [ ] statistical
- [ ] operational
- [ ] negotiable
- [ ] faulty

Day 55　形容詞11

Check 1　Listen 》CD-B20

☐ 0865
unpredictable
/ʌ̀nprɪdíktəbl/
Part 5, 6

形 **予測できない**(⇔predictable)
動 predict：〜を予測[予言、予想]する
名 prediction：(〜についての)予測、予報、予言、予想(about [of] 〜)

☐ 0866
instructive
/ɪnstrʌ́ktɪv/
Part 5, 6

形 **有益な**、ためになる(≒useful)
名 instruction：❶(〜s)使用[取扱]説明書　❷(通例〜s)(〜せよという)指示、命令(to do)　❸教育
動 instruct：(instruct A to doで)Aに〜するように指示[命令、指図]する

☐ 0867
organizational
/ɔ̀ːrɡənɪzéɪʃənəl/
ビジネス問題

形 **組織の**[に関する]
名 organization：組織(体)、団体
動 organize：❶(催しなど)を計画[準備]する　❷(団体など)を組織する
形 organized：❶組織化された　❷(人が)有能な

☐ 0868
conclusive
/kənklúːsɪv/
Part 7

形 (事実・証拠などが)**決定的な**(≒decisive)(⇔inconclusive)
名 conclusion：❶結論　❷結末
動 conclude：❶〜と結論する　❷〜を(…で)終了させる(with . . .)

☐ 0869
given
/ɡívən/
Part 7

形 **特定[既定]の**、定められた
名 既知の事実[状況]
前 〜を考慮に入れると
接 (しばしばgiven thatで)〜と仮定すると

☐ 0870
manifest
/mǽnəfèst/
Part 5, 6

形 **明らかな**、はっきりした(≒obvious)
名 乗客名簿　●政治などの「マニフェスト」はmanifesto
動 〜を明らかにする；〜を表す
名 manifestation：表れ、表現；(病気の)兆候

☐ 0871
superb
/supə́ːrb/
Part 2, 3

形 **素晴らしい**、見事な(≒excellent)

☐ 0872
disturbing
/dɪstə́ːrbɪŋ/
Part 7

形 **憂慮すべき**、平静を乱す、不安にさせる
名 disturbance：❶妨害[邪魔](物)　❷(社会の)騒動、混乱
動 disturb：❶(平静など)を乱す、妨げる　❷〜に迷惑をかける

continued
▼

マラソンで例えると、本書は今、ゴールまで残り10キロ地点。一番苦しい所だけど、ラストスパートをかけてゴールを目指そう！

☐ 聞くだけモード　Check 1
☐ しっかりモード　Check 1 ▶ 2
☐ かんぺきモード　Check 1 ▶ 2 ▶ 3

Check 2　Phrase

☐ an unpredictable economic climate（予測できない経済情勢）

☐ an instructive experience（有益な経験）

☐ an organizational tree（組織系統図）
☐ organizational ability（組織能力）

☐ conclusive evidence [proof]（決定的な証拠、確証）
☐ win a conclusive victory（決定的な勝利を収める）

☐ at a given time [place]（定められた時間［場所］に）

☐ a manifest mistake（明らかな誤り）
☐ become manifest（明らかになる）

☐ a superb performance（見事な演奏）

☐ disturbing news（憂慮すべきニュース）
☐ It is disturbing that ～.（～とは憂慮すべきことだ）

Check 3　Sentence

☐ Mountain weather is often unpredictable.（山の天気は予測できないことが多い）

☐ The book is informative, instructive, and readable.（その本は情報量が多く、有益で、そして読みやすい）

☐ The company announced sweeping organizational and management changes.（その会社は全面的な組織変更と経営陣の交代を発表した）

☐ A series of inspections failed to find conclusive evidence that Iraq possessed weapons of mass destruction.（一連の査察ではイラクが大量破壊兵器を保有しているとの確証は得られなかった）

☐ Weather is the state of the atmosphere at a given time and place.（天気とは特定の時間と場所における大気の状態のことだ）

☐ Some people say that the war in Iraq is a manifest failure.（イラク戦争は明らかな失敗だと言う人もいる）

☐ Dinner at the restaurant was superb.（そのレストランでの夕食は素晴らしかった）

☐ The present economic situation bears disturbing similarities to the start of the Great Depression.（現在の経済状況は大恐慌の始まりと似た憂慮すべき点がある）

continued ▼

Day 55

Check 1   Listen)) CD-B20

□ 0873
solvent
/sálvənt/
ビジネス問題

形 (負債などの)**支払い能力がある**(⇔insolvent, bankrupt)
名 solvency：支払い能力(のあること)

□ 0874
disruptive
/disrʌ́ptiv/
Part 7

形 (行動などが)**破壊的な**、妨害する、邪魔をする
名 disruption：混乱、中断
動 disrupt：〜を混乱[中断]させる

□ 0875
pertinent
/pə́ːrtənənt/
Part 7

形 (当面の問題に)**関連のある**(to 〜)；適切[妥当]な(≒relevant)(⇔irrelevant)

□ 0876
vocational
/voukéiʃənl/
ビジネス問題

形 **職業(上)の**(≒occupational)
名 vocation：❶天職 ❷職業

□ 0877
assorted
/əsɔ́ːrtid/
Part 5, 6

形 **詰め合わせの**；種々雑多の

□ 0878
integral
/íntigrəl/
❶アクセント注意
Part 5, 6

形 (〜に)**不可欠な**、なくてはならない(to 〜)(≒necessary, indispensable, essential)

□ 0879
on-the-job
/ánðədʒɑ̀b/
ビジネス問題

形 **実地の**、職場での、勤務中の(≒hands-on)

□ 0880
comprehensible
/kàmprihénsəbl/
Part 5, 6

形 (〜にとって)**分かりやすい**；理解できる(to 〜)
⊕ comprehensive(包括的な)と混同しないように注意
名 comprehension：理解(力)
動 comprehend：〜を(十分に)理解する

Day 54)) CD-B19
Quick Review
答えは右ページ下

- □ 衛生の
- □ 統合された
- □ 海外の
- □ 差し迫った
- □ 活気のある
- □ 暫定的な
- □ 不景気の
- □ 目立つ
- □ 実行可能な
- □ 不規則な
- □ 拘束力のある
- □ 値段が高過ぎる
- □ 一貫性のない
- □ 耐えられる
- □ 詐欺的な
- □ 近隣の

Check 2 Phrase	Check 3 Sentence
☐ a solvent company（支払い能力のある会社）	☐ Every company is struggling to remain solvent.（すべての企業は支払い能力を維持しようと奮闘している）
☐ disruptive activities（破壊的な行動）	☐ The student is displaying disruptive behavior in class.（その生徒は授業を妨害するような行動を取っている）
☐ pertinent information（関連情報） ☐ a pertinent question（適切な質問）	☐ The information is pertinent to the investigation of the accident.（その情報は事故の調査に関係するものだ）
☐ vocational training [education]（職業訓練[教育]） ☐ a vocational school（職業学校）	☐ The government should promote vocational training to young people.（政府は若者に対する職業訓練を促進するべきだ）
☐ assorted cheeses（チーズの詰め合わせ） ☐ bags in assorted sizes（さまざまなサイズのバッグ）	☐ Our assorted handmade chocolates are always a welcome gift.（当社の手作りチョコレートの詰め合わせはいつでも喜ばれる贈り物です）●広告の表現
☐ an integral part of ~（〜に不可欠な部分）	☐ Collaboration is integral to the success of the project.（そのプロジェクトの成功には協力が不可欠だ）
☐ on-the-job training（実地訓練） ●略はOJT	☐ A minimum of one year of on-the-job experience is required.（最低1年の実地の職業経験が要求される）●求人広告の表現
☐ comprehensible explanation（分かりやすい説明）	☐ She can speak or write comprehensible English.（彼女は分かりやすい英語を話したり書いたりできる）

Day 54 CD-B19
Quick Review
答えは左ページ下

☐ hygienic ☐ robust ☐ viable ☐ inconsistent
☐ integrated ☐ interim ☐ erratic ☐ tolerable
☐ offshore ☐ depressed ☐ binding ☐ fraudulent
☐ imminent ☐ noticeable ☐ overpriced ☐ neighboring

CHAPTER 1
CHAPTER 2
CHAPTER 3
CHAPTER 4
CHAPTER 5
CHAPTER 6
CHAPTER 7
CHAPTER 8
CHAPTER 9

Day 56　形容詞12

Check 1　Listen 》CD-B21

☐ 0881
inclusive
/inklú:siv/
Part 5, 6

形 ❶(料金などが)**すべてを含んだ**(≒all-inclusive)
❷(～を)含めて(of ～)(⇔exclusive：除いた)
動include：～を含む
前including：～を含めて

☐ 0882
ethical
/éθikəl/
Part 7

形 **倫理**[道徳]**の**；倫理[道徳]的な(≒moral)(⇔unethical)
名ethics：倫理、道徳

☐ 0883
ubiquitous
/ju:bíkwətəs/
ビジネス問題

形 **至る所にある**[いる]、遍在する(≒omnipresent)

☐ 0884
legendary
/lédʒəndèri/
Part 4

形 ❶**伝説に残るような**、有名な(≒famous)　❷伝説上の
名legend：❶伝説　❷伝説的人物

☐ 0885
formidable
/fɔ́:rmidəbl/
Part 5, 6

形 ❶(問題などが)**手に負えない**、手ごわい　❷恐ろしい

☐ 0886
commemorative
/kəmémərèitiv/
Part 5, 6

形 **記念の**、記念となる
名commemoration：❶記念(すること)　❷記念式[祭、式典]；記念物
動commemorate：～を記念する、祝う

☐ 0887
optimal
/áptəməl/
Part 5, 6

形 **最善**[最上、最適]**の**(≒best, optimum)
動optimize：❶～を最大限に利用する　❷(プログラム)を最適化する

☐ 0888
uninterrupted
/ʌnintərʌ́ptid/
Part 5, 6

形 **絶え間ない**、連続した(≒continuous)
動interrupt：～を遮る、妨げる

continued
▼

チャンツを聞いているだけでは、正しい発音はなかなか身につかない。つぶやくだけでもOKなので、必ず口を動かそう！

☐ 聞くだけモード　Check 1
☐ しっかりモード　Check 1 ▶ 2
☐ かんぺきモード　Check 1 ▶ 2 ▶ 3

Check 2　Phrase

☐ an inclusive fee [charge]（すべてを含んだ料金）
☐ be inclusive of taxes（[料金などが]税を含んでいる）

☐ an ethical problem（倫理上の問題）
☐ ethical education（道徳教育）

☐ the ubiquitous bird（どこにでもいる鳥）⊕スズメやハトなど

☐ the legendary concert（伝説に残るようなコンサート）
☐ a legendary hero（伝説上の英雄）

☐ a formidable opponent [adversary, enemy]（手ごわい相手）
☐ a formidable weapon（恐ろしい兵器）

☐ a commemorative medal（記念メダル）

☐ an optimal choice（最善の選択）
☐ optimal conditions（最適条件）

☐ uninterrupted rain（絶え間のない雨）
☐ for 20 uninterrupted years（20年間連続して）

Check 3　Sentence

☐ The inclusive cost for the trip is $98 per person.（その旅行のすべてを含んだ費用は1人98ドルだ）

☐ Employees must conduct themselves according to the highest ethical standards.（従業員らは最高の倫理規範に従って行動しなければならない）

☐ Computers have become ubiquitous in our life.（コンピューターは私たちの生活の中で至る所に存在するようになった）

☐ Chicago is legendary for its music, particularly jazz and blues.（シカゴは音楽、特にジャズとブルースで有名だ）

☐ The task of finding reasonably priced healthcare insurance was very formidable.（手ごろな値段の医療保険を見つける仕事はとても大変だった）

☐ Japan's first commemorative stamp was issued in 1894.（日本最初の記念切手は1894年に発行された）

☐ The optimal temperature for storing wine is between 12 and 17 degrees Celsius.（ワインを保存する最適温度はセ氏12度から17度の間だ）

☐ The TV station broadcast uninterrupted coverage of the presidential inaugural ceremony.（そのテレビ局は大統領就任式を中断なしで放送した）

continued ▼

Day 56

Check 1　Listen 》CD-B21

0889
incoming
/ínkʌmiŋ/
Part 4

形 ❶**新入りの**、新任の　❷(電話などが)入ってくる

0890
resourceful
/risɔ́ːrsfəl/
ビジネス問題

形 **臨機の才のある**、機知[工夫]に富んだ
名 resource：(通例～s)資源；資産

0891
impending
/impéndiŋ/
Part 5, 6

形 **差し迫った**、今にも起こりそうな(≒imminent)

0892
discouraging
/diskə́ːridʒiŋ/
ビジネス問題

形 **思わしくない**、落胆させる
名 discouragement：落胆、がっかりさせること[もの]
動 discourage：❶～を落胆させる；～のやる気をなくさせる　❷(discourage A from doingで)Aに～するのをやめさせる、思いとどまらせる

0893
accomplished
/əkámplist/
Part 4

形 ❶**熟達[熟練]した**(≒skilled, skillful)　❷(事実が)既成[既定]の
名 accomplishment：❶業績、功績、実績　❷完成、成就、達成
動 accomplish：～を成し遂げる、完遂[成就]する

0894
marginal
/máːrdʒinl/
Part 7

形 ❶**不十分な**、わずかな　❷限界収益点の　❸欄外の
名 margin：❶利ざや、販売利益、マージン　❷(ページの)余白、欄外　❸(得票数などの)差

0895
unforeseen
/ʌ̀nfɔːrsíːn/
Part 7

形 **予期しない**、思いがけない、不測の(≒unexpected)
動 foresee：～を予見する、見越す
形 foreseeable：予見[予知、予測]できる

0896
interdepartmental
/ìntərdipàːrtméntl/
ビジネス問題

形 **各部局間の**
名 department：❶(会社などの)部、課、部門　❷(大学の)学科、学部

Day 55 》CD-B20
Quick Review
答えは右ページ下

- □ 予測できない
- □ 有益な
- □ 組織の
- □ 決定的な
- □ 特定の
- □ 明らかな
- □ 素晴らしい
- □ 憂慮すべき
- □ 支払い能力がある
- □ 破壊的な
- □ 関連のある
- □ 職業の
- □ 詰め合わせの
- □ 不可欠な
- □ 実地の
- □ 分かりやすい

Check 2　Phrase

- ☐ incoming freshmen(新入生)
- ☐ an incoming call(かかってくる電話)

- ☐ a resourceful employee(臨機の才のある従業員)

- ☐ impending doom(差し迫った破滅)
- ☐ one's impending retirement(間近に迫った退職[引退])

- ☐ discouraging results(思わしくない結果)

- ☐ an accomplished pianist(熟達したピアニスト)
- ☐ an accomplished fact(既成事実)

- ☐ a marginal improvement(不十分な改善)
- ☐ marginal profits(限界利益)

- ☐ unforeseen consequences(予期せぬ結果)
- ☐ unforeseen circumstances(不測の事態)

- ☐ an interdepartmental project(部局間プロジェクト)

Check 3　Sentence

- ☐ The incoming president will face a number of difficult challenges.(新大統領は多くの困難な課題に直面するだろう)

- ☐ He is a shrewd and resourceful manager.(彼は敏腕で臨機の才がある部長だ)

- ☐ He has announced his impending retirement from politics.(彼は近々政界から引退することを発表した)

- ☐ Stock prices plummeted following discouraging sales reports from many of the nation's retailers.(国内小売業者の多くの思わしくない売上報告を受けて株価は急落した)

- ☐ He was an accomplished violinist and composer.(彼は名バイオリニストであり作曲家だった)

- ☐ The automaker reported a marginal increase in sales from a year ago.(その自動車メーカーは前年比でわずかに売り上げが伸びたことを報じた)

- ☐ The concert was canceled due to unforeseen circumstances.(そのコンサートは不測の事態のため中止になった)

- ☐ In hospitals, interdepartmental communication is essential to the continuity of care for patients.(病院においては、部局間の連絡が患者の看護の継続に不可欠だ)

Day 55 》CD-B20　Quick Review　答えは左ページ下

- ☐ unpredictable
- ☐ instructive
- ☐ organizational
- ☐ conclusive
- ☐ given
- ☐ manifest
- ☐ superb
- ☐ disturbing
- ☐ solvent
- ☐ disruptive
- ☐ pertinent
- ☐ vocational
- ☐ assorted
- ☐ integral
- ☐ on-the-job
- ☐ comprehensible

CHAPTER 1
CHAPTER 2
CHAPTER 3
CHAPTER 4
CHAPTER 5
CHAPTER 6
CHAPTER 7
CHAPTER 8
CHAPTER 9

Day 57　形容詞13

Check 1　Listen))) CD-B22

☐ 0897
adjoining
/ədʒɔ́iniŋ/
Part 5, 6

形 **隣の**、隣り合った
動 adjoin：〜の隣にある

☐ 0898
negligible
/néglidʒəbl/
Part 5, 6

形 **ごくわずかな**；無視できるほどの、取るに足らない
名 neglect：❶無視、軽視　❷怠慢
動 neglect：❶〜を無視[軽視]する　❷(仕事など)を怠る

☐ 0899
exorbitant
/igzɔ́:rbətənt/
Part 5, 6

形 (値段などが)**法外な**、途方もない

☐ 0900
behavioral
/bihéivjərəl/
Part 7

形 **行動の**[に関する]
名 behavior：❶振る舞い、行儀　❷行動
動 behave：振る舞う、行動する

☐ 0901
hardworking
/há:rdwə́:rkiŋ/
ビジネス問題

形 **勤勉な**、よく働く[勉強する] (≒ diligent, industrious) (⇔ idle, lazy)

☐ 0902
bullish
/búliʃ/
ビジネス問題

形 ❶(相場が)**上向きの**、強気の (⇔ bearish：[相場が]弱気の)　❷楽観的な

☐ 0903
renewable
/rinjú:əbl/
Part 7

形 ❶**再生**[回復、復活]**できる**　❷更新[継続、延長]できる
名 renewal：❶更新　❷再開
動 renew：❶(契約など)を更新する　❷〜を再開する

☐ 0904
understaffed
/ʌ̀ndərstǽft/
ビジネス問題

形 **人員**[人手、職員]**不足の** (⇔ overstaffed)

continued
▼

Quick Reviewは使ってる? 昨日覚えた表現でも、記憶に残っているとは限らない。学習の合間に軽くチェックするだけでも効果は抜群!

☐ 聞くだけモード　Check 1
☐ しっかりモード　Check 1 ▶ 2
☐ かんぺきモード　Check 1 ▶ 2 ▶ 3

Check 2　Phrase

☐ an adjoining building(隣の建物)

☐ a negligible difference(ごくわずかな違い)
☐ a negligible amount(取るに足らない量)

☐ an exorbitant price(法外な価格)

☐ behavioral psychology(行動心理学)

☐ a hardworking student(勤勉な生徒)

☐ the bullish stock market(上向きの株式市場)
☐ be bullish about the future(将来を楽観している)

☐ renewable energy(再生可能エネルギー)
☐ a renewable contract(更新可能な契約)

☐ an understaffed hospital(職員不足の病院)

Check 3　Sentence

☐ I booked adjoining hotel rooms for myself and my parents.(私は自分と両親用にホテルの隣り合った部屋を予約した)

☐ His experience in politics is negligible.(彼の政治経験はごくわずかだ)

☐ Housing prices are exorbitant in this area.(この地域の住宅価格は法外だ)

☐ The student has behavioral problems.(その生徒は行動に問題がある)

☐ Loyal and hardworking employees are the best asset of any company.(忠実で勤勉な従業員は企業の最高の資産だ)

☐ The stock market goes through bullish and bearish cycles.(株式市場は強気と弱気の循環を繰り返す)

☐ Paper is a renewable natural resource.(紙は再生可能な天然資源だ)

☐ The healthcare industry is severely understaffed.(医療産業は深刻な人手不足だ)

continued ▼

Day 57

Check 1 Listen))) CD-B22

☐ 0905 dogmatic
/dɔːgmǽtik/
Part 7

形 **独断[独善]的な**
名 dogma: 教義、教理

☐ 0906 plenary
/plíːnəri/
Part 7

形 ❶**全員出席の** ❷(権力が)絶対的な

☐ 0907 inaccessible
/ìnəksésəbl/
Part 5, 6

形 ❶(場所などが)(〜にとって)**近づきにくい**(to 〜)
❷(〜にとって)分かりにくい、理解しづらい(to 〜)
名 access: ❶接近 ❷利用[入手]する権利[機会]
動 access: ❶〜にアクセスする ❷〜に接近する

☐ 0908 top-of-the-line
/tápəvðəláin/
ビジネス問題

形 (あるメーカーの)**最高級品の**、最高価格の

☐ 0909 fledgling
/flédʒliŋ/
ビジネス問題

形 **新参の**、未熟な、経験のない
名 (巣立ちしたばかりの)ひな鳥

☐ 0910 arcane
/ɑːrkéin/
Part 5, 6

形 (普通の人には)**難解な**、深遠で分かりにくい

☐ 0911 lengthy
/léŋkθi/
❶発音注意
Part 5, 6

形 ❶(話などが)**長ったらしい** ❷非常に長い
名 length: 長さ
動 lengthen: 〜を長くする、延長する

☐ 0912 congressional
/kəŋgréʃənl/
Part 5, 6

形 (通例C〜)(米国)**議会[国会]の**
名 congress: (C〜)(米国の)国会、連邦議会
名 congressman: (しばしばC〜)(米国の)国会議員、(特に)下院議員

Day 56))) CD-B21
Quick Review
答えは右ページ下

☐ すべてを含んだ ☐ 手に負えない ☐ 新入りの ☐ 熟達した
☐ 倫理の ☐ 記念の ☐ 臨機の才のある ☐ 不十分な
☐ 至る所にある ☐ 最善の ☐ 差し迫った ☐ 予期しない
☐ 伝説に残るような ☐ 絶え間ない ☐ 思わしくない ☐ 各部局間の

Check 2 Phrase

- □ a dogmatic person（独善的な人）

- □ a plenary session [meeting]（全員出席の会議、本会議、総会）
- □ plenary powers（全権）

- □ an area inaccessible to cars（車では近づけない地域）
- □ a book inaccessible to ordinary people（普通の人では理解しづらい本）

- □ top-of-the-line products（最高級品）

- □ a fledgling business [company]（新参企業）
- □ a fledgling teacher（新米教師）

- □ an arcane theory [formula]（難解な理論[公式]）

- □ a lengthy speech（長ったらしいスピーチ）
- □ a lengthy recession（長引く景気後退）

- □ a congressional committee（議会の委員会）
- □ a Congressional district（下院選挙区）

Check 3 Sentence

- □ Researchers should avoid making dogmatic generalizations based on their findings.（研究者は調査結果に基づいた独断的な一般化を避けなければならない）

- □ The European Parliament will hold a plenary session next week.（欧州議会は来週、本会議を開く予定だ）

- □ The Arctic is one of the most inaccessible and mysterious places on Earth.（北極圏は地上で最も近づきにくく神秘的な場所の1つだ）

- □ The store specializes in top-of-the-line computers using only the latest and best hardware.（その店は最新かつ最高品質のハードウエアを使った最高級のコンピューターを専門に扱っている）

- □ It is difficult for fledgling businesses to survive in the current economic climate.（現在の経済状況で新参企業が生き残るのは難しい）

- □ The world of finance is full of arcane terminology.（金融の世界は難解な専門用語に満ちている）

- □ Today's meeting was quite lengthy.（今日の会議はかなり長かった）

- □ Congressional elections will be held next year.（連邦議会選挙が来年行われる）

Day 56))) CD-B21
Quick Review
答えは左ページ下

- □ inclusive
- □ ethical
- □ ubiquitous
- □ legendary
- □ formidable
- □ commemorative
- □ optimal
- □ uninterrupted
- □ incoming
- □ resourceful
- □ impending
- □ discouraging
- □ accomplished
- □ marginal
- □ unforeseen
- □ interdepartmental

CHAPTER 1
CHAPTER 2
CHAPTER 3
CHAPTER 4
CHAPTER 5
CHAPTER 6
CHAPTER 7
CHAPTER 8
CHAPTER 9

Day 58　形容詞14

Check 1　Listen))) CD-B23

☐ 0913
nutritious
/njuːtríʃəs/
Part 7

形 **栄養のある**、栄養に富んだ
名 nutrition：栄養；栄養補給[摂取]
名 nutrient：栄養物、栄養素

☐ 0914
functional
/fʌ́ŋkʃənl/
Part 5, 6

形 ❶**実用的な**(≒practical)、便利な(≒useful)　❷機能の
名 function：❶(〜の)機能、働き(of 〜)　❷(社会的)行事
動 function：(〜の)機能[役割]を果たす(as 〜)

☐ 0915
incompetent
/inkάmpətənt/
Part 2, 3

形 **無能な**、不適任な(⇔competent)
名 無能力者、不適格者
名 incompetence：無能力、不適格

☐ 0916
gigantic
/dʒaigǽntik/
❶発音注意
Part 5, 6

形 **巨大な**：莫大な

☐ 0917
accommodating
/əkάmədèitiŋ/
Part 7

形 **親切な**、世話好きな
名 accommodation：(通例〜s)宿泊設備
動 accommodate：❶(建物などが)(人)を収容できる　❷(要求など)を受け入れる

☐ 0918
exemplary
/igzémpləri/
Part 7

形 ❶**模範的な**、手本とすべき　❷見せしめの、戒めの

☐ 0919
coin-operated
/kɔ́inὰpəreitid/
Part 4

形 (機械が)**コイン式の**、自動販売式の

☐ 0920
improper
/imprάpər/
Part 5, 6

形 **適切[妥当]でない**(⇔proper)

continued
▼

今日でChapter 6は最後！ 時間に余裕があったら、章末のReviewにも挑戦しておこう。忘れてしまった単語も結構あるのでは?!

☐ 聞くだけモード　Check 1
☐ しっかりモード　Check 1 ▶ 2
☐ かんぺきモード　Check 1 ▶ 2 ▶ 3

Check 2　Phrase

☐ a nutritious diet（栄養のある食事）

☐ functional clothing（実用的な服）
☐ a functional disorder（機能障害）

☐ an incompetent doctor（無能な医者）

☐ a gigantic rock（巨大な岩）
☐ a gigantic debt（莫大な負債）

☐ accommodating hotel staff（親切なホテルの従業員たち）

☐ exemplary deeds（模範的な行い）
☐ an exemplary punishment（見せしめの罰、懲戒）

☐ a coin-operated locker（コインロッカー）

☐ improper behavior（不適切な行動）
☐ It is improper to do ~.（~するのは適切ではない）

Check 3　Sentence

☐ Fruit and vegetables are highly nutritious.（果物と野菜は非常に栄養がある）

☐ "Being" functional is better than "looking" functional.（実用的で「あること」は実用的に「見えること」よりも優れている）

☐ Incompetent teachers should be dismissed.（能力のない教師は解雇されるべきだ）

☐ The temple is famous for its gigantic statue of Buddha.（その寺は巨大な仏像で有名だ）

☐ He is accommodating and easy to work with.（彼は親切で一緒に働きやすい）

☐ She was cited for her exemplary teaching skills.（彼女は模範的な指導能力で表彰された）

☐ Five coin-operated laundry machines are located in the basement.（地下にはコイン式の洗濯機が5台置かれている）

☐ It would be improper for me to comment on the issue at this point.（現時点で私がその問題についてコメントするのは適切ではないだろう）

continued
▼

Check 1 Listen)) CD-B23

0921 restrictive
/rɪstríktɪv/
Part 5, 6

形 **制限[限定]的な**
名 restriction：(~に対する)制限、限定 (on ~)
動 restrict：~を(...に)制限[限定]する (to ...)
形 restricted：(~に)制限された (to ~)

0922 nonrefundable
/nànrɪfʌ́ndəbl/
ビジネス問題

形 **払い戻しが利かない**
名 refund：払い戻し(金)
動 refund：(料金など)を払い戻す

0923 de facto
/diː fǽktou/
Part 4

形 **事実上の**
副 事実上(は)、実際には

0924 resilient
/rɪzíljənt/
Part 5, 6

形 ❶(病気・逆境などから)**立ち直り[回復]の早い**
❷弾力のある

0925 firsthand
/fə́ːrsthǽnd/
ビジネス問題

形 **直接の**、じかの ➕ secondhandは「間接の」
副 直接に、じかに

0926 abdominal
/æbdɑ́mənl/
Part 7

形 **腹部の**
名 (~s)腹筋
名 abdomen：腹部

0927 impassable
/ɪmpǽsəbl/
Part 1

形 (悪天候などのために)**通行不能の** (⇔passable)
名 pass：通行(許可)証
動 pass：❶(議案など)を可決する、通過させる ❷~を(...に)手渡す (to ...) ❸~に合格する ❹(時が)過ぎる

0928 punitive
/pjúːnətɪv/
Part 5, 6

形 ❶**懲罰[懲戒]的な** ❷(課税などが)過酷な
名 punishment：(~に対する)処罰、刑罰 (for ~)
動 punish：(punish A for BでAをB(悪事など)のかどで罰する、処罰する

Day 57)) CD-B22
Quick Review
答えは右ページ下

- ☐ 隣の
- ☐ ごくわずかな
- ☐ 法外な
- ☐ 行動の
- ☐ 勤勉な
- ☐ 上向きの
- ☐ 再生できる
- ☐ 人員不足の
- ☐ 独断的な
- ☐ 全員出席の
- ☐ 近づきにくい
- ☐ 最高級品の
- ☐ 新参の
- ☐ 難解な
- ☐ 長ったらしい
- ☐ 議会の

Check 2 Phrase

- ☐ **restrictive** regulations [measures]（制限規定[措置]）

- ☐ a **nonrefundable** airline ticket（払い戻しが利かない航空券）

- ☐ a **de facto** government [parent]（事実上の政府[親]）

- ☐ a **resilient** person（立ち直りの早い人）
- ☐ a **resilient** rubber ball（弾力のあるゴムボール）

- ☐ **firsthand** knowledge（[経験から]直接得た知識）

- ☐ **abdominal** pains [cramps]（腹痛[腹部のけいれん]）

- ☐ make many streets **impassable**（[洪水などが]多くの通りを通行不能にする）

- ☐ **punitive** actions [measures]（処罰措置）
- ☐ **punitive** taxes（過酷な税）

Check 3 Sentence

- ☐ **Restrictive** diets can lead to nutritional deficiencies.（食事制限は栄養不足につながることがある）

- ☐ Deposits are usually **nonrefundable**.（手付金は通常、払い戻しが利かない）

- ☐ English is the **de facto** official language of India.（英語はインドの事実上の公用語だ）

- ☐ Brazil's economy proved **resilient** to the global slowdown.（世界的な景気後退に対してブラジル経済は回復が早いことが分かった）

- ☐ **Firsthand** experience is better than learning from a book.（実体験は本から学ぶことより優れている）

- ☐ Sudden **abdominal** pain is often an indicator of serious disease.（突然の腹痛は深刻な病気の兆候であることが多い）

- ☐ The road is **impassable** due to flooding.（道路は洪水で通行不能になっている）

- ☐ The UN Security Council imposed **punitive** sanctions on the country.（国連安全保障理事会はその国に対して懲罰的な制裁措置を課した）

Day 57))) CD-B22
Quick Review
答えは左ページ下

- ☐ adjoining
- ☐ negligible
- ☐ exorbitant
- ☐ behavioral
- ☐ hardworking
- ☐ bullish
- ☐ renewable
- ☐ understaffed
- ☐ dogmatic
- ☐ plenary
- ☐ inaccessible
- ☐ top-of-the-line
- ☐ fledgling
- ☐ arcane
- ☐ lengthy
- ☐ congressional

CHAPTER 1
CHAPTER 2
CHAPTER 3
CHAPTER 4
CHAPTER 5
CHAPTER 6
CHAPTER 7
CHAPTER 8
CHAPTER 9

Chapter 6 Review

左ページの(1)〜(20)の形容詞の同意・類義語（≒）、反意・反対語（⇔）を右ページのA〜Tから選び、カッコの中に答えを書き込もう。意味が分からないときは、見出し番号を参照して復習しておこう（答えは右ページ下）。

- □ (1) eminent (0818) ≒は？（　　）
- □ (2) barren (0820) ⇔は？（　　）
- □ (3) provisional (0831) ≒は？（　　）
- □ (4) occupational (0835) ≒は？（　　）
- □ (5) invaluable (0837) ≒は？（　　）
- □ (6) faulty (0848) ≒は？（　　）
- □ (7) imminent (0852) ≒は？（　　）
- □ (8) tolerable (0862) ≒は？（　　）
- □ (9) instructive (0866) ≒は？（　　）
- □ (10) conclusive (0868) ≒は？（　　）
- □ (11) integral (0878) ≒は？（　　）
- □ (12) ethical (0882) ≒は？（　　）
- □ (13) ubiquitous (0883) ≒は？（　　）
- □ (14) optimal (0887) ≒は？（　　）
- □ (15) uninterrupted (0888) ≒は？（　　）
- □ (16) accomplished (0893) ≒は？（　　）
- □ (17) hardworking (0901) ≒は？（　　）
- □ (18) bullish (0902) ⇔は？（　　）
- □ (19) understaffed (0904) ⇔は？（　　）
- □ (20) functional (0914) ≒は？（　　）

A. famous
B. diligent
C. bearable
D. best
E. temporary
F. continuous
G. moral
H. defective
I. skilled
J. precious
K. useful
L. bearish
M. impending
N. fertile
O. practical
P. decisive
Q. omnipresent
R. vocational
S. overstaffed
T. essential

【解答】(1) A (2) N (3) E (4) R (5) J (6) H (7) M (8) C (9) K (10) P
(11) T (12) G (13) Q (14) D (15) F (16) I (17) B (18) L (19) S (20) O

CHAPTER 7

副詞：必修48

Chapter 7では、TOEIC必修の副詞48をチェック。このChapterが終われば、単語編は終了です。ここまで来れば、語彙力は1万語オーバーレベル。これからは積極的にアウトプットしていきましょう！

Day 59 【副詞1】
▸ 270
Day 60 【副詞2】
▸ 274
Day 61 【副詞3】
▸ 278
Chapter 7 Review
▸ 282

TOEIC的格言

Experience is the best teacher.

経験は最良の師。

Day 59　副詞1

Check 1　Listen 》CD-B24

□ 0929
respectively
/rispéktivli/
Part 7

副 **それぞれ**、各自　⊕通例、文尾で用いる
形 respective：それぞれの、各自の

□ 0930
separately
/sépərətli/
Part 4

副 **別々に**、個々に；(〜から)離れて(from 〜)
名 separation：❶分離　❷別離；(夫婦の)別居
動 separate：❶〜を分ける、引き離す　❷(separate A from Bで)AをBから引き離す；AをBから区別する
形 separate：(〜から)離れた(from 〜)

□ 0931
temporarily
/tèmpərérəli/
Part 5, 6

副 **一時的に**
形 temporary：一時的な、臨時の；つかの間の

□ 0932
allegedly
/əlédʒidli/
Part 7

副 **伝えられるところでは**(≒reportedly)、申し立てによると
名 allegation：(特に証拠のない)申し立て、主張
動 allege：(証拠なしに)〜だと断言[主張]する
形 alleged：❶申し立てられた　❷疑わしい

□ 0933
locally
/lóukəli/
Part 2, 3

副 **地元で**、この[その]土地で
形 local：❶地元の、現地の　❷各駅停車の

□ 0934
closely
/klóusli/
Part 5, 6

副 ❶**密接に**；親密に　❷綿密に、念入りに
形 close：❶(〜に)近い(to 〜)　❷親密な　❸(調査などが)綿密な

□ 0935
regrettably
/rigrétəbli/
Part 7

副 **遺憾ながら**、残念なことには(≒unfortunately)
名 regret：後悔
動 regret：❶〜を後悔する、残念に思う　❷(regret doingで)〜したことを後悔する、残念に思う　❸(regret to doで)残念ながら〜する

□ 0936
fluently
/flú:əntli/
Part 7

副 **流ちょうに**、すらすらと
名 fluency：(言葉の)流ちょうさ
形 fluent：❶(be fluent inで)(言葉)を流ちょうに話せる、(言葉)に堪能である　❷(言葉が)流ちょうな

continued
▼

Chapter 7では、3日をかけて必修副詞48をチェック。まずはCDでチャンツを聞いて、単語を「耳」からインプット！

- □ 聞くだけモード　Check 1
- □ しっかりモード　Check 1 ▶ 2
- □ かんぺきモード　Check 1 ▶ 2 ▶ 3

Check 2　Phrase & Sentence

□ Japan and South Korea came first and second respectively.（日本と韓国がそれぞれ1位と2位になった）

□ interview witnesses separately（目撃者たちと1人ずつ面接する）
□ live separately from one's parents（両親と離れて生活する）

□ be temporarily out of service（一時的に使用中止になっている）

□ The suspect allegedly embezzled $10,000 from the company.（伝えられるところでは、容疑者は会社から1万ドルを横領した）

□ Think globally, act locally.（地球規模で考え、地元で活動しよう）❶環境活動などのスローガン

□ closely resemble 〜（〜によく似ている）
□ closely examine 〜（〜を綿密に調査する）

□ Regrettably, the event was canceled due to bad weather.（残念なことにそのイベントは悪天候のため中止になった）

□ speak French fluently（フランス語を流ちょうに話す）

Check 3　Sentence

□ I played piano and he played violin respectively.（私はピアノを、彼はバイオリンをそれぞれ弾いた）

□ The married couple decided to live separately.（その夫婦は別居することを決めた）

□ The store is closed temporarily for remodeling.（その店は改装のため一時的に閉店している）

□ He was arrested for allegedly stealing money from one of the clients.（伝えられるところでは、彼は顧客の1人から金を盗んだ容疑で逮捕された）

□ The company employs about 500 workers locally.（その会社は現地で約500人の労働者を雇用している）

□ Stress and lack of sleep are closely connected.（ストレスと睡眠不足は密接に関連している）

□ If you do not receive a response within 10 days, then regrettably your application has been unsuccessful.（10日以内に返答がなければ、遺憾ながら貴殿の応募は不合格です）❶求人広告の表現

□ We are looking for an accountant who speaks English and Spanish fluently.（当社では英語とスペイン語を流ちょうに話す会計士を求めています）❶求人広告の表現

continued ▼

Day 59

Check 1　Listen))) CD-B24

□ 0937
virtually
/və́ːrtʃuəli/
Part 5, 6

副 **ほとんど**、ほぼ（≒almost）
形 virtual：❶実質上の、事実上の　❷仮想の；インターネット上の

□ 0938
entirely
/intáiərli/
Part 5, 6

副 **完全に**、全く、すっかり（≒completely, totally）
形 entire：全体[全部]の

□ 0939
unanimously
/juːnǽnəməsli/
❶発音注意
Part 5, 6

副 **満場一致で**　⊕anonymously（匿名で）と混同しないように注意
形 unanimous：❶満場[全員]一致の　❷(～で)意見が一致して(in ～)

□ 0940
barely
/béərli/
Part 5, 6

副 **辛うじて**、何とか、わずかに　⊕hardly, scarcely（ほとんど～しない[ない]）との使い分けに注意

□ 0941
obviously
/ábviəsli/
Part 2, 3

副 **明らかに**（≒clearly, evidently）
形 obvious：❶明らかな、明白な　❷見え透いた

□ 0942
cordially
/kɔ́ːrdʒəli/
❶発音注意
Part 7

副 ❶**心から**、心を込めて　❷ひどく、強烈に
形 cordial：心からの、誠心誠意の

□ 0943
worldwide
/wə́ːrldwáid/
Part 7

副 **世界中で**[に]、世界的に　⊕「全国的に」はnationwide
形 世界中の、世界的な

□ 0944
individually
/ìndəvídʒuəli/
Part 4

副 **個別に**、1人[1つ]ずつ
名 individual：個人
形 individual：❶個々の　❷個人の

Day 58))) CD-B23
Quick Review
答えは右ページ下

- □ 栄養のある
- □ 実用的な
- □ 無能な
- □ 巨大な
- □ 親切な
- □ 模範的な
- □ コイン式の
- □ 適切でない
- □ 制限的な
- □ 払い戻しが利かない
- □ 事実上の
- □ 立ち直りの早い
- □ 直接の
- □ 腹部の
- □ 通行不能の
- □ 懲罰的な

Check 2 Phrase & Sentence

- □ be virtually impossible（ほとんど不可能である）
- □ virtually everyone（ほぼ全員）

- □ be entirely different from ~（〜と全く違う）
- □ be not entirely recovered（完全に回復したわけではない）

- □ unanimously approve ~（〜を満場一致で承認する）

- □ barely escape ~（辛うじて〜を免れる）
- □ be barely 15（わずか15歳である）

- □ The calculation is obviously wrong.（その計算は明らかに間違っている）

- □ Yours cordially = Cordially yours（敬具）
- □ cordially dislike ~（〜をひどく嫌う）

- □ a company doing business worldwide（世界中でビジネスを行っている会社）

- □ interview applicants individually（応募者たちと個別に面接する）
- □ wrap cookies individually（クッキーを1つずつ包む）

Check 3 Sentence

- □ The actor was virtually unknown before the movie's debut.（その俳優は映画デビューする前はほとんど知られていなかった）

- □ It was entirely my fault.（それは完全に私の誤りだった）

- □ The proposal was approved unanimously.（その提案は満場一致で承認された）

- □ The company could barely manage to sustain last year's profits.（その会社は辛うじて昨年の収益を維持することができた）

- □ Obviously, she doesn't like me.（明らかに彼女は私のことを気に入っていない）

- □ You are cordially invited to our wedding on March 29.（3月29日の私たちの結婚式に心からお招きいたします）●招待状の表現

- □ Global warming is impacting wildlife worldwide.（地球温暖化は世界中で野生生物に影響を及ぼしている）

- □ The new employees were introduced to the board individually.（新入社員は重役たちに1人ずつ紹介された）

Day 58 》CD-B23
Quick Review
答えは左ページ下

- □ nutritious
- □ functional
- □ incompetent
- □ gigantic
- □ accommodating
- □ exemplary
- □ coin-operated
- □ improper
- □ restrictive
- □ nonrefundable
- □ de facto
- □ resilient
- □ firsthand
- □ abdominal
- □ impassable
- □ punitive

CHAPTER 1
CHAPTER 2
CHAPTER 3
CHAPTER 4
CHAPTER 5
CHAPTER 6
CHAPTER 7
CHAPTER 8
CHAPTER 9

Day 60　副詞2

Check 1　Listen))) CD-B25

☐ 0945
effectively
/iféktivli/
Part 4

副 ❶**効果的に**、有効に　❷事実上(≒in effect)
名 effect：❶影響；(原因に対する)結果　❷(〜に対する)効果(on [upon] 〜)　❸(〜s)個人資産、身の回り品
形 effective：効果的な、有効な

☐ 0946
accordingly
/əkɔ́ːrdiŋli/
Part 7

副 ❶**それに応じて**　❷それ故に、従って(≒therefore, consequently)

☐ 0947
initially
/iníʃəli/
Part 5, 6

副 **最初**(のうち)**は**、初めに
名 initial：頭文字
形 initial：最初の
動 initiate：(計画など)を始める

☐ 0948
considerably
/kənsídərəbli/
❶アクセント注意
Part 5, 6

副 **かなり**、随分
名 consideration：考慮、考察
動 consider：❶〜をよく考える、熟慮[熟考]する　❷(consider doingで)〜することをよく考える
形 considerable：(数量などが)かなりの、相当な

☐ 0949
reportedly
/ripɔ́ːrtidli/
Part 4

副 **報道**[報告、うわさ]**によると**、伝えられるところによると(≒allegedly)
名 report：❶報告(書)　❷報道
動 report：❶〜を報告する　❷〜を報道する　❸(report toで)〜の部下である；〜に出頭する

☐ 0950
accidentally
/æksədéntəli/
Part 5, 6

副 **誤って**、偶然に(≒by accident)
名 accident：❶事故　❷偶然
形 accidental：偶然の

☐ 0951
inevitably
/inévətəbli/
Part 5, 6

副 **必然的に**、必ず
名 inevitable：(the 〜)避けられないこと[もの]
形 inevitable：避けられない、不可避の、必然の

☐ 0952
ultimately
/ʌ́ltəmətli/
Part 5, 6

副 **最終的に**、結局、最後に(≒finally)
名 ultimate：(the 〜)(〜において)究極のもの(in 〜)
形 ultimate：❶究極の、最終[最後]の　❷最高の

continued
▼

難しい語彙ばかりで挫折しそう?! でも、ここでやめてはモッタイナイ! 今日が終われば、あと10日。あきらめずにガンバロウ!

☐ 聞くだけモード　Check 1
☐ しっかりモード　Check 1 ▶ 2
☐ かんぺきモード　Check 1 ▶ 2 ▶ 3

Check 2　　Phrase & Sentence

☐ **cope effectively with** ~（~に効果的に対処する）
☐ **be effectively bankrupt**（事実上破産している）

☐ He is an adult and should be treated **accordingly**.（彼は大人なのだから、それ相応に扱われるべきだ）

☐ **Initially**, she wanted to be a veterinarian.（最初は、彼女は獣医になりたかった）

☐ **be considerably more expensive than** ~（~よりかなり値段が高い）

☐ **Reportedly**, four people were killed in the car accident.（その自動車事故で4人が死亡したと報じられている）

☐ **accidentally break a vase**（誤って花瓶を割る）
☐ **accidentally on purpose**（偶然を装って）

☐ An improving economy will **inevitably** lead to higher interest rates.（景気の回復は必然的に高金利につながるだろう）

☐ **Ultimately**, everything will work out fine.（最終的にはすべてがうまくいくだろう）

Check 3　　Sentence

☐ The drug works more **effectively** when taken on a daily basis.（その薬は毎日服用するとより効き目がある）

☐ The economy is recovering gradually and **accordingly** many companies are aggressive in their recruiting activities.（経済が徐々に回復しているので、多くの企業は採用活動に積極的だ）

☐ The economic crisis turned out to be more serious than **initially** thought.（経済危機は当初考えられていたよりも深刻であることが分かった）

☐ Oil prices have dropped **considerably** over the past year.（原油価格はこの1年でかなり下がった）

☐ The automaker has **reportedly** been considering a merger with GM.（その自動車メーカーはGMとの合併を検討中だと伝えられている）

☐ She **accidentally** locked herself out of the house.（誤って鍵がかかってしまい彼女は家に入れなくなった）

☐ The current economic downturn will **inevitably** have an impact on the tourism industry.（現在の景気の低迷は必ず観光業界に影響を及ぼすだろう）

☐ **Ultimately**, you'll have to decide what is best for you.（結局のところ、何が最善かはあなたが決めなくてはならない）

continued ▼

Day 60

Check 1　Listen))) CD-B25

0953 drastically /dræstikli/ Part 5, 6
副 **徹底的に**、思い切って
形 drastic：(行動・処置などが)徹底的な、思い切った

0954 periodically /pìəriάdikəli/ Part 5, 6
副 **定期的に**；周期的に
名 period：❶期間、時期　❷時代
名 periodical：定期刊行物、雑誌
形 periodical：定期刊行(物)の
形 periodic：周期的な；定期的な

0955 continuously /kəntínjuəsli/ Part 5, 6
副 **連続して**、連続的に、間断なく
名 continuity：連続性
動 continue：❶続く　❷~を続ける　❸(continue to do [doing]で)~し続ける
形 continuous：絶え間のない

0956 meanwhile /míːnwàil/ Part 2, 3
副 **その間に**；それまでは(≒ in the meanwhile, in the meantime)

0957 commonly /kάmənli/ Part 7
副 **一般に**、通例
形 common：❶一般的な　❷共通[共有]の　❸よくある、普通の

0958 unconditionally /ʌ̀nkəndíʃənli/ Part 7
副 **無条件で**(⇔ conditionally：条件つきで)
名 condition：❶(通例 ~s)(~の)(必要)条件(of [for] ~)　❷(~s)状況、事情；状態
形 conditional：条件つきの
形 unconditional：無条件の

0959 exceptionally /iksépʃənli/ Part 5, 6
副 **例外的に**、特別に、異常に
名 exception：例外
形 exceptional：❶非常に優れた　❷例外的な
副 except：~を除いて、~以外は

0960 purely /pjúərli/ Part 5, 6
副 ❶**全く**、完全に(≒ completely)　❷単に(≒ only)
形 pure：❶全くの　❷(学問などが)純粋な、理論的な

Day 59))) CD-B24　Quick Review　答えは右ページ下

- □ それぞれ
- □ 別々に
- □ 一時的に
- □ 伝えられるところでは
- □ 地元で
- □ 密接に
- □ 遺憾ながら
- □ 流ちょうに
- □ ほとんど
- □ 完全に
- □ 満場一致で
- □ 辛うじて
- □ 明らかに
- □ 心から
- □ 世界中で
- □ 個別に

Check 2   Phrase & Sentence

- ☐ cut costs **drastically**(徹底的に経費を削減する)

- ☐ test the equipment **periodically**(定期的に設備を検査する)

- ☐ work **continuously** for 24 hours(24時間連続して働く)

- ☐ We are in for a bumpy ride. **Meanwhile**, fasten your seat belts.(でこぼこ道に入ります。その間はシートベルトを締めてください)

- ☐ a **commonly** held belief(一般に抱かれた考え)
- ☐ be **commonly** known as ~(一般に~として知られている)

- ☐ surrender **unconditionally**(無条件降伏する)

- ☐ an **exceptionally** cold winter(例年になく寒い冬)
- ☐ an **exceptionally** gifted child(非常に才能の優れた子ども)

- ☐ **purely** by chance(全く偶然に)
- ☐ **purely** for financial reasons(単に金銭的な理由で)

Check 3   Sentence

- ☐ The company has **drastically** restructured its organization.(その会社は徹底的に組織を改革した)

- ☐ The information contained within this site is updated **periodically**.(このサイトに掲載されている情報は定期的に更新される)

- ☐ It has been raining almost **continuously** for three days.(ほぼ絶え間なく3日間雨が降り続いている)

- ☐ I'm starting work in April. **Meanwhile**, I'm travelling around the US.(私は4月に働き始める。それまでは、アメリカ中を旅するつもりだ)

- ☐ Stress fractures are **commonly** experienced by athletes.(疲労骨折は運動選手によく起こる)

- ☐ The $100 registration fee is fully and **unconditionally** refundable on request.(100ドルの登録料は要求があり次第、全額が無条件で返金される)

- ☐ She was **exceptionally** admitted to the Royal Conservatory of Music.(彼女は王立音楽院への入学を例外的に認められた)

- ☐ Participation in the charity event is **purely** voluntary.(その慈善行事への参加は完全に自由だ)

Day 59))) CD-B24
Quick Review
答えは左ページ下

- ☐ respectively
- ☐ separately
- ☐ temporarily
- ☐ allegedly
- ☐ locally
- ☐ closely
- ☐ regrettably
- ☐ fluently
- ☐ virtually
- ☐ entirely
- ☐ unanimously
- ☐ barely
- ☐ obviously
- ☐ cordially
- ☐ worldwide
- ☐ individually

CHAPTER 1 | CHAPTER 2 | CHAPTER 3 | CHAPTER 4 | CHAPTER 5 | CHAPTER 6 | **CHAPTER 7** | CHAPTER 8 | CHAPTER 9

Day 61　副詞3

Check 1　Listen 》CD-B26

0961 financially /fainǽnʃəli/
ビジネス問題

副 **財政[金銭]的に**
名 finance：❶(~s)財源、資金；財務状態　❷財政、財務
動 finance：~に資金を供給する
形 financial：❶財務の、財政上の；金銭上の　❷金融の

0962 vaguely /véigli/
Part 5, 6

副 **ぼんやりと**、漠然と
形 vague：❶(考えなどが)はっきりしない、漠然とした　❷(形などが)ぼんやりした

0963 profoundly /prəfáundli/
Part 5, 6

副 **深く**；大いに
形 profound：❶(影響などが)重大[重要]な；意味深い　❷(悲しみなどが)深い

0964 sufficiently /səfíʃəntli/
Part 5, 6

副 **十分に**
名 sufficiency：❶十分なこと、充足　❷十分な蓄え[資産]
形 sufficient：(~に/…するのに)十分な、足りる(for ~/to do)

0965 comparatively /kəmpǽrətivli/
Part 5, 6

副 **比較的**(に)、比較して(≒ relatively)
名 comparison：(~との)比較(with [to] ~)
動 compare：(compare A to [with] Bで)❶AをBと比較する　❷AをBに例える
形 comparable：(be comparable to [with])~と同等である

0966 mutually /mjú:tʃuəli/
Part 7

副 **互いに**、相互に
形 mutual：❶相互の、互いの　❷共通の

0967 voluntarily /vɑ̀ləntéərəli/
Part 5, 6

副 **自発的に**
名 volunteer：志願者、ボランティア
動 volunteer：❶(~を)進んで引き受ける(for ~)　❷(volunteer to doで)~しようと進んで申し出る
形 voluntary：ボランティアの、自発的な

0968 exponentially /èkspounénʃəli/
Part 7

副 **急激に**、幾何級数的に
形 exponential：急激な、幾何級数的な

continued
▼

今日でChapter 7は最後！ 時間に余裕があったら、章末のReviewにも挑戦しておこう。忘れてしまった単語も結構あるのでは?!

- ☐ 聞くだけモード Check 1
- ☐ しっかりモード Check 1 ▶ 2
- ☐ かんぺきモード Check 1 ▶ 2 ▶ 3

Check 2　Phrase

☐ be financially sound（財政的に堅実である）
☐ be financially independent（経済的に独立している）

☐ be vaguely familiar（[主語のことを]何となくは知っている）

☐ be profoundly moved by ~（~に深く感動する）
☐ change profoundly（大きく変化する）

☐ recover sufficiently（十分に回復する）

☐ be comparatively warm（比較的暖かい）
☐ comparatively speaking（比較して言うと）

☐ a mutually agreed decision（互いに同意した決定）
☐ mutually exclusive [contradictory]（互いに矛盾する、相いれない）

☐ voluntarily participate in ~（自発的に~に参加する）
☐ voluntarily surrender to the police（警察に自首する）

☐ increase [decrease] exponentially（急激に増加[減少]する）

Check 3　Sentence

☐ The proposal is not financially viable.（その提案は財政的に実行可能ではない）

☐ I vaguely remember watching the movie.（私はその映画を見たことをぼんやりと覚えている）

☐ The travel industry was profoundly affected by the terrorist attacks of September 11, 2001.（旅行産業は2001年9月11日のテロ攻撃によって深刻な影響を受けた）

☐ You should eat, sleep, and exercise sufficiently to maintain your health.（健康を維持するために十分に食べ、睡眠を取り、そして運動すべきだ）

☐ The exam was comparatively easy.（その試験は比較的簡単だった）

☐ The business partnership is mutually beneficial to both companies.（その事業提携は両社にとって互いに利益がある）

☐ He was not fired, but left voluntarily.（彼は解雇されたのではなく、自主的に辞職した）

☐ The world's population has been growing exponentially in recent centuries.（世界の人口はここ数世紀で急増している）

continued ▼

Day 61

Check 1　Listen))) CD-B26

0969 partially
/pá:rʃəli/
Part 5, 6

副 部分的に、一部分は(≒partly)
名 part : ❶部分　❷役目；役
形 partial : ❶部分[局部]的な　❷(~が)とても好きな(to ~)　❸(~を)えこひいきする(to [toward] ~)

0970 concisely
/kənsáisli/
❶アクセント注意
Part 5, 6

副 簡潔に(≒briefly)
形 concise : 簡潔な

0971 oddly
/ádli/
Part 7

副 ❶奇妙に　❷奇妙なことに、不思議なことには(≒oddly enough)
形 odd : ❶奇妙な　❷奇数の

0972 deliberately
/dilíbərətli/
Part 5, 6

副 ❶故意に、わざと(≒on purpose, intentionally)　❷慎重に
動 deliberate : ❶~を熟考する　❷(deliberate about [on, over]で)~について熟考する
形 deliberate : ❶意図[計画]的な、故意の　❷慎重な

0973 preferably
/préfərəbli/
Part 7

副 できれば、希望を言えば
名 preference : ❶好み　❷優先
動 prefer : ❶(…より)~を好む(to …)　❷(prefer to doで)~することが好きである
形 preferable : (be preferable toで)~より好ましい

0974 inadvertently
/ìnədvə́:rtntli/
Part 5, 6

副 不注意で、うっかりして
形 inadvertent : うっかりした、偶然の

0975 unexpectedly
/ʌ̀nikspéktidli/
Part 5, 6

副 思いがけなく、突然に、不意に
形 unexpected : 思いがけない、予期しない

0976 notably
/nóutəbli/
Part 5, 6

副 ❶特に(≒especially, particularly)　❷著しく、明白に
形 notable : (~で)注目すべき；有名な(for ~)

Day 60))) CD-B25　Quick Review　答えは右ページ下

- ☐ 効果的に
- ☐ それに応じて
- ☐ 最初は
- ☐ かなり
- ☐ 報道によると
- ☐ 誤って
- ☐ 必然的に
- ☐ 最終的に
- ☐ 徹底的に
- ☐ 定期的に
- ☐ 連続して
- ☐ その間に
- ☐ 一般に
- ☐ 無条件で
- ☐ 例外的に
- ☐ 全く

Check 2　Phrase

- □ partially agree with ~(~に部分的に賛成する)
- □ a partially destroyed house (半壊した家)

- □ summarize the information concisely(情報を簡潔に要約する)
- □ to put it concisely(簡潔に言うと)

- □ behave oddly(奇妙な行動をする)
- □ an oddly dressed man(奇妙な服装をした男性)

- □ lie deliberately(故意にうそをつく)
- □ speak deliberately(慎重に話す)

- □ want a computer, preferably a laptop(コンピューターが欲しい、できればラップトップがいい)

- □ inadvertently cut a power cable(不注意で電源ケーブルを切断する)
- □ inadvertently or deliberately (不注意にせよ故意にせよ)

- □ die unexpectedly(急死する)

- □ be notably important(特に重要である)
- □ increase notably(著しく増加する)

Check 3　Sentence

- □ Global warming is partially due to greenhouse gas emissions.(地球温暖化の一部は温室効果ガスの排出に原因がある)

- □ Articles should be written clearly and concisely.(記事は明確かつ簡潔に書かれなければならない)

- □ Oddly, the accident wasn't on the news.(奇妙なことにその事故は報道されなかった)

- □ The police determined that the fire had been set deliberately.(その火事は意図的に起こされたと警察は断定した)

- □ Customer service experience is required, preferably in hotel work or a related field.(顧客サービスの経験、できればホテルでの仕事もしくは関連分野でのものが必須である)●求人広告の表現

- □ He has inadvertently deleted important files.(彼は重要なファイルをうっかり削除してしまった)

- □ The test results were unexpectedly good.(テストの結果は思いがけないほどよかった)

- □ France is famous for many things, notably wine.(フランスは多くのことで有名だが、特にワインで有名だ)

Day 60))) CD-B25
Quick Review
答えは左ページ下

- □ effectively
- □ accordingly
- □ initially
- □ considerably
- □ reportedly
- □ accidentally
- □ inevitably
- □ ultimately
- □ drastically
- □ periodically
- □ continuously
- □ meanwhile
- □ commonly
- □ unconditionally
- □ exceptionally
- □ purely

CHAPTER 1
CHAPTER 2
CHAPTER 3
CHAPTER 4
CHAPTER 5
CHAPTER 6
CHAPTER 7
CHAPTER 8
CHAPTER 9

Chapter 7 Review

左ページの(1)～(14)の副詞の同意・類義語［熟語］（≒）、反意・反対語（⇔）を右ページのA～Nから選び、カッコの中に答えを書き込もう。意味が分からないときは、見出し番号を参照して復習しておこう（答えは右ページ下）。

- □ (1) allegedly (0932) ≒は？（　　）
- □ (2) regrettably (0935) ≒は？（　　）
- □ (3) virtually (0937) ≒は？（　　）
- □ (4) entirely (0938) ≒は？（　　）
- □ (5) obviously (0941) ≒は？（　　）
- □ (6) accidentally (0950) ≒は？（　　）
- □ (7) ultimately (0952) ≒は？（　　）
- □ (8) meanwhile (0956) ≒は？（　　）
- □ (9) unconditionally (0958) ⇔は？（　　）
- □ (10) comparatively (0965) ≒は？（　　）
- □ (11) partially (0969) ≒は？（　　）
- □ (12) concisely (0970) ≒は？（　　）
- □ (13) deliberately (0972) ≒は？（　　）
- □ (14) notably (0976) ≒は？（　　）

A. conditionally
B. by accident
C. partly
D. almost
E. especially
F. completely
G. unfortunately
H. relatively
I. finally
J. briefly
K. in the meantime
L. reportedly
M. intentionally
N. clearly

【解答】(1) L (2) G (3) D (4) F (5) N (6) B (7) I (8) K (9) A (10) H (11) C (12) J (13) M (14) E

CHAPTER 8
動詞句

Chapter 8からは「熟語編」が始まります。このChapterでは、動詞表現112を見ていきましょう。ここが終われば、TOEIC990点＝満点はすぐそこに見えてくる！

TOEIC的格言

Nothing great is easy.
偉大なことで簡単なものはない。

Day 62【動詞句1】「動詞＋副詞［前置詞］」型1
▶286
Day 63【動詞句2】「動詞＋副詞［前置詞］」型2
▶290
Day 64【動詞句3】「動詞＋副詞［前置詞］」型3
▶294
Day 65【動詞句4】「動詞＋A＋前置詞＋B」型1
▶298
Day 66【動詞句5】「動詞＋A＋前置詞＋B」型2
▶302
Day 67【動詞句6】「be動詞＋形容詞＋前置詞」型1
▶306
Day 68【動詞句7】「be動詞＋形容詞＋前置詞」型2
▶310
Chapter 8 Review
▶314

Day 62　動詞句1
「動詞＋副詞［前置詞］」型1

Check 1　Listen ») CD-B27

□ 0977
subscribe to
Part 2, 3

❶ **〜を定期購読する**　❷（通例疑問・否定文で）〜に同意する
图subscription：（〜の）定期購読（料）(to 〜)
图subscriber：（〜の）定期購読者(to 〜)；（電話などの）加入者

□ 0978
enroll in [at, for]
Part 5, 6

〜に入学[入会]する
图enrollment：❶入学[登録]者数　❷入学、入会

□ 0979
merge with
ビジネス問題

（会社などが）**〜と合併する**
图merger：（〜との）（企業の）合併(with 〜)

□ 0980
conform to [with]
Part 5, 6

（規則など）**に従う**（≒ obey, follow, comply with, abide by）

□ 0981
bid for
ビジネス問題

〜に入札する
图bid：❶（工事などの）入札(for 〜)　❷（〜のための）企て、試み(for 〜)
图bidder：入札者、競り手

□ 0982
pull over
Part 2, 3

❶ **車を片側に寄せる**　❷（車など）を片側に寄せる

□ 0983
collide with
Part 5, 6

〜と衝突する、ぶつかる（≒ crash into）
图collision：（〜との／…の間の）衝突(with 〜/between …)

□ 0984
mark down
ビジネス問題

〜を値下げする

continued
▼

Chapter 8では、動詞句112をチェック。まずは、3日をかけて「動詞＋副詞［前置詞］」型の表現を見ていこう。

☐ 聞くだけモード　Check 1
☐ しっかりモード　Check 1 ▶ 2
☐ かんぺきモード　Check 1 ▶ 2 ▶ 3

Check 2　Phrase

☐ subscribe to two newspapers（新聞を2紙定期購読する）
☐ subscribe to his point of view（彼の意見に同意する）

☐ enroll in a vocational school（職業学校に入学する）
☐ enroll in a book club（読書クラブに入会する）

☐ merge with the parent company（親会社と合併する）

☐ conform to school rules（校則に従う）

☐ bid for public works（公共事業に入札する）

☐ pull over for an ambulance（救急車を通すために車を道の片側に寄せる）
☐ pull over a speeding car（スピード違反の車を止めさせる）

☐ collide with a car（車と衝突する）

☐ mark merchandise down（商品を値下げする）

Check 3　Sentence

☐ What magazines do you subscribe to?（どんな雑誌を定期購読していますか?）

☐ She enrolled in [at] Columbia University last year.（彼女は去年、コロンビア大学に入学した）

☐ In 1998, Daimler-Benz merged with Chrysler to form Daimler Chrysler.（1998年にダイムラーベンツはクライスラーと合併して、ダイムラークライスラーとなった）

☐ All employees must conform to certain ethical and legal standards.（全従業員は定められた倫理規範および法定基準に従わなければならない）

☐ Five contractors have bid for the project.（5つの建設業者がそのプロジェクトに入札した）

☐ Please pull over in front of the bank.（その銀行の前に車を止めてください）

☐ The car collided with a utility pole.（その車は電柱に衝突した）

☐ Everything has been marked down by 30 percent!（全品30パーセント引き!）●広告の表現

continued
▼

Day 62

Check 1　Listen))) CD-B27

☐ 0985
struggle with [against]
Part 5, 6

(難事など)**と闘う**、〜に取り組む
名struggle：苦闘、努力

☐ 0986
adhere to
Part 5, 6

❶(規則など)**を厳守する**　❷(考えなど)に固執する
名adherence：❶(規則などの)厳守(to 〜)　❷(〜に対する)固執、執着(to 〜)
名adherent：(〜の)支持者(of 〜)

☐ 0987
hand out
Part 1

〜を(…に)**配る**、分配する(to ...)(≒ distribute, pass out)
名handout：(講演などの)配付資料、プリント

☐ 0988
rule out
Part 5, 6

❶**〜を除外[排除]する**(≒ exclude)；〜を拒否する
❷〜を不可能にする、妨げる

☐ 0989
go with
Part 2, 3

〜に似合う、〜と調和する、釣り合う(≒ suit, match)

☐ 0990
interact with
Part 5, 6

〜と交流する、触れ合う、情報を伝え合う
名interaction：(〜との)交流(with [between, among] 〜)
形interactive：対話式の；双方向の

☐ 0991
cater to [for]
Part 7

〜に必要な物を提供する、〜の要求を満たす
名catering：仕出し
名caterer：(宴会などの)仕出し屋、配膳業者

☐ 0992
turn around
ビジネス問題

(経済など)**を好転させる**
名turnaround：(企業業績などの)好転、(黒字への)転換

Day 61))) CD-B26
Quick Review
答えは右ページ下

☐ 財政的に　☐ 比較的　☐ 部分的に　☐ できれば
☐ ぼんやりと　☐ 互いに　☐ 簡潔に　☐ 不注意で
☐ 深く　☐ 自発的に　☐ 奇妙に　☐ 思いがけなく
☐ 十分に　☐ 急激に　☐ 故意に　☐ 特に

Check 2　Phrase

- ☐ struggle with crime（犯罪と闘う）
- ☐ struggle with a difficult problem（難題に取り組む）

- ☐ adhere to the terms of the contract（契約の条項を厳守する）
- ☐ adhere to one's opinion（自分の意見に固執する）

- ☐ hand out food to homeless people（食べ物をホームレスの人々に配る）

- ☐ rule out the possibility of ～（～の可能性を排除する）
- ☐ rule out a return to ～（～への復帰を不可能にする）

- ☐ a wine that goes with fish（魚に合うワイン）

- ☐ interact with guests（来客たちと交流する）

- ☐ a restaurant catering to families（家族向けのレストラン）

- ☐ turn the economy around（経済を好転させる）

Check 3　Sentence

- ☐ The company has been struggling with high energy and labor costs.（その会社は高いエネルギー費と人件費に苦労している）

- ☐ Employees must adhere to company rules.（従業員は社則を厳守しなければならない）

- ☐ The man is handing out leaflets.（男性はちらしを配っている）

- ☐ Syria has ruled out the resumption of peace talks with Israel.（シリアはイスラエルとの和平交渉の再開を拒否した）

- ☐ What kind of bag goes with this dress?（どんなバッグがこのドレスに似合うかしら?）

- ☐ Working parents don't have enough time to interact with their children.（共働きの親は子どもと触れ合う時間が十分にない）

- ☐ The retail store caters mainly to young females.（その小売店は若い女性を主に相手にしている）

- ☐ The new CEO turned the company around in a year.（新CEOは1年でその会社を立て直した）

Day 61))) CD-B26
Quick Review
答えは左ページ下

- ☐ financially
- ☐ vaguely
- ☐ profoundly
- ☐ sufficiently
- ☐ comparatively
- ☐ mutually
- ☐ voluntarily
- ☐ exponentially
- ☐ partially
- ☐ concisely
- ☐ oddly
- ☐ deliberately
- ☐ preferably
- ☐ inadvertently
- ☐ unexpectedly
- ☐ notably

Day 63 動詞句2「動詞＋副詞［前置詞］」型2

Check 1　Listen 》CD-B28

□ 0993
elaborate on
Part 7

〜について詳しく述べる
名 elaboration：念入りに作ること；推敲
形 elaborate：❶精巧［精密］な、手の込んだ　❷入念な
副 elaborately：精巧に、入念に

□ 0994
bring out
ビジネス問題

❶（製品など）**を市場に出す**、発表する　❷（…の）（才能など）を引き出す（in ...）

□ 0995
plug in
Part 1

（電気器具）**をコンセントにつなぐ**、〜のプラグを差し込む
名 plug：❶プラグ　❷コンセント

□ 0996
culminate in [with]
Part 7

ついに〜となる（≒end in, result in）、〜で最高潮に達する
名 culmination：（通例the 〜）最高点、絶頂

□ 0997
work out
Part 2, 3

❶（問題など）**を解く**、解決する（≒solve）　❷（費用など）を計算［算定］する（≒calculate）　❸〜を理解する（≒understand）　❹うまくいく　❺練習［運動］する
名 workout：（練習）運動、トレーニング

□ 0998
carry over [forward]
Part 7

（ある金額など）**を繰り越す**、持ち越す

□ 0999
prevail in [among]
Part 5, 6

〜に普及している、広がっている　✚prevail over [against]は「〜に勝つ、勝る」
名 prevalence：普及；流行
形 prevailing：広く行き渡っている、一般的な

□ 1000
bargain with
ビジネス問題

〜と交渉［取引］**する**（≒negotiate with）
名 bargain：❶バーゲン品、特価品　❷取引；協約、協定

continued
▼

「動詞＋副詞[前置詞]」型の表現は「丸ごと1つの動詞」として覚えることが大切。そのためにも「聞いて音読する」ことを忘れずに！

- □ 聞くだけモード　Check 1
- □ しっかりモード　Check 1 ▶ 2
- □ かんぺきモード　Check 1 ▶ 2 ▶ 3

Check 2　Phrase

□ elaborate on the reasons for ~（～の理由について詳しく述べる）

□ bring out a new car（新車を市場に出す）
□ bring out the best in him（彼の最高の力を引き出す）

□ plug in the DVD player（DVDプレーヤーをコンセントにつなぐ）

□ culminate in the civil war（[対立などが]ついに内戦となる）

□ work out the math problems（数学の問題を解く）
□ work out the total cost of the project（プロジェクトの総費用を計算する）

□ carry over the balance（残高を繰り越す）

□ customs prevailing in the region（その地域に普及している習慣）

□ refuse to bargain with terrorists（テロリストらと取引するのを拒む）

Check 3　Sentence

□ The minister refused to elaborate on the status of the talks.（その大臣は会談の状況について詳述するのを拒んだ）

□ Apple brought out the first PC in the mid-70s.（アップル社は70年代中盤に最初のパソコンを市場に出した）

□ The man is plugging in the appliance.（男性は電気器具をコンセントにつないでいる）

□ The Watergate scandal culminated in the resignation of President Richard Nixon.（ウォーターゲート事件はついにはリチャード・ニクソン大統領の辞任へとつながった）

□ You must work out your own destiny.（自分の運命は自分で決めなければならない）

□ Employees can carry over up to 160 hours of unused paid vacation to the next year.（従業員は未消化の有給休暇を160時間まで次年度へ繰り越すことができる）

□ A pessimistic mood prevails in the stock market.（悲観的な雰囲気が株式市場に広がっている）

□ Unions bargained with employers for regular wage increases.（各労働組合は定期昇給を求めて雇用側と交渉した）

continued
▼

Day 63

Check 1　Listen)) CD-B28

1001 go in for
Part 2, 3

❶**〜に参加する**(≒join, take part in, participate in)；〜を受ける　❷〜を好む、趣味とする

1002 discriminate against
Part 5, 6

〜を差別する
名discrimination：(〜に対する)差別(待遇)(against 〜)

1003 reside in
Part 7

〜に住む、居住する(≒live in, dwell in, inhabit)
名residence：❶居住、滞在　❷邸宅、住宅
名resident：居住者、在住者
形resident：居住[在住]している
形residential：住宅[居住]の

1004 converse with
Part 5, 6

〜と話をする、談話する
名conversation：会話、対話、対談
形conversational：会話(体)の

1005 excel in [at]
Part 5, 6

〜に秀でている、ずば抜けている
名excellence：(〜における)優秀さ、卓越(in 〜)
形excellent：素晴らしい、非常に優れた

1006 fill in for
Part 2, 3

〜の代理[代行]をする(≒substitute for)

1007 inquire into
Part 7

〜を調査する、調べる(≒look into, investigate)
⊕inquire aboutは「〜について尋ねる、問い合わせる」
名inquiry：❶(〜についての)問い合わせ、質問(about 〜)　❷(事件などの)調査(into 〜)

1008 move on to
Part 4

(次の話題など)に移る

Day 62)) CD-B27　Quick Review　答えは右ページ下

- □ 〜を定期購読する
- □ 〜に入学する
- □ 〜と合併する
- □ 〜に従う
- □ 〜に入札する
- □ 車を片側に寄せる
- □ 〜と衝突する
- □ 〜を値下げする
- □ 〜と闘う
- □ 〜を厳守する
- □ 〜を配る
- □ 〜を除外する
- □ 〜に似合う
- □ 〜と交流する
- □ 〜に必要な物を提供する
- □ を好転させる

Check 2　Phrase

- ☐ **go in for** cosmetic surgery（整形手術を受ける）
- ☐ **go in for** soccer（サッカーが好きである）

- ☐ **discriminate against** minorities（少数民族を差別する）

- ☐ **reside in** Chicago（シカゴに住む）

- ☐ **converse with** him on the subject（その問題について彼と話をする）

- ☐ **excel in** math（数学に秀でている）

- ☐ **fill in for** a sick colleague（病気の同僚の代理をする）

- ☐ **inquire into** the cause of the accident（その事故の原因を調査する）

- ☐ **move on to** a new topic（新しい話題に移る）

Check 3　Sentence

- ☐ Are you planning to **go in for** the competition?（その競技会に参加するつもりですか?）

- ☐ We must not **discriminate against** people with disabilities.（障害のある人々を差別してはならない）

- ☐ My family currently **resides in** San Francisco.（私の家族は現在サンフランシスコに住んでいる）

- ☐ Teachers should have more opportunities to **converse with** their students.（教師たちは生徒たちと話をする機会をもっと持つべきだ）

- ☐ She especially **excels in** English.（彼女はとりわけ英語に秀でている）

- ☐ Linda **filled in for** Jack while he was on vacation.（ジャックが休暇中にリンダが彼の代理をした）

- ☐ The police **inquired into** the suspect's background.（警察は容疑者の経歴を調査した）

- ☐ Let's **move on to** the next item on the agenda.（議題の次の項目に移りましょう）

Day 62))) CD-B27
Quick Review
答えは左ページ下

- ☐ subscribe to
- ☐ enroll in
- ☐ merge with
- ☐ conform to
- ☐ bid for
- ☐ pull over
- ☐ collide with
- ☐ mark down
- ☐ struggle with
- ☐ adhere to
- ☐ hand out
- ☐ rule out
- ☐ go with
- ☐ interact with
- ☐ cater to
- ☐ turn around

Day 64　動詞句3
「動詞＋副詞［前置詞］」型3

Check 1　Listen » CD-B29

□ 1009
originate in [from]
Part 5, 6

〜から生じる、起こる、始まる
名 origin：❶起源；由来　❷(しばしば〜s)生まれ、血統
名 original：(the 〜)原物、原作
形 original：❶最初の　❷独創的な　❸原作の
副 originally：❶最初は、初めは　❷出身は

□ 1010
hand over
Part 5, 6

❶**〜を(…に)譲り渡す**(to . . .)　❷〜を(…に)手渡す(to . . .)

□ 1011
cut down (on)
ビジネス問題

〜を減らす、削減する(≒reduce)

□ 1012
wrap up
Part 2, 3

❶**〜を終える**、仕上げる(≒finish, complete)　❷〜を包む、包装する
名 wrap：(食品保存用の)ラップ

□ 1013
pull together
Part 4

協力する、協調する(≒cooperate)

□ 1014
call off
Part 2, 3

(予定の催しなど)**を中止する**(≒cancel)

□ 1015
settle on [upon]
Part 5, 6

〜を決定する、〜を選ぶ(≒decide)
名 settlement：❶妥協、合意　❷植民地、開拓地　❸移民、植民　❹支払い、決済

□ 1016
draw on [upon]
Part 5, 6

〜に頼る、〜を利用する

continued
▼

Quick Reviewは使ってる？ 昨日覚えた表現でも、記憶に残っているとは限らない。学習の合間に軽くチェックするだけでも効果は抜群！

- □ 聞くだけモード　Check 1
- □ しっかりモード　Check 1 ▶ 2
- □ かんぺきモード　Check 1 ▶ 2 ▶ 3

Check 2　　Phrase

- □ originated in England in the 18th century（[産業革命は]18世紀にイギリスから始まった）

- □ hand over the command（指揮権を譲り渡す）
- □ hand over a document to him（書類を彼に手渡す）

- □ cut down the number of employees（従業員数を減らす）

- □ wrap up the meeting（会議を終える）
- □ wrap up a present（プレゼントを包装する）

- □ pull together to complete the project（そのプロジェクトを終えるために協力する）

- □ call off the search for ~（~の捜索を中止する）

- □ settle on a date for the election（選挙日を決定する）
- □ settle on a new leader（新しい指導者を選ぶ）

- □ draw on one's experience（経験に頼る、経験を利用する）

Check 3　　Sentence

- □ The Internet originated in the United States.（インターネットはアメリカから始まった）

- □ The company handed over its camera business to Sony.（その会社はカメラ事業をソニーに譲渡した）

- □ We must cut down production costs to stay competitive.（我が社は競争力を維持し続けるために製造コストを削減しなければならない）

- □ I hope to wrap up the rest of the work within the next month.（私はその仕事の残りを来月中に終えたいと思っている）

- □ We must all pull together to get through this economic crisis.（私たちはこの経済危機を乗り越えるために全員で協力しなければならない）

- □ The competition was called off due to heavy rain.（その競技会は豪雨のため中止になった）

- □ We haven't settled on a name for the baby yet.（私たちは赤ちゃんの名前をまだ決めていない）

- □ She has a wealth of knowledge to draw on.（彼女には頼りになる知識が豊富にある）

continued
▼

CHAPTER 1
CHAPTER 2
CHAPTER 3
CHAPTER 4
CHAPTER 5
CHAPTER 6
CHAPTER 7
CHAPTER 8
CHAPTER 9

Day 64

Check 1 Listen 》CD-B29

1017 speculate in
ビジネス問題

(株など)**に投機する**、〜を思惑買い[売り]する
图speculation：❶推測、推量 ❷投機、思惑買い
图speculator：投機[投資]家

1018 buy out
ビジネス問題

(会社など)**を買収する**(≒acquire)
图buyout：買収

1019 put together
Part 5, 6

❶(計画など)**をまとめる** ❷(部品など)を組み立てる

1020 defer to
Part 5, 6

(敬意を払って)**〜に従う**、譲る(≒yield to)

1021 pass out
Part 1

❶**〜を**(…に)**配る**、分配する(to ...)(≒distribute, hand out) ❷気絶する、意識を失う

1022 check with
Part 2, 3

〜に相談する、尋ねる(≒consult with)

1023 consist in
Part 5, 6

(本質的なものが)**〜にある**、存在する(≒lie in)
➕consist ofは「〜から成り立つ、構成される」

1024 factor in
Part 7

〜を計算に入れる：〜を要因[要素]の1つとして含める
图factor：(〜の)要素、要因(in 〜)

Day 63 》CD-B28
Quick Review
答えは右ページ下

- □ 〜について詳しく述べる
- □ 〜を市場に出す
- □ 〜をコンセントにつなぐ
- □ ついに〜となる
- □ 〜を解く
- □ 〜を繰り越す
- □ 〜に普及している
- □ 〜と交渉する
- □ 〜に参加する
- □ 〜を差別する
- □ 〜に住む
- □ 〜と話をする
- □ 〜に秀でている
- □ 〜の代理をする
- □ 〜を調査する
- □ 〜に移る

Check 2 Phrase

- □ speculate in real estate（不動産に投機する）

- □ buy out a competing company（競合会社を買収する）

- □ put together a plan（計画をまとめる）
- □ put together an engine（エンジンを組み立てる）

- □ defer to one's boss（上司に従う）
- □ defer to the court's decision（裁判所の判決に従う）

- □ pass out test booklets to students（テスト冊子を生徒たちに配る）
- □ pass out in shock（ショックで気絶する）

- □ check with a lawyer（弁護士に相談する）

- □ consist in living in accord with nature（[幸福などが]自然と調和して生きることにある）

- □ factor in changes in interest rates（金利の変動を計算に入れる）

Check 3 Sentence

- □ He made a fortune by speculating in stocks.（彼は株に投機して一財産を作った）

- □ The bank announced its intention to buy out the US-based insurance company.（その銀行はアメリカに本社がある保険会社を買収する意図があることを発表した）

- □ It took three months to put together a new business plan.（新しい事業計画をまとめるのに3カ月かかった）

- □ We should defer to him on this issue.（私たちはこの問題については彼に従うべきだ）

- □ The woman is passing out fliers.（女性はちらしを配っている）

- □ He checked with his boss if his vacation schedule could be changed.（彼は休暇の予定が変えられるかどうか上司に相談した）

- □ Love consists in giving without getting in return.（愛は見返りを受けずに与えることに存在する）

- □ You must factor in labor costs when calculating the cost of the repairs.（修理費を計算する際には人件費を計算に入れなければならない）

Day 63))) CD-B28
Quick Review
答えは左ページ下

- □ elaborate on
- □ bring out
- □ plug in
- □ culminate in
- □ work out
- □ carry over
- □ prevail in
- □ bargain with
- □ go in for
- □ discriminate against
- □ reside in
- □ converse with
- □ excel in
- □ fill in for
- □ inquire into
- □ move on to

Day 65 動詞句4
「動詞＋A＋前置詞＋B」型1

Check 1　　Listen)) CD-B30

□ 1025
notify A of B
Part 5, 6

AにBを知らせる、通知[通告]する(≒inform A of [about] B)
名notification：通知、通告

□ 1026
donate A to B
Part 5, 6

AをBに寄付[寄贈]する(≒contribute A to [toward] B)
名donation：❶(〜への)寄付、寄贈(to 〜)　❷(〜への)寄付金、寄贈品(to 〜)
名donor：❶寄贈者　❷(臓器などの)提供者；献血者

□ 1027
designate A as [for] B
Part 7

AをBに指名[任命、指定]する
名designation：指名、任命、指定

□ 1028
reimburse A for B
ビジネス問題

AにB(経費など)を返済する
名reimbursement：払い戻し、返済

□ 1029
prescribe A for B
Part 7

A(薬)をB(人・病気)に処方する
名prescription：処方箋

□ 1030
subtract A from B
Part 7

AをBから引く(≒deduct A from B)(⇔add A to B：AをBに加える)
名subtraction：引くこと；引き算

□ 1031
hook up A to B
Part 2, 3

AをBに接続する、つなぐ(≒connect A to B)
名hook：かぎ、留め金、フック

□ 1032
allocate A for B
Part 5, 6

AをBのために取っておく、充てる、計上する
⊕allocate A to Bは「AをBに割り当てる」
名allocation：割り当て、配分；割当量[額]

continued
▼

今日と明日は、「動詞＋A＋前置詞＋B」型の表現をチェック！　まずはCDでチャンツを聞いて、表現を「耳」からインプットしよう。

☐ 聞くだけモード　Check 1
☐ しっかりモード　Check 1 ▶ 2
☐ かんぺきモード　Check 1 ▶ 2 ▶ 3

Check 2　Phrase

☐ **notify** employees **of** schedule changes（従業員に予定の変更を知らせる）

☐ **donate** $2,000 **to** the Red Cross（2000ドルを赤十字社に寄付する）

☐ **designate** him **as** team leader（彼をチームリーダーに指名する）

☐ **reimburse** him **for** all expenses（彼に全経費を返済する）

☐ **prescribe** a drug **for** a patient [cough]（薬を患者に処方する［せき薬を処方する］）

☐ **subtract** 4 **from** 6（6から4を引く）

☐ **hook up** an external hard drive **to** a laptop（外づけハードドライブをラップトップコンピューターに接続する）

☐ **allocate** money **for** future expenses（将来の出費のためにお金を取っておく）

Check 3　Sentence

☐ Employees were **notified of** the layoffs via e-mail.（従業員らは電子メールで解雇を知らされた）

☐ All proceeds from the event will be **donated to** local charities.（そのイベントの全収益は地元の慈善団体に寄付される予定だ）

☐ Machu Picchu was **designated as** a World Heritage Site in 1983.（マチュピチュは1983年に世界遺産に指定された）

☐ Employees are **reimbursed for** travel and business related expenses.（従業員は交通費および業務に関連した経費を返済される）

☐ Tamiflu is often **prescribed for** flu.（タミフルはインフルエンザに処方されることが多い）

☐ **Subtract** 11 **from** 28 and you have 17. ＝11 **subtracted from** 28 equals 17.（28引く11は17）

☐ Do you know how to **hook up** my computer **to** the Internet?（私のコンピューターをどうやってインターネットに接続するか分かりますか？）

☐ The government **allocated** $30 million **for** disaster relief.（政府は災害救援に3000万ドルを充てた）

continued
▼

Day 65

Check 1　Listen))) CD-B30

1033
integrate A **with** B
Part 5, 6

AをBと統合する、結びつける（≒ combine A with B）
名 integration：統合
形 integrated：統合［一体化］された

1034
diagnose A **with** [as] B
Part 2, 3

AをBと診断する
名 diagnosis：診断

1035
allot A **to** B
Part 7

AをBに割り当てる、分配する（≒ assign A to B, allocate A to B）
名 allotment：割り当て、分配

1036
interpret A **as** B
Part 5, 6

AをBだと解釈［理解］する
名 interpretation：❶解釈、説明　❷通訳
名 interpreter：通訳者

1037
compensate A **for** B
Part 5, 6

AにB（損害など）**の補償［賠償］をする**　⊕ compensate for は「（損失など）の埋め合わせをする」
名 compensation：❶（～に対する）補償［賠償］（金）（for ～）　❷報酬

1038
exclude A **from** B
Part 5, 6

AをBから締め出す；AをBから除外する
名 exclusion：（～からの）除外、排除（from ～）
形 exclusive：❶独占的な　❷排他的な　❸高級な
副 exclusively：専ら、全く～のみ；独占［排他］的に
前 excluding：～を除いて

1039
adjust A **to** B
Part 5, 6

AをBに合わせる、適合させる
名 adjustment：❶調整、調節　❷適応
形 adjustable：調節［調整］できる

1040
dispense A **to** B
Part 4

AをBに分配する、分け与える
名 dispenser：❶自動販売機　❷（銀行の）自動支払機

Day 64))) CD-B29
Quick Review
答えは右ページ下

- □ ～から生じる
- □ ～を譲り渡す
- □ ～を減らす
- □ ～を終える
- □ 協力する
- □ ～を中止する
- □ ～を決定する
- □ ～に頼る
- □ ～に投機する
- □ ～を買収する
- □ ～をまとめる
- □ ～に従う
- □ ～を配る
- □ ～に相談する
- □ ～にある
- □ ～を計算に入れる

Check 2　Phrase

- ☐ integrate play with learning（遊びを学習と統合する）

- ☐ diagnose him with [as having] diabetes（彼を糖尿病と診断する）

- ☐ allot tasks to everyone（全員に仕事を割り当てる）

- ☐ interpret his remarks as a threat（彼の発言を脅迫と解釈する）

- ☐ compensate him for damage（彼に損害の補償をする）

- ☐ exclude women from politics（女性を政治から締め出す）
- ☐ exclude his name from the list（彼の名前をリストから除外する）

- ☐ adjust the seat to a comfortable position（座席を快適な位置に合わせる）
- ☐ adjust oneself to the new environment（新しい環境に慣れる）

- ☐ dispense medications to patients（患者たちに薬を分配する）

Check 3　Sentence

- ☐ You can easily integrate text with graphics with this software.（このソフトウエアを使えば文字を画像と簡単に組み合わせることができる）

- ☐ She was diagnosed with appendicitis.（彼女は盲腸と診断された）

- ☐ Twenty minutes was allotted to each speaker.（各演説者に20分が割り当てられた）

- ☐ I interpreted his silence as tacit approval.（私は彼の沈黙を暗黙の了解だと解釈した）

- ☐ Employees are entitled to be compensated for work-related injuries.（従業員は仕事に関連したけがの補償を受ける権利がある）

- ☐ The student has been excluded from school for misbehavior.（その生徒は非行が原因で停学になっている）

- ☐ Please adjust your monitor settings to "1024 x 768" resolution.（モニターの設定を「1024×768」の解像度に合わせてください）

- ☐ The volunteers dispensed food and clothing to the disaster victims.（ボランティアたちは食料と衣服を被災者たちに配った）

Day 64))) CD-B29
Quick Review
答えは左ページ下

- ☐ originate in
- ☐ hand over
- ☐ cut down
- ☐ wrap up
- ☐ pull together
- ☐ call off
- ☐ settle on
- ☐ draw on
- ☐ speculate in
- ☐ buy out
- ☐ put together
- ☐ defer to
- ☐ pass out
- ☐ check with
- ☐ consist in
- ☐ factor in

Day 66 動詞句5 「動詞＋A＋前置詞＋B」型2

Check 1　Listen)) CD-B31

1041
levy A on B
ビジネス問題
▶ **A(税金など)をBに課す**、賦課する(≒ impose A on B)
名 levy：(～に対する)徴税(on ～)

1042
instill A in [into] B
Part 7
▶ **A(思想など)をBに徐々に教え込む**

1043
adorn A with B
Part 5, 6
▶ **AをBで飾る**(≒ decorate A with B)

1044
allocate A to B
Part 5, 6
▶ **AをBに割り当てる**、配分する(≒ assign A to B, allot A to B)　✚allocate A for Bは「AをBのために取っておく」
名 allocation：割り当て、配分；割当量[額]

1045
relay A to B
Part 4
▶ **A(伝言など)を(中継ぎして)Bに伝える**、中継する
名 relay：❶(スポーツの)リレー　❷中継装置

1046
exchange A with B
Part 5, 6
▶ **AをB(人)と取り交わす**、交換し合う　✚exchange A for Bは「A(物)をB(物)と交換する」
名 exchange：❶交換　❷両替；為替

1047
earmark A for B
Part 7
▶ **A(資金など)をBのために取っておく**、充てる(≒ allocate A for B)

1048
nominate A for [as] B
Part 5, 6
▶ **AをBに推薦[指名]する**
名 nomination：推薦[指名、任命]する[される]こと
名 nominee：推薦[指名、任命]された人、候補者

continued
▼

「動詞＋A＋前置詞＋B」型の表現は、Aを主語にした受け身の文で使われることも多い。その場合の語順もしっかり押さえておこう。

☐ 聞くだけモード　Check 1
☐ しっかりモード　Check 1 ▶ 2
☐ かんぺきモード　Check 1 ▶ 2 ▶ 3

Check 2　Phrase

☐ levy a tax on alcohol（アルコール飲料に税金を課す）

☐ instill responsibility in children（責任を子どもたちに徐々に教え込む）

☐ adorn a room with flowers（部屋を花で飾る）
☐ adorn oneself with ~（~で身を飾る）

☐ allocate jobs to employees（仕事を従業員に割り当てる）

☐ relay the message to him（その伝言を彼に伝える）

☐ exchange greetings [words] with ~（~とあいさつ[言葉]を交わす）

☐ earmark funds for future use（資金を将来使うために取っておく）

☐ be nominated for president（大統領候補に推薦される）

Check 3　Sentence

☐ Personal income tax is levied on income earned between January 1 and December 31.（個人所得税は1月1日から12月31日の間に得られた収入に対して課せられる）

☐ Teachers should instill moral values in students.（教師は道徳的価値観を生徒に少しずつ教えなければならない）

☐ The Christmas tree was adorned with many ornaments.（そのクリスマスツリーはたくさんの装飾品で飾られていた）

☐ Approximately 20 percent of the national budget was allocated to social security.（国家予算の約20パーセントが社会保障に割り当てられた）

☐ I relayed my boss's instructions to my team.（私は上司の指示を仲間に伝えた）

☐ The president exchanged views with the Japanese prime minister.（大統領は日本の首相と意見を交換し合った）

☐ Approximately 6 percent of GDP will be earmarked for education.（GDPの約6パーセントが教育に充てられる予定だ）

☐ The actor was nominated for an Academy Award.（その俳優はアカデミー賞にノミネートされた）

continued ▼

Day 66

Check 1 Listen))) CD-B31

□ 1049
immerse A in B
Part 5, 6

AをBに浸す、沈める
名immersion: ❶没頭 ❷(〜に)浸すこと(in 〜)

□ 1050
caution A about [against] B
Part 5, 6

AにBを用心させる、警告[注意]する(≒warn A of [about] B)
名caution: ❶用心、注意、警戒 ❷警告
形cautious: (be cautious about [of]で)〜に注意[用心]深い、慎重である

□ 1051
characterize A as B
Part 5, 6

AをBであると述べる、見なす、描く
名character: ❶性格、個性 ❷登場人物 ❸文字
名characteristic: (通例〜s)特徴、特性、特質
形characteristic: ❶典型[特徴]的な ❷(be characteristic ofで)〜に特有[特徴的]である

□ 1052
exempt A from B
ビジネス問題

AのB(義務など)を免除する(≒excuse A from B)
名exemption: ❶(課税対象からの)控除(額) ❷(〜の)免除(from 〜)
形exempt: (be exempt fromで)〜を免除されている

□ 1053
weigh A against B
Part 7

AをBと比較検討[考察]する
名weight: ❶重さ;体重 ❷重み

□ 1054
abbreviate A as [to] B
Part 7

AをBに短縮[省略]する
名abbreviation: (〜の)省略形、略語(of [for] 〜)

□ 1055
reprimand A for B
Part 5, 6

AをBの理由で叱責[懲戒]する(≒accuse A of B, blame A for B, criticize A for B, condemn A for B, rebuke A for B)
名reprimand: 叱責、懲戒

□ 1056
prop up A against B
Part 1

AをBに寄りかける、もたせかける
名prop: 支え、支柱

Day 65))) CD-B30
Quick Review
答えは右ページ下

□AにBを知らせる □AをBに処方する □AをBと統合する □AにBの補償をする
□AをBに寄付する □AをBから引く □AをBと診断する □AをBから締め出す
□AをBに指名する □AをBに接続する □AをBに割り当てる □AをBに合わせる
□AにBを返済する □AをBのために取っておく □AをBだと解釈する □AをBに分配する

Check 2 Phrase

- □ **immerse** cabbage **in** boiling water（キャベツを熱湯に浸す）
- □ **immerse oneself in** ~（[仕事など]に没頭する）

- □ **caution** him **about** speeding（彼にスピードの出し過ぎを注意する）

- □ **characterize** the situation **as** serious（状況を深刻だと述べる）

- □ **exempt** him **from** the exam（彼の試験を免除する）

- □ **weigh** costs **against** benefits（経費を収益と比較検討する）

- □ **be abbreviated as** CEO（[Chief Executive Officer＝最高経営責任者は] CEOに短縮される）

- □ **reprimand** him **for** breaking a company policy（会社の方針を破った理由で彼を叱責する）

- □ **prop up** a ladder **against** the wall（はしごを壁に寄りかける）

Check 3 Sentence

- □ **Immerse** the eggs **in** cold water before peeling them.（殻をむく前に、卵を冷水に浸してください）

- □ The police have **cautioned** senior citizens **about** telephone fraud.（警察は高齢者に電話詐欺に用心するよう呼びかけている）

- □ The analyst **characterized** the Chinese economy **as** "overheated."（そのアナリストは中国経済を「インフレ気味」だと述べた）

- □ Some types of non-profit organizations are **exempted from** paying income tax.（ある種の非営利団体は所得税の支払いを免除されている）

- □ Economic benefits must be **weighed against** potential dangers to the environment.（経済的利益は自然環境に与え得る危険と比較検討されなければならない）

- □ Gigabyte is often **abbreviated as** GB.（ギガバイトはしばしばGBに短縮される）

- □ Her boss **reprimanded** her **for** arriving at work late.（彼女の上司は職場に遅刻したことで彼女を叱責した）

- □ The bicycle is **propped up against** a fence.（自転車がフェンスに寄りかけられている）

Day 65 》CD-B30
Quick Review
答えは左ページ下

- □ notify A of B
- □ donate A to B
- □ designate A as B
- □ reimburse A for B
- □ prescribe A for B
- □ subtract A from B
- □ hook up A to B
- □ allocate A for B
- □ integrate A with B
- □ diagnose A with B
- □ allot A to B
- □ interpret A as B
- □ compensate A for B
- □ exclude A from B
- □ adjust A to B
- □ dispense A to B

CHAPTER 1
CHAPTER 2
CHAPTER 3
CHAPTER 4
CHAPTER 5
CHAPTER 6
CHAPTER 7
CHAPTER 8
CHAPTER 9

Day 67　動詞句6
「be動詞＋形容詞＋前置詞」型1

Check 1　Listen))) CD-B32

1057
be eligible for
Part 5, 6

〜の資格がある
名 eligibility：適格、適任

1058
be grateful (to A) **for**
Part 4

(Aに)〜のことで感謝している
副 gratefully：感謝して、喜んで

1059
be liable for
Part 7

〜に対して法的責任がある (≒ be responsible for)
名 liability：❶(〜に対する)法的責任(for 〜)　❷(〜ies)負債、債務

1060
be commensurate with
ビジネス問題

〜に相応[対応]している、ふさわしい

1061
be exempt from
Part 7

〜を免除されている (≒ be immune from)
名 exemption：❶(課税対象からの)控除(額)　❷(〜の)免除(from 〜)
動 exempt：(exempt A from Bで)AのB(義務など)を免除する

1062
be affiliated with [to]
ビジネス問題

〜の系列下である、〜に付属している
名 affiliate：系列[関連]会社、付属機関

1063
be frustrated with [at]
Part 5, 6

〜に不満を持っている、いら立っている
名 frustration：欲求不満、フラストレーション
動 frustrate：〜をいら立たせる
形 frustrating：いら立たしい

1064
be fed up with
Part 2, 3

〜にうんざりしている、あきあきしている (≒ be tired of, be sick of, be bored with, be weary of)

continued
▼

今日と明日は、「be動詞＋形容詞＋前置詞」型の表現をチェック！　まずはCDでチャンツを聞いて、表現を「耳」からインプット！

- ☐ 聞くだけモード　Check 1
- ☐ しっかりモード　Check 1 ▶ 2
- ☐ かんぺきモード　Check 1 ▶ 2 ▶ 3

Check 2　Phrase

☐ be eligible for child care leave（育児休暇をもらう資格がある）

☐ be grateful for his support（彼の支援に感謝している）

☐ be liable for a debt（負債を支払う法的責任がある）

☐ punishment commensurate with the crime（犯罪に相応した刑罰）

☐ be exempt from military service（兵役を免除されている）

☐ a hospital affiliated with the university（その大学の付属病院）

☐ be frustrated with one's job（仕事に不満を持っている）

☐ be fed up with his complaints（彼の愚痴にうんざりしている）

Check 3　Sentence

☐ People over 65 are eligible for Medicare.（65歳以上の人々はメディケア[=高齢者医療保険制度]を受ける資格がある）

☐ I am really grateful for your advice.（ご助言に本当に感謝しています）

☐ Manufacturers are liable for damages or injuries caused by their products.（メーカーは製品が原因の損害やけがに対して法的責任がある）

☐ Salary is commensurate with your experience and qualifications.（給与は経験と資格に応じる）◆求人広告の表現

☐ Registered religious organizations are exempt from income tax.（認可された宗教法人は所得税を免除されている）

☐ The station is affiliated with NBC.（その放送局はNBC系列だ）

☐ More and more people have grown frustrated with politics.（より多くの人々が政治に不満を持つようになっている）

☐ She is getting fed up with her job.（彼女は仕事にうんざりしてきている）

continued ▼

Day 67

Check 1 Listen 》CD-B32

☐ 1065
be comparable to [with]
Part 5, 6

～と(ほぼ)同等である(≒ be similar to)
图 comparison：(～との)比較(with [to] ～)
動 compare：(compare A to [with] Bで)❶AをBと比較する ❷AをBに例える
副 comparatively：比較的(に)

☐ 1066
be preferable to
Part 5, 6

～より好ましい、望ましい
图 preference：❶好み ❷優先
動 prefer：❶(…より)～を好む(to ...) ❷(prefer to do で)～することが好きである
副 preferably：できれば、希望を言えば

☐ 1067
be averse to
Part 5, 6

～を(ひどく)嫌っている ❶しばしば否定文で用いられ、「嫌いではない＝好きだ」を表す

☐ 1068
be contingent on [upon]
Part 7

～次第である、～を条件としている(≒ be dependent on)

☐ 1069
be incompatible with
Part 7

❶(事が)**～と相いれない**、両立しない、矛盾している ❷～と互換性がない

☐ 1070
be crammed with
Part 1

～でいっぱいである

☐ 1071
be stranded at [in, on]
Part 4

～に取り残されている、立ち往生している

☐ 1072
be applicable to
Part 5, 6

～に適用[応用]できる
图 application：❶申し込み(書) ❷適用、応用
動 apply：❶(apply forで)～を申し込む ❷(apply toで)(規則などが)～に適用される；～に申し込む ❸(apply A to Bで)AをBに適用[応用、利用]する

Day 66 》CD-B31
Quick Review
答えは右ページ下

☐ AをBに課す ☐ AをBに伝える ☐ AをBに浸す ☐ AをBと比較検討する
☐ AをBに徐々に教え込む ☐ AをBと取り交わす ☐ AにBを用心させる ☐ AをBに短縮する
☐ AをBで飾る ☐ AをBのために取っておく ☐ AをBであると述べる ☐ AをBの理由で叱責する
☐ AをBに割り当てる ☐ AをBに推薦する ☐ AのBを免除する ☐ AをBに寄りかける

Check 2 Phrase

☐ be comparable to ~ in size [quality]（～と規模[品質]が同等である）

☐ be preferable to anything else（ほかの何よりも望ましい）

☐ be not averse to the occasional glass of wine（時々ワインを飲むのは嫌いではない＝好きだ）

☐ be contingent on the weather（[予定などが]天気次第である）

☐ be incompatible with the facts（事実と矛盾している）
☐ software incompatible with Windows Vista（ウィンドウズビスタと互換性のないソフトウエア）

☐ be crammed with commuters（[電車などが]通勤者でいっぱいである）

☐ people stranded at sea（海に取り残された人々）

☐ rules applicable to all employees（全従業員に適用される規則）

Check 3 Sentence

☐ Our prices are comparable to other supermarkets.（当店の価格はほかのスーパーマーケットと同じだ）

☐ Peaceful coexistence is definitely preferable to war.（平和的共存のほうが戦争より絶対に好ましい）

☐ He is averse to taking advice from others.（彼はほかの人からアドバイスされるのが嫌いだ）

☐ Success is contingent on one's own efforts.（成功はその人自身の努力次第だ）

☐ Some people say that the market economy is incompatible with sustainable development.（市場経済は持続可能な開発と相いれないと言う人もいる）

☐ The store is crammed with shoppers.（その店は買い物客でごった返している）

☐ Thousands of passengers were stranded at the airport due to cancellations.（欠航のため何千人もの乗客が空港で足止めを食った）

☐ The legislation is applicable to companies with more than 50 employees.（その法律は従業員50人以上の企業に適用される）

Day 66))) CD-B31
Quick Review
答えは左ページ下

☐ levy A on B
☐ instill A in B
☐ adorn A with B
☐ allocate A to B
☐ relay A to B
☐ exchange A with B
☐ earmark A for B
☐ nominate A for B
☐ immerse A in B
☐ caution A about B
☐ characterize A as B
☐ exempt A from B
☐ weigh A against B
☐ abbreviate A as B
☐ reprimand A for B
☐ prop up A against B

CHAPTER 1
CHAPTER 2
CHAPTER 3
CHAPTER 4
CHAPTER 5
CHAPTER 6
CHAPTER 7
CHAPTER 8
CHAPTER 9

Day 68 動詞句7
「be動詞＋形容詞＋前置詞」型2

Check 1　Listen)) CD-B33

1073
be vulnerable to
Part 5, 6

❶(人が)**〜に弱点がある**、傷つきやすい(⇔be invulnerable to)　❷(場所などが)(攻撃などに)弱い

1074
be immune from
Part 7

〜を免れている、免除されている(≒be exempt from)　◆be immune toは「(伝染病などに)免疫がある；〜に影響されない」
名immunity：❶(病気などに対する)免疫(性)(against [to] 〜)　❷(義務などの)免除、免責(from 〜)

1075
be adept at [in]
Part 5, 6

〜がうまい、〜に熟達[熟練]している(≒be good at)
名adept：(〜の)達人、名人(at [in] 〜)

1076
be skeptical about [of]
Part 5, 6

〜を疑っている、〜に懐疑的である
名skeptic：懐疑論者、疑い深い人
名skepticism：懐疑的な態度

1077
be dissatisfied with
Part 5, 6

〜に満足していない、不満である(⇔be satisfied with)
名dissatisfaction：(〜に対する)不満、不平(with 〜)

1078
be devoted to
Part 5, 6

〜に献身[専念]**している**(≒be dedicated to, be committed to)
名devotion：(〜への)献身、専念(to 〜)
動devote：❶(devote A to Bで)A(時間など)をBにささげる　❷(devote oneself toで)〜に専念する

1079
be accountable for
Part 7

〜についての(説明する)**責任がある**(≒be responsible for)
名accountability：説明責任
動account：(account forで)❶(ある割合)を占める　❷〜(の理由・原因)を説明する

1080
be adaptable to
Part 7

〜に適合[適応、順応]**できる**
名adaptation：(〜への)適合、適応(to 〜)
動adapt：❶(adapt A to Bで)AをBに適合[適応、順応]させる　❷(adapt toで)(環境など)に適応[順応]する

continued
▼

今日でChapter 8は最後！ 時間に余裕があったら、章末のReviewにも挑戦しておこう。忘れてしまった表現も結構あるのでは?!

□ 聞くだけモード　Check 1
□ しっかりモード　Check 1 ▶ 2
□ かんぺきモード　Check 1 ▶ 2 ▶ 3

Check 2　Phrase

□ be vulnerable to temptation（誘惑に弱い）
□ a position vulnerable to attack（攻撃に弱い場所）

□ be immune from taxation（税を免除されている）

□ be adept at sewing（裁縫がうまい）

□ be skeptical about the credibility of ～（～の信憑性を疑っている）

□ be dissatisfied with one's job（仕事に満足していない）

□ be devoted to one's study（学業に専念している）

□ be accountable for errors（過失についての説明責任がある）

□ be adaptable to change（変化に適応できる）

Check 3　Sentence

□ She is vulnerable to pressure.（彼女はプレッシャーに弱い）

□ The officer will be immune from prosecution.（その役人は起訴を免れるだろう）

□ She is very adept at English.（彼女は英語がとても上手だ）

□ Some economists are skeptical about the feasibility of the government's economic plan.（政府の経済計画の実現性を疑っている経済学者もいる）

□ According to the survey, more than a third of respondents are dissatisfied with their salaries.（その調査によると、回答者の3分の1以上が給料に満足していない）

□ She is devoted to helping the poor.（彼女は貧者の救済に献身している）

□ Management must be accountable for their decisions and actions.（経営陣は自らの決定と行動の責任を負わなければならない）

□ The workout is adaptable to all fitness levels.（そのトレーニングはすべての健康レベルに適合できる）

continued
▼

Day 68

Check 1 Listen)) CD-B33

□ 1081
be reconciled with
Part 5, 6

〜と和解[仲直り]する
名reconciliation：(〜の間の／…との)和解、調和(between 〜/with ...)

□ 1082
be appreciative of
Part 4

〜に感謝している(≒be grateful for, be thankful for)
名appreciation：❶感謝 ❷(〜の)正しい理解(of 〜) ❸(資産などの)値上がり
動appreciate：❶〜を感謝する ❷〜を正当に評価する ❸価格[相場]が上がる

□ 1083
be equipped with
Part 4

〜が備えつけられている、装備されている
名equipment：(集合的に)装置、器具類

□ 1084
be identical to [with]
Part 7

〜と全く同じである ❶be similar toは「〜と(よく)似ている」

□ 1085
be attentive to
Part 5, 6

❶**〜に注意深い** ❷〜に思いやりがある、気を使う
名attention：❶(〜への)注意(to 〜) ❷(〜への)配慮(to 〜)

□ 1086
be infected with
Part 2, 3

〜に感染している
名infection：❶伝染病、感染症 ❷伝染、感染
形infectious：伝染性の、伝染病の

□ 1087
be allergic to
Part 2, 3

❶**〜に対してアレルギーがある** ❷〜が大嫌いである
名allergy：(〜に対する)アレルギー(to 〜)

□ 1088
be enthusiastic about
Part 2, 3

〜に熱中している、夢中になっている
名enthusiasm：(〜に対する)熱意、熱狂、強い興味(for 〜)
名enthusiast：熱中している人

Day 67)) CD-B32
Quick Review
答えは右ページ下

- □ 〜の資格がある
- □ 〜のことで感謝している
- □ 〜に対して法的責任がある
- □ 〜に相応している
- □ 〜を免除されている
- □ 〜の系列下である
- □ 〜に不満を持っている
- □ 〜にうんざりしている
- □ 〜と同等である
- □ より好ましい
- □ 〜を嫌っている
- □ 〜次第である
- □ 〜と相いれない
- □ 〜でいっぱいである
- □ 〜に取り残されている
- □ 〜に適用できる

Check 2　Phrase

- [ ] be reconciled with one's former enemy（以前の敵と和解する）

- [ ] be appreciative of her kindness（彼女の親切に感謝している）

- [ ] be equipped with furniture（家具が備えつけられている）

- [ ] be nearly [almost] identical to ～（～とほぼ全く同じである）

- [ ] be attentive to what is being said（話されていることを注意深く聞く）
- [ ] be attentive to guests（客に気を使う）

- [ ] be infected with tuberculosis（結核に感染している）

- [ ] be allergic to milk（牛乳に対してアレルギーがある）
- [ ] be allergic to math（数学が大嫌いである）

- [ ] be enthusiastic about golf（ゴルフに熱中している）

Check 3　Sentence

- [ ] He wants to be reconciled with his girlfriend.（彼はガールフレンドと仲直りしたいと思っている）

- [ ] I am truly appreciative of your support and understanding.（あなたのご支援とご理解に心から感謝しています）

- [ ] All hotel rooms are equipped with satellite TV, telephone, and Internet connection.（ホテルの全室には衛星テレビ、電話、そしてインターネット接続が装備されている）

- [ ] My car is identical to his.（私の車は彼の車と全く同じだ）

- [ ] You should be more attentive to your health.（あなたは健康にもっと注意したほうがいい）

- [ ] About one in five Americans is infected with influenza every year.（毎年、アメリカ人の約5人に1人がインフルエンザに感染する）

- [ ] I'm allergic to cedar pollen.（私はスギ花粉アレルギーだ）

- [ ] My child is enthusiastic about going to school every day.（私の子どもは毎日学校に行くことに夢中になっている）

Day 67))) CD-B32
Quick Review
答えは左ページ下

- [ ] be eligible for
- [ ] be grateful for
- [ ] be liable for
- [ ] be commensurate with
- [ ] be exempt from
- [ ] be affiliated with
- [ ] be frustrated with
- [ ] be fed up with
- [ ] be comparable to
- [ ] be preferable to
- [ ] be averse to
- [ ] be contingent on
- [ ] be incompatible with
- [ ] be crammed with
- [ ] be stranded at
- [ ] be applicable to

Chapter 8 Review

左ページの(1)〜(20)の熟語の同意熟語・類義熟語（または同意語・類義語）（≒）、反意熟語・反対熟語（⇔）を右ページのA〜Tから選び、カッコの中に答えを書き込もう。意味が分からないときは、見出し番号を参照して復習しておこう（答えは右ページ下）。

- [ ] (1) conform to (0980) ≒は？ (   )
- [ ] (2) hand out (0987) ≒は？ (   )
- [ ] (3) go with (0989) ≒は？ (   )
- [ ] (4) culminate in (0996) ≒は？ (   )
- [ ] (5) bargain with (1000) ≒は？ (   )
- [ ] (6) fill in for (1006) ≒は？ (   )
- [ ] (7) wrap up (1012) ≒は？ (   )
- [ ] (8) pull together (1013) ≒は？ (   )
- [ ] (9) call off (1014) ≒は？ (   )
- [ ] (10) notify A of B (1025) ≒は？ (   )
- [ ] (11) subtract A from B (1030) ⇔は？ (   )
- [ ] (12) integrate A with B (1033) ≒は？ (   )
- [ ] (13) levy A on B (1041) ≒は？ (   )
- [ ] (14) allocate A to B (1044) ≒は？ (   )
- [ ] (15) reprimand A for B (1055) ≒は？ (   )
- [ ] (16) be liable for (1059) ≒は？ (   )
- [ ] (17) be fed up with (1064) ≒は？ (   )
- [ ] (18) be contingent on (1068) ≒は？ (   )
- [ ] (19) be adept at (1075) ≒は？ (   )
- [ ] (20) be dissatisfied with (1077) ⇔は？ (   )

A. combine A with B
B. suit
C. cancel
D. be responsible for
E. end in
F. be satisfied with
G. inform A of B
H. distribute
I. cooperate
J. blame A for B
K. impose A on B
L. negotiate with
M. be dependent on
N. finish
O. be tired of
P. obey
Q. add A to B
R. assign A to B
S. be good at
T. substitute for

【解答】 (1) P (2) H (3) B (4) E (5) L (6) T (7) N (8) I (9) C (10) G
(11) Q (12) A (13) K (14) R (15) J (16) D (17) O (18) M (19) S (20) F

CHAPTER 9
形容詞句・副詞句

Chapter 9では、数語で1つの形容詞・副詞の働きをする熟語をチェック。どれも「固まり」で覚えるのがポイントです。本書も残りわずか2日。ゴールを目指してラストスパートをかけましょう！

Day 69【形容詞句・副詞句1】
▶ 318
Day 70【形容詞句・副詞句2】
▶ 322
Chapter 9 Review
▶ 326

TOEIC的格言

All's well that ends well.

終わりよければすべてよし。
[直訳] よく終わるものはすべてよい。

Day 69 形容詞句・副詞句1

Check 1　Listen 》CD-B34

□ 1089
in demand
ビジネス問題

需要がある
名demand：❶(〜の)需要(for 〜)　❷(〜を求める)要求(for 〜)
動demand：〜を(…に)要求する(of [from] . . .)
形demanding：❶(仕事が)きつい　❷(人が)要求の厳しい

□ 1090
in the meantime
Part 4

その間に：それまでは(≒ meanwhile, in the meanwhile)　➕for the meantimeは「差し当たって、今のところは」

□ 1091
at any rate
Part 2, 3

とにかく、いずれにしても(≒ anyway)

□ 1092
from scratch
Part 2, 3

ゼロから、最初から
名scratch：ひっかき傷、かすり傷

□ 1093
in the long run
Part 4

長い目で見れば、結局は(≒ eventually, in the end)
(⇔ in the short run：短期的に見れば)

□ 1094
at stake
Part 5, 6

❶**危険に瀕して**(≒ at risk)　❷賭けられて
名stake：賭け

□ 1095
on hand
Part 2, 3

❶**手元にある**、手持ちの　❷出席して、近くに居合わせて　➕at handは「(空間・時間的に)近くに[の]」

□ 1096
across the board
ビジネス問題

一律に、全面的に
形across-the-board：一律の、全面的な

continued
▼

Chapter 9では、2日をかけて形容詞句・副詞句32をチェック。まずはCDでチャンツを聞いて、表現を「耳」からインプットしよう。

- □ 聞くだけモード　Check 1
- □ しっかりモード　Check 1 ▶ 2
- □ かんぺきモード　Check 1 ▶ 2 ▶ 3

Check 2　　Phrase & Sentence

□ **be in great demand**(非常に需要がある)
□ **goods in demand**(需要のある商品)

□ He will be here soon, so **in the meantime**, please wait here.(彼は間もなくやって来ますので、その間ここでお待ちください)

□ That's what he said, **at any rate**.(とにかく、それが彼の言ったことだ)

□ **start from scratch**(ゼロから出発する)
□ **restart from scratch**(最初からやり直す)

□ Hard work will pay off **in the long run**.(長い目で見れば、勤勉は報われる)

□ The company's survival is **at stake**.(その会社の存続が危機に瀕している)

□ I have enough cash **on hand** to buy a new car.(私は新車を買うのに十分な現金が手元にある)

□ **cut spending across the board**(支出を一律に削減する)

Check 3　　Sentence

□ Healthcare jobs are always **in demand**.(医療職は常に需要がある)

□ **In the meantime**, take care of yourself.(それまで、お元気で)❶別れのあいさつ

□ **At any rate**, we must leave right now.(とにかく、私たちは今すぐ出発しなければならない)

□ He built the business **from scratch** and became very successful.(彼はゼロから事業を築き、大成功を収めた)

□ **In the long run**, the economy will return to its normal state.(長い目で見れば、経済は通常の状態に戻るだろう)

□ My future is **at stake** here.(今こそ私の未来がかかっている)

□ A doctor and a nurse will be **on hand** in case of emergency.(医者と看護師1人ずつが緊急事態に備えて出席する予定だ)

□ The automaker cut salaries **across the board** by 10 percent.(その自動車メーカーは給与を一律に10パーセント下げた)

continued
▼

Day 69

Check 1 Listen 》CD-B34

□ 1097 **all told** Part 7	**合計**[総計]**で**、全部で
□ 1098 **among other things** Part 5, 6	**とりわけ**、特に(≒ among others, above all, in particular)
□ 1099 **as it is** Part 2, 3	**そのままにして**
□ 1100 **at a stretch** Part 5, 6	**連続して**、立て続けに(≒ continuously) 名stretch:一続きの期間
□ 1101 **at this rate** Part 2, 3	**この調子で**(は)、この分だと 名rate:速度、ペース
□ 1102 **first thing** Part 2, 3	**いの一番に**、何よりも先に
□ 1103 **on offer** ビジネス問題	**売りに出されて**(≒ on sale, on the market) 名offer:売り込み
□ 1104 **in question** Part 7	**問題になっている**、当該の(≒ at issue) 名question:問題

Day 68 》CD-B33
Quick Review
答えは右ページ下

- □ 〜に弱点がある
- □ 〜がうまい
- □ 〜を疑っている
- □ 〜に満足していない
- □ 〜を免れている
- □ 〜に献身している
- □ 〜に適合できる
- □ 〜と和解する
- □ 〜についての責任がある
- □ 〜に感謝している
- □ 〜が備えつけられている
- □ 〜と全く同じである
- □ 〜に注意深い
- □ 〜に感染している
- □ 〜に対してアレルギーがある
- □ 〜に熱中している

Check 2 Phrase & Sentence

- ☐ **All told**, 32 people died in the earthquake.(合計で32人がその地震で死亡した)

- ☐ They discussed, **among other things**, the future of the automobile industry.(彼らは、とりわけ自動車産業の未来について話し合った)

- ☐ leave ~ **as it is**(~をそのままにしておく)
- ☐ take ~ **as it is**(~をあるがままに受け入れる)

- ☐ for three days **at a stretch**(3日間連続して)

- ☐ **At this rate** I will never get to work on time.(この調子では絶対に時間通りに職場には着かないだろう)

- ☐ I'll call you **first thing** tomorrow morning.(明日の朝一番にあなたにお電話します)

- ☐ the house **on offer**(売りに出されている家)

- ☐ the person **in question**(問題となっている人物、当人)

Check 3 Sentence

- ☐ There were 40 participants, **all told**.(総勢40人の出席者がいた)

- ☐ I like sports and I like skiing **among other things**.(私はスポーツが好きだが、特にスキーが好きだ)

- ☐ Your essay is well organized **as it is**.(あなたの小論文はそのままでもよくまとまっている)

- ☐ She worked for 40 hours **at a stretch** without sleep.(彼女は40時間立て続けに寝ずに働いた)

- ☐ If the population increases **at this rate**, it will cause many problems for society.(人口がこの調子で増加すれば、社会に多くの問題を引き起こすだろう)

- ☐ I will go to the bank **first thing** on Monday morning.(私は月曜日の朝一番に銀行に行くつもりだ)

- ☐ A wide range of famous brands are **on offer** at reduced prices.(さまざまな有名ブランド商品が値引きされて売られている)

- ☐ The mayor didn't comment on the development project **in question**.(市長は問題となっている開発計画についてコメントしなかった)

Day 68 » CD-B33
Quick Review
答えは左ページ下

- ☐ be vulnerable to
- ☐ be immune from
- ☐ be adept at
- ☐ be skeptical about
- ☐ be dissatisfied with
- ☐ be devoted to
- ☐ be accountable for
- ☐ be adaptable to
- ☐ be reconciled with
- ☐ be appreciative of
- ☐ be equipped with
- ☐ be identical to
- ☐ be attentive to
- ☐ be infected with
- ☐ be allergic to
- ☐ be enthusiastic about

Day 70 形容詞句・副詞句2

Check 1　Listen)) CD-B35

□ 1105
in the doldrums
ビジネス問題

(事が)**停滞状態で**
名 doldrums：(the ～)停滞状態

□ 1106
in the first place
Part 4

まず第一に、そもそも(≒ first, firstly)

□ 1107
in writing
ビジネス問題

文書で、書面で　❶「口頭で」は orally

□ 1108
in droves
Part 7

大挙して、群れを成して
名 drove：(～s)大群衆

□ 1109
on one's hands and knees
Part 1

四つんばいになって
名 knee：ひざ

□ 1110
on request
Part 7

申し込み[請求]があり次第
名 request：要請

□ 1111
on the road
Part 2, 3

旅行[出張]中で

□ 1112
out of service
Part 1

使用[運転]中止になって(⇔ in service)

continued
▼

今日で『キクタンTOEIC Test Score 990』も最後。ここまで続けてくれて本当にありがとう！ We're proud of you!!

- ☐ 聞くだけモード　Check 1
- ☐ しっかりモード　Check 1 ▶ 2
- ☐ かんぺきモード　Check 1 ▶ 2 ▶ 3

Check 2　Phrase & Sentence

☐ The global economy is in the doldrums. (世界経済は停滞している)

☐ In the first place, I would like to express my sincere appreciation to you. (まず第一に、あなたに心から感謝の意を表したいと思います)

☐ put ~ in writing (~を文書化する)
☐ get an agreement in writing (書面で承諾を得る)

☐ gather in droves (大挙して集まる)

☐ crawl on one's hands and knees (四つんばいになってはう、[赤ん坊が]はいはいする)

☐ A laundry and dry cleaning service is available on request. (申し込みがあれば、洗濯とドライクリーニングのサービスが利用できる)

☐ He has been on the road for nearly a month. (彼は1カ月近く旅行に出たままだ)

☐ be currently out of service (現在、使用中止になっている)

Check 3　Sentence

☐ The housing market remains in the doldrums. (住宅市場は依然として停滞したままだ)

☐ You shouldn't have said that to her in the first place. (そもそもあなたはそのことを彼女に言うべきではなかった)

☐ An employment contract must be concluded in writing. (雇用契約は文書で結ばれなければならない)

☐ The spectators arrived in droves to watch the race. (そのレースを見ようと観客たちが大挙して到着した)

☐ The woman is on her hands and knees. (女性は四つんばいになっている)

☐ An application form will be sent on request. (請求があり次第、申込書が送られる)

☐ I used to be on the road at least 10 days a month for my old job. (私は前の仕事では1カ月に少なくとも10日は出張に出たものだった)

☐ The escalator is out of service. (そのエスカレーターは使用中止になっている)

continued
▼

Day 70

Check 1　Listen))) CD-B35

□ 1113
around the clock
Part 7

24時間ぶっ通しで
形 around-the-clock：24時間連続[営業]の

□ 1114
behind [at] the wheel
Part 1

車を運転して
名 wheel：(車の)ハンドル

□ 1115
at fault
Part 5, 6

(~の)**責任[罪]がある**(for [in] ~)
名 fault：(過失の)責任

□ 1116
at no time
Part 5, 6

決して~ない[しない]　● in no timeは「すぐに」

□ 1117
beyond one's control
Part 5, 6

どうすることもできない、手に負えない
名 control：制御

□ 1118
on the market
ビジネス問題

売りに出されて(≒ on sale, on offer)

□ 1119
out of commission
Part 2, 3

使用不能の
名 commission：任務

□ 1120
at a moment's notice
Part 7

すぐに、直ちに、即座に
名 notice：通知

Day 69))) CD-B34
Quick Review
答えは右ページ下

- □ 需要がある
- □ その間に
- □ とにかく
- □ ゼロから
- □ 長い目で見れば
- □ 危険に瀕して
- □ 手元にある
- □ 一律に
- □ 合計で
- □ とりわけ
- □ そのままにして
- □ 連続して
- □ この調子で
- □ いの一番に
- □ 売りに出されて
- □ 問題になっている

Check 2　Phrase & Sentence

- □ work around the clock(24時間ぶっ通しで働く)

- □ the man behind the wheel(運転手)

- □ be at fault for the accident(その事故の責任がある)

- □ At no time have I ever said such a thing.(私はそんなことは決して言っていない) ⊕at no timeが文頭に来ると、疑問文の語順に倒置される

- □ circumstances beyond her control(彼女にはどうすることもできない事情)

- □ put ~ on the market(~を売りに出す)
- □ come on the market(売り出される)

- □ put ~ out of commission(~を使用不能にする)

- □ be ready to leave at a moment's notice(すぐに出発する準備ができている)

Check 3　Sentence

- □ The store is open around the clock.(その店は24時間営業だ)

- □ The woman is behind the wheel.(女性は車を運転している)

- □ The court found the defendant at fault for infringing on copyright laws.(裁判所は被告に著作権侵害の罪があるとの判決を下した)

- □ At no time was he told about the danger of asbestos.(アスベストの危険について彼は決して知らされなかった)

- □ The global economic situation is beyond the government's control.(世界の経済情勢は政府の手に負えなくなっている)

- □ We will put our house on the market.(私たちは自宅を売りに出す予定だ)

- □ My car is currently out of commission.(私の車は現在、使えなくなっている)

- □ We are prepared to respond to emergency situations at a moment's notice.(私たちは緊急事態にすぐに対応する準備ができている)

Day 69))) CD-B34
Quick Review
答えは左ページ下

- □ in demand
- □ in the meantime
- □ at any rate
- □ from scratch
- □ in the long run
- □ at stake
- □ on hand
- □ across the board
- □ all told
- □ among other things
- □ as it is
- □ at a stretch
- □ at this rate
- □ first thing
- □ on offer
- □ in question

CHAPTER 1
CHAPTER 2
CHAPTER 3
CHAPTER 4
CHAPTER 5
CHAPTER 6
CHAPTER 7
CHAPTER 8
CHAPTER 9

Chapter 9 Review

左ページの(1)〜(10)の熟語の同意熟語・類義熟語（または同意語・類義語）（≒）、反意熟語・反対熟語（⇔）を右ページのA〜Jから選び、カッコの中に答えを書き込もう。意味が分からないときは、見出し番号を参照して復習しておこう（答えは右ページ下）。

- ☐ (1) in the meantime (1090) ≒は? (　　)
- ☐ (2) at any rate (1091) ≒は? (　　)
- ☐ (3) in the long run (1093) ≒は? (　　)
- ☐ (4) at stake (1094) ≒は? (　　)
- ☐ (5) among other things (1098) ≒は? (　　)
- ☐ (6) at a stretch (1100) ≒は? (　　)
- ☐ (7) on offer (1103) ≒は? (　　)
- ☐ (8) in question (1104) ≒は? (　　)
- ☐ (9) in the first place (1106) ≒は? (　　)
- ☐ (10) out of service (1112) ⇔は? (　　)

Day 70 CD-B35　Quick Review　答えは右ページ下

- ☐ 停滞状態で
- ☐ まず第一に
- ☐ 文書で
- ☐ 大挙して
- ☐ 四つんばいになって
- ☐ 申し込みがあり次第
- ☐ 旅行中で
- ☐ 使用中止になって
- ☐ 24時間ぶっ通しで
- ☐ 車を運転して
- ☐ 責任がある
- ☐ 決して〜ない
- ☐ どうすることもできない
- ☐ 売りに出されて
- ☐ 使用不能の
- ☐ すぐに

A. above all
B. continuously
C. anyway
D. at issue
E. firstly
F. eventually
G. in service
H. at risk
I. meanwhile
J. on the market

【解答】(1) I (2) C (3) F (4) H (5) A (6) B (7) J (8) D (9) E (10) G

Day 70))) CD-B35
Quick Review
答えは左ページ下

- [ ] in the doldrums
- [ ] in the first place
- [ ] in writing
- [ ] in droves
- [ ] on one's hands and knees
- [ ] on request
- [ ] on the road
- [ ] out of service
- [ ] around the clock
- [ ] behind the wheel
- [ ] at fault
- [ ] at no time
- [ ] beyond one's control
- [ ] on the market
- [ ] out of commission
- [ ] at a moment's notice

ねぇねぇ、どれくらい覚えてる？
Hey, how many do you remember?

Index

＊見出しとして掲載されている単語・熟語は赤字、それ以外のものは黒字で示されています。それぞれの語の右側にある数字は、見出し番号を表しています。赤字の番号は、見出しとなっている番号を示します。

Index

A

- a shred of 0718
- **abate** 0735
- abbreviate 0625
- **abbreviate A as B** 1054, 0625
- abbreviate A to B 0625, 1054
- **abbreviation** 0625, 1054
- abdomen 0926
- **abdominal** 0926
- abide by 0980
- **abolish** 0721
- abolition 0721
- **abound** 0814
- above all 1098
- abundance 0814
- abundant 0814
- **accelerate** 0347, 0245, 0803
- acceleration 0347
- accelerator 0347
- acceptance 0061, 0479
- access 0907
- accident 0078, 0482, 0950
- accidental 0950
- **accidentally** 0950
- **acclaim** 0469
- accommodate 0917
- **accommodating** 0917
- accommodation 0917
- accomplish 0893
- **accomplished** 0893
- accomplishment 0893
- **accordingly** 0946
- account 0503, 1079
- account for 0503, 1079
- **accountability** 0503, 1079
- **accuracy** 0119
- accurate 0119
- accurately 0119
- accuse A of B 1055
- acknowledge 0132
- **acknowledgment** 0132
- acquire 1018
- **across the board** 1096
- across-the-board 1096
- **activate** 0760
- active 0760
- activity 0760
- **acumen** 0654
- acute 0382
- adapt 1080
- adapt A to B 1080
- adapt to 1080
- adaptation 1080
- add 0255
- add A to B 1030
- **additive** 0633
- adept 1075
- adhere 0590
- **adhere to** 0986, 0590
- **adherence** 0590, 0986
- adherent 0590, 0986
- **adjacent** 0358
- adjoin 0897
- **adjoining** 0897
- **adjourn** 0336
- adjournment 0336
- adjust 0316
- **adjust A to B** 1039
- adjustable 1039
- adjustment 1039
- **administer** 0715, 0564
- administration 0564, 0715
- administrative 0564, 0715
- **administrator** 0564, 0715
- **adopt** 0206
- **adoption** 0206
- **adorn A with B** 1043
- **adversary** 0604, 0376
- **adverse** 0376, 0604
- advertise 0743
- advocacy 0029
- **advocate** 0029
- **affiliate** 0039, 1062
- **affirm** 0729, 0815
- affirmation 0729
- affirmative 0729
- **affluence** 0575, 0406
- **affluent** 0406, 0575
- age 0528
- aged 0528
- **agenda** 0022
- **aggravate** 0345, 0802
- aggravation 0345
- **aging** 0528
- agree 0754
- aircraft 0155
- airplane 0155
- **all told** 1097
- **allegation** 0216, 0932
- allege 0216, 0932
- alleged 0216, 0932
- **allegedly** 0932, 0216, 0949
- allergic 0126
- **allergy** 0126, 1087
- **alleviate** 0269, 0290
- alleviation 0269
- alliance 0225
- allied 0225
- all-inclusive 0881
- allocate 0515
- **allocate A for B** 1032, 0515, 1044, 1047
- **allocate A to B** 1044, 0515, 1032, 1035
- **allocation** 0515, 1032, 1044
- **allot A to B** 1035, 1044
- allotment 1035
- **ally** 0225
- ally oneself to 0225
- ally oneself with 0225
- almost 0937
- alter 0162
- **alteration** 0162
- **alternate** 0363

☐ alternate A with B		0363
☐ alternative		0363
☐ **altitude**		**0034**
☐ amazing		0391
☐ ambiguity		0388
☐ **ambiguous**		**0388**
☐ ambiguously		0388
☐ **ameliorate**		**0789**
☐ amelioration		0789
☐ **amend**	**0257,**	**0190**
☐ **amendment**	**0190,**	**0257**
☐ **amenity**		**0166**
☐ **among other things**		
		1098
☐ among others		1098
☐ **anecdote**		**0688**
☐ announce		0743
☐ annoy		0313
☐ **annuity**		**0599**
☐ anonymous		0371
☐ anonymously		0939
☐ anyway		1091
☐ **apparel**		
	0187, 0105,	0135
☐ appeal		0601
☐ appendix		0071
☐ **appliance**		**0025**
☐ **applicant**		**0018**
☐ application	0018,	1072
☐ apply	0018,	1072
☐ apply A to B		1072
☐ apply for	0018,	1072
☐ apply to	0018,	1072
☐ **appraisal**	**0537,**	**0744**
☐ **appraise**	**0744,**	**0537**
☐ appreciate		1082
☐ appreciation		1082
☐ approval		0061
☐ **approximate**		**0460**
☐ approximately		0460
☐ **aptitude**		**0113**
☐ arbitrate		0084
☐ **arbitration**		**0084**
☐ arbitrator		0084
☐ **arcane**		**0910**

☐ **archive**		**0623**
☐ **arise**	**0251,**	**0326**
☐ **around the clock**		**1113**
☐ around-the-clock		1113
☐ **arouse**	**0326,**	**0251**
☐ arrange		0805
☐ **artisan**		**0588**
☐ **as it is**		**1099**
☐ ascent		0622
☐ ask		0761
☐ aspect		0471
☐ assess		0744
☐ assessment		0537
☐ asset		0037
☐ assign A to B	1035,	1044
☐ associate		0189
☐ **assorted**		**0877**
☐ assume		0282
☐ **asthma**		**0671**
☐ **at a moment's notice**		
		1120
☐ **at a stretch**		**1100**
☐ **at any rate**		**1091**
☐ **at fault**		**1115**
☐ at hand		1095
☐ at issue		1104
☐ **at no time**		**1116**
☐ at risk		1094
☐ **at stake**		**1094**
☐ at the wheel		1114
☐ **at this rate**		**1101**
☐ attach	0089,	0804
☐ attach A to B		0089
☐ **attachment**		**0089**
☐ attention		1085
☐ **attire**	0135, 0105,	0187
☐ attitude		0113
☐ **attorney**		**0157**
☐ attract		0349
☐ **audit**	**0031,**	**0176**
☐ **auditor**	**0176,**	**0031**
☐ **auditorium**		**0122**
☐ **authentic**		**0386**
☐ authenticate		0386
☐ authenticity		0386

☐ authority		0523
☐ authorize		0764
☐ **autograph**		**0081**
☐ available		0823
☐ avenue		0642
☐ **avert**		**0742**
☐ **aviation**		**0495**
☐ avoid		0551
☐ avoid doing		0551
☐ **avoidance**		**0551**
☐ **await**		**0338**
☐ **awning**		**0530**

B

☐ **bachelor**		**0612**
☐ **ballot**		**0118**
☐ bankrupt		
	0042, 0840,	0873
☐ **bankruptcy**	**0042,**	**0691**
☐ **barely**		**0940**
☐ bargain		1000
☐ **bargain with**		**1000**
☐ **barren**		**0820**
☐ barrow		0504
☐ base		0637
☐ **be accountable for**		
		1079
☐ **be adaptable to**		**1080**
☐ **be adept at**		**1075**
☐ be adept in		1075
☐ be affiliated to	0039,	1062
☐ **be affiliated with**		
	1062,	0039
☐ **be allergic to**		
	1087,	0126
☐ **be applicable to**		**1072**
☐ **be appreciative of**		**1082**
☐ **be attentive to**		**1085**
☐ **be averse to**		**1067**
☐ be bored with		1064
☐ be cautious about		1050
☐ be cautious of		1050
☐ be characteristic of		1051
☐ **be commensurate**		
	with	**1060**

どれだけチェックできた？ 1 ☐ 2 ☐

☐ be committed to	1078		1069	☐ best	0887
☐ **be comparable to**		☐ be inconsistent with	0861	☐ **bet**	0333
	1065, 0965	☐ be indicative of	0077	☐ betting	0333
☐ be comparable with		☐ **be infected with**	1086	☐ **beverage**	0002
	0965, 1065	☐ be invulnerable to	1073	☐ **beyond one's control**	
☐ be consistent with	0861	☐ **be liable for** 1059, 0037			1117
☐ **be contingent on**		☐ be liable to do	0037	☐ **bias**	0069, 0447
	1068, 0078	☐ be obliged to do	0404	☐ **biased**	0447, 0069
☐ be contingent upon		☐ be occupied with		☐ **bid**	0014, 0543, 0981
	0078, 1068		0649, 0821	☐ bid A for B	0014, 0543
☐ **be crammed with** 1070		☐ be optimistic about	0502	☐ **bid for** 0981, 0014, 0543	
☐ be credited for	0230	☐ **be preferable to**		☐ **bidder** 0543, 0014, 0981	
☐ be credited with	0230		1066, 0973	☐ **bilateral**	0454
☐ be dedicated to		☐ be prepared to do	0832	☐ **bin**	0477
	0060, 1078	☐ be presumed to do	0282	☐ bind	0859
☐ be dependent on	1068	☐ be projected to do	0191	☐ bind A to do	0859
☐ be depressed about	0855	☐ **be reconciled with**		☐ **binding**	0859
☐ be depressed over	0855		1081, 0346	☐ blame A for B	1055
☐ be descended from	0622	☐ be relieved to do	0290	☐ **blizzard**	0481
☐ **be devoted to**	1078	☐ be responsible for		☐ bloom	0617
☐ **be dissatisfied with**			1059, 1079	☐ board	0550
	1077	☐ be satisfied with	1077	☐ **boarding**	0550
☐ **be eligible for**	1057	☐ be sick of	1064	☐ boat	0155
☐ **be enthusiastic about**		☐ be similar to 1065, 1084		☐ bogus	0439
	1088	☐ **be skeptical about**		☐ book	0488
☐ be equal to	0800		1076	☐ **booking**	0488
☐ **be equipped with** 1083		☐ be skeptical of	1076	☐ bookkeeper	0621
☐ **be exempt from**		☐ **be stranded at**	1071	☐ **bookkeeping**	0621
	1061, 0199, 1052, 1074	☐ be stranded in	1071	☐ booklet	0005
☐ **be fed up with**	1064	☐ be stranded on	1071	☐ border	0499
☐ be fluent in	0936	☐ be thankful for	1082	☐ boss	0047
☐ be frustrated at	1063	☐ be tired of	1064	☐ **bother**	0313
☐ **be frustrated with**		☐ **be vulnerable to** 1073		☐ bother doing	0313
	1063	☐ be weary of	1064	☐ bother to do	0313
☐ be good at	1075	☐ bear	0722	☐ **boulevard**	0642
☐ **be grateful for**		☐ bearable	0862	☐ **bounce**	0709
	1058, 1082	☐ bearish	0902	☐ **boundary**	0499
☐ be grateful to A for	1058	☐ **beep**	0517	☐ **brand-new**	0416
☐ be hesitant to do	0201	☐ beginner	0662	☐ **breadth**	0569
☐ **be identical to**	1084	☐ behave	0900	☐ break	0131
☐ be identical with	1084	☐ behavior	0900	☐ break through	0054
☐ **be immune from**		☐ **behavioral**	0900	☐ **breakthrough**	0054
	1074, 1061	☐ **behind the wheel** 1114		☐ bribe	0100
☐ be immune to	1074	☐ **benchmark**	0559	☐ **bribery**	0100
☐ **be incompatible with**		☐ **beneficiary**	0527	☐ briefly	0970

どれだけチェックできた？ 1 ☐ 2 ☐

☐ bring out	0994	☐ cause	0291, 0799	☐ clerk	0385
☐ brisk	0390	☐ caution	1050	☐ client	0573
☐ broad	0341	☐ caution A about B	1050	☐ close	0485, 0934
☐ broaden	0341	☐ caution A against B	1050	☐ closed	0485
☐ brochure	0005	☐ cautious	1050	☐ closely	0934
☐ brokerage	0594	☐ cease	0281	☐ closing	0485
☐ brokerage firm	0594	☐ cease doing	0281	☐ closure	0485
☐ brokerage house	0594	☐ cease to do	0281	☐ cloth	0139, 0178
☐ broom	0617	☐ celebrate	0713	☐ clothes	0105, 0135, 0187
☐ browse	0271	☐ cellphone	0398	☐ clothing	0105, 0135, 0187
☐ browser	0271	☐ census	0473	☐ clutter	0529
☐ buffet	0698	☐ center	0571	☐ coincide	0090, 0754
☐ bulk	0062	☐ centerpiece	0659	☐ coincide with	0090
☐ bulky	0062	☐ cereal	0561	☐ coincidence	0090
☐ bulletin	0066	☐ certificate	0146, 0253	☐ coincident	0090
☐ bullish	0902	☐ certified	0253	☐ coincidental	0090
☐ business	0104, 0202	☐ certify	0253	☐ coin-operated	0919
☐ buy out	1018	☐ challenge	0822	☐ collaborate	0259, 0194
☐ buyout	0137, 1018	☐ challenging	0822	☐ collaborate to do	0194, 0259
☐ by accident	0950	☐ change	0099, 0278, 0320	☐ collaboration	0194, 0259
		☐ changeable	0455	☐ collaborator	0194, 0259
		☐ character	1051	☐ collateral	0544
		☐ characteristic	1051	☐ colleague	0189
		☐ characterize A as B	1051	☐ collection	0589
		☐ charity	0666	☐ collide	0231
		☐ cheap	0394	☐ collide with	0983, 0231
		☐ check	0247	☐ collision	0231, 0983
		☐ check with	1022	☐ combine A with B	1033
		☐ chemist's	0043	☐ command	0523
		☐ chore	0035	☐ commemorate	0713, 0886
		☐ chronic	0382	☐ commemoration	0713, 0886
		☐ citation	0195	☐ commemorative	0886, 0713
		☐ citizen	0574	☐ commend	0798
		☐ citizenship	0574	☐ commendable	0798
		☐ civilization	0151	☐ commendation	0798
		☐ civilize	0151	☐ comment	0563
		☐ civilized	0151	☐ comment on	0563
		☐ claim	0469	☐ commentary	0563
		☐ clarify	0276, 0402	☐ commerce	0104
		☐ clear	0221, 0400, 0402	☐ commercial	0104
		☐ clearance	0221		
		☐ clearance sale	0221		
		☐ clearly	0941		
		☐ clerical	0385		

C

☐ copyright	0518
☐ cafeteria	0629
☐ calculate	0997
☐ call off	1014
☐ can	0477
☐ cancel	0172, 1014
☐ cancellation	0172
☐ canteen	0629
☐ capital bonus	0011
☐ cardboard	0507
☐ career	0557
☐ careful	0380
☐ cargo	0115
☐ carousel	0605
☐ carry forward	0998
☐ carry over	0998
☐ catastrophe	0680
☐ catastrophic	0680
☐ cater	0209
☐ cater for	0209, 0991
☐ cater to	0991, 0209
☐ caterer	0209, 0991
☐ catering	0209, 0991

☐ commission	1119
☐ common	0393, 0957
☐ **commonly**	0957
☐ communication	0180
☐ **commute**	0243, 0128
☐ **commuter**	0128, 0243
☐ company	0202
☐ comparable	0965
☐ **comparatively**	0965, 1065
☐ compare	0965, 1065
☐ compare A to B	0965, 1065
☐ compare A with B	0965, 1065
☐ comparison	0965, 1065
☐ **compartment**	0161
☐ **compensate A for B**	1037
☐ compensate for	0712, 1037
☐ compensation	1037
☐ **competence**	0514
☐ competent	0514, 0915
☐ compilation	0266
☐ **compile**	0266
☐ **complement**	0263
☐ complementary	0263, 0354
☐ complete	1012
☐ completely	0938, 0960
☐ **compliance**	0205, 0210
☐ compliment	0263, 0354
☐ **complimentary**	0354
☐ comply	0205
☐ comply with	0205, 0980
☐ comprehend	0880
☐ **comprehensible**	0880, 0366
☐ comprehension	0880
☐ **comprehensive**	0366, 0880
☐ comprise	0303
☐ compromise	0467
☐ compulsory	0356, 0404

☐ conceal	0768
☐ **concede**	0324, 0467
☐ **concession**	0467, 0324
☐ concise	0970
☐ **concisely**	0970
☐ conclude	0868
☐ conclusion	0868
☐ **conclusive**	0868
☐ **concur**	0754
☐ concurrent	0754
☐ condemn A for B	1055
☐ condition	0958
☐ conditional	0958
☐ conditionally	0958
☐ condo	0076
☐ **condominium**	0076
☐ conduct	0490
☐ **conductor**	0490
☐ **confectionery**	0647
☐ **confer**	0725
☐ confidence	0357, 0580
☐ **confidential**	0357, 0580
☐ **confidentiality**	0580, 0357
☐ confidentially	0357, 0580
☐ confirm	0196, 0247
☐ **confirmation**	0196
☐ **confiscate**	0306, 0611, 0759
☐ **confiscation**	0611, 0306
☐ **conform to**	0980
☐ conform with	0980
☐ confusion	0103
☐ **congested**	0434, 0134
☐ **congestion**	0134, 0434
☐ **conglomerate**	0170
☐ congress	0912
☐ **congressional**	0912
☐ congressman	0912
☐ connect	0706
☐ connect A to B	1031
☐ **consecutive**	0355
☐ consecutively	0355
☐ consequently	0946
☐ conservation	0300

☐ **conserve**	0300
☐ consider	0378, 0948
☐ consider doing	0378, 0948
☐ considerable	0378, 0948
☐ **considerably**	0948
☐ **considerate**	0378
☐ consideration	0378, 0948
☐ **consist in**	1023
☐ consist of	1023
☐ consistent	0861
☐ **consolidate**	0292, 0536
☐ **consolidation**	0536, 0292
☐ consortia	0624
☐ **consortium**	0624
☐ **constitute**	0303
☐ constitution	0303
☐ constitutional	0303
☐ constrain	0560
☐ **constraint**	0560
☐ construct	0462
☐ construction	0462
☐ **constructive**	0462
☐ consult with	1022
☐ contagion	0441
☐ **contagious**	0441
☐ contaminant	0756
☐ **contaminate**	0756, 0741
☐ contamination	0756
☐ **contingency**	0078
☐ contingent	0078
☐ continue	0955
☐ continue doing	0955
☐ continue to do	0955
☐ continuity	0955
☐ continuous	0888, 0955
☐ **continuously**	0955, 1100
☐ **contractor**	0143
☐ contradict	0505
☐ **contradiction**	0505
☐ contradictory	0505
☐ contribute	0597
☐ contribute A to B	

		0597, 1026	☐ criminal	0644	☐ **deduce**	0767
☐ contribute A toward B			☐ criteria	0538	☐ deduce A from B	0767
		0597, 1026	☐ **criterion**	**0538**	☐ **deduct** **0255**, 0403, 0478
☐ contribute to	0597	☐ critic	0556, 0684	☐ deduct A from B	1030
☐ contribution	0597	☐ criticize A for B	1055	☐ **deductible**
☐ **contributor**	**0597**	☐ crossing	0020		0403, 0255, 0478
☐ control	0316, 1117	☐ **crude**	**0397**	☐ **deduction**
☐ **convene**	**0719**	☐ **cubicle**	**0109**		**0478**, 0199, 0255, 0403,
☐ conversation	1004	☐ **cuisine**	**0234**		0767
☐ conversational	1004	☐ **culminate in**	**0996**	☐ **deem**	**0351**
☐ **converse with**	**1004**	☐ culminate with	0996	☐ deep	0420
☐ cooking	0234	☐ culmination	0996	☐ **default**	**0487**
☐ cooperate	1013	☐ **culprit**	**0644**	☐ defect	0092, 0374
☐ copy	0087	☐ cultivate	0558	☐ **defective**	**0374**, 0848
☐ **copyright**	**0518**	☐ cultivated	0558	☐ defense	0645
☐ cordial	0942	☐ **cultivation**	**0558**	☐ defer	0310
☐ **cordially**	**0942**	☐ **curb**	**0261**, 0307	☐ **defer**	**0319**, 0310
☐ correct	0589	☐ **curtail**	**0328**, 0315	☐ **defer to**	1020
☐ **correction**	**0589**	☐ custodian	0200	☐ **defiance**	**0673**
☐ correctly	0589	☐ **custody**	**0200**	☐ defiant	0673
☐ correspond	0180	☐ custom	0427	☐ deficit	0049
☐ correspond to	0180	☐ **customary**	**0427**	☐ defy	0673
☐ correspond with	0180	☐ customer	0573	☐ **degradation**	**0672**
☐ **correspondence**	**0180**	☐ **cut down**	**1011**	☐ degrade	0672
☐ correspondent	0180	☐ cut down on	1011	☐ delay	0319, 0581, 0780
☐ corridor	0509			☐ **delegate**	**0140**, 0552
☐ cost	0044, 0425, 0697	**D**		☐ **delegation**	**0552**, 0140
☐ **costly**	**0425**	☐ damp	0448	☐ **delete**	**0284**
☐ **counterfeit**	**0439**	☐ danger	0064	☐ deletion	0284
☐ **courier**	**0094**	☐ dangerous	0360	☐ deliberate	0972
☐ court	0675	☐ **de facto**	**0923**	☐ deliberate about	0972
☐ **courtyard**	**0695**	☐ **debacle**	**0703**	☐ deliberate on	0972
☐ **coworker**	**0189**	☐ **debris**	**0508**, 0539	☐ deliberate over	0972
☐ crack down on	0570	☐ debt	0220	☐ **deliberately**	**0972**
☐ **crackdown**	**0570**	☐ **debtor**	**0220**, 0230	☐ delicate	0364
☐ **craft**	**0155**	☐ decelerate	0347	☐ delinquency	0841
☐ craftsman	0155, 0588	☐ decide	1015	☐ **delinquent**	**0841**
☐ craftsmanship	0155	☐ decisive	0868	☐ demand	1089
☐ crash into	0983	☐ decorate A with B	1043	☐ demanding	1089
☐ **crease**	**0603**	☐ decrease		☐ **demolish**	**0330**
☐ **credential**	**0215**		0315, 0328, 0758, 0781	☐ demolition	0330
☐ **credibility**	**0690**	☐ dedicate	0060	☐ demonstrate	0193
☐ credible	0391, 0690	☐ dedicate A to B	0060	☐ **demonstration**	**0193**
☐ credit	0230	☐ dedicated	0060	☐ demonstrator	0193
☐ **creditor**	**0230**, 0220	☐ **dedication**	**0060**	☐ **denounce**	**0343**

☐ denunciation	0343	
☐ deny	0729	
☐ department	0896	
☐ depend	0453	
☐ depend on	0453	
☐ **dependable**	**0453**	
☐ dependence	0453	
☐ **depict**	**0776**	
☐ depiction	0776	
☐ **depose**	**0784**	
☐ deposition	0784	
☐ **depot**	**0600**	
☐ depress	0855	
☐ **depressed**	**0855**	
☐ depression	0855	
☐ depth	0569	
☐ deregulate	0316	
☐ **derogatory**	**0829**	
☐ descend	0622	
☐ **descent**	**0622**	
☐ describe	0776	
☐ **designate A as B**	**1027**	
☐ designate A for B	1027	
☐ designation	1027	
☐ destiny	0685	
☐ destroy	0330	
☐ destructive	0462	
☐ **detach**	**0804**	
☐ detached	0804	
☐ detachment	0804	
☐ **detain**	**0297**	
☐ detect	0653	
☐ detection	0653	
☐ detective	0653	
☐ **detector**	**0653**	
☐ detention	0297	
☐ **deter**	**0310**, 0319	
☐ deter A from doing	0310	
☐ **deteriorate**	**0258**	
☐ deterioration	0258	
☐ determine	0334	
☐ deterrent	0310	
☐ **detour**	**0016**, 0582	
☐ develop	0708	
☐ devote	1078	

☐ devote A to B	1078	
☐ devote oneself to	1078	
☐ devotion	0060, 1078	
☐ **diabetes**	**0501**	
☐ diabetic	0501	
☐ diagnose	0165	
☐ diagnose A as B		
	0165, 1034	
☐ **diagnose A with B**		
	1034, 0165	
☐ diagnoses	0165	
☐ **diagnosis**	**0165**, 1034	
☐ **dictate**	**0334**	
☐ dictation	0334	
☐ difference	0465	
☐ different	0400	
☐ **differentiate**	**0770**	
☐ differentiation	0770	
☐ dig	0809	
☐ **digit**	**0224**	
☐ digital	0224	
☐ dignify	0545	
☐ **dignitary**	**0658**	
☐ **dignity**	**0545**	
☐ **diligence**	**0535**	
☐ diligent	0535, 0901	
☐ diligently	0535	
☐ **dilute**	**0734**	
☐ dilution	0734	
☐ **dimension**	**0471**	
☐ **dine**	**0286**, 0568	
☐ **diner**	**0568**, 0286	
☐ dinner	0286, 0568	
☐ **dip**	**0317**, 0327	
☐ **diploma**	**0146**	
☐ diplomacy	0579	
☐ **diplomat**	**0579**	
☐ diplomatic	0579	
☐ **directory**	**0074**	
☐ **discard**	**0273**	
☐ disclose	0480, 0768	
☐ **disclosure**	**0480**	
☐ **disconnect**	**0706**	
☐ discontinuation	0264	
☐ **discontinue**	**0264**	

☐ discourage	0613, 0892	
☐ discourage A from doing		
	0613, 0892	
☐ **discouragement**		
	0613, 0892	
☐ **discouraging**		
	0892, 0613	
☐ **discreet**	**0380**, 0048	
☐ **discrepancy**	**0465**	
☐ **discretion**	**0048**, 0380	
☐ **discriminate**	**0295**	
☐ **discriminate against**		
	1002, 0295	
☐ discrimination	0295, 1002	
☐ disease	0103	
☐ dismiss	0175	
☐ dismiss A as B	0175	
☐ **dismissal**	**0175**	
☐ disobey	0268	
☐ **disorder**	**0103**	
☐ disordered	0103	
☐ disorderly	0103	
☐ **dispatch**	**0304**	
☐ **dispel**	**0793**	
☐ **dispense A to B**	**1040**	
☐ dispenser	1040	
☐ **disperse**	**0249**	
☐ disposable	0150	
☐ **disposal**	**0150**	
☐ dispose	0150	
☐ dispose of	0150	
☐ **disregard**	**0339**	
☐ **disrupt**	**0325**, 0874	
☐ disruption	0325, 0874	
☐ **disruptive**	**0874**, 0325	
☐ dissatisfaction	1077	
☐ **disseminate**	**0748**	
☐ **distinct**	**0400**	
☐ distinction	0400	
☐ distinguish		
	0295, 0400, 0770	
☐ distinguish A from B	0400	
☐ distinguished	0426, 0818	
☐ **distract**	**0349**, 0513	
☐ distracting	0349, 0513	

☐ distraction	0513, 0349	
☐ distribute	0987, 1021	
☐ disturb	0208, 0872	
☐ disturbance	0208, 0872	
☐ disturbing	0872, 0208	
☐ diverse	0289	
☐ diversify	0289	
☐ diversity	0289	
☐ dividend	0011	
☐ division	0148	
☐ divorce	0123	
☐ doctor	0612	
☐ dogma	0905	
☐ dogmatic	0905	
☐ doldrums	1105	
☐ donate A to B	1026	
☐ donation	1026	
☐ donor	1026	
☐ doom	0685	
☐ dormitory	0542	
☐ dosage	0186	
☐ dose	0186	
☐ downpour	0681	
☐ downside	0693	
☐ downsize	0315, 0328	
☐ downsizing	0315	
☐ downswing	0167	
☐ downturn	0167	
☐ drastic	0953	
☐ drastically	0953	
☐ draw on	1016	
☐ draw upon	1016	
☐ drop	0733	
☐ drought	0145	
☐ drove	1108	
☐ drugstore	0043	
☐ due	0368	
☐ duplicate	0087	
☐ durability	0384	
☐ durable	0384	
☐ duration	0492	
☐ during	0492	
☐ dustpan	0617	
☐ dwell in	1003	
☐ dwindle	0758	

E

☐ eagerness	0634	
☐ earlier	0365	
☐ earmark A for B	1047	
☐ ease	0332	
☐ easily	0332	
☐ easy	0332	
☐ effect	0945	
☐ effective	0945	
☐ effectively	0945	
☐ elaborate	0993	
☐ elaborate on	0993	
☐ elaborately	0993	
☐ elaboration	0993	
☐ elevation	0034	
☐ eligibility	1057	
☐ embezzle	0730	
☐ embezzlement	0730	
☐ embrace	0301	
☐ eminence	0818	
☐ eminent	0818, 0426, 0852	
☐ emission	0114, 0283	
☐ emit	0283, 0114, 0272	
☐ emphasis	0270	
☐ emphasize	0270, 0352	
☐ emphatic	0270	
☐ empower	0764	
☐ enact	0293	
☐ enclose	0154	
☐ enclosure	0154	
☐ encounter	0322	
☐ encourage	0232	
☐ encourage A to do	0232	
☐ encouragement	0232	
☐ encouraging	0232	
☐ end	0241, 0260	
☐ end in	0996	
☐ endanger	0298, 0392	
☐ endangered	0392, 0421	
☐ endemic	0096	
☐ endorse	0242, 0213	
☐ endorsement	0213, 0242	

☐ enemy	0604	
☐ energize	0782	
☐ energy	0782	
☐ enforce	0275	
☐ enforcement	0275	
☐ enhance	0252, 0609	
☐ enhancement	0609, 0252	
☐ enlarge	0279	
☐ enlargement	0279	
☐ enroll	0235	
☐ enroll at	0235, 0978	
☐ enroll for	0235, 0978	
☐ enroll in	0978, 0235	
☐ enrollment	0235, 0978	
☐ entail	0810	
☐ enterprise	0202	
☐ enthusiasm	0634, 1088	
☐ enthusiast	1088	
☐ entire	0938	
☐ entirely	0938	
☐ entrepreneur	0052	
☐ envisage	0786	
☐ envision	0786	
☐ epicenter	0641	
☐ epidemic	0096	
☐ equal	0800	
☐ equality	0652, 0800	
☐ equalize	0800	
☐ equipment	1083	
☐ erase	0284	
☐ erratic	0858, 0844	
☐ escort	0344	
☐ especially	0976	
☐ essential	0878	
☐ estimate	0195, 0763, 0806	
☐ ethical	0882	
☐ ethics	0882	
☐ evacuate	0244, 0229	
☐ evacuation	0229, 0244	
☐ evaluate	0744	
☐ evaluation	0537	
☐ event	0482	
☐ eventually	1093	
☐ evidently	0941	

どれだけチェックできた？ 1 ☐ 2 ☐

☐ evocative	0779	
☐ evoke	0779	
☐ exaggerate	0308	
☐ exaggerated	0308	
☐ exaggeration	0308	
☐ examination	0164	
☐ examine	0705	
☐ excavate	0809	
☐ excavation	0809	
☐ excel	0248, 0595	
☐ excel at	0595, 1005	
☐ excel in	1005, 0595	
☐ excellence	0595, 1005	
☐ excellent	0595, 0871, 1005	
☐ except	0959	
☐ exception	0959	
☐ exceptional	0959	
☐ exceptionally	0959	
☐ exchange	1046	
☐ exchange A for B	1046	
☐ exchange A with B	1046	
☐ exclude	0988	
☐ exclude A from B	1038	
☐ excluding	1038	
☐ exclusion	1038	
☐ exclusive	0881, 1038	
☐ exclusively	1038	
☐ excursion	0472	
☐ excuse	0199, 0601	
☐ excuse A from B	1052	
☐ exemplary	0918	
☐ exemplification	0796	
☐ exemplify	0796	
☐ exempt	0199, 1052, 1061	
☐ exempt A from B	1052, 0199, 1061	
☐ exemption	0199, 0478, 1052, 1061	
☐ exercise	0337	
☐ exert	0337	
☐ exert oneself	0337	
☐ exertion	0337	
☐ exorbitant	0899	
☐ expand	0217	
☐ expanse	0217	
☐ expansion	0217	
☐ expedite	0803, 0245, 0347	
☐ expend	0044	
☐ expenditure	0044, 0697	
☐ expense	0044, 0697	
☐ expensive	0394, 0425	
☐ expert	0083, 0556	
☐ expertise	0083	
☐ expiration	0470, 0241	
☐ expire	0241, 0470	
☐ exponential	0968	
☐ exponentially	0968	
☐ expose	0768	
☐ extinct	0421, 0108, 0392	
☐ extinction	0108, 0421	
F		
☐ fable	0670	
☐ fabric	0139, 0178	
☐ fabricate	0696	
☐ fabrication	0696	
☐ fabulous	0836	
☐ facilitate	0245, 0347, 0803	
☐ faction	0655	
☐ factional	0655	
☐ factor	1024	
☐ factor in	1024	
☐ fake	0386, 0439	
☐ famous	0426, 0818, 0884	
☐ farewell	0525	
☐ fatal	0685	
☐ fatality	0685	
☐ fate	0685	
☐ fated	0685	
☐ fateful	0685	
☐ fault	0092, 0848, 1115	
☐ faulty	0848, 0374	
☐ feasibility	0436	
☐ feasible	0436, 0857	
☐ feat	0701	
☐ feedback	0628	
☐ fellow worker	0189	
☐ fertile	0820	
☐ fierce	0827	
☐ fiercely	0827	
☐ fill in for	1006	
☐ finally	0952	
☐ finance	0961	
☐ financial	0961	
☐ financially	0961	
☐ fingerprint	0661	
☐ finish	1012	
☐ first	1106	
☐ first thing	1102	
☐ firsthand	0925	
☐ firstly	1106	
☐ fiscal	0361	
☐ fit	0125	
☐ fitness	0125	
☐ fixture	0576	
☐ flagship	0699	
☐ flaw	0092, 0370	
☐ flawed	0092, 0370	
☐ flawless	0370, 0092	
☐ fledgling	0909	
☐ flier	0226, 0179	
☐ flounder	0788	
☐ flourish	0331, 0707	
☐ fluctuate	0320, 0099	
☐ fluctuation	0099, 0320	
☐ fluency	0936	
☐ fluent	0936	
☐ fluently	0936	
☐ flyer	0226	
☐ fold	0603, 0708	
☐ follow	0980	
☐ following	0407, 0464	
☐ footing	0637	
☐ for the meantime	1090	
☐ forefront	0660	
☐ foresee	0745, 0895	
☐ foreseeable	0745, 0895	
☐ foretell	0791	
☐ forfeit	0759, 0306	
☐ former	0842	
☐ formidable	0885	

☐ fragile	0364	
☐ frail	0364	
☐ fraud	0147, 0863	
☐ fraudulent	0863, 0147	
☐ free	0354	
☐ freight	0115	
☐ friction	0117	
☐ from scratch	1092	
☐ frustrate	1063	
☐ frustrating	1063	
☐ frustration	1063	
☐ function	0914	
☐ functional	0914	
☐ fund	0584	
☐ funding	0584	
☐ fund-raise	0694	
☐ fund-raiser	0694	
☐ fund-raising	0694	

G

☐ gadget	0133	
☐ gage	0183	
☐ gala	0679	
☐ gateway	0632	
☐ gather	0484	
☐ gathering	0484, 0160	
☐ gauge	0183	
☐ gear	0516	
☐ gene	0593	
☐ generic	0458	
☐ genetic	0411	
☐ genetically	0411	
☐ genetics	0411	
☐ genuine	0386	
☐ get rid of	0273	
☐ get together	0160	
☐ get-together	0160, 0484	
☐ gifted	0461	
☐ gigantic	0916	
☐ given	0869	
☐ given that	0869	
☐ glimmer	0648	
☐ go in for	1001	
☐ go on	0826	

☐ go with	0989	
☐ goods	0013	
☐ goodwill	0702	
☐ gourmet	0449	
☐ government	0585	
☐ graduate	0111	
☐ grain	0561	
☐ grand	0531	
☐ grandeur	0531	
☐ gratefully	1058	
☐ gratuity	0618	
☐ gross	0430	
☐ guarantee	0015	
☐ gym	0565	
☐ gymnasium	0565	

H

☐ habitat	0238	
☐ habitual	0427	
☐ hallway	0509	
☐ hamper	0717, 0724	
☐ hand out	0987, 0506, 1021	
☐ hand over	1010	
☐ handout	0506, 0987	
☐ hands-on	0444, 0879	
☐ hardly	0940	
☐ hardworking	0901	
☐ hassle	0687	
☐ hassle A to do	0687	
☐ hasten	0245, 0347, 0803	
☐ hatch	0812	
☐ hazard	0064, 0360	
☐ hazardous	0360, 0064	
☐ health	0125	
☐ hectic	0417	
☐ helm	0643	
☐ hemisphere	0181	
☐ hereditary	0593	
☐ heredity	0593	
☐ hesitant	0201	
☐ hesitate	0201	
☐ hesitate to do	0201	
☐ hesitation	0201	
☐ highlight	0270, 0352	

☐ hinder	0724, 0717	
☐ hindrance	0724	
☐ hint	0583	
☐ home loan	0058	
☐ honest	0399	
☐ honesty	0072	
☐ hook	1031	
☐ hook up A to B	1031	
☐ horizontal	0399, 0424	
☐ housekeeper	0555	
☐ housekeeping	0555	
☐ hub	0571	
☐ humid	0448, 0177	
☐ humidity	0177, 0448	
☐ hustle	0687	
☐ hygiene	0635, 0849	
☐ hygienic	0849, 0635, 0843	
☐ hypotheses	0534	
☐ hypothesis	0534	
☐ hypothetical	0534	

I

☐ idle	0901	
☐ ignore	0339	
☐ illness	0103	
☐ imagine	0786	
☐ immature	0342	
☐ immerse A in B	1049	
☐ immersion	1049	
☐ immigrant	0127	
☐ immigrate	0127	
☐ immigration	0127, 0686	
☐ imminence	0852	
☐ imminent	0852, 0818, 0891	
☐ immunity	1074	
☐ impassable	0927	
☐ impending	0891, 0852	
☐ imperative	0834	
☐ implement	0520	
☐ implementation	0520	
☐ implication	0169	
☐ imply	0169	
☐ impolite	0397	

☐ impose A on B	1041	☐ **incorporate**	0311	☐ inject	0222
☐ **improper**	0920	☐ incorporation	0311	☐ inject A into B	0222
☐ improve	0258, 0789	☐ **incredible**	0391	☐ **injection**	0222
☐ **in demand**	1089	☐ incredibly	0391	☐ inquire about	1007
☐ **in droves**	1108	☐ increment	0408	☐ **inquire into**	1007
☐ in effect	0945	☐ **incur**	0254	☐ inquiry	1007
☐ in jeopardy	0298	☐ indicate	0077	☐ insolvency	0840
☐ in no time	1116	☐ indication	0077	☐ **insolvent**	0840, 0873
☐ in particular	1098	☐ indicative	0077	☐ inspect	0705
☐ **in question**	1104	☐ **indicator**	0077	☐ install	0110
☐ in service	1112	☐ indispensable	0878	☐ **installation**	0110, 0614
☐ **in the doldrums**	1105	☐ individual	0944	☐ **installment**	0614, 0110
☐ in the end	1093	☐ **individually**	0944	☐ **instill A in B**	1042
☐ **in the first place**	1106	☐ **induce**	0291	☐ instill A into B	1042
☐ in the interim	0854	☐ induce A to do	0291	☐ instinct	0156
☐ **in the long run**	1093	☐ inducement	0046, 0291	☐ instruct	0866
☐ **in the meantime**	1090, 0956	☐ induction	0291	☐ instruct A to do	0866
☐ in the meanwhile	0956, 1090	☐ industrious	0901	☐ instruction	0866
☐ in the short run	1093	☐ **inequality**	0652	☐ **instructive**	0866
☐ **in writing**	1107	☐ inevitable	0951	☐ **insulate**	0749
☐ **inaccessible**	0907	☐ **inevitably**	0951	☐ insulation	0749
☐ inaccuracy	0119	☐ **inexpensive**	0394	☐ insurance	0541
☐ inadvertent	0974	☐ infamous	0451	☐ insure	0541
☐ **inadvertently**	0974	☐ infection	1086	☐ **insurer**	0541
☐ **inaugurate**	0329	☐ infectious	0441, 1086	☐ **intact**	0413
☐ inauguration	0329	☐ **infer**	0314	☐ **intake**	0240
☐ **incentive**	0046	☐ inference	0314	☐ **integral**	0878
☐ **incidence**	0553, 0482	☐ **influx**	0591	☐ integrate	0850
☐ incident	0482, 0553	☐ inform	0428	☐ **integrate A with B**	1033, 0850
☐ **inclement**	0408	☐ inform A about B	1025	☐ **integrated**	0850, 1033
☐ inclination	0102	☐ inform A of B	0428, 1025	☐ integration	0850, 1033
☐ include	0301, 0311, 0881	☐ informant	0428	☐ **integrity**	0072
☐ including	0881	☐ information	0428	☐ intense	0353
☐ **inclusive**	0881, 0366	☐ **informative**	0428	☐ intensify	0353
☐ **incoming**	0889	☐ **infringe**	0774, 0689	☐ intensity	0353
☐ incompetence	0514, 0915	☐ infringe on	0689, 0774	☐ **intensive**	0353
☐ **incompetent**	0915	☐ infringe upon	0689, 0774	☐ intensively	0353
☐ inconclusive	0868	☐ **infringement**	0689, 0774	☐ intentionally	0972
☐ inconsiderate	0378	☐ inhabit	0188, 1003	☐ **interact with**	0990
☐ inconsistency	0861	☐ **inhabitant**	0188	☐ interaction	0990
☐ **inconsistent**	0861	☐ **in-house**	0445	☐ interactive	0990
☐ **inconvenience**	0027	☐ initial	0947	☐ **interdepartmental**	0896
☐ inconvenient	0027	☐ **initially**	0947	☐ interfere	0475
		☐ initiate	0947		

☐ interfere in	0475	☐ junction	0020	☐ limit	0261, 0307, 0496
☐ interfere with	0475			☐ **limitation**	0496, 0499
☐ **interference**	0475	**K**		☐ liquidate	0691
☐ **interim**	0854, 0831	☐ **keynote**	0664	☐ **liquidation**	0691
☐ **intermission**	0131	☐ knee	1109	☐ **literacy**	0567
☐ **intern**	0218, 0149			☐ literate	0567
☐ internship	0218	**L**		☐ litigate	0627
☐ **interpret**	0752	☐ labor force	0494	☐ **litigation**	0627
☐ **interpret A as B**		☐ **lag**	0581	☐ live in	1003
	1036, 0752	☐ **landlord**	0682, 0522	☐ local	0933
☐ interpretation	0752, 1036	☐ **landmark**	0030	☐ **locally**	0933
☐ interpreter	0752, 1036	☐ lane	0546	☐ logistic	0197
☐ interrupt	0888	☐ **lapse**	0636	☐ logistical	0197
☐ interruption	0208	☐ lasting	0384	☐ **logistics**	0197
☐ intersect	0020	☐ **latitude**	0669	☐ longitude	0669
☐ **intersection**	0020	☐ **latter**	0842	☐ look into	1007
☐ interval	0131	☐ lawful	0401	☐ love	0089
☐ introduce	0824	☐ **lawsuit**	0059, 0627	☐ lower	0315, 0328
☐ introduction	0824	☐ lawyer	0157	☐ **lucrative**	0373
☐ **introductory**	0824	☐ lay out	0214	☐ **lumber**	0152
☐ **intuition**	0156	☐ layoff	0692	☐ **luxurious**	0377
☐ **invaluable**	0837	☐ **layout**	0214	☐ luxury	0377
☐ **inventory**	0006	☐ lazy	0901		
☐ investigate	0498, 1007	☐ **leaflet**	0179, 0226	**M**	
☐ investigation	0498	☐ lecture	0608	☐ magazine	0204
☐ **investigator**	0498	☐ **lecturer**	0608	☐ magnificence	0531
☐ investor	0619	☐ legal	0401	☐ make efforts	0337
☐ **invoice**	0008	☐ legend	0884	☐ make up	0303
☐ **ironic**	0825	☐ **legendary**	0884	☐ make up for	0712
☐ ironically	0825	☐ legitimacy	0401	☐ **malfunction**	0040
☐ irony	0825	☐ **legitimate**	0401	☐ **mandate**	0523, 0356
☐ irrational	0415	☐ length	0569, 0911	☐ **mandatory**	
☐ **irregular**	0844, 0858	☐ lengthen	0911		0356, 0404, 0523
☐ irregularity	0844	☐ **lengthy**	0911	☐ **manifest**	0870
☐ irregularly	0844	☐ less	0781	☐ manifestation	0870
☐ **irrelevant**	0442, 0875	☐ lessee	0522	☐ manifesto	0870
☐ item	0766	☐ **lessen**	0781	☐ mansion	0076
☐ **itemize**	0766	☐ lesser	0781	☐ many	0432
☐ **itinerary**	0003	☐ levy	1041	☐ margin	0894
		☐ **levy A on B**	1041	☐ **marginal**	0894
J		☐ **liability**	0037, 1059	☐ **mark down**	0984
☐ **jeopardize**	0298	☐ liable	0037	☐ market	0456
☐ jeopardy	0298	☐ **liaison**	0512	☐ **marketable**	0456
☐ job	0557	☐ lie	0696	☐ marriage	0123
☐ join	1001	☐ lie in	1023	☐ master	0612

どれだけチェックできた？ 1 ☐ 2 ☐

☐ match	0989
☐ **maternity**	0838
☐ **mature**	0342
☐ maturity	0342
☐ maximal	0288, 0830
☐ **maximize**	0288, 0296
☐ maximum	0288
☐ means	0548
☐ **meanwhile**	0956, 1090
☐ measurement	0471
☐ media	0548
☐ mediation	0084
☐ **medium**	0548
☐ meeting	0160, 0484
☐ **meltdown**	0646
☐ memo	0171
☐ **memorable**	0423
☐ memoranda	0171
☐ **memorandum**	0171
☐ **mentor**	0586
☐ **merchandise**	0013
☐ merchandising	0013
☐ merchant	0013
☐ merge	0021, 0292
☐ **merge with**	0979, 0021
☐ **merger**	0021, 0979
☐ merry-go-round	0605
☐ mess	0383, 0529
☐ mess up	0383
☐ **messy**	0383
☐ metropolis	0452
☐ **metropolitan**	0452
☐ migrant	0686
☐ migrate	0686
☐ **migration**	0686
☐ **mileage**	0097
☐ **mingle**	0778
☐ **minimal**	0830, 0296
☐ **minimize**	
0296, 0288, 0830	
☐ minimum	0296, 0830
☐ **miscellaneous**	0435
☐ **misplace**	0738
☐ mistake	0667
☐ misunderstand	0606

☐ **misunderstanding**	
	0606
☐ misunderstood	0606
☐ **mobile**	0398
☐ modern	0792
☐ modernization	0792
☐ **modernize**	0792
☐ moist	0448
☐ **momentum**	0521
☐ moral	0032, 0882
☐ **morale**	0032
☐ moratoria	0678
☐ **moratorium**	0678
☐ **mortgage**	0058
☐ motivation	0046
☐ motive	0046
☐ **move on to**	1008
☐ **mow**	0305
☐ mower	0305
☐ multilateral	0454
☐ **multinational**	0409
☐ **multiple**	0432
☐ multiplication	0432
☐ multiply	0432
☐ multiply A by B	0432
☐ **municipal**	0359
☐ municipality	0359
☐ **mutual**	0393, 0966
☐ **mutually**	0966, 0393
☐ **myriad**	0630

N

☐ nationalize	0777
☐ **nationwide**	0463, 0943
☐ nearby	0358
☐ nearness	0578
☐ neat	0383
☐ necessarily	0710
☐ necessary	0710, 0878
☐ **necessitate**	0710
☐ necessitate doing	0710
☐ neglect	0174, 0898
☐ **negligence**	0174
☐ negligent	0174
☐ **negligible**	0898

☐ **negotiable**	0847
☐ negotiate	0847
☐ negotiate with	1000
☐ negotiation	0847
☐ neighbor	0864
☐ neighborhood	0526, 0864
☐ **neighboring**	0864, 0358
☐ net	0430
☐ next	0358
☐ **nominal**	0437
☐ nominate A as B	1048
☐ **nominate A for B**	1048
☐ nomination	1048
☐ nominee	1048
☐ **nonrefundable**	0922
☐ notable	0976
☐ **notably**	0976
☐ notice	0856, 1120
☐ **noticeable**	0856
☐ noticeably	0856
☐ notification	1025
☐ notify	0856
☐ **notify A of B**	1025, 0856
☐ notoriety	0451
☐ **notorious**	0451
☐ notoriously	0451
☐ **novice**	0662
☐ **nurture**	0723
☐ nutrient	0163, 0913
☐ **nutrition**	0163, 0913
☐ **nutritious**	0913, 0163

O

☐ obedience	
	0205, 0210, 0237
☐ obey	0980
☐ obligation	0404
☐ **obligatory**	0404, 0356
☐ oblige	0404
☐ **obscure**	0402
☐ obscurity	0402
☐ **observance**	0210, 0205
☐ observation	0210
☐ observatory	0210
☐ observe	0210

☐ obtain	0772	☐ optimize	0887	☐ overstaffed	0904
☐ obvious	0870, 0941	☐ optimum	0887	☐ **overture**	**0683**
☐ **obviously**	**0941**	☐ oral	0419	☐ **overview**	**0640**
☐ **occupancy**	**0649**, 0821	☐ orally	1107	☐ owner	0674
☐ occupant	0649, 0821	☐ order	0523	**P**	
☐ occupation	0557, 0835	☐ **ordinance**	**0236**		
☐ **occupational**		☐ organization	0867	☐ pack	0813
	0835, 0876	☐ **organizational**	**0867**	☐ pamphlet	0005
☐ **occupied**	**0821**	☐ organize	0867	☐ pandemic	0096
☐ occupy	0649, 0821	☐ organized	0867	☐ part	0185, 0969
☐ occur	0482	☐ orient	0227	☐ partial	0969
☐ occur to	0482	☐ orient oneself to	0227	☐ **partially**	**0969**
☐ **occurrence**	**0482**, 0553	☐ orient oneself toward		☐ participate in	1001
☐ odd	0971		0227	☐ particularly	0976
☐ **oddly**	**0971**	☐ **orientation**	**0227**	☐ **partition**	**0148**
☐ oddly enough	0971	☐ origin	1009	☐ partly	0969
☐ offender	0644	☐ original	1009	☐ pass	0927
☐ offer	1103	☐ originally	1009	☐ **pass out**	**1021**, 0987
☐ **offset**	**0712**	☐ originate from	1009	☐ passable	0927
☐ **offshore**	**0851**	☐ **originate in**	**1009**	☐ paternity	0838
☐ oil	0466	☐ **out of commission**		☐ path	0546
☐ omnipresent	0883		**1119**	☐ **pathway**	**0546**
☐ **on hand**	**1095**	☐ **out of service**	**1112**	☐ **patron**	**0573**, 0112
☐ **on offer**	**1103**, 1118	☐ **outfit**	**0105**, 0135, 0187	☐ **patronage**	**0112**, 0573
☐ **on one's hands and**		☐ **outing**	**0472**	☐ pause	0131
knees	**1109**	☐ **outlay**	**0697**	☐ pay	0182
☐ on purpose	0972	☐ **outlet**	**0085**, 0240	☐ **paycheck**	**0101**
☐ **on request**	**1110**	☐ **outline**	**0318**	☐ payoff	0100
☐ on sale	1103, 1118	☐ **outnumber**	**0807**	☐ **payroll**	**0067**
☐ **on the market**		☐ out-of-date	0405	☐ **pedestrian**	**0007**
	1118, 1103	☐ outrage	0431	☐ **penetrate**	**0302**
☐ **on the road**	**1111**	☐ **outraged**	**0431**	☐ penetration	0302
☐ one-way	0381	☐ **outrageous**	**0431**	☐ pension	0599
☐ **ongoing**	**0826**	☐ **outsource**	**0771**	☐ period	0204, 0954
☐ only	0960	☐ outsourcing	0771	☐ periodic	0204, 0954
☐ **on-the-job**	**0879**, 0444	☐ **overcharge**	**0285**	☐ **periodical**	**0204**, 0954
☐ opening	0142	☐ **overdue**	**0368**	☐ **periodically** **0954**, 0204
☐ operate	0846	☐ **overestimate**		☐ **perk**	**0596**
☐ operation	0846		0763, 0806	☐ permission	0061
☐ **operational**	**0846**	☐ **overhaul**	**0728**	☐ perquisite	0596
☐ opponent	0604, 0651	☐ overprice	0860	☐ perspective	0474
☐ **optimal**	**0887**	☐ **overpriced**	**0860**	☐ **pertinent**	**0875**
☐ **optimism**	**0502**	☐ **oversee**	**0335**, 0277	☐ pessimism	0502
☐ optimist	0502	☐ **overshadow**	**0797**	☐ **petition**	**0050**
☐ optimistic	0502	☐ **oversight**	**0667**	☐ **petroleum**	**0466**

- [ ] **pharmaceutical**
  0410, 0043, 0075
- [ ] **pharmacist**
  0075, 0043, 0410
- [ ] **pharmacy**
  0043, 0075, 0410
- [ ] **phenomenal** 0459
- [ ] phenomenon 0459
- [ ] **philanthropy** 0666
- [ ] **photocopier** 0129
- [ ] photocopy 0129
- [ ] picnic 0472
- [ ] plague 0096
- [ ] plane 0155
- [ ] **plaque** 0532
- [ ] **plea** 0601
- [ ] plead 0601
- [ ] plead for 0601
- [ ] plead with A to do 0601
- [ ] **pledge** 0616
- [ ] pledge to do 0616
- [ ] **plenary** 0906
- [ ] plight 0223
- [ ] plug 0995
- [ ] **plug in** 0995
- [ ] **plumber** 0091
- [ ] **plummet** 0769, 0775
- [ ] plunge 0769, 0775
- [ ] **ply** 0816, 0524
- [ ] point 0583
- [ ] point at 0583
- [ ] point of view 0474
- [ ] **pointer** 0583
- [ ] pollutant 0741
- [ ] **pollute** 0741, 0756
- [ ] pollution 0741
- [ ] poor 0406
- [ ] portray 0776
- [ ] postgraduate 0111
- [ ] postpone
  0319, 0336, 0780
- [ ] **poultry** 0620
- [ ] practical 0914
- [ ] praise 0469, 0798
- [ ] precaution 0323
- [ ] precede 0212, 0389, 0407
- [ ] **precedent**
  0212, 0389, 0407
- [ ] **preceding**
  0407, 0212, 0389, 0464
- [ ] precious 0837
- [ ] **precipitation** 0631
- [ ] precision 0119
- [ ] **predecessor** 0038
- [ ] **predicament** 0223
- [ ] predict 0446, 0791, 0865
- [ ] **predictable** 0446, 0865
- [ ] prediction 0446, 0865
- [ ] prefer 0973, 1066
- [ ] prefer to do 0973, 1066
- [ ] preferable 0973
- [ ] **preferably** 0973, 1066
- [ ] preference 0973, 1066
- [ ] prejudice 0069
- [ ] **premium** 0001
- [ ] preparation 0832
- [ ] **preparatory** 0832
- [ ] prepare 0832
- [ ] prepare for 0832
- [ ] prepare to do 0832
- [ ] **prerequisite** 0184
- [ ] **prescribe A for B** 1029
- [ ] prescription 1029
- [ ] preserve 0300
- [ ] prestige 0396
- [ ] **prestigious** 0396
- [ ] presumably 0282
- [ ] **presume** 0282
- [ ] presumption 0282
- [ ] prevail 0817
- [ ] prevail against 0817, 0999
- [ ] prevail among 0817, 0999
- [ ] **prevail in** 0999, 0817
- [ ] prevail over 0817, 0999
- [ ] **prevailing** 0817, 0999
- [ ] prevalence 0817, 0999
- [ ] prevalent 0817
- [ ] prevent
  0457, 0717, 0724, 0742
- [ ] prevent A from doing 0457
- [ ] prevention 0457
- [ ] **preventive** 0457
- [ ] previous 0365
- [ ] primary 0828
- [ ] **prior** 0365
- [ ] prior to 0365
- [ ] priority 0365
- [ ] private 0777
- [ ] privatization 0777
- [ ] **privatize** 0777
- [ ] **probation** 0598
- [ ] **procrastinate** 0783
- [ ] **procure** 0772
- [ ] profession 0557
- [ ] profitable 0373
- [ ] **profound** 0420, 0963
- [ ] **profoundly** 0963, 0420
- [ ] project 0191
- [ ] **projection** 0191
- [ ] **proliferate** 0676
- [ ] **proliferation** 0676
- [ ] prominent 0426, 0818
- [ ] promise 0616
- [ ] promise to do 0280
- [ ] **proofread** 0309
- [ ] proofreader 0309
- [ ] proofreading 0309
- [ ] prop 1056
- [ ] **prop up A against B** 1056
- [ ] proper 0920
- [ ] **proponent** 0651
- [ ] **proprietor** 0674
- [ ] prosecute 0645
- [ ] **prosecution** 0645
- [ ] prosecutor 0645
- [ ] prospect 0367
- [ ] **prospective** 0367
- [ ] **prospectus** 0519
- [ ] **prosper** 0707, 0331
- [ ] prosperity 0707
- [ ] prosperous 0707
- [ ] protect 0323
- [ ] **prototype** 0120

☐ **provisional** 0831, 0854	☐ rationale 0415	☐ **reimbursement**
☐ **proximity** 0578	☐ raw 0397	0093, 0010, 0098, 1028
☐ **publication** 0491	☐ **reaffirm** 0815	☐ **reinforce** 0267
☐ publicity 0743	☐ reaffirmation 0815	☐ reinforcement 0267
☐ **publicize** 0743	☐ real 0386	☐ reject 0479
☐ publish 0491	☐ **rearrange** 0805	☐ **rejection** 0479
☐ publisher 0491	☐ reason 0665	☐ relatively 0965
☐ **pull over** 0982	☐ reasonable 0415, 0665	☐ relay 1045
☐ **pull together** 1013	☐ **reasoning** 0665	☐ **relay A to B** 1045
☐ **pundit** 0556, 0684	☐ **rebate** 0098	☐ relevant 0442, 0875
☐ punish 0928	☐ **rebound** 0747, 0709	☐ reliability 0690
☐ punish A for B 0928	☐ rebuke A for B 1055	☐ reliable 0453
☐ punishment 0928	☐ recall 0726	☐ relief 0290
☐ **punitive** 0928	☐ **recipient** 0065	☐ **relieve** 0290, 0269, 0332
☐ pure 0960	☐ **recollect** 0726	☐ relieve A of B 0290
☐ **purely** 0960	☐ recollect doing 0726	☐ relieved 0290
☐ put off 0319, 0336, 0780	☐ recollection 0726	☐ **relinquish** 0720
☐ **put together** 1019	☐ recommend 0798	☐ remainder 0136
	☐ **reconcile** 0346	☐ remember 0726
Q	☐ reconciliation 0346, 1081	☐ remind 0136
☐ qualification 0362	☐ rectangle 0440	☐ remind A about B 0136
☐ **qualified** 0362	☐ **rectangular** 0440	☐ remind A of B 0136
☐ qualify 0362	☐ **redeem** 0801	☐ **reminder** 0136
☐ qualify as 0362	☐ redemption 0801	☐ **remit** 0272, 0168, 0283
☐ qualify for 0362	☐ **redress** 0794	☐ **remittance** 0168, 0272
☐ **quarantine** 0615	☐ reduce	☐ remunerate 0182
☐ quarter 0079, 0379	0315, 0328, 0740, 1011	☐ **remuneration** 0182
☐ **quarterly** 0379	☐ **redundancy** 0692	☐ remunerative 0182
☐ question 1104	☐ redundant 0692	☐ renew 0045, 0903
☐ **questionnaire** 0056	☐ **refill** 0086	☐ **renewable** 0903, 0045
☐ **quota** 0158	☐ refined 0397	☐ **renewal** 0045, 0903
☐ **quotation** 0195	☐ **refund**	☐ **renovate** 0262, 0051
☐ quote 0195	0010, 0093, 0098, 0922	☐ **renovation** 0051, 0262
	☐ refundable 0010	☐ renown 0426
R	☐ **regime** 0585	☐ **renowned** 0426, 0818
☐ radiate 0080	☐ regret 0935	☐ repeat 0500
☐ **radiation** 0080	☐ regret doing 0935	☐ repeated 0500
☐ **raft** 0510	☐ regret to do 0935	☐ repeatedly 0500
☐ rafting 0510	☐ **regrettably** 0935	☐ **repertoire** 0656
☐ **rake** 0736	☐ regular 0844	☐ **repetition** 0500
☐ rare 0704	☐ **regulate** 0316	☐ repetitive 0500
☐ rarely 0704	☐ regulation 0316	☐ report 0949
☐ **rarity** 0704	☐ reimburse 0093	☐ report to 0949
☐ rate 1101	☐ **reimburse A for B**	☐ **reportedly** 0949, 0932
☐ **rational** 0415	1028, 0093	☐ represent 0776

☐ reprimand 1055	☐ review 0684	☐ **seniority** 0198
☐ **reprimand A for B** 1055	☐ **reviewer** 0684, 0556	☐ separate 0930
☐ request 0050, 0601, 1110	☐ revise 0070	☐ separate A from B 0930
☐ requirement 0184	☐ **revision** 0070	☐ **separately** 0930
☐ requisite 0184	☐ **revitalize** 0765	☐ separation 0930
☐ reservation 0488	☐ revolution 0755	☐ **serial** 0418
☐ **reservoir** 0610	☐ revolutionary 0755	☐ set back 0116
☐ **reside in** 1003	☐ **revolutionize** 0755	☐ **setback** 0116
☐ residence 1003	☐ reward 0182	☐ **settle on** 1015
☐ resident 0188, 1003	☐ rich 0406	☐ settle upon 1015
☐ residential 1003	☐ risk 0064, 0298	☐ settlement 1015
☐ resign 0144	☐ **robust** 0853	☐ share 0095
☐ **resignation** 0144	☐ **round-trip** 0381	☐ **shareholder** 0095
☐ **resilient** 0924	☐ **rubble** 0539, 0508	☐ shelf 0780
☐ resource 0890	☐ rude 0397	☐ **shelve** 0780
☐ **resourceful** 0890	☐ **rule out** 0988	☐ ship 0004, 0155
☐ respectful 0375	**S**	☐ **shipment** 0004
☐ **respective** 0375, 0929	☐ **safeguard** 0323	☐ shipping 0004
☐ **respectively** 0929, 0375	☐ **sag** 0733	☐ **shortcut** 0582, 0016
☐ respond 0554	☐ salary 0101, 0182	☐ shorten 0328
☐ respond to 0554	☐ **sanction** 0061	☐ shot 0222
☐ **respondent** 0554	☐ **sanitary** 0843, 0849	☐ **showdown** 0638
☐ response 0554	☐ sanitation 0843	☐ **shred** 0718
☐ responsibility 0037, 0503	☐ sarcastic 0825	☐ **shuttle** 0524, 0816
☐ **restrain** 0307, 0261	☐ saturate 0592	☐ **sightseeing** 0489
☐ restrain oneself from doing 0307	☐ **saturation** 0592	☐ sightseer 0489
☐ restrained 0307	☐ scarcely 0940	☐ sign 0081
☐ restraint 0261, 0307	☐ scenery 0412	☐ signature 0081
☐ restrict 0921	☐ **scenic** 0412	☐ **simulate** 0714
☐ restricted 0921	☐ scratch 1092	☐ simulation 0714
☐ restriction 0560, 0921	☐ screen 0572	☐ sink 0733
☐ **restrictive** 0921	☐ **screening** 0572	☐ **sip** 0757
☐ restructure 0233	☐ **script** 0239	☐ size 0471
☐ **restructuring** 0233	☐ **scrub** 0265	☐ skeptic 1076
☐ result in 0996	☐ **scrutinize** 0705, 0164	☐ skepticism 1076
☐ resume 0282	☐ **scrutiny** 0164, 0705	☐ skill 0155
☐ retail 0073, 0107	☐ seaweed 0785	☐ skilled 0893
☐ retailer 0107, 0483	☐ **secondary** 0828	☐ skillful 0893
☐ **retailer** 0107, 0483	☐ secondhand 0925	☐ **skyrocket** 0739
☐ retrieval 0256	☐ security 0544	☐ **slash** 0750
☐ **retrieve** 0256	☐ **segment** 0185	☐ slug 0395
☐ **reunion** 0138	☐ **semester** 0079	☐ **sluggish** 0395
☐ **revamp** 0790	☐ **semiconductor** 0607	☐ **slump** 0731
☐ reveal 0768	☐ senior 0198	☐ snowstorm 0481
		☐ **soak** 0327, 0317

どれだけチェックできた？ 1 ☐ 2 ☐

☐ soaking	0327	☐ **staple**	0153, 0476	☐ subscribe	0019, 0124
☐ **soar**	0312	☐ **stapler**	0476, 0153	☐ **subscribe to**	0977, 0019, 0124
☐ socket	0085	☐ start up	0663	☐ **subscriber**	0124, 0019, 0977
☐ **solicit**	0761	☐ **start-up**	0663	☐ **subscription**	0019, 0124, 0977
☐ solicitor	0761	☐ station	0600	☐ **subsequent**	0464, 0407
☐ solve	0997	☐ stationary	0033	☐ subsequently	0464
☐ solvency	0873	☐ **stationery**	0033	☐ **subside**	0753
☐ **solvent**	0873, 0840	☐ **statistical**	0845	☐ **subsidiary**	0009
☐ **souvenir**	0055	☐ statistically	0845	☐ **subsidize**	0727, 0082
☐ space	0369	☐ statistician	0845	☐ **subsidy**	0082, 0727
☐ **spacious**	0369	☐ statistics	0845	☐ substitute	0363
☐ **spawn**	0799	☐ stimulate	0497, 0782	☐ substitute for	1006
☐ spec	0017	☐ **stimulation**	0497	☐ subtract	0255
☐ special	0088	☐ stimulus	0497	☐ **subtract A from B**	1030
☐ specialize	0088	☐ **stir**	0746	☐ subtraction	1030
☐ specialize in	0088	☐ stockholder	0095	☐ succeed	0331, 0707
☐ **specialty**	0088	☐ **stool**	0700	☐ successive	0355
☐ specific	0017	☐ stop	0281	☐ successor	0038
☐ **specification**	0017	☐ **stopover**	0486	☐ sufficiency	0964
☐ specify	0017	☐ storehouse	0600	☐ sufficient	0964
☐ **specimen**	0562	☐ straight	0355	☐ **sufficiently**	0964
☐ **speculate**	0287, 0619	☐ **strait**	0626	☐ suit	0059, 0627, 0989
☐ speculate about	0287, 0619	☐ strata	0657	☐ **suite**	0141
☐ **speculate in**	1017, 0287, 0619	☐ **strategic**	0429	☐ sum up	0294
☐ speculate on	0287, 0619	☐ strategically	0429	☐ **summarize**	0294
☐ speculation	0287, 0619, 1017	☐ strategist	0429	☐ summary	0294
☐ **speculator**	0619, 0287, 1017	☐ **strategy**	0429	☐ summon	0719
☐ spending	0044, 0697	☐ **stratum**	0657	☐ **superb**	0871
☐ sphere	0181	☐ **streamline**	0340	☐ superior	0047
☐ spoken	0419	☐ strengthen	0267, 0292	☐ **supervise**	0277, 0023, 0335
☐ square	0440	☐ stress	0270, 0352	☐ supervision	0023, 0277, 0667
☐ stability	0737	☐ stretch	1100	☐ **supervisor**	0023, 0277
☐ **stabilize**	0737	☐ **stroll**	0811	☐ supervisory	0023, 0277
☐ stable	0737	☐ stroller	0811	☐ **supplement**	0071
☐ stagnant	0677	☐ strong	0853	☐ supplement A with B	0071
☐ stagnate	0677	☐ structure	0139	☐ supplementary	0071
☐ **stagnation**	0677	☐ struggle	0985	☐ **supplier**	0028
☐ **stake**	0207, 1094	☐ struggle against	0985	☐ supply	0028
☐ standard	0183, 0559	☐ **struggle with**	0985	☐ supply A with B	0028
☐ standpoint	0474	☐ **subdue**	0787, 0751	☐ support	0795
☐ **standstill**	0549	☐ subdued	0787		
		☐ **submission**	0237		
		☐ submit	0237		
		☐ submit to	0237		
		☐ **subordinate**	0047		

どれだけチェックできた？ 1 ☐ 2 ☐

☐ supporter	0573	☐ testimony	0732	☐ **trustee**	0566
☐ suppose	0282	☐ **textile**	0178, 0139	☐ **tuition**	0053
☐ **suppress**	0751, 0787	☐ therefore	0946	☐ tuition fee	0053
☐ suppression	0751	☐ **thrive**	0331, 0707	☐ **tumble**	0775, 0769
☐ **surcharge**	0057	☐ thriving	0331	☐ tumult	0668
☐ **surge**	0219	☐ throw away	0273	☐ **turbulence**	0068
☐ **surpass**	0248	☐ tidy	0383	☐ turbulent	0068
☐ **surplus**	0049	☐ timber	0152	☐ **turmoil**	0668
☐ suspect	0644	☐ tip	0583, 0618	☐ **turn around**	0992, 0533
☐ suspend	0159	☐ **token**	0228	☐ turn out	0493
☐ **suspension**	0159	☐ **tolerable**	0862, 0422	☐ **turnaround**	0533, 0992
☐ sustain	0450	☐ tolerance	0422, 0862	☐ **turnout**	0493
☐ sustainability	0450	☐ **tolerant**	0422, 0862	☐ **turnover**	0173
☐ **sustainable**	0450	☐ tolerate	0422, 0862	**U**	
☐ sweep	0839	☐ toll	0372	☐ **ubiquitous**	0883
☐ **sweeping**	0839	☐ **toll-free**	0372	☐ **ultimate**	0443, 0952
☐ sweets	0647	☐ tone	0517	☐ **ultimately**	0952, 0443
☐ **synergy**	0587	☐ **top-of-the-line**	0908	☐ **unanimous**	0371, 0939
☐ **synthetic**	0438	☐ total	0430	☐ **unanimously**	
T		☐ totally	0938		0939, 0371
☐ **tag**	0106	☐ **tow**	0299	☐ **unavailable**	0823
☐ take over	0137	☐ **toxic**	0414	☐ unbelievable	0391
☐ take part in	1001	☐ toxin	0414	☐ unclear	0402
☐ **takeover**	0137	☐ trade	0104	☐ unconditional	0958
☐ talent	0113, 0461	☐ train	0149	☐ **unconditionally**	0958
☐ **talented**	0461	☐ **trainee**	0149, 0218	☐ uncover	0768
☐ **tariff**	0121	☐ training	0149	☐ **undercharge**	0285
☐ teaching	0053	☐ **transact**	0348	☐ **underestimate**	
☐ **temporarily**	0931	☐ transaction	0348		0806, 0763
☐ temporary		☐ transcribe	0203	☐ **undergraduate**	0111
	0831, 0854, 0931	☐ **transcript**	0203	☐ **underline**	0352, 0270
☐ tenancy	0522	☐ transcription	0203	☐ **undermine**	0711
☐ **tenant**	0522, 0682	☐ **transit**	0024	☐ **underpin**	0795
☐ tend	0102	☐ transition	0024	☐ underpinning	0795
☐ tend to do	0102	☐ transitional	0024	☐ underscore	0270, 0352
☐ **tendency**	0102	☐ translate	0752	☐ **understaffed**	0904
☐ **tentative**	0387	☐ **transparency**	0602	☐ understand	0997
☐ tentatively	0387	☐ transparent	0602	☐ **undertake**	0280
☐ term	0079	☐ **traverse**	0808	☐ undertake to do	0280
☐ **terminate**	0260	☐ trend	0102	☐ undertaking	0280
☐ termination	0260	☐ **tribunal**	0675	☐ unethical	0882
☐ tertiary	0828	☐ **tribute**	0650	☐ unexpected	0895, 0975
☐ **testify**	0732	☐ **trigger**	0321	☐ **unexpectedly**	0975
☐ **testimonial**	0547	☐ trim	0740	☐ **unfold**	0708
		☐ trimester	0079		

☐ **unforeseen** 0895, 0745	☐ various 0278, 0432	☐ **warranty** 0015
☐ unfortunately 0935	☐ **vary** 0278, 0455, 0833	☐ **waste** 0130
☐ unilateral 0454	☐ **vend** 0773, 0026	☐ wasteful 0130
☐ **uninterrupted** 0888	☐ **vendor** 0026, 0773	☐ watch over 0277, 0335
☐ unoccupied 0821	☐ ventilate 0577	☐ wealth 0575
☐ **unpack** 0813	☐ **ventilation** 0577	☐ wealthy 0406
☐ **unprecedented** 0389, 0212, 0407	☐ **venue** 0036	☐ **weave** 0716
☐ **unpredictable** 0865, 0446	☐ **verbal** 0419	☐ **weed** 0785
	☐ verification 0247	☐ **weigh A against B** 1053
☐ unrelated 0442	☐ **verify** 0247	☐ weight 1053
☐ unrest 0103	☐ **vertical** 0424, 0399	☐ well-known 0426, 0818
☐ untidy 0383	☐ **veto** 0762	☐ wheel 1114
☐ **unveil** 0768	☐ viability 0857	☐ **wheelbarrow** 0504
☐ up to date 0405	☐ **viable** 0857, 0436	☐ **wholesale** 0073, 0483
☐ **upcoming** 0433	☐ **vicinity** 0526	☐ **wholesaler** 0483, 0073, 0107
☐ **update** 0246	☐ **viewpoint** 0474	☐ width 0569
☐ **upgrade** 0274	☐ **violate** 0268, 0774	☐ **withhold** 0250
☐ **upheaval** 0211	☐ violation 0268	☐ without cease 0281
☐ **upright** 0399, 0424	☐ violator 0268	☐ **withstand** 0722
☐ **upside** 0693	☐ virtual 0937	☐ wonderful 0391
☐ **up-to-date** 0405, 0246	☐ **virtually** 0937	☐ work force 0494
☐ upturn 0167	☐ vision 0819	☐ **work out** 0997
☐ **usage** 0540	☐ **visionary** 0819	☐ work together 0259
☐ useful 0866, 0914	☐ vitalize 0765	☐ **workforce** 0494
☐ **usher** 0639	☐ **vocation** 0557, 0876	☐ workout 0997
	☐ **vocational** 0876, 0557, 0835	☐ **workplace** 0041
V	☐ **voluntarily** 0967	☐ **worldwide** 0943, 0463
☐ **vacancy** 0142	☐ voluntary 0356, 0404, 0967	☐ worse 0802
☐ vacant 0142		☐ **worsen** 0802, 0258, 0345
☐ **vaccination** 0063	☐ volunteer 0967	
☐ vaccine 0063	☐ volunteer to do 0967	☐ wrap 1012
☐ vague 0402, 0962	☐ voting 0118	☐ **wrap up** 1012
☐ **vaguely** 0962	☐ **voucher** 0192	☐ wrinkle 0603
☐ valid 0468, 0511	☐ vow 0616	☐ written 0419
☐ validate 0468, 0511		
☐ **validation** 0511, 0468	**W**	**Y**
☐ **validity** 0468, 0511	☐ wage 0101, 0182	☐ yield to 1020
☐ valuable 0837	☐ wait for 0338	
☐ value 0837	☐ **waive** 0350	**Z**
☐ valueless 0837	☐ waiver 0350	☐ **zeal** 0634
☐ **variable** 0455, 0278, 0833	☐ walker 0007	☐ zealous 0634
	☐ **warehouse** 0012, 0600	
☐ variation 0278	☐ warn A about B 1050	
☐ **varied** 0833, 0455	☐ warn A of B 1050	

聞いて覚える英単語
キクタン TOEIC® Test Score 990

発行日	2009年5月30日（初版） 2015年5月28日（第13刷）
編著	一杉武史
編集	英語出版編集部
英文校正	Peter Branscombe、Joel Weinberg、Owen Schaefer
アートディレクション	細山田 光宣
デザイン	若井夏澄（細山田デザイン事務所）
イラスト	shimizu masashi (gaimgraphics)
ナレーション	Greg Dale、Julia Yermakov、紗川じゅん
音楽制作	東海林 敏行（onetrap）
録音・編集	千野幸男（有限会社ログスタジオ）
CDプレス	株式会社 学研教育アイ・シー・ティー
DTP	株式会社 秀文社
印刷・製本	図書印刷株式会社
発行者	平本照麿
発行所	株式会社 アルク 〒168-8611　東京都杉並区永福2-54-12 TEL：03-3327-1101　FAX：03-3327-1300 Email：csss@alc.co.jp Website：http://www.alc.co.jp/

・落丁本、乱丁本は弊社にてお取り替えいたしております。アルクお客様センター（電話：03-3327-1101　受付時間：平日9時～17時）までご相談ください。
・本書の全部または一部の無断転載を禁じます。
・著作権法上で認められた場合を除いて、本書からのコピーを禁じます。
・定価はカバーに表示してあります。

©2009 Takeshi Hitosugi/ALC PRESS INC.
shimizu masashi (gaimgraphics)/Toshiyuki Shoji (onetrap)
Printed in Japan.
PC：7009039
ISBN：978-4-7574-1594-2

地球人ネットワークを創る
アルクのシンボル
「地球人マーク」です。